Ultimate Recipes

Italian

Ultimate Recipes

Italian

DP

DEMPSEY
PARR

This is a Dempsey Parr Book
This edition published in 2000

Dempsey Parr is an imprint of Parragon

Parragon
Queen Street House
4 Queen Street
Bath BA1 1HE, UK

ISBN 1-84084-969-X

Printed in Indonesia

Produced by Haldane Mason, London

Notes

Use all metric or all imperial quantities, as the two are not interchangeable.
Cup measurements in this book are for American cups. Tablespoons are assumed to be 15 ml.
Unless otherwise stated, milk is assumed to be full fat, eggs are medium and pepper is freshly
ground black pepper.

The nutritional information provided for each recipe is per serving or per portion.
Optional ingredients, variations or serving suggestions have not been included in the
calculations. The times given for each recipe are an approximate guide only as the
preparation times may differ as a result of the type of oven used.

Contents

Introduction 10

Soups

Starters

Snacks & Light Meals

Snacks & Light Meals (continued)

Fish & Seafood

Meat

Poultry & Game

Vegetables

Salads

Salads
(continued)

Pasta

Rice &
Grains

Pizzas & Breads

Desserts

Introduction

Italian food, including the many pasta dishes, pizzas and risottos, as well as the decadent desserts, are enjoyed all around the world. This inspirational cookbook aims to bring a little bit of Italy into your kitchen!

Glorious sunlight, spectacular beaches, luscious countryside, rugged mountains, world-famous museums and art galleries, elegant designer shops, picturesque villages, and magnificent cities—if this were not enough, Italy also boasts one of the longest and finest culinary traditions in the whole of Europe.

The ancient Romans loved good food and plenty of it, vying with each other to produce increasingly lavish and outlandish banquets. One of the earliest cookbooks written by Apicius, a gourmet in the first century, includes an appalling recipe for dormouse stuffed with walnuts! Overseas trade as the Roman Empire expanded brought new ingredients, and agriculture began to flourish at home. However, even then, wine production was just as prodigious as it is today.

With the collapse of the Roman Empire, the diet returned to plainer fare, relying on the wealth of cereals, fruit, and vegetables that could be cultivated on the fertile plains. However, with the Renaissance, an interest in and enthusiasm for fine food revived and, once again, there were wealthy families who presided over extravagant banquets.

Italian pastry cooks were valued throughout the courts of Europe and were generally acknowledged as the best in the world. When Catherine de' Medici went to Paris to marry the future King Henri II, she took an army of Italian cooks with her and changed French culinary traditions irrevocably. A new middle class developed who also took an interest in eating well, creating a bourgeois cuisine characterized by fresh flavors and simple, unsauced dishes. The poor, of course, continued with a peasant subsistence.

The very finest produce and freshest ingredients still characterize Italian cuisine as a whole.

Introduction

Although modern transportation makes it possible for more exotic ingredients to travel across the world, Italian cooking still centers on home-grown produce. Over 60 percent of the land is devoted to crops and pasture. With a climate that ranges from very cold in the Alps and Apennines to semitropical along the coast of the Ligurian Sea, the range of produce is extensive: olives, oranges, lemons, figs, grapes, pomegranates, almonds, wheat, potatoes, tomatoes, sugar beet, corn, and rice.

Livestock includes cattle and buffalo, sheep, goats, pigs, and chickens. In a single year, Italy produces nearly 6.5 million tonnes of wine, nearly 2.5 million tonnes of olives, about 500,000 tonnes of olive oil, over 4.5 million tonnes of tomatoes, and 120 million chickens. An impressive amount, you'll agree!

The introduction to this book continues to explore Italy, region by region, to discover the different types of food that are identified with a specific area of the country. Seasonal ingredients are also examined to provide the reader with as much insight into the type of produce used by the very discerning people of Italy.

Ragu Sauce

3 tablespoons olive oil

3 tablespoons butter

2 large onions, chopped

4 celery stalks, thinly sliced

6 ounces bacon, chopped

2 garlic cloves, chopped

1 pound 2 ounces ground
    lean beef

2 tablespoons tomato paste

1 tablespoon all-purpose flour

14-ounce can chopped tomatoes

⅔ cup beef stock

⅔ cup red wine

2 teaspoons dried oregano

½ teaspoon freshly grated nutmeg

salt and pepper

1 Heat the oil and butter in a pan over medium heat. Add the onions, celery, and bacon and fry for 5 minutes, stirring.

2 Stir in the garlic and ground beef and cook, stirring until the meat has lost its redness. Lower the heat and cook for 10 minutes, stirring.

3 Increase the heat to medium, stir in the tomato paste and the flour and cook for 1–2 minutes. Stir in the tomatoes, stock, and wine and bring to a boil, stirring. Season and stir in the oregano and nutmeg. Cover and simmer for 45 minutes, stirring. The sauce is now ready to use.

Regional Cooking

To talk about Italian cuisine is somewhat misleading, as it is not a single entity. The country has been united only since 17 March, 1861 and Italians still have a powerful sense of their regional identity.

Regional cuisine is a source of pride and considerable competition. Sicilians are dismissed as *mangimaccaroni* (pasta eaters), while they express their contempt for Neapolitan cooking with the term *mangiafoglie* (vegetable eaters). Each region bases its cuisine on local ingredients, so the best ham comes from the area where pigs are raised, fish and seafood feature in coastal regions, butter is used in dishes from the north of Italy where there is dairy farming, while olive oil is characteristic of southern recipes.

Abruzzi & Molise

This was once a single region and although it has now been divided into two separate provinces, they remain closely associated. Located in northern Italy to the east of Rome, the area is well-known for its high-quality cured meats and cheese. The cuisine is traditional and also features lamb and fish, and seafood in the coastal areas. Peperoncino a tiny, fiery hot, dried red chili is from Abruzzi.

Basilicata

If the Italian peninsula looks like a boot, Basilicata is located on the arch of the foot. The landscape is rugged and inhospitable, with a considerable part of the region being over 6,500 feet above sea level.

Regional Cooking

It is hardly surprising, therefore, that the cuisine is warming and filling, featuring substantial soups in particular. Cured meats, pork, lamb, and game are typical ingredients and freshwater fish are abundant in the more mountainous areas.

Calabria

In the south, on Italy's toe, Calabria is a region of dramatic contrasts—superb beaches and towering mountains. Excellent fish and seafood typify the local cuisine, which is well known for its swordfish and tuna dishes. Fruit and vegetables are abundant, particularly oranges, lemons, eggplants, and olives. Like other southern regions, desserts are a specialty, often based on local figs, honey, or almonds.

Campania

Naples on the west coast is the home of pizza, now known across the world from Sydney to New York, and the region bases many of its other dishes on the wonderful sun-ripened tomatoes grown locally. Fish and seafood feature strongly in the Neapolitan diet and robust herb-flavored stews, redolent with garlic, are popular. Pastries and fruit desserts are also characteristic.

Emilia-Romagna

A central Italian province, Emilia-Romagna's capital is the beautiful medieval city of Bologna, nicknamed *la grassa*, the fat city, and home to some of the best restaurants in the country. A gourmet paradise, the region is famous for Parmesan cheese and prosciutto ham from Parma, balsamic vinegar from the area around Modena, cotechino, mortadella, and other cured meats and, of course, *spaghetti alla bolognese.* Butter, cream, and other dairy products feature

in the fine food of
the region and a wide range of
pasta dishes is popular.

Lazio

Capital of the region and the
country, Rome is a cosmopolitan and
sophisticated city with some of the
best restaurants—and ice cream
parlors—in Europe. Fruit and
vegetables are abundant
and lamb and veal dishes
are characteristic of the
region, which is famous for
saltimbocca, which literally means
"jump in the mouth". Here, they
have perfected the art of preparing
high-quality ingredients in simple,
but delicious ways that retain the
individual flavors. A Roman specialty
is *supplì al telefono*—"telephone
wires"—mozzarella cheese wrapped
in balls of cooked rice and deep-
fried. The mozzarella is stringy, hence
the name of the dish.

Liguria

A northern province with a long
coastline, Liguria is well known for
its superb fish and seafood. It is also
said to produce the best basil in the
whole of Italy and it is where pesto
sauce was first invented. The ancient
port of Genoa was one of the first
places in Europe to import Asian
spices, and highly seasoned dishes
are still particularly characteristic of
this area.

Lombardy

An important rice-growing region in
northwest Italy, this is the home of
risotto, and there are probably as
many variations of this dish as there
are cooks. Dairy produce features in
the cuisine and Lombardy is credited
with the invention of butter, as well
as mascarpone cheese. Vegetable
soups, stews, and pot roasts are
characteristic of this region.
Bresaola, cured raw beef, is a local

Regional Cooking

specialty that is often served wrapped around soft goat cheese.

Marche

With its long coastline and high mountains, this region is blessed with both abundant seafood and game. Pasta, pork, and olives also feature and methods of preparation are even more elaborate than those of neighboring Umbria.

Piedmont

On the borders of France and Switzerland, Piedmont in the northwest is strongly influenced by its neighbors. A fertile, arable region, it is well known for rice, polenta, and gnocchi, and is said to grow the finest onions in Italy. Gorgonzola, one of the world's greatest cheeses, comes from this region although, sadly, the little village that gave it its name has now been subsumed by the urban sprawl of Milan. Piedmontese garlic is said to be the best in Italy and the local white truffles are a gourmet's dream.

Puglia

On the heel of Italy, this region produces excellent olives, herbs, vegetables, and fruit, particularly melons and figs. Fish and seafood are abundant and the region is known for its oyster and mussel dishes. Calzone, a sort of inside out pizza, was invented here.

Sardinia

This Mediterranean island is famous for its luxurious desserts and extravagant pastries, many of them featuring honey, nuts, and home-grown fruit. Hardly surprisingly, fish and seafood—tuna, eel, mullet, sea bass, lobster, and mussels—are central to Sardinian cuisine, and spit-roasted suckling pig is the national dish served on feast days. *Sardo* is a mild-tasting pecorino cheese produced in Sardinia.

Sicily

Like their southern neighbors, Sicilians have a sweet tooth, which they indulge with superb cakes, desserts and ice cream, often incorporating locally grown almonds, pistachios, and citrus fruits. Pasta dishes are an important part of the diet, and fish and seafood, including tuna, swordfish, and mussels, feature prominently.

Trentino Alto-Adage

A mountainous region in the north-east, Trentino has been strongly influenced by its Austrian neighbor. Smoked sausage and dumplings are characteristic of the cuisine, which is also well known for its filled pasta.

Tuscany

The fertile plains of Tuscany are ideal for farming and the region produces superb fruit and vegetables. Cattle are raised here and both steak and veal dishes feature on the Tuscan menu, together with a wide range of game. Tripe is a local specialty and *Panforte di Siena*, a traditional Christmas cake made with honey and nuts, comes from the city of Siena. A grain known as *farro* is grown almost exclusively in Tuscany, where it is used to make a nourishing soup.

Umbria

Pork, lamb, game, and freshwater fish, prepared and served simply but deliciously, characterize the excellent cuisine of the region. Fragrant black truffles are a feature and Umbrian cooking makes good use of its high-quality olive oil. Umbria is also famous for *imbrecciata*, a hearty and warming soup made with lentils, garbanzo beans, and navy beans.

Veneto and Friuli

An intensively farmed area in the north-east of Italy, this region produces cereals and almost 20 per cent of the country's wine.

Polenta and risotto feature in the cuisine, as well as an extensive range of fish and seafood. *Risi e bisi*, rice and peas, is a traditional dish, which was served every year at the Doge's banquet in Venice to honor the city's patron saint, Mark.

Ingredients

Whatever regional variations there may be, all the cuisines of Italy have one thing in common—the use of the freshest and best seasonal ingredients. Choosing and buying meat, fish, vegetables, and fruit are as important as the way they are prepared and cooked.

Cheese

Bel Paese

Its name means "beautiful country" and it is a very creamy, mild-flavored cheese with a waxy yellow rind. It maybe eaten on its own or used for cooking.

Dolcelatte

This is a very creamy, delicate-tasting type of Gorgonzola. Its name means "sweet milk".

Fontina

A mild, nutty-tasting cheese with a creamy texture, genuine fontina is produced from the unpasteurized milk of cattle grazed on alpine herbs and grass in the Val d'Aosta. When fresh, it is delicious eaten on its own and the sharp cheese is excellent for cooking.

Gorgonzola

Strictly speaking, this cheese should be called Stracchino Gorgonzola. It is a creamy cheese with green-blue veining and its flavor can range from mild to strong. Delicious on its own, it can also be used in pasta sauces and stirred into polenta.

Mascarpone

This is a triple cream cheese from Lombardy that can be used for making cheesecakes and other desserts. It also adds richness to risotto and pasta sauces.

Mozzarella

No Italian kitchen would be complete without a supply of this moist, white, egg-shaped cheese. Traditionally made from buffalo milk, it is the ideal cheese for cooking and is also used in salads with tomatoes and fresh basil. It originated in the area around Naples, which still produces the best mozzarella, but it is now made throughout Italy, often from cow's milk.

Parmesan

Probably the best-known Italian cheese, Parmesan is extensively used in cooking. Parmigiano Reggiano is produced under strictly controlled conditions in a closely defined area. It is always aged for a minimum of two years, but this may be extended up to seven years. A cow's milk cheese, it is hard with a granular, flaky texture and a slightly nutty flavor. It is best bought in a single piece and grated as required.

Pecorino

A hard or semi-hard ewe's milk cheese, pecorino is widely used in cooking. It has a sharp flavor and a granular texture rather like Parmesan. Pecorino pepato from Sicily is studded with black peppercorns.

Provolone

Eaten on its own when fresh, provolone is also perfect for cooking, as it has a stringy texture when melted. It is made from different types of milk—the strongest being made from goat milk. Buffalo milk is often used in the south of Italy. Cylindrical or oval, it varies considerably in size and is often seen hanging from the ceiling in Italian delicatessens.

Ricotta

Literally translated as "recooked", ricotta is a soft white curd cheese originally made from goat or ewe's milk. It is more often made from cow's milk these days. It is widely used for both savory and sweet dishes and is classically paired with spinach.

Cured Meats

Bresaola

This salt-cured, air-dried beef is usually served in thin slices as an antipasto. It is similar to prosciutto in flavor, but not so salty.

Mortadella

Considered to be one of the finest Italian sausages, mortadella is also the largest with a diameter that may reach 18 inches. It has a smooth texture and a fairly bland flavor. It is usually eaten in sandwiches or as an

Ingredients

antipasto, but may also be added to risottos or pasta sauces shortly before the end of the cooking time.

Pancetta

Made from belly of pork, this resembles unsmoked bacon. It is very fatty and is used in a wide variety of dishes, particularly spaghetti alla carbonara. Smoked pancetta is also available.

Prosciutto

This salted, air-dried ham does not need any cooking. The drying process may take up to two years. Prosciutto di Parma, also known as Parma ham, is produced under strictly controlled conditions in a closely defined area between Taro and Baganza from pigs fed on the whey from the process of making Parmesan cheese. San Daniele is a leaner prosciutto with a very

distinctive flavor that is produced in Friuli. Prosciutto cotto is a cooked ham, often flavored with herbs. Prosciutto is traditionally served with melon or figs as an antipasto, but is also used in veal dishes, risottos, and various pasta sauces.

Salami

Salami are all made from pork, but there is an almost infinite variety of types which vary according to how finely or coarsely the meat is ground, the proportion of lean meat to fat, the seasoning and spices, and the length of drying time. Some of the best-known varieties are the quite coarse salame milano, salame sardo, a hotly spiced sausage from Sardinia, salame napoletano, flavored with black and red pepper, salame fiorentina, a coarse-cut Tuscan salame flavored with fennel seeds and pepper, and salame

di Felino from the Emilia-Romagna region, a very lean salame delicately flavored with garlic and white wine.

Sausages

Most Italian sausages are made from pork, but both venison and wild boar are sometimes used. There must be hundreds of different varieties from every region of the country. Cotechino is a large, lightly spiced sausage, weighing about 2¼ pounds. It is usually boiled and served hot with lentils or beans. Luganega is a mildly spiced, long, coiled sausage that is sold by the meter. Zampone is a pig's trotter stuffed with ground pork. Traditionally, it is boiled, sliced into rings and served with lentils. It is one of the classic ingredients of bollito misto.

Mushrooms

Collecting wild mushrooms is a national pastime and drugstores throughout the country will identify species if there is any doubt whether they are edible varieties.

Caesar's mushrooms

These are large mushrooms with orange caps and were once the favorites of Roman emperors. They are difficult to find outside Italy.

Chanterelles

These slightly frilly, orange-yellow mushrooms have a delicate flavor and aroma. They are now cultivated and are widely available in supermarkets.

Porcini

Also known as ceps or boletus mushrooms, these have a superb flavor. They can grow to be huge, weighing as much as 1 pound 2 ounces each. Young mushrooms may be eaten raw and larger specimens are delicious broiled. Dried porcini are available from Italian delicatessens and although they are very expensive, you need only a small quantity.

Pasta

Plain & filled pasta

There are hundreds of different types of pasta and new shapes are being produced all the time. Basic pasta is made from hard durum wheat flour and water, while pasta all'uova is enriched with eggs. Additional ingredients, such as spinach, tomatoes, and squid ink, are used to flavor and color it.

It is worth buying fresh pasta, called maccheroni, in Italy, if you have access to a good Italian delicatessen, and the stuffed varieties available in supermarkets are often quite good. Otherwise, commercially available, fresh, unfilled pasta is not really any better than the dried variety. There is no definitive list of names and the same shape may be called different things in various regions. Some have delightfully descriptive names: capelli d'angelo (angel's hair), dischi volante (flying saucers), linguine di passeri (sparrows' tongues), and strozzapreti (priest strangler), for example.

There are no hard-and-fast rules about which pasta should be served with which sauce. As a guide, long, thin types of pasta, such as fettuccine, tagliatelle, spaghetti, and taglioni, are best for delicate, olive-oil-based and seafood sauces. Short, fat pasta shapes, such as lumache, conchiglie, and penne, or curly shapes, such as farfalle and fusilli,

Ingredients

are best for meat sauces, as they trap the pieces. Tomato-based sauces go with virtually any pasta shape. Tiny pasta shapes, such as stellete, pepe bucato, and risi, are used for soups.

Pasta may be stuffed with cheese, meat, fish, chicken, sun-dried tomatoes, and any number of other fillings. Traditionally, ravioli are square, tortelli are round and tortelloni resemble the shape of Venus's navel! Flat pasta is used to make baked dishes, such as lasagne al forno.

Gnocchi

These are rather like little dumplings and are served as a first course in a similar way to pasta, either in soup or with a sauce. They are made from a variety of ingredients: milled durum wheat, potatoes, flour, or spinach and ricotta. They are available from Italian delicatessens and are easy to make at home.

Basic Pasta Dough

Making your own pasta dough is time consuming but immensely satisfying. You will need plenty of space for the rolled-out dough, and somewhere to hang it to dry.

SERVES 4

INGREDIENTS

1 cup all-purpose flour,
     plus extra for dusting

⅔ cup fine semolina

1 teaspoon salt

1 tablespoons olive oil

2 eggs

2–3 tablespoons hot water

1 Sift the flour, semolina, and salt into a bowl and make a well in the center. Pour in half of the oil and add the eggs. Add 1 tablespoon of hot water and, using your fingertips, work to form a smooth dough. Sprinkle on a little more water if necessary to make the dough pliable.

2 Lightly dust a board with flour, turn the dough out and knead it until it is elastic and silky. This could take 10–15 minutes. Dust the dough with more flour if your fingers become too sticky.

3 Alternatively, put the eggs, 1 tablespoon hot water, and the oil in the bowl of a food processor and process for a few seconds. Add the flour, semolina, and salt and process until smooth. Sprinkle on a little more hot water if necessary to make the dough pliable. Transfer to an electric mixer and knead using the dough hook for 2–3 minutes.

4 Divide the dough into 2 equal pieces. Cover a counter with a clean cloth or dish cloth and dust it liberally with flour. Place one portion of the dough on the floured cloth and roll it out as thinly and evenly as possible, stretching the dough gently until the pattern of the weave shows through. Cover it with a cloth and roll out the second piece in a similar way.

5 Use a ruler and a sharp knife blade to cut long, thin strips for noodles, or small confectionery cutters to cut rounds, stars, or an assortment of other decorative shapes.

6 Cover the dough shapes with a clean cloth and leave them in a cool place (not the refrigerator) for 30–45 minutes to become partly dry. To dry ribbons, place a dish cloth over the back of a chair and hang the ribbons over it.

Olive Oil

Arguably the best olive oil in the world comes from Italy and each region produces an oil with a different flavor. The oil is made by pressing the pulp of ripe olives. The first pressing, with no additional processing, produces extra virgin olive oil. This is the highest quality and is carefully regulated. It is the best oil to use for salad dressings.

The next quality, virgin olive oil, may also be used for dressings and is good for cooking. It has slightly higher level of acidity than extra virgin, but still has a good flavor.

Other types of olive oil are usually refined and may have been heat-treated. They can be used for cooking, but should not be used in dressings.

Rice & Grains

Polenta

A kind of cornmeal, polenta is a staple in northern Italy. There, it is available in an astonishing range of degrees of coarseness, but elsewhere there are two main types—coarse and fine. It is boiled to make a kind of porridge and can then be cooled and left to set, before being broiled, fried, or baked. It is very versatile and can be used for both savory and sweet dishes. Traditionally, polenta was cooked in a large copper pan and had to be stirred for at least 1 hour. Nowadays, quick-cook polenta is available.

Rice

Italy produces a wide range of types of rice in greater quantities than any other European country. Superfino rice is a round grain type used for risottos. It can absorb a large amount of liquid, swelling to three times its size during cooking, while still retaining its shape and texture. This is what gives the dish its unique and characteristic creaminess. Carnaroli, arborio and vialone nano are especially fine varieties. Semifino rice is used for soups and salads. Italians never serve food on a bed of rice, but may sometimes serve plain boiled rice with butter and cheese as a separate dish.

Vegetables & Pulses

Artichokes

Globe artichokes are cultivated throughout Italy and grow wild on Sicily. Naples is credited with the first cultivation and, nowadays, they are regarded as a Roman specialty, being served twice deep-fried. Tiny plants may be eaten raw or braised

Ingredients

with olive oil and fresh herbs. Larger artichokes are boiled and served with a dressing or stuffed.

Eggplants

Originally regarded with great suspicion, eggplants are now integral to Italian cooking, especially in the southern part of the country. They may be cooked in a wide of variety of ways and add depth of flavor and color to many dishes.

Beans

Navy, cannellini and borlotti, black-eyed peas (known as fagioli coll'occhio), fava beans, garbanzo beans, and other legumes are eaten all over Italy, although Tuscans are renowned for being bean-eaters. They are incorporated in substantial stews and soups or may be served as a simple side dish or salad dressed with a little extra virgin olive oil.

Zucchini

Widely used in northern Italian cooking, zucchini combine well with many other typically Mediterranean ingredients, such as tomatoes and eggplants. They may be served cold as an antipasto, stuffed, or deep-fried. They are often sold with their flowers still attached.

Fennel

Also known as Florence fennel, this aniseed-flavored bulb is one the most important ingredients in Italian cooking. It is served raw with a vinaigrette or with cheese at the end of a meal, and may be cooked in a wide variety of ways, including sautéing, braising in wine, and baking.

Onions

Sweet red onions are delicious raw and add color to cooked dishes.

White onions have a stronger flavor and yellow onions are mild-tasting. Baby white onions are traditionally cooked in a sour-sweet sauce—agrodolce—and usually served as an antipasto.

Bell Peppers

Capsicums or sweet bell peppers are invariably sun-ripened in Italy and, while they do not always have the uniform shape of greenhouse-grown bell peppers, they have a depth of flavor that is unsurpassed. They are served raw or roasted as an antipasto, and roasted or stuffed as a hot dish. They are classically partnered with anchovies, eggplants, capers, olives or tomatoes.

Radicchio

This bitter-tasting, red-leafed member of the chicory family is nearly always cooked in Italy, rather than being included in salads. It may be broiled or stuffed and baked, and is quite frequently used as a pizza topping.

Arugula

Now enjoying a rediscovered popularity in Britain and America, arugula has never lost favor in Italy, where it grows wild. It is also cultivated, but the homegrown variety has a better flavor. It is usually served in salads or on its own with a dressing of balsamic vinegar and olive oil. It is sometimes cooked like spinach, but tends to lose its pungency.

Spinach

Spinach and its close relatives Swiss chard and spinach beet are used in a wide variety of Italian dishes. Anything described as alla fiorentina is likely to contain it. Young leaves are eaten raw in salads and spinach is typically paired with ricotta in pasta and pancake fillings. It is also

classically combined with eggs, fish, chicken, and veal.

Squash

A huge variety of squashes, from tiny butternuts to massive pumpkins, are used in northern Italian cooking for both savory and sweet dishes, including soups, risottos, stuffed pasta, and dessert pies. Deep-fried pumpkin flowers in batter are also served.

Tomatoes

Many different varieties of tomatoes have been grown throughout Italy since the sixteenth century and it is difficult to imagine an Italian kitchen without them. Plum tomatoes are probably the most familiar and they have a firm texture that is less watery than other varieties, which makes them ideal for cooking. They may be served raw, typically partnering mozzarella cheese and fresh basil in

an insalata tricolore, and are used to add both color and flavor to a range of dishes. Italian tomatoes are always sun ripened and have a truly unmistakable flavor.

Sun-dried tomatoes have an intense flavor and are sold dry in packets or preserved in oil. These days, commercially produced sun-dried tomatoes have, in fact, been air-dried by machine, although sometimes it is possible to obtain the genuine article. If they are to be used for cooking, they should be soaked in hot water first.

Passata is a pulp made from sieved tomatoes. It has a strong flavor and may be fine or coarse. It is useful for soups and sauces and can be used as substitute for fresh tomatoes in slow-cooked dishes. Tomato paste is made from puréed tomatoes and has a less intense flavor than passata.

Basic Recipes

These recipes form the basis of several of the dishes contained throughout this book. Many of these basic recipes can be made in advance and stored in the refrigerator until required.

Basic Tomato Sauce

2 tablespoons olive oil

1 small onion, chopped

1 garlic clove, chopped

14-ounce can diced tomatoes

2 tablespoons chopped parsley

1 teaspoon dried oregano

2 bay leaves

2 tablespoons tomato paste

1 teaspoon sugar

salt and pepper

1 Heat the oil in a pan over a medium heat and fry the onion for 2–3 minutes, or until translucent. Add the garlic and fry for 1 minute.

2 Stir in the chopped tomatoes, parsley, oregano, bay leaves, tomato paste, and sugar, and season with salt and pepper to taste.

3 Bring the sauce to a boil, then simmer, uncovered, for 15–20 minutes, or until the sauce has reduced by half. Taste the sauce and adjust the seasoning if necessary. Discard the bay leaves just before serving.

Béchamel Sauce

1¼ cups milk

2 bay leaves

3 cloves

1 small onion

¼ cup butter, plus extra for greasing

6 tablespoons all-purpose flour

1¼ cups light cream

large pinch of freshly grated nutmeg

salt and pepper

1 Pour the milk into a small pan and add the bay leaves. Press the cloves into the onion, add to the pan and bring the milk to a boil. Remove the pan from the heat and set aside to cool.

2 Strain the milk into a pitcher and rinse the pan. Melt the butter in the pan and stir in the flour. Stir for 1 minute, then gradually pour on the milk, stirring constantly. Cook the sauce for 3 minutes, then pour on the cream and bring it to a boil. Remove from the heat and season with nutmeg, salt, and pepper to taste.

Lamb Sauce

2 tablespoons olive oil

1 large onion, sliced

2 celery stalks, thinly sliced

1 pound 2 ounces lean lamb, ground

3 tablespoons tomato paste

5½ ounces bottled sun-dried tomatoes, drained and chopped

1 teaspoon dried oregano

1 tablespoon red wine vinegar

⅔ cup chicken stock

salt and pepper

1 Heat the oil in a skillet over medium heat and fry the onion and celery until the onion is translucent, about 3 minutes. Add the lamb and fry, stirring frequently, until it browns.

2 Stir in the tomato paste, sun-dried tomatoes, oregano, red wine vinegar, and stock. Season with salt and pepper to taste.

3 Bring to a boil and cook, uncovered, for 20 minutes, or until the meat has absorbed the stock. Taste and adjust the seasoning if necessary.

Cheese Sauce

2 tablespoons butter

1 tablespoon all-purpose flour

1 cup milk

2 tablespoons light cream

pinch of freshly grated nutmeg

½ cup grated sharp Cheddar

1 tablespoon freshly grated Parmesan

salt and pepper

1 Melt the butter in a pan, stir in the flour, and cook for 1 minute. Gradually pour on the milk, stirring all the time. Stir in the cream and season the sauce with nutmeg, salt, and pepper to taste.

2 Simmer the sauce for 5 minutes to reduce, then remove it from the heat and stir in the cheeses. Stir until the cheeses have melted and blended into the sauce.

Espagnole Sauce

2 tablespoons butter

¼ cup all-purpose flour

1 teaspoon tomato paste

1 cup hot veal stock

1 tablespoon Madeira

1½ teaspoons white wine vinegar

2 tablespoons olive oil

3 tablespoons diced bacon

1 small carrot, diced

2 tablespoons diced onion

2 tablespoons diced celery

2 tablespoons diced leek

2 tablespoons diced fennel

1 fresh thyme sprig

1 bay leaf

1 Melt the butter in a pan, add the flour, and cook, stirring, until lightly colored. Add the tomato paste, then gradually stir in the hot veal stock, Madeira, and white wine vinegar and cook for 2 minutes.

2 Heat the oil in a separate pan, add the bacon, carrot, onion, celery, leek, fennel, thyme sprig, and bay leaf, and fry until the vegetables have softened. Remove the vegetables from the pan with a slotted spoon and drain thoroughly. Add the vegetables to the sauce and simmer for 4 hours, stirring occasionally. Strain the sauce before using.

Italian Red Wine Sauce

⅔ cup Brown Stock

(see page 30)

⅔ cup Espagnole Sauce

(see left)

½ cup red wine

2 tablespoons red wine vinegar

4 tablespoons shallots, chopped

1 bay leaf

1 thyme sprig

pepper

1 First make a demi-glace sauce. Put the Brown Stock and Espagnole Sauce in a pan and heat for 10 minutes, stirring occasionally.

2 Meanwhile, put the red wine, red wine vinegar, shallots, bay leaf, and thyme in a pan, bring to a boil, and reduce by three-quarters.

3 Strain the demi-glace sauce and add to the pan containing the Red Wine Sauce and simmer for 20 minutes, stirring occasionally. Season with pepper to taste and strain the sauce before using.

Basic Recipes

Italian Cheese Sauce

2 tablespoons butter

¼ cup all-purpose flour

1¼ cups hot milk

pinch of nutmeg

pinch of dried thyme

2 tablespoons white wine vinegar

3 tablespoons heavy cream

½ cup grated mozzarella cheese

⅔ cup grated Parmesan cheese

1 teaspoon mustard

2 tablespoons sour cream

salt and pepper

1 Melt the butter in a pan and stir in the flour. Cook, stirring, over a low heat until the roux is light in color and crumbly in texture. Stir in the hot milk and cook, stirring, for 15 minutes, until thick and smooth.

2 Add the nutmeg, thyme, and white wine vinegar and season to taste. Stir in the heavy cream and mix well.

3 Stir in the cheeses, mustard, and sour cream and mix until the cheeses have melted and blended into the sauce.

Fish Stock

2 pounds non-oily fish pieces, such as heads, tails, trimmings, and bones

⅔ cup white wine

1 onion, chopped

1 carrot, sliced

1 celery stalk, sliced

4 black peppercorns

1 bouquet garni

7½ cups water

1 Put the fish pieces, wine, onion, carrot, celery, black peppercorns, bouquet garni, and water in a large pan and simmer for 30 minutes, stirring occasionally. Strain and blot the fat from the surface with paper towels before using the stock.

Garlic Mayonnaise

2 garlic cloves, crushed

8 tablespoons mayonnaise

chopped parsley

salt and pepper

1 Put the mayonnaise in a small bowl. Add the garlic and parsley and season with salt and pepper to taste and mix together well.

Brown Stock

2 pounds veal bones and shin of beef

1 leek, sliced

1 onion, chopped

1 celery stick, sliced

1 carrot, sliced

1 bouquet garni

⅔ cup white wine vinegar

1 thyme sprig

7½ cups cold water

1 Roast the veal bones and shin of beef in their own juices in the oven for 40 minutes.

2 Transfer the bones to a large pan and add the leeks, onion, celery, carrots, bouquet garni, white wine vinegar, and thyme and cover with the water. Simmer over very low heat for about 3 hours. Strain and blot the fat from the surface with paper towels before using.

How to Use This Book

Each recipe contains a wealth of useful information, including a breakdown of nutritional quantities, preparation and cooking times, and level of difficulty. All of this information is explained in detail below.

This amount of time represents the actual cooking time.

The nutritional information provided for each recipe is per serving or per portion. Optional ingredients, variations, or serving suggestions have not been included in the calculations.

The number of chef's hats represents the difficulty of each recipe, ranging from easy (1 chef's hat) to difficult (5 chef's hats).

This amount of time represents the preparation of ingredients, including cooling, chilling, and soaking times.

The ingredients for each recipe are listed in the order in which they are used.

The method is clearly explained with step-by-step instructions that are easy to follow.

The method is illustrated with step-by-step photographs, making the recipe easy to follow.

A full-color photograph of the finished dish.

Variations and cook's tips provide useful information regarding ingredients or cooking techniques.

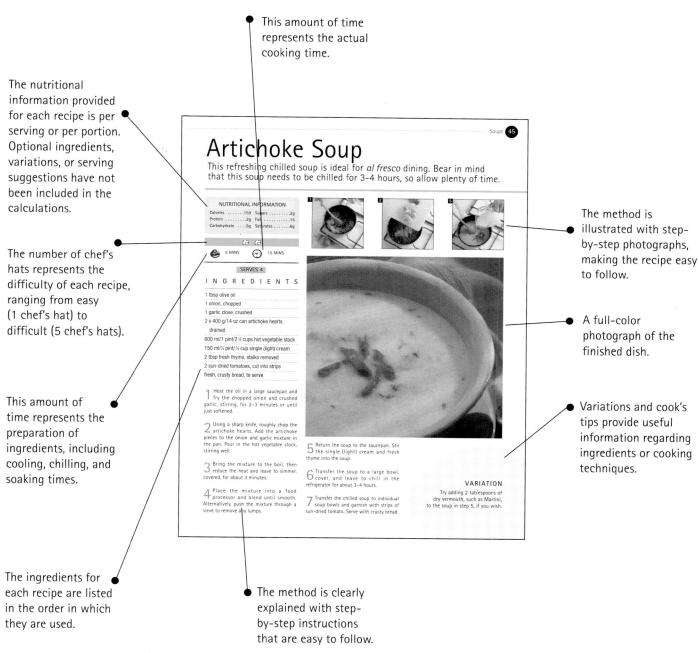

Soups 45

Artichoke Soup

This refreshing chilled soup is ideal for *al fresco* dining. Bear in mind that this soup needs to be chilled for 3-4 hours, so allow plenty of time.

NUTRITIONAL INFORMATION

Calories ....159 Sugars 2g
Protein ....2g Fat 15
Carbohydrate ....5g Saturates 6g

5 MINS   15 MINS

SERVES 4

INGREDIENTS

1 tbsp olive oil
1 onion, chopped
1 garlic clove, crushed
2 x 400 g/14 oz can artichoke hearts, drained
600 ml/1 pint/2 ½ cups hot vegetable stock
150 ml/¼ pint/⅔ cup single (light) cream
2 tbsp fresh thyme, stalks removed
2 sun-dried tomatoes, cut into strips
fresh, crusty bread, to serve

1 Heat the oil in a large saucepan and fry the chopped onion and crushed garlic, stirring, for 2–3 minutes or until just softened.

2 Using a sharp knife, roughly chop the artichoke hearts. Add the artichoke pieces to the onion and garlic mixture in the pan. Pour in the hot vegetable stock, stirring well.

3 Bring the mixture to the boil, then reduce the heat and leave to simmer, covered, for about 3 minutes.

4 Place the mixture into a food processor and blend until smooth. Alternatively, push the mixture through a sieve to remove any lumps.

5 Return the soup to the saucepan. Stir the single (light) cream and fresh thyme into the soup.

6 Transfer the soup to a large bowl, cover, and leave to chill in the refrigerator for about 3–4 hours.

7 Transfer the chilled soup to individual soup bowls and garnish with strips of sun-dried tomato. Serve with crusty bread.

VARIATION

Try adding 2 tablespoons of dry vermouth, such as Martini, to the soup in step 5, if you wish.

Soups

Soups are an important part of the Italian cuisine. They vary in consistency from light and delicate to hearty main meal soups. Texture is always apparent—Italians rarely serve smooth soups. Some may be partially puréed but the identity of the ingredients is never entirely obliterated. There are regional characteristics, too. In the north, soups  are often based on rice, while in Tuscany, thick bean- or bread-based soups are popular. Tomato, garlic, and pasta soups are typical of the south. Minestrone is known worldwide, but the best-known version probably comes from Milan. However, all varieties are full of vegetables and are delicious and satisfying. Fish soups also abound in one guise or another, and most of these are village specialties, so the variety is unlimited and always tasty.

Tuscan Onion Soup

This soup is best made with white onions, which have a mild flavor. If you cannot get hold of them, try using large Spanish onions instead.

NUTRITIONAL INFORMATION

Calories	390	Sugars	.........0g
Protein	.........9g	Fat	..........33g
Carbohydrate	...15g	Saturates	......14g

5–10 MINS   40–45 MINS

SERVES 4

I N G R E D I E N T S

1¾ ounces pancetta ham, diced

1 tablespoon olive oil

4 large white onions, sliced thinly into rings

3 garlic cloves, chopped

3½ cups hot chicken or
   ham stock

4 slices ciabatta or other Italian bread

3 tablespoons butter

¾ cup grated Swiss or Cheddar cheese

salt and pepper

 Dry fry the pancetta in a large saucepan for 3–4 minutes until it begins to brown. Remove the pancetta from the pan and set aside until required.

 Add the oil to the pan and cook the onions and garlic over high heat for 4 minutes. Reduce the heat, cover, and cook for 15 minutes or until the onions are lightly caramelized.

3 Add the stock to the saucepan and bring to a boil. Reduce the heat and leave the mixture to simmer, covered, for about 10 minutes.

4 Toast the slices of ciabatta on both sides, under a preheated broiler, for 2–3 minutes or until golden. Spread the ciabatta with butter and top with the Swiss or Cheddar cheese. Cut the bread into bite-size pieces.

5 Add the reserved pancetta to the soup and season with salt and pepper to taste.

6 Pour into 4 soup bowls and top with the toasted bread.

COOK'S TIP

Pancetta is similar to bacon, but it is air- and salt-cured for about 6 months. Pancetta is available from most delicatessens and some large supermarkets. If you cannot obtain pancetta, use unsmoked bacon instead.

Pumpkin Soup

This thick, creamy soup has a wonderful, warming golden color.
It is flavored with orange and thyme.

NUTRITIONAL INFORMATION

Calories 111   Sugars 4g
Protein . . . . .2g   Fat 6g
Carbohydrate . . . .5g   Saturates 2g

 10 MINS   35–40 MINS

SERVES 4

I N G R E D I E N T S

2 tablespoons olive oil

2 medium onions, chopped

2 garlic cloves, chopped

2 pounds pumpkin, peeled and cut into
  1-inch chunks

6 ¼ cups boiling vegetable or chicken stock

finely grated rind and juice of 1 orange

3 tablespoons fresh thyme, stalks removed

⅔ cup milk

salt and pepper

crusty bread, to serve

1 Heat the olive oil in a large saucepan. Add the onions to the pan and cook for 3–4 minutes or until softened. Add the garlic and pumpkin and cook for a further 2 minutes, stirring well.

2 Add the boiling vegetable or chicken stock, orange rind and juice, and 2 tablespoons of the thyme to the pan. Leave to simmer, covered, for 20 minutes or until the pumpkin is tender.

3 Place the mixture in a food processor and blend until smooth. Alternatively, mash the mixture with a potato masher until smooth. Season to taste.

4 Return the soup to the saucepan and add the milk. Reheat the soup for 3–4 minutes or until it is piping hot but not boiling.

5 Sprinkle with the remaining fresh thyme just before serving.

6 Divide the soup among 4 warm soup bowls and serve with lots of fresh crusty bread.

COOK'S TIP

Pumpkins are usually large vegetables. To make things a little easier, ask the food store to cut a chunk off for you. Alternatively, make double the quantity and freeze the soup for up to 3 months.

Cream of Artichoke Soup

A creamy soup with the unique, subtle flavoring of Jerusalem artichokes and a garnish of grated carrots for extra crunch.

NUTRITIONAL INFORMATION

Calories 19   Sugars 0g
Protein ....0.4g   Fat 2g
Carbohydrate ...0.7g   Saturates 0.7g

 10–15 MINS   55–60 MINS

SERVES 6

INGREDIENTS

1 pound 10 ounces Jerusalem artichokes

1 lemon, sliced thickly

¼ cup butter or margarine

2 onions, chopped

1 garlic clove, crushed

5½ cups chicken or
   vegetable stock

2 bay leaves

¼ teaspoon ground mace or ground nutmeg

1 tablespoon lemon juice

⅔ cup light cream

salt and pepper

TO GARNISH

coarsely grated carrot

chopped fresh parsley or cilantro

1 Peel and slice the artichokes. Put into a bowl of water with the lemon slices.

2 Melt the butter or margarine in a large saucepan. Add the onions and garlic and fry gently for 3–4 minutes until soft but not colored.

3 Drain the artichokes (discarding the lemon) and add to the pan. Mix well and cook gently for 2–3 minutes without allowing to color.

4 Add the stock, seasoning, bay leaves, mace or nutmeg, and lemon juice. Bring slowly to a boil, then cover, and simmer gently for about 30 minutes until the vegetables are very tender.

5 Discard the bay leaves. Cool the soup slightly, then press through a strainer or blend in a food processor until smooth. If liked, a little of the soup may be only partially puréed and added to the rest of the puréed soup, to give extra texture.

6 Pour into a clean pan and bring to a boil. Adjust the seasoning and stir in the cream. Reheat gently without boiling. Garnish with grated carrot and chopped parsley or cilantro.

Vegetable & Bean Soup

This wonderful combination of cannellini beans, vegetables, and vermicelli is made even richer by the addition of pesto and dried mushrooms.

NUTRITIONAL INFORMATION

Calories ....294 Sugars 2g
Protein ....11g Fat 16g
Carbohydrate ...30g Saturates 2g

  30 MINS   30 MINS

SERVES 4

INGREDIENTS

1 small eggplant

2 large tomatoes

1 potato, peeled

1 carrot, peeled

1 leek

15-ounce can cannellini beans

3¾ cups hot vegetable or
   chicken stock

2 teaspoons dried basil

½ ounce dried porcini mushrooms,
   soaked for 10 minutes in enough warm
   water to cover

¼ cup vermicelli

3 tablespoons pesto (see page 53 or
   use ready-made)

freshly grated Parmesan cheese, to serve
   (optional)

1 Slice the eggplant into rounds about ½ inch thick, then cut each round into 4 pieces.

2 Cut the tomatoes and potato into small dice. Cut the carrot into sticks, about 1 inch long and cut the leek into rings.

3 Place the cannellini beans and their liquid in a large saucepan. Add the eggplant, tomatoes, potatoes, carrot, and leek, stirring to mix.

4 Add the stock to the pan and bring to a boil. Reduce the heat and leave to simmer for 15 minutes.

5 Add the basil, dried mushrooms and their soaking liquid, and the vermicelli

and simmer for 5 minutes or until all of the vegetables are tender.

6 Remove the pan from the heat and stir in the pesto.

7 Serve with freshly grated Parmesan cheese, if using.

Garbanzo Bean Soup

A thick vegetable soup which is a delicious meal in itself. Serve with Parmesan cheese and warm sun-dried-tomato-flavored ciabatta bread.

NUTRITIONAL INFORMATION

Calories 297	Sugars 0g
Protein 11g	Fat 18g
Carbohydrate . . .24g	Saturates 2g

 5 MINS   15 MINS

SERVES 4

I N G R E D I E N T S

2 tablespoons olive oil

2 leeks, sliced

2 zucchini, diced

2 garlic cloves, crushed

2 x 14-ounce cans diced tomatoes

1 tablespoon tomato paste

1 fresh bay leaf

3 ¾ cups chicken stock

14-ounce can garbanzo beans, drained and rinsed

8 ounces spinach

salt and pepper

TO SERVE

Parmesan cheese

sun-dried tomato bread

1 Heat the oil in a large saucepan, add the leeks and zucchini, and cook briskly for 5 minutes, stirring constantly.

2 Add the garlic, tomatoes, tomato paste, bay leaf, stock, and garbanzo beans. Bring to a boil and simmer for 5 minutes.

3 Shred the spinach finely, add to the soup, and cook for 2 minutes. Season.

4 Remove the bay leaf from the soup and discard.

5 Serve the soup with freshly grated Parmesan cheese and sun-dried tomato bread.

COOK'S TIP

Garbanzo beans, also known as chick peas, are used extensively in North African cuisine and are also found in Italian, Spanish, Middle Eastern, and Indian cooking. They have a deliciously nutty flavor with a firm texture and are an excellent canned product.

Potato & Pesto Soup

Fresh pesto is a treat to the taste buds and very different in flavor from that available from supermarkets. Store fresh pesto in the refrigerator.

NUTRITIONAL INFORMATION

Calories 548	Sugars 0g	
Protein 11g	Fat 52g	
Carbohydrate . . .10g	Saturates 18g	

  5–10 MINS   50 MINS

SERVES 4

I N G R E D I E N T S

3 slices bacon

1 pound russet potatoes

1 pound onions

2 tablespoons olive oil

2 tablespoons butter

2 ½ cups chicken stock

2 ½ cups milk

1 cup dried conchigliette pasta

⅔ cup heavy cream

chopped fresh parsley

salt and pepper

freshly grated Parmesan cheese and garlic
bread, to serve

P E S T O   S A U C E

1 cup finely chopped fresh parsley

2 garlic cloves, crushed

¼ cup pine nuts, crushed

2 tablespoons chopped fresh basil leaves

⅔ cup freshly grated Parmesan cheese

white pepper

⅔ cup olive oil

1 To make the pesto sauce, put all of the ingredients in a blender or food processor and process for 2 minutes, or blend by hand using a pestle and mortar.

2 Finely chop the bacon, potatoes, and onions. Fry the bacon in a large pan over a medium heat for 4 minutes. Add the butter, potatoes and onions and cook for 12 minutes, stirring constantly.

3 Add the stock and milk to the pan, bring to a boil and simmer for 10 minutes. Add the conchigliette and simmer for a further 10–12 minutes.

4 Blend in the cream and simmer for 5 minutes. Add the parsley, salt and pepper, and 2 tablespoons pesto sauce. Transfer to serving bowls and serve with Parmesan cheese and fresh garlic bread.

Creamy Tomato Soup

This quick and easy creamy soup has a lovely fresh tomato flavor. Basil leaves complement tomatoes perfectly.

NUTRITIONAL INFORMATION

Calories 218   Sugars 10g
Protein ....3g   Fat 19g
Carbohydrate ...10g   Saturates 11g

5 MINS   25–30 MINS

SERVES 4

I N G R E D I E N T S

3 tablespoons butter

1 pound 9 ounces ripe tomatoes, preferably
   plum, roughly chopped

3¾ cups hot vegetable stock

½ cup ground almonds

⅔ cup milk or light cream

1 teaspoon sugar

2 tablespoons shredded basil leaves

salt and pepper

1 Melt the butter in a large saucepan. Add the tomatoes and cook for 5 minutes until the skins start to wrinkle. Season to taste with salt and pepper.

2 Add the stock to the pan, bring to a boil, cover, and simmer for 10 minutes.

3 Meanwhile, under a preheated broiler, lightly toast the ground almonds until they are golden-brown. This will take only 1-2 minutes, so watch them closely.

4 Remove the soup from the heat, place in a food processor, and blend the mixture to form a smooth consistency. Alternatively, mash the soup with a potato masher until smooth.

5 Pass the soup through a strainer to remove any tomato skin or pips.

6 Place the soup in the pan and return to the heat. Stir in the milk or cream, toasted ground almonds, and sugar. Warm the soup through and add the shredded basil leaves just before serving.

7 Transfer the creamy tomato soup to warm soup bowls and serve hot.

COOK'S TIP

Very fine bread crumbs can be used instead of the ground almonds, if you prefer. Toast them in the same way as the almonds and add with the milk or cream in step 6.

Calabrian Mushroom Soup

The Calabrian Mountains in southern Italy provide large amounts of wild mushrooms that are rich in flavor and color.

NUTRITIONAL INFORMATION

Calories ....452 Sugars 5g
Protein ....15g Fat 26g
Carbohydrate ...42g Saturates 12g

5 MINS   25–30 MINS

SERVES 4

I N G R E D I E N T S

2 tbsp olive oil

1 onion, chopped

1 lb mixed mushrooms, such as porcini, oyster, and button

1¼ cup milk

3¾ cups hot vegetable stock

8 slices of rustic bread or French stick

2 garlic cloves, minced

3 tbsp butter, melted

2¾ oz Swiss cheese, finely grated

salt and pepper

1 Heat the oil in a large skillet and cook the onion for 3–4 minutes or until soft and golden.

2 Wipe each mushroom with a damp cloth and cut any large mushrooms into smaller, bite-size pieces.

3 Add the mushrooms to the pan, stirring quickly to coat them in the oil.

4 Add the milk to the pan, bring to a boil, cover, and leave to simmer for about 5 minutes. Gradually stir in the hot vegetable stock and season with salt and pepper to taste.

5 Under a preheated broiler, toast the bread on both sides until golden.

6 Mix together the garlic and butter and spoon generously over the toast.

7 Place the toast in the bottom of a large tureen or divide it among 4 individual serving bowls and pour over the hot soup. Top with the grated Swiss cheese and serve at once.

COOK'S TIP

Mushrooms absorb liquid, which can lessen the flavor and affect cooking properties. Wipe them carefully with a damp cloth rather than rinsing them in water.

Green Soup

This fresh-tasting soup with green beans, cucumber, and watercress can be served warm or chilled on a hot summer day.

NUTRITIONAL INFORMATION

Calories 121   Sugars 2g
Protein . . . . .2g   Fat 8g
Carbohydrate . . .10g   Saturates 1g

  5 MINS   25–30 MINS

SERVES 4

I N G R E D I E N T S

1 tablespoon olive oil

1 onion, chopped

1 garlic clove, chopped

7 ounces potato, peeled and cut into
    1-inch cubes

3 cups vegetable or chicken stock

1 small cucumber or ½ large cucumber, cut
    into chunks

3-ounce bunch watercress

4 ½ ounces green beans, trimmed
    and halved lengthwise

salt and pepper

VARIATION

Try using 4½ ounces snow peas or sugar snap peas instead of the beans, if you prefer.

1 Heat the oil in a large pan and fry the onion and garlic for 3–4 minutes or until softened.

2 Add the cubed potato and fry for a further 2–3 minutes.

3 Stir in the stock, bring to a boil, and leave to simmer for 5 minutes.

4 Add the cucumber to the pan and cook for a further 3 minutes or until the potatoes are tender. Test by inserting the tip of a knife into the potato cubes—it should pass through easily.

5 Add the watercress and allow to wilt. Then place the soup in a food processor and blend until smooth. Alternatively, before adding the watercress, mash the soup with a potato masher and push through a strainer, then chop the watercress finely and stir into the soup.

6 Bring a small pan of water to a boil and steam the beans for 3–4 minutes or until tender.

7 Add the beans to the soup, season, and warm through.

Bean & Pasta Soup

A dish with proud Mediterranean origins, this soup is a winter warmer. Serve with warm, crusty bread and, if you like, a slice of cheese.

NUTRITIONAL INFORMATION

Calories ....463 Sugars 5g
Protein ....13g Fat 33g
Carbohydrate ...30g Saturates 7g

 5–10 MINS   1¼ HOURS

SERVES 4

INGREDIENTS

1¼ cup dried navy beans, soaked, drained, and rinsed

4 tablespoons olive oil

2 large onions, sliced

3 garlic cloves, chopped

14-ounce can diced tomatoes

1 teaspoon dried oregano

1 teaspoon tomato paste

3¾ cups water

¾ cup small dried pasta shapes, such as fusilli or conchigliette

4½ ounces sun-dried tomatoes, drained and sliced thinly

1 tablespoon chopped cilantro, or flat-leaf parsley

2 tablespoons freshly grated Parmesan

salt and pepper

1 Put the soaked beans into a large pan, cover with cold water, and bring them to a boil. Boil rapidly for 15 minutes to remove any harmful toxins. Drain the beans in a colander.

2 Heat the oil in a pan over medium heat and fry the onions until they are just beginning to change color. Stir in the garlic and cook for 1 further minute. Stir in the diced tomatoes, oregano, and the tomato paste and pour on the water. Add the beans, bring to a boil, and cover the pan. Simmer for 45 minutes or until the beans are almost tender.

3 Add the pasta, season the soup with salt and pepper to taste, and stir in the sun-dried tomatoes. Return the soup to a boil, partly cover the pan, and continue cooking for 10 minutes, or until the pasta is nearly tender.

4 Stir in the chopped cilantro or parsley. Taste the soup and adjust the seasoning if necessary. Transfer to a warm soup tureen to serve. Sprinkle with the cheese and serve hot.

Tomato & Pasta Soup

Plum tomatoes are ideal for making soups and sauces as they have denser, less watery flesh than rounder varieties.

NUTRITIONAL INFORMATION

Calories	503	Sugars	........16g
Protein	.........9g	Fat	.........28g
Carbohydrate	...59g	Saturates	......17g

  5 MINS   50–55 MINS

SERVES 4

I N G R E D I E N T S

4 tablespoons unsalted butter

1 large onion, chopped

2½ cups vegetable stock

2 pounds Italian plum tomatoes, peeled and roughly chopped

pinch of baking soda

2 cups dried fusilli

1 tablespoon sugar

⅔ cup heavy cream

salt and pepper

fresh basil leaves, to garnish

1 Melt the butter in a large pan, add the onion, and fry for 3 minutes, stirring. Add 1¼ cups of vegetable stock to the pan, with the chopped tomatoes and baking soda. Bring the soup to a boil and simmer for 20 minutes.

VARIATION

To make orange and tomato soup, simply use half the quantity of vegetable stock, topped up with the same amount of fresh orange juice and garnish the soup with orange rind.

  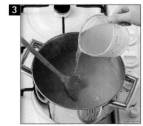

2 Remove the pan from the heat and set aside to cool. Purée the soup in a blender or food processor and pour through a fine strainer back into the saucepan.

3 Add the remaining vegetable stock and the fusilli to the pan, and season to taste with salt and pepper.

4 Add the sugar to the pan, bring to a boil, then lower the heat, and simmer for about 15 minutes.

5 Pour the soup into a warm tureen, swirl the heavy cream around the surface of the soup, and garnish with fresh basil leaves. Serve immediately.

Artichoke Soup

This refreshing chilled soup is ideal for *al fresco* dining. Bear in mind that this soup needs to be chilled for 3-4 hours, so allow plenty of time.

NUTRITIONAL INFORMATION

Calories 159   Sugars 2g
Protein . . . . .2g   Fat 15
Carbohydrate . . . .5g   Saturates 6g

🍽 5 MINS   🕐 15 MINS

SERVES 4

I N G R E D I E N T S

1 tablespoon olive oil

1 onion, chopped

1 garlic clove, crushed

2 x 14-ounce cans artichoke hearts,
   drained

2½ cups hot vegetable stock

⅔ cup light cream

2 tablespoons fresh thyme, stalks removed

2 sun-dried tomatoes, cut into strips

fresh, crusty bread, to serve

1 Heat the oil in a large saucepan and fry the chopped onion and crushed garlic, stirring, for 2–3 minutes or until just softened.

2 Using a sharp knife, roughly chop the artichoke hearts. Add the artichoke pieces to the onion and garlic mixture in the pan. Pour in the hot vegetable stock, stirring well.

3 Bring the mixture to a boil, then reduce the heat, and simmer, covered, for about 3 minutes.

4 Place the mixture in a food processor and blend until smooth. Alternatively, push the mixture through a strainer to remove any lumps.

5 Return the soup to the saucepan. Stir the light cream and fresh thyme into the soup.

6 Transfer the soup to a large bowl, cover, and leave to chill in the refrigerator for about 3–4 hours.

7 Transfer the chilled soup to individual soup bowls and garnish with strips of sun-dried tomato. Serve with crusty bread.

VARIATION

Try adding 2 tablespoons of dry vermouth, such as Martini, to the soup in step 5, if you wish.

Minestrone & Pasta Soup

Italian cooks have created some very heart-warming soups and this is the most famous of all.

NUTRITIONAL INFORMATION

Calories 231	Sugars 3g
Protein 8g	Fat 16g
Carbohydrate . . .14g	Saturates 7g

10 MINS   1¾ HOURS

SERVES 10

INGREDIENTS

3 garlic cloves

3 large onions

2 celery stalks

2 large carrots

2 large potatoes

3 ½ ounces green beans

3 ½ ounces zucchini

4 tablespoons butter

¼ cup olive oil

⅓ cup finely diced bacon

7 cups vegetable or chicken stock

1 bunch fresh basil, finely chopped

3 ½ ounces chopped tomatoes

2 tablespoons tomato paste

3 ½ ounces Parmesan cheese rind

¾ cup dried spaghetti, broken up

salt and pepper

freshly grated Parmesan cheese,
   to serve

1 Finely chop the garlic, onions, celery, carrots, potatoes, beans, and zucchini.

2 Heat the butter and oil together in a large saucepan, add the bacon, and cook for 2 minutes.

3 Add the garlic and onion and fry for 2 minutes, then stir in the celery, carrots, and potatoes, and fry for a further 2 minutes.

4 Add the beans to the pan and fry for 2 minutes. Stir in the zucchini and fry for a further 2 minutes. Cover the pan and cook all the vegetables, stirring frequently, for 15 minutes.

5 Add the stock, basil, tomatoes, tomato paste, and cheese rind and season to taste. Bring to a boil, lower the heat, and simmer for 1 hour. Remove and discard the cheese rind.

6 Add the spaghetti to the pan and cook for 20 minutes. Serve in large, warm soup bowls; sprinkle with freshly grated Parmesan cheese.

Red Bean Soup

Beans feature widely in Italian soups, making them hearty and tasty. The beans need to be soaked overnight, so prepare well in advance.

NUTRITIONAL INFORMATION

Calories 184	Sugars 5g
Protein 4g	Fat 11g
Carbohydrate . . .19g	Saturates 2g

5–10 MINS   3¾ HOURS

SERVES 6

I N G R E D I E N T S

1 cup dried red kidney beans,
    soaked overnight

7½ cups water

1 large ham bone

2 carrots, chopped

1 large onion, chopped

2 celery stalks, sliced thinly

1 leek, trimmed, washed and sliced

1–2 bay leaves

2 tablespoons olive oil

2–3 tomatoes, peeled and chopped

1 garlic clove, crushed

1 tablespoon tomato paste

4½ tablespoons arborio or Italian rice

4–6 ounces green cabbage,
    shredded finely

salt and pepper

1 Drain the beans and place them in a saucepan with enough water to cover. Bring to a boil, then boil for 15 minutes to remove any harmful toxins. Reduce the heat and simmer for 45 minutes.

2 Drain the beans and put into a clean saucepan with the water, ham bone, carrots, onion, celery, leek, bay leaves, and olive oil. Bring to a boil, then cover, and simmer for 1 hour or until the beans are very tender.

3 Discard the bay leaves and bone, reserving any ham pieces from the bone. Remove a small cupful of the beans and reserve. Purée or process the soup in a food processor or blender, or push through a coarse strainer, and return to a clean saucepan.

4 Add the tomatoes, garlic, tomato paste, and rice and season to taste with salt and pepper. Bring back to a boil and simmer for about 15 minutes or until the rice is tender.

5 Add the cabbage and reserved beans and ham, and continue to simmer for 5 minutes. Adjust the seasoning and serve very hot. If liked, a piece of toasted crusty bread may be put in the base of each soup bowl before ladling in the soup. If the soup is too thick, add a little boiling water or stock.

Brown Lentil & Pasta Soup

In Italy, this soup is called *Minestrade Lentiche*. A *minestra* is a soup cooked with pasta; here, farfalline, a small bow-shaped variety, is used.

NUTRITIONAL INFORMATION

Calories 225	Sugars 1g	
Protein 13g	Fat 8g	
Carbohydrate . . .27g	Saturates 3g	

 5 MINS   25 MINS

SERVES 4

INGREDIENTS

4 slices rindless bacon, cut into
  small squares

1 onion, chopped

2 garlic cloves, crushed

2 celery stalks, chopped

½ cup farfalline or spaghetti,
  broken into small pieces

14-ounce can brown lentils, drained

5 cups hot ham or
  vegetable stock

2 tablespoons chopped, fresh mint

1 Place the bacon in a large skillet, together with the onions, garlic, and celery. Dry fry for 4–5 minutes, stirring, until the onion is tender and the bacon is just beginning to brown.

2 Add the pasta to the skillet and cook, stirring, for about 1 minute to coat the pasta in the oil.

3 Add the lentils and the stock and bring to a boil. Reduce the heat and leave to simmer for 12–15 minutes or until the pasta is tender.

4 Remove the skillet from the heat and stir in the chopped fresh mint.

5 Transfer the soup to warm soup bowls and serve immediately.

COOK'S TIP

If you prefer to use dried lentils, add the stock before the pasta and cook for 1–1¼ hours until the lentils are tender. Add the pasta and cook for a further 12–15 minutes.

Minestrone Soup

Minestrone translates as "big soup" in Italian. It is made all over Italy, but this version comes from Livorno, a port on the western coast.

NUTRITIONAL INFORMATION

Calories 311   Sugars 8g
Protein . . . . .12g   Fat 19g
Carbohydrate . . .26g   Saturates 5g

10 MINS   30 MINS

SERVES 4

I N G R E D I E N T S

1 tablespoon olive oil

3 ½ ounces pancetta ham, diced

2 medium onions, chopped

2 garlic cloves, crushed

1 potato, peeled and cut into ½-inch cubes

1 carrot, peeled and cut into chunks

1 leek, sliced into rings

¼ green cabbage, shredded

1 celery stalk, chopped

1-pound can diced tomatoes

7-ounce can small navy beans,
    drained and rinsed

2 ½ cups hot ham or chicken stock,
    diluted with 2 ½ cups boiling water

bouquet garni (2 bay leaves, 2 sprigs
    rosemary and 2 sprigs thyme,
    tied together)

salt and pepper

freshly grated Parmesan cheese,
    to serve

1 Heat the olive oil in a large saucepan. Add the diced pancetta, chopped onions, and garlic and fry for about 5 minutes, stirring, or until the onions are soft and golden.

2 Add the prepared potato, carrot, leek, cabbage, and celery to the saucepan. Cook for a further 2 minutes, stirring frequently to coat all of the vegetables in the oil.

3 Add the tomatoes, small navy beans, hot ham or chicken stock, and bouquet garni to the pan, stirring to mix. Leave the soup to simmer, covered, for 15–20 minutes or until all of the vegetables are just tender.

4 Remove the bouquet garni, season with salt and pepper to taste, and serve with plenty of freshly grated Parmesan cheese.

Spinach & Mascarpone Soup

Spinach is the basis for this delicious soup, but use sorrel or watercress instead for a pleasant change.

NUTRITIONAL INFORMATION

Calories 537	Sugars 2g
Protein 6g	Fat 53g
Carbohydrate 9g	Saturates 29g

5 MINS   35 MINS

SERVES 4

I N G R E D I E N T S

¼ cup butter

1 bunch green onions, trimmed
   and chopped

2 celery stalks, chopped

12 ounces spinach or sorrel, or
   3 bunches watercress

3¾ cups vegetable stock

1 cup mascarpone cheese

1 tablespoon olive oil

2 slices thick-cut bread, cut into cubes

½ teaspoon caraway seeds

salt and pepper

sesame bread sticks, to serve

1 Melt half the butter in a very large saucepan. Add the green onions and celery and cook gently for about 5 minutes, or until softened.

2 Pack the spinach, sorrel, or watercress into the saucepan. Add the vegetable stock and bring to a boil, then reduce the heat, and simmer, covered, for 15–20 minutes.

3 Transfer the soup to a blender or food processor and blend until smooth, or pass through a strainer. Return to the saucepan.

4 Add the mascarpone cheese to the soup and heat gently, stirring, until smooth and blended. Taste and season with salt and pepper.

5 Heat the remaining butter with the oil in a skillet. Add the bread cubes and fry in the hot oil until golden brown, adding the caraway seeds toward the end of cooking, so that they do not burn.

6 Ladle the soup into 4 warm bowls. Sprinkle with the croûtons and serve at once, accompanied by the sesame bread sticks.

VARIATIONS

Any leafy vegetable can be used to make this soup to give variations to the flavor. For anyone who grows their own vegetables, it is the perfect recipe for experimenting with a glut of produce. Try young beet leaves or surplus lettuces for a change.

Tuscan Bean Soup

A thick and creamy soup that is based on a traditional Tuscan recipe. If you use dried beans, the preparation and cooking times will be longer.

NUTRITIONAL INFORMATION

Calories	250	Sugars 4g
Protein	. . . . .13g	Fat 10g
Carbohydrate	. . .29g	Saturates 2g

2 MINS   10 MINS

SERVES 4

INGREDIENTS

1¼ cups dried lima beans, soaked
   overnight, or 2 x 14-ounce cans
   lima beans

1 tablespoon olive oil

2 garlic cloves, crushed

1 vegetable or chicken stock cube,
   crumbled

⅔ cup milk

2 tablespoons chopped fresh oregano

salt and pepper

1   If you are using dried beans that have been soaked overnight, drain them thoroughly. Bring a large pan of water to a boil, add the beans, and boil for 10 minutes. Cover the pan and simmer for a further 30 minutes or until tender. Drain the beans, reserving the cooking liquid. If you are using canned beans, drain them thoroughly and reserve the liquid.

2   Heat the oil in a large skillet and fry the garlic for 2–3 minutes or until just beginning to brown.

3   Add the beans and 1⅔ cups of the reserved liquid to the skillet, stirring constantly. You may need to add a little water if there is insufficient liquid and the mixture is too stiff. Stir in the crumbled stock cube. Bring the mixture to a boil and then remove the pan from the heat.

4   Place the bean mixture in a food processor and blend to form a smooth purée. Alternatively, mash the bean mixture to a smooth consistency. Season to taste with salt and pepper and stir in the milk.

5   Pour the soup back into the pan and gently heat to just below boiling point. Stir in the chopped oregano just before serving.

Ravioli alla Parmigiana

This soup is traditionally served at Easter and Christmas in the province of Parma.

SERVES 4

INGREDIENTS

10 ounces Basic Pasta Dough (see page 24)

5 cups veal stock

freshly grated Parmesan cheese, to serve

FILLING

½ cup Espagnole Sauce (see page 29)

1 cup freshly grated Parmesan cheese

1½ cups fine white bread crumbs

2 eggs

1 small onion, finely chopped

1 teaspoon freshly grated nutmeg

1 Make the Basic Pasta Dough (see page 24) and the Espagnole Sauce (see page 29).

2 Carefully roll out 2 sheets of the pasta dough and cover with a damp dish cloth while you are making the filling for the ravioli.

3 To make the filling, place the freshly grated Parmesan cheese, fine white bread crumbs, eggs, Espagnole Sauce, finely chopped onion, and the freshly grated nutmeg in a large mixing bowl, and mix together well.

4 Place spoonfuls of the filling at regular intervals on 1 sheet of pasta dough. Cover with the second sheet of pasta dough, then cut into squares, and seal the edges.

5 Bring the veal stock to a boil in a large saucepan.

6 Add the ravioli to the pan and cook for about 15 minutes.

7 Transfer the soup and ravioli to warm serving bowls and serve, generously sprinkled with Parmesan cheese.

COOK'S TIP

It is advisable to prepare the Basic Pasta Dough (see page 24) and the Espagnole Sauce (see page 29) well in advance, or buy ready-made equivalents if you are short of time.

Minestrone with Pesto

This version of minestrone contains cannellini beans—these need to be soaked overnight, so prepare in advance.

NUTRITIONAL INFORMATION

Calories ....604 Sugars 3g
Protein ....26g Fat 45g
Carbohydrate ...24g Saturates 11g

🍲 10–15 MINS 🕐 1¾ HOURS

SERVES 6

INGREDIENTS

1 cup dried cannellini beans,
  soaked overnight

10 cups water or stock

1 large onion, chopped

1 leek, trimmed and sliced thinly

2 celery stalks, sliced very thinly

2 carrots, chopped

3 tablespoons olive oil

2 tomatoes, peeled and chopped roughly

1 zucchini, trimmed and
  sliced thinly

2 potatoes, diced

¾ cup dried elbow macaroni (or other small
  macaroni)

salt and pepper

4–6 tablespoons freshly grated Parmesan,
to serve

PESTO

2 tablespoons pine nuts

5 tablespoons olive oil

2 bunches basil, stems removed

4–6 garlic cloves, crushed

1 cup grated Romano or Parmesan

1 Drain the beans, rinse, and put in a pan with the water or stock. Bring to a boil, cover, and simmer for 1 hour.

2 Add the onion, leek, celery, carrots, and oil. Cover and simmer for about 4–5 minutes.

3 Add the tomatoes, zucchini, potatoes, macaroni, and seasoning. Cover and continue to simmer for about 30 minutes.

4 Meanwhile, make the pesto. Fry the pine nuts in 1 tablespoon of the oil until pale brown, then drain. Put the basil into a food processor or blender, with the nuts and garlic. Process until well chopped. Alternatively, chop finely by hand and pound with a pestle and mortar. Gradually add the remaining oil until smooth. Turn into a bowl, add the cheese and seasoning, and mix thoroughly.

5 Stir 4½ teaspoons of the pesto into the soup until well blended. Simmer for a further 5 minutes and adjust the seasoning. Serve very hot, sprinkled with the cheese.

Fish Soup

There are many varieties of fish soup in Italy, some including shellfish. This one, from Tuscany, is more like a chowder.

NUTRITIONAL INFORMATION

Calories 305   Sugars 3g
Protein . . . . .47g   Fat 7g
Carbohydrate . . . .11g   Saturates 1g

 5–10 MINS   1 HOUR

SERVES 6

I N G R E D I E N T S

2¼ pounds assorted prepared fish
   (including mixed fish fillets, squid, etc.)

2 onions, sliced thinly

2 celery stalks, sliced thinly

a few sprigs of parsley

2 bay leaves

⅔ cup white wine

4 cups water

2 tablespoons olive oil

1 garlic clove, crushed

1 carrot, chopped finely

14-ounce can peeled tomatoes, puréed

2 potatoes, chopped

1 tablespoon tomato paste

1 teaspoon chopped fresh oregano or
   ½ teaspoon dried oregano

12 ounces fresh mussels

6 ounces peeled shrimp

2 tablespoons chopped fresh parsley

salt and pepper

crusty bread, to serve

1 Cut the fish into slices and put into a pan with half the onion and celery, the parsley, bay leaves, wine, and water. Bring to a boil, cover, and simmer for 25 minutes.

2 Strain the fish stock and discard the vegetables. Skin the fish, remove any bones, and reserve the flesh.

3 Heat the oil in a pan. Fry the remaining onion and celery with the garlic and carrot until soft but not colored, stirring occasionally. Add the puréed canned tomatoes, potatoes, tomato paste, oregano, reserved stock, and seasoning. Bring to a boil and simmer for about 15 minutes or until the potato is almost tender.

4 Meanwhile, thoroughly scrub the mussels. Add the mussels to the pan with the shrimp and simmer for about 5 minutes or until the mussels have opened (discard any that remain closed).

5 Return the fish to the soup with the chopped parsley, bring back to a boil, and simmer for 5 minutes. Adjust the seasoning.

6 Serve the soup in warm bowls with chunks of fresh crusty bread, or put a toasted slice of crusty bread in the bottom of each bowl before adding the soup. If possible, remove a few half shells from the mussels before serving.

Mussel & Potato Soup

This quick and easy soup would make a delicious summer lunch, served with fresh crusty bread.

NUTRITIONAL INFORMATION

Calories 804	Sugars 3g
Protein 17g	Fat 68g
Carbohydrate . . .32g	Saturates 38g

 10 MINS   35 MINS

SERVES 4

I N G R E D I E N T S

1 pound 10 ounces mussels

2 tablespoons olive oil

7 tablespoons butter

2 slices rindless fatty bacon, chopped

1 onion, chopped

2 garlic cloves, crushed

½ cup all-purpose flour

1 pound potatoes, thinly sliced

1 cup dried conchigliette pasta

1 ¼ cups heavy cream

1 tablespoon lemon juice

2 egg yolks

salt and pepper

TO GARNISH

2 tablespoons finely chopped
   fresh parsley

lemon wedges

1 Debeard the mussels and scrub them under cold water for 5 minutes. Discard any mussels that do not close immediately when sharply tapped.

2 Bring a large pan of water to a boil, add the mussels, oil, and a little pepper. Cook until the mussels open. (discard any mussels that remain closed).

3 Drain the mussels, reserving the cooking liquid. Remove the mussels from their shells.

4 Melt the butter in a large saucepan, add the bacon, onion, and garlic, and cook for 4 minutes. Carefully stir in the flour. Measure 5 cups of the reserved cooking liquid and stir it into the pan.

5 Add the potatoes to the pan and simmer for 5 minutes. Add the conchigliette and simmer for a further 10 minutes.

6 Add the cream and lemon juice, season to taste with salt and pepper, then add the mussels to the pan.

7 Carefully blend the egg yolks with 1-2 tablespoons of the remaining cooking liquid, stir into the pan, and cook for 4 minutes.

8 Ladle the soup into 4 warm individual soup bowls, garnish with the chopped fresh parsley and lemon wedges, and serve at once.

Italian Fish Stew

This robust stew is full of Mediterranean flavors. If you do not want to prepare the fish yourself, ask your local fish store to do it for you.

NUTRITIONAL INFORMATION

Calories 236	Sugars 4g	
Protein 20g	Fat 7g	
Carbohydrate ...25g	Saturates 1g	

 5–10 MINS   25 MINS

SERVES 4

INGREDIENTS

2 tablespoons olive oil

2 red onions, finely chopped

1 garlic clove, crushed

2 zucchini, sliced

14-ounce can diced tomatoes

3¾ cups fish or vegetable stock

¾ cup dried pasta shapes

12 ounces firm white fish, such as cod,
   haddock, or hake

1 tablespoon chopped fresh basil or
   oregano or 1 teaspoon dried oregano

1 teaspoon grated lemon rind

1 tablespoon cornstarch

1 tablespoon water

salt and pepper

sprigs of fresh basil or oregano,
   to garnish

1 Heat the oil in a large saucepan and fry the onions and garlic for 5 minutes. Add the zucchini and cook for 2–3 minutes, stirring often.

2 Add the tomatoes and stock to the saucepan and bring to a boil. Add the pasta, cover, and reduce the heat. Simmer for 5 minutes.

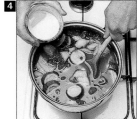

3 Skin and bone the fish, then cut it into chunks. Add to the saucepan, with the basil or oregano and lemon rind, and cook gently for 5 minutes until the fish is opaque and flakes easily (take care not to overcook it).

4 Blend the cornstarch with the water and stir into the stew. Cook gently for 2 minutes, stirring, until thickened. Season with salt and pepper to taste and ladle into 4 warm soup bowls. Garnish with basil or oregano sprigs and serve at once.

Italian Seafood Soup

This colorful mixed seafood soup would be superbly complemented by a dry white wine.

NUTRITIONAL INFORMATION

Calories . . . . .668 Sugars 3g
Protein . . . . .48g Fat 43g
Carbohydrate . . .21g Saturates 25g

5 MINS   55 MINS

SERVES 4

INGREDIENTS

4 tablespoons butter

1 pound assorted fish fillets, such as
    salmon and red snapper

1 pound prepared
    seafood, such as
    squid and shrimp

8 ounces fresh crab meat

1 large onion, sliced

¼ cup all-purpose flour

5 cups fish stock

1 cup dried pasta shapes, such as ditalini
    or elbow macaroni

1 tablespoon anchovy paste

grated rind and juice of 1 orange

¼ cup dry sherry

1 ¼ cups heavy cream

salt and pepper

crusty brown bread, to serve

1 Melt the butter in a large saucepan, add the fish fillets, seafood, crab meat, and onion and cook gently over low heat for 6 minutes.

2 Add the flour to the seafood mixture, stirring thoroughly to prevent any lumps from forming.

3 Gradually add the stock, stirring, until the soup comes to a boil. Reduce the heat and simmer for 30 minutes.

4 Add the pasta to the pan and cook for a further 10 minutes.

5 Stir in the anchovy paste, orange rind, orange juice, sherry, and heavy cream.

Season to taste with salt and pepper and mix well.

6 Heat the soup until completely warmed through.

7 Transfer the soup to a tureen or to warm soup bowls and serve with crusty brown bread.

Lemon & Chicken Soup

This delicately flavored summer soup is surprisingly easy to make, and tastes delicious.

NUTRITIONAL INFORMATION

Calories	506	Sugars	.........4g
Protein	........19g	Fat	..........31g
Carbohydrate	...41g	Saturates	......19g

 5–10 MINS   1¼ HOURS

SERVES 4

INGREDIENTS

4 tablespoons butter

8 shallots, thinly sliced

2 carrots, thinly sliced

2 celery stalks, thinly sliced

8 ounces boneless chicken breasts, finely chopped

3 lemons

5 cups chicken stock

2 cups dried spaghetti, broken into small pieces

⅔ cup heavy cream

salt and white pepper

TO GARNISH

fresh parsley sprig

3 lemon slices, halved

COOK'S TIP

You can prepare this soup up to the end of step 3 in advance, so that all you need do before serving is heat it through before adding the pasta and the finishing touches.

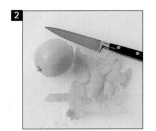

1 Melt the butter in a large saucepan. Add the shallots, carrots, celery, and chicken and cook over low heat, stirring occasionally, for 8 minutes.

2 Thinly pare the lemons and blanch the lemon rind in boiling water for 3 minutes. Squeeze the juice from the lemons.

3 Add the lemon rind and juice to the pan, together with the chicken stock. Bring slowly to a boil over low heat and simmer for 40 minutes, stirring occasionally.

4 Add the spaghetti to the pan and cook for 15 minutes. Season to taste with salt and white pepper and add the cream. Heat through, but do not allow the soup to boil or it will curdle.

5 Pour the soup into a tureen or individual bowls, garnish with the parsley and half slices of lemon, and serve at once.

Chicken & Pasta Broth

This satisfying soup makes a good lunch or supper dish and you can use any vegetables you like. Children will love the tiny pasta shapes.

NUTRITIONAL INFORMATION

Calories 185	Sugars 5g
Protein 17g	Fat 5g
Carbohydrate ...20g	Saturates 1g

5 MINS   15-20 MINS

SERVES 6

INGREDIENTS

12 ounces boneless chicken breasts

2 tablespoons sunflower oil

1 medium onion, diced

1½ cups diced carrots

9 ounces cauliflower flowerets

3¾ cups chicken stock

2 teaspoons dried mixed herbs

1 cup small dried pasta shapes

salt and pepper

Parmesan cheese (optional) and crusty
    bread, to serve

1 Using a sharp knife, finely dice the chicken, discarding any skin.

2 Heat the oil in a large saucepan and quickly sauté the chicken, onion, carrots, and cauliflower until they are lightly colored.

3 Stir in the chicken stock and dried mixed herbs and bring to a boil.

4 Add the pasta shapes to the pan and return to a boil. Cover the pan and leave the broth to simmer for 10 minutes, stirring occasionally to prevent the pasta shapes from sticking together.

5 Season the broth with salt and pepper to taste and sprinkle with Parmesan cheese, if using. Serve the broth with fresh crusty bread.

COOK'S TIP

You can use any small pasta shapes for this soup—try conchigliette or ditalini or even spaghetti broken up into small pieces. To make a fun soup for children you could add animal-shaped or alphabet pasta.

Chicken & Bean Soup

This hearty and nourishing soup, combining garbanzo beans and chicken, is an ideal starter for a family supper.

NUTRITIONAL INFORMATION

Calories	347	Sugars	2g
Protein	28g	Fat	11g
Carbohydrate	37g	Saturates	4g

5 MINS   1¾ HOURS

SERVES 4

I N G R E D I E N T S

2 tablespoons butter

3 green onions, chopped

2 garlic cloves, crushed

1 fresh marjoram sprig, finely chopped

12 ounces boneless chicken breasts, diced

5 cups chicken stock

12-ounce can garbanzo beans, drained

1 bouquet garni

1 red bell pepper, diced

1 green bell pepper, diced

1 cup small dried pasta shapes,
    such as elbow macaroni

salt and white pepper

croutons, to serve

COOK'S TIP

If you prefer, you can use dried garbanzo beans. Cover with cold water and set aside to soak for 5–8 hours or overnight. Drain and add the beans to the soup, according to the recipe, and allow an additional 30 minutes– 1 hour cooking time.

1 Melt the butter in a large saucepan. Add the green onions, garlic, sprig of fresh marjoram, and the diced chicken and cook, stirring frequently, over medium heat for 5 minutes.

2 Add the chicken stock, garbanzo beans, and bouquet garni and season with salt and white pepper.

3 Bring the soup to a boil, lower the heat, and simmer for about 2 hours.

4 Add the diced bell peppers and pasta to the pan, then simmer for a further 20 minutes.

5 Transfer the soup to a warm tureen. To serve, ladle the soup into individual serving bowls and serve immediately, garnished with the croutons.

Tuscan Veal Broth

Veal plays an important role in Italian cuisine and there are dozens of recipes for all cuts of this meat.

NUTRITIONAL INFORMATION

Calories . . . . . . .420 Sugars 5g
Protein . . . . .54g Fat 7g
Carbohydrate . . .37g Saturates 2g

2¼ HOURS   4¾ HOURS

SERVES 4

I N G R E D I E N T S

⅓ cup dried peas, soaked for
  2 hours and drained

2 pounds boned neck of veal, diced

5 cups beef or brown stock

2½ cups water

⅓ cup barley, washed

1 large carrot, diced

1 small turnip (about 6 ounces), diced

1 large leek, thinly sliced

1 red onion, finely chopped

3½ ounces chopped tomatoes

1 fresh basil sprig

1 cup dried vermicelli

salt and white pepper

1 Put the peas, veal, stock, and water into a large pan and bring to a boil over low heat. Using a slotted spoon, skim off any scum that rises to the surface.

2 When all of the scum has been removed, add the barley and a pinch of salt to the mixture. Simmer gently over a low heat for 25 minutes.

3 Add the carrot, turnip, leek, onion, tomatoes, and basil to the pan, and season with salt and pepper to taste. Leave to simmer for about 2 hours, skimming the surface from time to time to remove any scum. Remove the pan from the heat and set aside for 2 hours.

4 Set the pan over a medium heat and bring to a boil. Add the vermicelli and cook for 12 minutes. Season with salt and pepper to taste; remove and discard the basil. Ladle into soup bowls and serve immediately.

COOK'S TIP

The best brown stock is made with veal bones and shin of beef roasted with drippings in the oven for 40 minutes. Transfer the bones to a pan and add sliced leeks, onion, celery and carrots, a bouquet garni, white wine vinegar, and a thyme sprig and cover with cold water. Simmer over very low heat for 3 hours; strain before use.

Veal & Wild Mushroom Soup

Wild mushrooms are available commercially and an increasing range of cultivated varieties is now to be found in many supermarkets.

NUTRITIONAL INFORMATION

Calories	413	Sugars	.........3g
Protein	........28g	Fat	..........22g
Carbohydrate	...28g	Saturates	......12g

5 MINS 3¼ HOURS

SERVES 4

I N G R E D I E N T S

1 pound veal, thinly sliced

1 pound veal bones

5 cups water

1 small onion

6 peppercorns

1 teaspoon cloves

pinch of mace

5 ounces oyster and shiitake mushrooms,
    roughly chopped

⅔ cup heavy cream

1 cup dried vermicelli

1 tablespoon cornstarch

3 tablespoons milk

salt and pepper

COOK'S TIP

You can make this soup
with the more inexpensive
cuts of veal, such as breast or
neck slices. These are lean and the
long cooking time ensures that the
meat is really tender.

1 Put the veal, bones and water into a large saucepan. Bring to a boil and lower the heat. Add the onion, peppercorns, cloves, and mace and simmer for about 3 hours, until the veal stock is reduced by one-third.

2 Strain the stock, skim off any fat on the surface with a slotted spoon, and pour the stock into a clean saucepan. Add the veal meat to the pan.

3 Add the mixed mushrooms and heavy cream, bring to a boil over low heat, and then leave to simmer for 12 minutes, stirring occasionally.

4 Meanwhile, cook the vermicelli in lightly salted boiling water for 10 minutes or until tender, but still firm to the bite. Drain and keep warm.

5 Mix the cornstarch and milk to form a smooth paste. Stir into the soup to thicken. Season to taste with salt and pepper and just before serving, add the vermicelli. Transfer the soup to a warm tureen and serve immediately.

 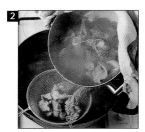 

Veal & Ham Soup

Veal and ham is a classic combination, complemented here with the addition of sherry to create a richly-flavored Italian soup.

NUTRITIONAL INFORMATION

Calories	.501	Sugars	.10g
Protein	.38g	Fat	.18g
Carbohydrate	..28g	Saturates	.10g

  5 MINS   3¼ HOURS

SERVES 4

I N G R E D I E N T S

4 tablespoons butter

1 onion, diced

1 carrot, diced

1 celery stalk, diced

1 pound veal, very thinly sliced

1 pound ham, thinly sliced

½ cup all-purpose flour

4½ cups beef stock

1 bay leaf

8 black peppercorns

pinch of salt

3 tablespoons red currant jelly

⅔ cup cream sherry

1 cup dried vermicelli

garlic croutons (see Cook's Tip), to serve

1 Melt the butter in a large pan. Add the onions, carrot, celery, veal, and ham and cook over low heat for 6 minutes.

2 Sprinkle over the flour and cook, stirring constantly, for a further 2 minutes. Gradually stir in the stock, then add the bay leaf, peppercorns, and salt. Bring to a boil and simmer for 1 hour.

3 Remove the pan from the heat and add the red currant jelly and cream sherry, stirring to combine. Set aside for about 4 hours.

4 Remove the bay leaf from the pan and discard. Reheat the soup over very low heat until warmed through.

5 Meanwhile, cook the vermicelli in a saucepan of lightly salted boiling water for 10–12 minutes. Stir the vermicelli into the soup and transfer to soup bowls. Serve with garlic croutons.

COOK'S TIP

To make garlic croutons, remove the crusts from 3 slices of day-old white bread. Cut the bread into ¼-inch cubes. Heat 3 tablespoons oil over a low heat and stir-fry 1–2 chopped garlic cloves for 1–2 minutes. Remove the garlic and add the bread. Cook, stirring frequently, until golden. Remove with a slotted spoon.

Starters

Starters are known as antipasto in Italy which is translated as meaning "before the main course". Antipasti usually come in three categories: meat, fish, and vegetables. There are many varieties of cold meats, including ham, invariably sliced paper-thin. All varieties of fish are popular in Italy, including inkfish, octopus, and cuttlefish. Seafood is also

highly prized, especially huge shrimp, mussels, and fresh sardines. Numerous vegetables feature in Italian cuisine and are an important part of the daily diet. They are served as a starter, as an accompaniment to main dishes, or as a course on their own. In Italy, vegetables are cooked only until "al dente" and still slightly crisp. This ensures that they retain more nutrients and the colors remain bright and appealing.

Roasted Bell Peppers

These bell peppers can be used as an *antipasto*, as a side dish, or as a relish to accompany meat and fish.

NUTRITIONAL INFORMATION

Calories 98   Sugars 13g
Protein ....3g   Fat 4g
Carbohydrate ...15g   Saturates 1g

🍅 5 MINS   🕐 40 MINS

SERVES 4

INGREDIENTS

2 each, red, yellow, and orange bell
    peppers

4 tomatoes, halved

1 tablespoon olive oil

3 garlic cloves, chopped

1 onion, sliced in rings

2 tablespoons fresh thyme

salt and pepper

1 Halve and deseed the bell peppers. Place them, cut-side down, on a cookie sheet and cook under a preheated broiler for 10 minutes.

2 Add the tomatoes to the cookie sheet and broil for 5 minutes, until the skins of the bell peppers and tomatoes are charred.

3 Put the bell peppers into a plastic bag for 10 minutes to sweat, which will make the skin easier to peel.

4 Remove the tomato skins and chop the flesh. Peel the skins from the bell peppers and slice the flesh into strips.

5 Heat the olive oil in a large, heavy-based skillet and fry the garlic and onion, stirring occasionally, for 3–4 minutes or until softened.

6 Add the bell peppers and tomatoes to the skillet and cook for 5 minutes. Stir in the fresh thyme and season to taste with salt and pepper.

7 Transfer to serving bowls and serve warm or chilled.

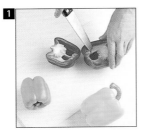

COOK'S TIP

Preserve bell peppers in the refrigerator by placing them in a sterilized jar and pouring olive oil over the top to seal. Or, heat ¼ cup white wine vinegar with a bay leaf and 4 juniper berries and bring to a boil. Pour over the bell peppers and set aside until cold. Pack into sterilized jars.

Sweet & Sour Baby Onions

This typical Sicilian dish combines honey and vinegar to give a sweet and sour flavor. Serve hot as an accompaniment or cold with cured meats.

NUTRITIONAL INFORMATION

Calories . . . . .131 Sugars 11g
Protein . . . . .2g Fat 6g
Carbohydrate . . .19g Saturates 1g

🥘 2 MINS   🕐 15 MINS

SERVES 4

I N G R E D I E N T S

12 ounces baby or pickling onions

2 tablespoons olive oil

2 fresh bay leaves, torn into strips

thinly pared rind of 1 lemon

1 tablespoon soft brown sugar

1 tablespoon liquid honey

4 tablespoons red wine vinegar

1 Soak the onions in a bowl of boiling water—this will make them easier to peel. Using a sharp knife, peel and halve the onions.

2 Heat the oil in a large skillet. Add the bay leaves and onions to the skillet and cook for 5–6 minutes over medium-high heat or until browned all over.

3 Cut the lemon rind into thin matchsticks. Add to the skillet with the sugar and honey. Cook for about 2–3 minutes, stirring occasionally, until the onions are lightly caramelized.

4 Add the red wine vinegar to the skillet, being careful because it will spit. Cook for about 5 minutes, stirring, or until the onions are tender and the liquid has all but disappeared.

5 Transfer the onions to a serving dish and serve at once.

COOK'S TIP

Adjust the piquancy of this dish to your liking by adding extra sugar for a sweeter, more caramelized taste or extra red wine vinegar for a sharper, tarter flavor.

Eggplant Rolls

Thin slices of eggplant are fried in olive oil and garlic, and then topped with pesto sauce and finely sliced mozzarella.

NUTRITIONAL INFORMATION

Calories	278	Sugars	.........2g
Protein	.........4g	Fat	..........28g
Carbohydrate	....2g	Saturates	.......7g

15-20 MINS   20 MINS

SERVES 4

I N G R E D I E N T S

2 eggplants, sliced thinly lengthwise

5 tablespoons olive oil

1 garlic clove, crushed

4 tablespoons pesto

1½ cups grated mozzarella

basil leaves, torn into pieces

salt and pepper

fresh basil leaves, to garnish

1 Sprinkle the eggplant slices liberally with salt and leave for 10–15 minutes to extract the bitter juices. Turn the slices over and repeat. Rinse well with cold water and drain on paper towels.

2 Heat the olive oil in a large skillet and add the garlic. Fry the eggplant slices lightly on both sides, a few at a time. Drain them on paper towels.

3 Spread the pesto on to one side of the eggplant slices. Top with the grated mozzarella, divided equally among them, and sprinkle with the torn basil leaves. Season to taste with a little salt and pepper. Carefully roll up the eggplant slices and secure with wooden toothpicks.

4 Arrange the eggplant rolls in a lightly greased ovenproof baking dish. Place in a preheated oven, 350°F, and bake for 8–10 minutes.

5 Transfer the eggplant rolls to a warm serving plate. Scatter with fresh basil leaves and serve at once.

Leek & Tomato Timbales

Angel-hair pasta, known as cappellini, is mixed with fried leeks, sun-dried tomatoes, fresh oregano, and beaten eggs, and baked in ramekins.

NUTRITIONAL INFORMATION

Calories 331   Sugars 10g
Protein . . . . .10g   Fat 21g
Carbohydrate . . .26g   Saturates 9g

5–10 MINS   50 MINS

SERVES 4

INGREDIENTS

3 ounces angel-hair pasta (cappellini)

2 tablespoons butter

1 tablespoon olive oil

1 large leek, sliced finely

½ cup sun-dried tomatoes in oil,
    drained and chopped

1 tablespoon chopped fresh oregano
    or 1 teaspoon dried oregano

2 eggs, beaten

⅓ cup light cream

1 tablespoon freshly grated
    Parmesan cheese

salt and pepper

sprigs of oregano, to garnish

lettuce leaves, to serve

SAUCE

1 small onion, chopped finely

1 small garlic clove, crushed

12 ounces tomatoes, peeled
    and chopped

1 teaspoon mixed dried Italian herbs

4 tablespoons dry white wine

1 Cook the pasta in plenty of boiling salted water for about 3 minutes until "al dente" (just tender). Drain and rinse with cold water to cool quickly.

2 Meanwhile, heat the butter and oil in a skillet. Gently fry the leek until softened, about 5–6 minutes. Add the sun-dried tomatoes and oregano, and cook for a further 2 minutes. Remove from the heat.

3 Add the leek mixture to the pasta. Stir in the beaten eggs, cream, and Parmesan. Season with salt and pepper. Divide among 4 greased ramekin dishes or dariole molds.

4 Place the dishes in a roasting pan with enough warm water to come halfway up their sides. Bake in a preheated oven, 350°F, for about 30 minutes, until set.

5 Meanwhile, make the tomato sauce. Fry the onion and garlic in the remaining butter and oil until softened. Add the tomatoes, herbs, and wine. Cover and cook gently for about 20 minutes until pulpy. Blend in a food processor until smooth, or press through a strainer.

6 Run a knife or small spatula around the edge of the ramekins, then turn out the timbales onto 4 warm serving plates. Pour over a little sauce and garnish with oregano. Serve with the lettuce leaves.

Baked Fennel Gratinati

Fennel is a common ingredient in Italian cooking. In this dish its distinctive flavor is offset by the smooth Béchamel Sauce.

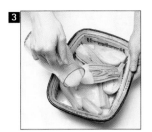

NUTRITIONAL INFORMATION

Calories 426	Sugars 9g
Protein 13g	Fat 35g
Carbohydrate ...16g	Saturates 19g

5–10 MINS   45 MINS

SERVES 4

INGREDIENTS

4 heads fennel

2 tablespoons butter

⅔ cup dry white wine

Béchamel Sauce (see page 28),
   enriched with 2 egg yolks

½ cup fresh white bread crumbs

3 tablespoons freshly grated Parmesan

salt and pepper

fennel fronds, to garnish

1 Remove any bruised or tough outer stalks of fennel and cut each head in half. Put into a saucepan of boiling salted water and simmer for 20 minutes until tender, then drain.

2 Butter an ovenproof dish liberally and arrange the drained fennel in it.

3 Mix the wine into the Béchamel Sauce and season with salt and pepper to taste. Pour over the fennel.

4 Sprinkle evenly with the bread crumbs and then the Parmesan.

5 Place in a preheated oven, 400°F, and bake for 20 minutes until the top is golden. Serve garnished with fennel fronds.

Stewed Artichokes

This is a traditional Roman dish. The artichokes are stewed in olive oil with fresh herbs.

NUTRITIONAL INFORMATION

Calories 129	Sugars 0g
Protein 4g	Fat 8g
Carbohydrate ...10g	Saturates 1g

5 MINS   50 MINS

SERVES 4

INGREDIENTS

4 small artichokes

olive oil

4 garlic cloves, peeled

2 bay leaves

finely grated rind and juice of 1 lemon

2 tablespoons fresh marjoram

lemon wedges, to serve

1 Using a sharp knife, carefully peel away the tough outer leaves surrounding the artichokes. Trim the stems to about 1 inch.

2 Using a knife, cut each artichoke in half and scoop out the choke (heart).

3 Place the artichokes in a large heavy-based pan. Pour over enough olive oil to half cover the artichokes in the pan.

4 Add the garlic cloves, bay leaves, and half of the grated lemon rind.

5 Start to heat the artichokes gently, cover the pan, and continue to cook over low heat for about 40 minutes. It is important that the artichokes should be stewed in the oil, not fried.

6 Once the artichokes are tender, remove them with a slotted spoon and

drain thoroughly. Remove the bay leaves and discard.

7 Transfer the artichokes to warm serving plates. Garnish the artichokes with the remaining grated lemon rind, fresh marjoram, and a little lemon juice. Serve with lemon wedges.

COOK'S TIP

To prevent the artichokes from oxidizing and turning brown before cooking, brush them with a little lemon juice. In addition, use the oil used for cooking the artichokes for salad dressings— it will impart a lovely lemon and herb flavor.

Eggplant Bake

This dish combines layers of eggplant, tomato sauce, mozzarella, and Parmesan cheese to create a very tasty starter.

NUTRITIONAL INFORMATION

Calories 232	Sugars 8g
Protein 10g	Fat 18g
Carbohydrate 8g	Saturates 6g

5 MINS   45 MINS

SERVES 4

INGREDIENTS

3–4 tablespoons olive oil

2 garlic cloves, crushed

2 large eggplants

3½ ounces mozzarella cheese, sliced thinly

1 cup sieved tomatoes

⅔ cup grated Parmesan cheese

1 Heat 2 tablespoons of the olive oil in a large skillet. Add the garlic and sauté for 30 seconds.

2 Slice the eggplants lengthwise. Add the slices to the pan and cook in the oil for 3–4 minutes on each side or until tender. (You will probably have to cook them in batches, so add the remaining oil as necessary.)

3 Remove the eggplants with a slotted spoon and drain well on absorbent paper towels.

4 Place a layer of eggplant slices in a shallow ovenproof dish. Cover the eggplants with a layer of mozzarella and then pour over a third of the sieved tomatoes. Continue layering in the same order, finishing with a layer of sieved tomatoes on top.

5 Generously sprinkle the grated Parmesan cheese over the top and bake in a preheated oven at 400°F for 25–30 minutes.

6 Transfer to serving plates and serve warm or chilled.

Bell Pepper Salad

Colorful marinated Mediterranean vegetables make a tasty starter. Serve with fresh bread or Tomato Toasts (see below).

NUTRITIONAL INFORMATION

Calories . . . . . . .234 Sugars 4g
Protein . . . . .6g Fat 17g
Carbohydrate . . .15g Saturates 2g

5–10 MINS   35 MINS

SERVES 4

I N G R E D I E N T S

1 onion

2 red bell peppers

2 yellow bell peppers

3 tablespoons olive oil

2 large zucchini, sliced

2 garlic cloves, sliced

1 tablespoon balsamic vinegar

1¾ ounces anchovy fillets, chopped

¼ cup black olives,
   halved and pitted

1 tablespoon chopped fresh basil

salt and pepper

T O M A T O   T O A S T S

French bread or baguette

1 garlic clove, crushed

1 tomato, peeled and chopped

2 tablespoons olive oil

1 Cut the onion into wedges. Core and deseed the bell peppers and cut into thick slices.

2 Heat the oil in a large heavy-based skillet. Add the onion, bell peppers, zucchini, and garlic and fry gently for 20 minutes, stirring occasionally.

3 Add the vinegar, anchovies, olives, and seasoning to taste, mix thoroughly and leave to cool.

4 Spoon on to individual plates and sprinkle with the basil.

5 To make the tomato toasts, cut the French bread diagonally into ½-inch slices.

6 Mix the garlic, tomato, oil, and seasoning together, and spread thinly over each slice of bread.

7 Place the bread on a cookie sheet, drizzle with the olive oil and bake in a preheated oven, 425°F, for 5–10 minutes until crisp. Serve the Tomato Toasts with the bell pepper salad.

Black Olive Pâté

This pâté is delicious served as a starter on Tomato Toasts (see page 73). It can also be served as a cocktail snack on small rounds of fried bread.

NUTRITIONAL INFORMATION

Calories	149	Sugars	.........1g
Protein	.........2g	Fat	..........14g
Carbohydrate	....4g	Saturates	.......6g

5 MINS   5 MINS

SERVES 4

I N G R E D I E N T S

1½ cups pitted juicy
black olives

1 garlic clove, crushed

finely grated rind of 1 lemon

4 tablespoons lemon juice

½ cup fresh bread crumbs

¼ cup cream cheese

salt and pepper

lemon wedges, to garnish

T O   S E R V E

thick slices of bread

mixture of olive oil and butter

1 Roughly chop the olives and mix with the garlic, lemon rind and juice, bread crumbs, and cream cheese. Pound the mixture until smooth, or place in a food processor and work until fully blended. Season to taste with salt and freshly ground black pepper.

2 Store the pâté in a screw-top jar and chill for several hours before using—this allows the flavors to develop.

3 For a delicious cocktail snack, use a pastry cutter to cut out small rounds from a thickly sliced loaf.

4 Fry the bread rounds in a mixture of olive oil and butter until they are a light golden brown color. Drain thoroughly on paper towels.

5 Top each round with a little of the pâté, garnish with lemon wedges, and serve immediately. This pâté will keep chilled in an airtight jar for up to 2 weeks.

Stuffed Artichokes

This specific recipe has been designed for microwave cooking. Use conventional cooking methods if you prefer.

NUTRITIONAL INFORMATION

Calories 189   Sugars 5g
Protein ....5g   Fat 11g
Carbohydrate ...17g   Saturates 1g

 15 MINUTES   1 HOUR

SERVES 4

I N G R E D I E N T S

4 artichokes

8 tablespoons water

4 tablespoons lemon juice

1 onion, chopped

1 garlic clove, crushed

2 tablespoons olive oil

2 cups mushrooms,
   chopped

½ cup pitted black olives, sliced

¼ cup sun-dried tomatoes in oil,
   drained and chopped (reserve the oil for
   drizzling)

1 tablespoon chopped fresh basil

1 cup fresh white bread crumbs

¼ cup pine nuts, toasted

salt and pepper

1 Cut the stalks and lower leaves off the artichokes. Snip off the leaf tips using scissors. Place 2 artichokes in a large bowl with half the water and half the lemon juice. Cover and cook on HIGH power for 10 minutes, turning the artichokes over halfway through, until a leaf pulls away easily from the base. Leave to stand, covered, for 3 minutes before draining. Turn the artichokes upside down and leave to cool. Repeat the process with the remaining artichokes.

2 Place the onion, garlic, and oil in a bowl. Cover and cook on HIGH power for 2 minutes, stirring once. Add the mushrooms, olives, and sun-dried tomatoes. Cover and cook on HIGH power for 2 minutes.

3 Stir in the basil, bread crumbs, and pine nuts. Season to taste.

4 Turn the artichokes the right way up and carefully pull the leaves apart.

Remove the purple-tipped central leaves. Using a teaspoon, scrape out the hairy choke (heart) and discard.

5 Divide the stuffing into 4 and spoon into the center of each artichoke. Push the leaves back around the stuffing.

6 Arrange in a shallow dish and drizzle over a little oil from the jar of sun-dried tomatoes. Cook on HIGH power for 7–8 minutes to reheat, turning the artichokes around halfway through. Serve.

Zucchini Fritters

These tasty little fritters are great with the sauce on page 69 as a relish for a cocktail party.

NUTRITIONAL INFORMATION

Calories	162	Sugars	.........2g
Protein	.........7g	Fat	...........6g
Carbohydrate	...20g	Saturates	.......2g

 5-10 MINS   20 MINS

MAKES 16-30

I N G R E D I E N T S

¾ cup self-rising flour

2 eggs, beaten

¼ cup milk

10 ½ ounces zucchini

2 tablespoons fresh thyme

1 tablespoon oil

salt and pepper

1 Sift the self-rising flour into a large bowl and make a well in the center. Add the eggs to the well, and using a wooden spoon, gradually draw in the flour.

2 Slowly add the milk to the mixture, stirring constantly to form a thick batter.

3 Meanwhile, wash the zucchini. Grate the zucchini over a layer of paper towels placed in a bowl to absorb some of the juices.

4 Add the zucchini, thyme, and salt and pepper to taste to the batter and mix thoroughly.

5 Heat the oil in a large, heavy-based skillet. Taking a tablespoon of the batter for a medium-sized fritter or half a tablespoon of batter for a smaller-sized fritter, spoon the mixture into the hot oil and cook, in batches, for 3-4 minutes on each side.

6 Remove the fritters with a perforated spoon and drain thoroughly on absorbent paper towels. Keep each batch of fritters warm in the oven while making the rest. Transfer to serving plates and serve hot.

VARIATION

Try adding ½ teaspoon of dried, crushed chilies to the batter in step 4 for spicier tasting fritters.

Spinach & Ricotta Patties

Nudo or naked is the word used to describe this mixture, which can also be made into thin pancakes or used as a filling for tortelloni.

NUTRITIONAL INFORMATION

Calories 374   Sugars 4g
Protein . . . . .16g   Fat 31g
Carbohydrate . . . .9g   Saturates 19g

5 MINS   30 MINS

SERVES 4

I N G R E D I E N T S

1 pound fresh spinach

9 ounces ricotta cheese

1 egg, beaten

2 teaspoon fennel seeds, lightly crushed

⅔ cup finely grated Romano or Parmesan
    cheese, plus extra to garnish

¼ cup all-purpose flour, mixed
    with 1 teaspoon dried thyme

5 tablespoons butter

2 garlic cloves, crushed

salt and pepper

tomato wedges, to serve

1 Wash the spinach and trim off any long stalks. Place in a pan, cover, and cook for 4–5 minutes until wilted. This will probably have to be done in batches as the volume of spinach is quite large. Place in a colander and leave to drain and cool.

2 Mash the ricotta and beat in the egg and the fennel seeds. Season with plenty of salt and pepper, then stir in the Romano or Parmesan cheese.

3 Squeeze as much excess water as possible from the spinach and finely chop the leaves. Stir the spinach into the cheese mixture.

4 Taking about 1 tablespoon of the spinach and cheese mixture, shape it into a ball, and flatten it slightly to form a patty. Gently roll in the seasoned flour. Continue this process until all of the mixture has been used up.

5 Half-fill a large skillet with water and bring to a boil. Carefully add the patties and cook for 3–4 minutes or until they rise to the surface. Remove with a perforated spoon.

6 Melt the butter in a pan. Add the garlic and cook for 2–3 minutes. Pour the garlic butter over the patties, season with freshly ground black pepper and serve at once.

Avocado Margherita

The colors of the tomatoes, basil, and mozzarella cheese in this patriotic recipe represent the colors of the Italian flag.

NUTRITIONAL INFORMATION

Calories	249	Sugars	.........2g
Protein	.........4g	Fat	..........24g
Carbohydrate	....4g	Saturates	.......6g

5–10 MINS   10–15 MINS

SERVES 4

INGREDIENTS

1 small red onion, sliced

1 garlic clove, crushed

1 tablespoon olive oil

2 small tomatoes

2 avocados, halved and pitted

4 fresh basil leaves, torn into shreds

2 ounces mozzarella cheese, sliced thinly

salt and pepper

fresh basil leaves, to garnish

mixed salad greens, to serve

1 Place the onion, garlic, and the olive oil in a bowl. Cover and cook on HIGH power for 2 minutes.

2 Meanwhile, skin the tomatoes by cutting a cross in the base of the tomatoes and placing them in a small bowl. Pour on boiling water and leave for about 45 seconds. Drain and then plunge into cold water. The skins will slide off without too much difficulty.

3 Arrange the avocado halves on a plate with the narrow ends pointed towards the center. Spoon the onions into the hollow of each half.

4 Cut and slice the tomatoes in half. Divide the tomatoes, basil and thin slices of mozzarella among the avocado halves. Season with salt and pepper to taste.

5 Cook on MEDIUM power for 5 minutes or until the avocados are heated through and the cheese has melted. Transfer the avocados to serving plates, garnish with basil leaves, and serve with mixed salad greens.

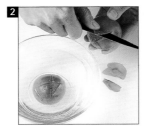

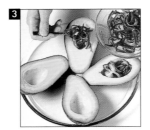

VARIATION

If you are using a combination microwave oven with broiler, arrange the avocados on the low rack of the broiler, or on the glass turntable. Cook on combination broiler 1 and LOW power for 8 minutes until browned and bubbling.

Deep-fried Risotto Balls

The Italian name for this dish translates as "telephone wires" which refers to the strings of melted mozzarella contained within the risotto balls.

NUTRITIONAL INFORMATION

Calories 280	Sugars 2g
Protein 5g	Fat 13g
Carbohydrate . . .35g	Saturates 3g

 5 MINS   35–40 MINS

SERVES 4

I N G R E D I E N T S

2 tablespoons olive oil

1 medium onion,
    finely chopped

1 garlic clove, chopped

½ red bell pepper, diced

¾ cup arborio rice, washed

1 teaspoon dried oregano

1 ⅔ cups hot vegetable or
    chicken stock

½ cup dry white wine

2 ¾ ounces mozzarella cheese

oil, for deep-frying

fresh basil sprig,
    to garnish

1 Heat the oil in a skillet and cook the onion and garlic for 3–4 minutes or until just softened.

2 Add the bell pepper, arborio rice, and oregano to the pan. Cook for 2–3 minutes, stirring to coat the rice in the oil.

3 Mix the stock together with the wine and add to the pan a ladleful at a time, waiting for the liquid to be absorbed by the rice before you add the next ladleful of liquid.

4 Once all of the liquid has been absorbed and the rice is tender (it should take about 15 minutes in total), remove the pan from the heat and leave until the mixture is cool enough to handle.

5 Cut the cheese into 12 pieces. Taking about 1 tablespoon of risotto, shape the mixture around the cheese pieces to make 12 balls.

6 Heat the oil until a cube of bread browns in 30 seconds. Cook the risotto balls, in batches of 4, for 2 minutes or until golden.

7 Remove the risotto balls with a perforated spoon and drain thoroughly on absorbent paper towels.. Garnish with a sprig of basil and serve the risotto balls hot.

Olive & Anchovy Pâté

The flavor of olives is accentuated by the anchovies. Serve the pâté as an appetizer on thin pieces of toast with a very dry white wine.

NUTRITIONAL INFORMATION

Calories 214	Sugars 1g
Protein 2g	Fat 22g
Carbohydrate 1g	Saturates 8g

5–10 MINS   35 MINS

SERVES 4

INGREDIENTS

1¼ cups black olives, pitted and chopped

finely grated rind and juice of 1 lemon

2 tablespoons butter

4 canned anchovy fillets, drained and rinsed

2 tablespoons extra virgin olive oil

2 tablespoons ground almonds

fresh herbs, to garnish

1 If you are making the pâté by hand, chop the olives very finely and then mash them along with the lemon rind, juice, and butter, using a fork or potato masher. Alternatively, place the roughly chopped olives, lemon rind, juice, and butter in a food processor and blend until all of the ingredients are finely chopped.

2 Chop the drained anchovies and add them to the olive and lemon mixture. Mash the pâté by hand or blend in a food processor for 20 seconds.

3 Gradually whisk in the olive oil and stir in the ground almonds. Place the black olive pâté in a serving bowl. Leave the pâté to chill in the refrigerator for about 30 minutes. Serve the pâté accompanied by thin pieces of toast, if wished.

COOK'S TIP

This pâté will keep for up to 5 days in a serving bowl in the refrigerator if you pour a thin layer of extra virgin olive oil over the top of the pâté to seal it. Then use the oil to brush on the toast before spreading the pâté.

Tuna Stuffed Tomatoes

Deliciously sweet roasted tomatoes are filled with homemade lemon mayonnaise and tuna.

NUTRITIONAL INFORMATION

Calories ....196 Sugars 2g
Protein ....9g Fat 17g
Carbohydrate ....2g Saturates 3g

5-10 MINS   25 MINS

SERVES 4

INGREDIENTS

4 plum tomatoes

2 tablespoons sun-dried tomato paste

2 egg yolks

2 teaspoon lemon juice

finely grated rind of 1 lemon

4 tablespoons olive oil

4-ounce can tuna, drained

2 tablespoons capers, rinsed

salt and pepper

TO GARNISH

2 sun-dried tomatoes, cut into strips

fresh basil leaves

1 Halve the tomatoes and scoop out the seeds. Divide the sun-dried tomato paste among the tomato halves and spread around the inside of the skin.

2 Place on a cookie sheet and roast in a preheated oven at 400°F for 12–15 minutes. Leave to cool slightly.

3 Meanwhile, make the mayonnaise. In a food processor, blend the egg yolks and lemon juice with the lemon rind until smooth. Once mixed and with the motor still running slowly, add the olive oil. Stop the processor as soon as the mayonnaise has thickened. Alternatively, use a hand whisk, beating the mixture continuously until it thickens.

4 Add the tuna and capers to the mayonnaise and season.

5 Spoon the tuna mayonnaise mixture into the tomato shells and garnish with sun-dried tomato strips and basil leaves. Return to the oven for a few minutes or serve chilled.

COOK'S TIP

For a picnic, do not roast the tomatoes, just scoop out the seeds, drain, cut side down on absorbent paper towels for 1 hour, and fill with the mayonnaise mixture. They are firmer and easier to handle this way. If you prefer, ready-made mayonnaise may be used instead— just stir in the lemon rind.

Mussels in White Wine

This soup of mussels, cooked in white wine with onions and cream, can be served as an appetizer or a main dish with plenty of crusty bread.

NUTRITIONAL INFORMATION

Calories 396	Sugars 2g	
Protein 23g	Fat 24g	
Carbohydrate 8g	Saturates 15g	

 5–10 MINS 25 MINS

SERVES 4

I N G R E D I E N T S

12 cups fresh mussels

¼ cup butter

1 large onion, chopped very finely

2–3 garlic cloves, crushed

1 ½ cups dry white wine

⅔ cup water

2 tablespoons lemon juice

good pinch of finely grated lemon rind

1 bouquet garni

1 tablespoon all-purpose flour

4 tablespoons light or thick cream

2–3 tablespoons chopped fresh parsley

salt and pepper

warm crusty bread, to serve

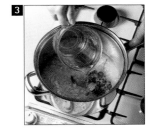

1 Scrub the mussels in several changes of cold water to remove all mud, sand, barnacles, etc. Pull off all the "beards." All of the mussels must be tightly closed; if they don't close when given a sharp tap, they must be discarded.

2 Melt half the butter in a large saucepan. Add the onion and garlic, and fry gently until soft but not colored.

3 Add the wine, water, lemon juice and rind, bouquet garni, and plenty of seasoning. Bring to a boil, then cover and simmer for 4–5 minutes.

4 Add the mussels to the pan, cover tightly, and simmer for 5 minutes, shaking the pan frequently, until all the mussels have opened. Discard any mussels which have not opened. Remove the bouquet garni.

5 Remove the empty half shell from each mussel. Blend the remaining butter with the flour and whisk into the soup, a little at a time. Simmer gently for 2–3 minutes until slightly thickened.

6 Add the cream and half the parsley to the soup and reheat gently. Adjust the seasoning. Ladle the mussels and soup into warm large soup bowls, sprinkle with the remaining parsley, and serve with plenty of warm crusty bread.

Deep-fried Seafood

Deep-fried seafood is popular all around the Mediterranean, where fish of all kinds is fresh and abundant.

NUTRITIONAL INFORMATION

Calories 393   Sugars 0.2g
Protein ....27g   Fat 26g
Carbohydrate ...12g   Saturates 3g

5 MINS   15 MINS

SERVES 4

INGREDIENTS

7 ounces prepared squid

7 ounces raw jumbo shrimp,
  peeled

5 ½ ounces white fish such as sole

oil, for deep-frying

⅓ cup all-purpose flour

1 teaspoon dried basil

salt and pepper

TO SERVE

garlic mayonnaise (see page 30)

lemon wedges

1 Carefully rinse the squid, shrimp, and fish under cold running water, completely removing any dirt or grit.

2 Using a sharp knife, slice the squid into rings, leaving the tentacles whole.

3 Heat the oil in a large saucepan to 350°–375°F or until a cube of bread browns in 30 seconds.

4 Place the flour in a bowl, add the basil, and season with salt and pepper to taste. Mix together well.

5 Roll the squid, shrimp, and fish in the seasoned flour until coated all over. Carefully shake off any excess flour.

6 Cook the seafood in the heated oil, in batches, for 2–3 minutes or until crispy and golden all over. Remove all of the seafood from the oil with a perforated spoon and leave to drain thoroughly on paper towels.

7 Transfer the deep-fried seafood to serving plates and serve with garlic mayonnaise (see page 30) and a few lemon wedges.

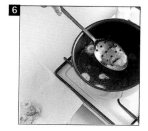

Pasta & Cheese Pots

A layered pasta, cheese, and prosciutto delight, complemented by a tomato and basil sauce. This recipe is adapted for the microwave.

NUTRITIONAL INFORMATION

Calories . . . . . . .286 Sugars 4g
Protein . . . . .9g Fat 17g
Carbohydrate . . .26g Saturates 7g

 15 MINS   35 MINS

SERVES 4

I N G R E D I E N T S

1 small onion, chopped

1 garlic clove, chopped

1 tablespoon olive oil

4 tomatoes, peeled (see page 78)
   and chopped

1 tablespoon tomato paste

4 fresh basil leaves, chopped

2 tablespoons butter

2 tablespoons dried brown bread crumbs

2 tablespoons chopped hazelnuts,
   lightly toasted

3 ounces dried angel-hair pasta

2 tablespoons all-purpose flour

⅔ cup milk

½ ounce blue cheese

2¾ ounces prosciutto, chopped

4 pitted black olives, chopped

salt and pepper

sprigs of fresh basil, to garnish

1 Place the onion, garlic, and oil in a bowl. Cover and cook on HIGH power for 3 minutes. Add the tomatoes and tomato paste and cook on HIGH power for 4 minutes, stirring halfway through. Add the basil and seasoning. Leave to stand, covered.

2 Place half of the butter in a small bowl and cook on HIGH power for 30 seconds until melted. Brush the insides of 4 ramekin dishes with the melted butter. Mix the bread crumbs and hazelnuts together and coat the insides of the ramekins. Set aside.

3 Break the pasta into 3 short lengths and place in a large bowl. Pour over enough boiling water to cover the pasta by 1 inch, and season lightly with salt. Cover and cook on HIGH power for 4 minutes, stirring halfway through. Leave to stand, covered, for 1 minute, then drain thoroughly.

4 Place the remaining butter, the flour, and milk in a small bowl. Cook on HIGH power for 2–2½ minutes until thickened, stirring well every 30 seconds. Crumble the cheese into the sauce and stir until melted. Season to taste.

5 Add the pasta to the sauce and mix well. Divide half the pasta mixture among the ramekins and top with the ham and olives. Spoon the remaining pasta mixture on top. Cook on MEDIUM power for 6 minutes. Leave to stand, uncovered, for 2 minutes before carefully turning out onto serving plates with the tomato sauce. Garnish with sprigs of basil.

Crostini alla Fiorentina

Serve as a starter, or simply spread on small pieces of crusty fried bread (crostini) as an appetizer with drinks.

NUTRITIONAL INFORMATION

Calories	393	Sugars	.........2g
Protein	........17g	Fat	..........25g
Carbohydrate	...19g	Saturates	.......9g

  10 MINS   40–45 MINS

SERVES 4

I N G R E D I E N T S

3 tablespoons olive oil

1 onion, chopped

1 celery stalk, chopped

1 carrot, chopped

1–2 garlic cloves, crushed

4½ ounces chicken livers

4½ ounces calf's, lamb's, or pig's liver

⅔ cup red wine

1 tablespoon tomato paste

2 tablespoons chopped fresh parsley

3–4 canned anchovy fillets, chopped finely

2 tablespoons stock or water

2–3 tablespoons butter

1 tablespoon capers

salt and pepper

small pieces of fried crusty bread, to serve

chopped parsley, to garnish

1 Heat the oil in a pan, add the onion, celery, carrot, and garlic, and cook gently for 4–5 minutes or until the onion is soft, but not colored.

2 Meanwhile, rinse and dry the chicken livers. Dry the calf's or other liver, and slice into strips. Add the liver to the pan and fry gently for a few minutes until the strips are well sealed on all sides.

3 Add half of the wine and cook until it has mostly evaporated. Then add the rest of the wine, tomato paste, half of the parsley, the anchovy fillets, stock or water, a little salt, and plenty of black pepper.

4 Cover the pan and leave to simmer, stirring occasionally, for about 15–20 minutes or until tender and most of the liquid has been absorbed.

5 Leave the mixture to cool a little, then either coarsely grind or put into a food processor and process to a chunky purée.

6 Return to the pan and add the butter, capers, and remaining parsley. Heat through gently until the butter melts. Adjust the seasoning and turn out into a bowl. Serve warm or cold spread on the slices of crusty bread and sprinkled with chopped parsley.

Figs & Prosciutto

This colorful fresh salad is delicious at any time of the year. Prosciutto di Parma is thought to be the best ham in the world.

NUTRITIONAL INFORMATION

Calories 121	Sugars 6g
Protein 1g	Fat 11g
Carbohydrate 6g	Saturates 2g

15 MINS   5 MINS

SERVES 4

I N G R E D I E N T S

1 bunch arugula

4 fresh figs

4 slices prosciutto

4 tablespoons olive oil

1 tablespoon fresh orange juice

1 tablespoon liquid honey

1 small red chili

1 Tear the arugula into more manageable pieces and arrange on 4 serving plates.

2 Using a sharp knife, cut each of the figs into quarters and place them on top of the arugula leaves.

3 Using a sharp knife, cut the prosciutto into strips and scatter over the arugula and figs.

4 Place the oil, orange juice, and honey in a screw-top jar. Shake the jar until the mixture emulsifies and forms a thick dressing. Transfer to a bowl.

5 Using a sharp knife, dice the chili, remembering not to touch your face before you have washed your hands (see Cook's Tip, below). Add the chopped chili to the dressing and mix well.

6 Drizzle the dressing over the prosciutto, arugula, and figs, tossing to mix well. Serve at once.

COOK'S TIP

Chilies can burn the skin for several hours after chopping, so it is advisable to wear gloves when you are handling the very hot varieties.

Preserved Meats (Salumi)

Mix an attractive selection of these preserved meats (salumi) with olives and marinated vegetables for extra color and variety.

NUTRITIONAL INFORMATION

Calories 227	Sugars 5g	
Protein 10g	Fat 19g	
Carbohydrate 5g	Saturates 1g	

 10 MINS   5–10 MINS

SERVES 4

INGREDIENTS

3 ripe tomatoes

3 ripe figs

1 small melon

2 ounces Italian salami, sliced thinly

4 thin slices mortadella ham

6 slices prosciutto

6 slices bresaola (see page 21)

4 fresh basil leaves, chopped

olive oil

½ cup marinated olives, pitted

freshly ground black pepper, to serve

1 Slice the tomatoes thinly and cut the figs into quarters.

2 Halve the melon, scoop out the seeds, and cut the flesh into wedges.

3 Arrange the meats on one half of a serving platter. Arrange the tomato slices in the center and sprinkle with the basil leaves and oil.

4 Cover the rest of the platter with the figs and melon and scatter the olives over the meats.

5 Serve with a little extra olive oil to drizzle over the bresaola, and sprinkle with coarsely ground black pepper.

Garbanzo Beans & Prosciutto

Prosciutto is used in this recipe. It is a cured ham, which is air- and salt-dried for up to 1 year. There are many different varieties available.

NUTRITIONAL INFORMATION

Calories 180	Sugars 2g	
Protein 12g	Fat 7g	
Carbohydrate ...18g	Saturates 1g	

10 MINS   15 MINS

SERVES 4

INGREDIENTS

1 tablespoon olive oil

1 medium onion, thinly sliced

1 garlic clove, chopped

1 small red bell pepper, deseeded and cut into thin strips

7 ounces prosciutto, cut into cubes

14-ounce can garbanzo beans, drained and rinsed

1 tablespoon chopped parsley, to garnish

crusty bread, to serve

COOK'S TIP

Whenever possible, use fresh herbs when cooking. They are becoming more readily available, especially since the introduction of "growing" herbs, small pots of herbs which you can buy from the supermarket or foodstore and grow at home. This ensures the herbs are fresh and also provides a continuous supply.

1 Heat the oil in a skillet. Add the onion, garlic, and bell pepper and cook for 3–4 minutes or until the vegetables have softened. Add the prosciutto to the skillet and fry for 5 minutes or until the prosciutto is just beginning to brown.

2 Add the garbanzo beans to the skillet and cook, stirring, for 2–3 minutes until warmed through.

3 Sprinkle with chopped parsley and transfer to warm serving plates. Serve with lots of fresh crusty bread.

Cured Meats, Olives, & Tomatoes

This is a typical *antipasto* dish with the cold cured meats, stuffed olives, and fresh tomatoes, basil, and balsamic vinegar.

NUTRITIONAL INFORMATION

Calories . . . . .312 Sugars 1g
Protein . . . . .12g Fat 28g
Carbohydrate . . . .2g Saturates 1g

10 MINS   5 MINS

SERVES 4

I N G R E D I E N T S

4 plum tomatoes

1 tablespoon balsamic vinegar

6 canned anchovy fillets, drained and rinsed

2 tablespoons capers, drained and rinsed

1 cup pitted green olives

6 ounces mixed cured meats, sliced

8 fresh basil leaves

1 tablespoon extra virgin olive oil

salt and pepper

crusty bread, to serve

1 Using a sharp knife, cut the tomatoes into evenly-sized slices. Sprinkle the tomato slices with the balsamic vinegar and a little salt and pepper to taste, and set aside.

2 Chop the anchovy fillets into pieces measuring about the same length as the olives.

3 Push a piece of anchovy and a caper into each olive.

4 Arrange the sliced meat on 4 individual serving plates together with the tomatoes, filled olives, and basil leaves.

5 Lightly drizzle the olive oil over the sliced meat, tomatoes, and olives.

6 Serve the cured meats, olives, and tomatoes with plenty of fresh crusty bread.

COOK'S TIP

The cured meats for this recipe are up to your individual taste. They can include a selection of prosciutto, pancetta, bresaola (dried salt beef) and salame di Milano (pork and beef sausage).

Snacks & Light Meals

Recipes for snacks and light meals offer something for every taste, including vegetables, meat, and fish dishes. These recipes are suitable for when you are not too hungry,

but still a bit peckish, or if you are in a hurry and want to eat something quick, but still nutritious and tasty. Try the mouthwatering Italian flavors of Tomato & Mozzarella Bruschetta or an Italian-style omelet—they are sure to satisfy even the most discerning tastebuds. All of the recipes in this chapter are quick to prepare and very easy to cook, and are sure to become staples in your Italian culinary repertoire.

Tomato & Mozzarella Bruschetta

These simple toasts are filled with color and flavor. They are great as a speedy starter or delicious as a light meal or snack.

NUTRITIONAL INFORMATION

Calories	232	Sugars	.........4g
Protein	.........4g	Fat	..........15g
Carbohydrate	...20g	Saturates	......8g

5–10 MINS   10 MINS

SERVES 4

INGREDIENTS

4 English muffins

4 garlic cloves, crushed

2 tablespoons butter

1 tablespoon chopped basil

4 large, ripe tomatoes

1 tablespoon tomato paste

8 pitted black olives, halved

1 ¾ ounces mozzarella cheese, sliced

salt and pepper

fresh basil leaves, to garnish

DRESSING

1 tablespoon olive oil

2 teaspoon lemon juice

1 teaspoon liquid honey

VARIATION

Use balsamic vinegar instead of the lemon juice for an authentic Italian flavor.

1 Cut the English muffins in half to give eight thick pieces. Toast the muffin halves under a hot broiler for 2–3 minutes until golden.

2 Mix the garlic, butter, and basil together and spread on to each English muffin half.

3 Cut a cross shape at the base of each tomato. Plunge the tomatoes in a bowl of boiling water—this will make the skin easier to peel. After a few minutes, pick each tomato up with a fork and peel away the skin. Chop the tomato flesh and mix with the tomato paste and olives. Divide the mixture between the English muffins.

4 Mix the dressing ingredients and drizzle over each English muffin. Arrange the mozzarella cheese on top and season to taste.

5 Return the muffins to the broiler for 1–2 minutes until the cheese melts.

6 Garnish with fresh basil leaves and serve at once.

Eggplant Sandwiches

Serve these sandwiches as a vegetarian main course for two or as a side dish to accompany other barbecued foods.

NUTRITIONAL INFORMATION

Calories 270	Sugars 4g	
Protein 10g	Fat 15g	
Carbohydrate . . .25g	Saturates 7g	

5 MINS   10–15 MINS

SERVES 2

INGREDIENTS

1 large eggplant

1 tablespoon lemon juice

3 tablespoons olive oil

1 cup grated mozzarella cheese

2 sun-dried tomatoes, chopped

salt and pepper

TO SERVE

Italian bread, such as focaccia or ciabatta

mixed salad greens

slices of tomato

1 Slice the eggplant into thin rounds.

2 Combine the lemon juice and olive oil in a small bowl and season the mixture with salt and pepper to taste.

3 Brush the eggplant slices with the oil and lemon juice mixture and barbecue over medium hot coals for 2–3 minutes, without turning, until they are golden on the underside.

4 Turn half of the eggplant slices over and sprinkle with cheese and chopped sun-dried tomatoes.

5 Place the remaining eggplant slices on top of the cheese and tomatoes, turning them so that the pale side is uppermost.

6 Barbecue for 1–2 minutes, then carefully turn the whole sandwich over and barbecue for 1–2 minutes. Baste with the oil mixture.

7 Serve the eggplant sandwiches with Italian bread, mixed salad greens, and a few slices of tomato.

VARIATION

Try Feta cheese instead of Mozzarella but omit the salt from the basting oil because Feta is quite salty. A creamy goat's cheese would be equally delicious.

Vegetable Kabobs

Brighten up a barbecue meal with these colorful kabobs. They are basted with a deliciously flavored oil.

NUTRITIONAL INFORMATION

Calories	142	Sugars	.........4g
Protein	.........1g	Fat	..........14g
Carbohydrate	....4g	Saturates	.......2g

15 MINS   15 MINS

SERVES 4

I N G R E D I E N T S

1 red bell pepper, deseeded

1 yellow bell pepper, deseeded

1 green bell pepper, deseeded

1 small onion

8 cherry tomatoes

3 ½ ounces exotic mushrooms

S E A S O N E D   O I L

6 tablespoons olive oil

1 clove garlic, crushed

½ teaspoon mixed dried herbs or
    herbes de Provence

 Cut the bell peppers into 1-inch pieces.

 Peel the onion and cut it into wedges, leaving the root end just intact to help keep the wedges together.

3 Thread the bell peppers, onion wedges, cherry tomatoes and mushrooms onto skewers, alternating the colors of the bell peppers.

4 To make the seasoned oil, mix together the olive oil, garlic, and mixed dried herbs in a a small bowl. Brush the seasoned oil mixture liberally over the kabobs.

5 Barbecue the kabobs over medium hot coals for 10–15 minutes, brushing with more of the seasoned oil and turning the skewers frequently.

6 Transfer the vegetable kabobs to warm serving plates. Serve the kabobs with walnut sauce (see Cook's Tip, left), if you wish.

COOK'S TIP

To make walnut sauce, work 1 cup walnuts in a food processor to form a paste. With the machine running, add ⅔ cup cream and 1 tablespoon oil. Season. Or, chop the walnuts, then pound them in a mortar to form a paste. Mix with the cream and oil, and season.

Bruschetta with Tomatoes

Using ripe tomatoes and the best olive oil will make this Tuscan dish absolutely delicious.

NUTRITIONAL INFORMATION

Calories 330   Sugars 4g
Protein ....8g   Fat 14g
Carbohydrate ...45g   Saturates 2g

15 MINS   5 MINS

SERVES 4

I N G R E D I E N T S

10½ ounces cherry tomatoes

4 sun-dried tomatoes

4 tablespoons extra virgin olive oil

16 fresh basil leaves, shredded

2 garlic cloves, peeled

8 slices ciabatta or other Italian bread

salt and pepper

1 Using a sharp knife, cut the cherry tomatoes in half.

2 Using a sharp knife, slice the sun-dried tomatoes into strips.

3 Place the cherry tomatoes and sun-dried tomatoes in a bowl. Add the olive oil and the shredded basil leaves and toss to mix well. Season to taste with a little salt and pepper.

4 Using a sharp knife, cut the garlic cloves in half. Lightly toast the ciabatta bread.

5 Rub the garlic, cut side down, over both sides of the lightly toasted ciabatta bread.

6 Top the ciabatta bread with the tomato mixture and serve at once.

Onion & Mozzarella Tarts

These individual tarts are delicious hot or cold and are great for lunchboxes or picnics.

NUTRITIONAL INFORMATION

Calories	327	Sugars	........3g
Protein	.........5g	Fat	.........23g
Carbohydrate	...25g	Saturates	.......9g

 45 MINS   45 MINS

SERVES 4

I N G R E D I E N T S

9 ounces puff pastry, thawed
   if frozen

2 medium red onions

1 red bell pepper

8 cherry tomatoes, halved

3½ ounces mozzarella cheese,
   cut into chunks

8 sprigs thyme

1 Roll out the pastry to make 3-inch squares. Using a sharp knife, trim the edges of the pastry, reserving the trimmings. Leave the pastry to chill in the refrigerator for 30 minutes.

2 Place the pastry squares on a cookie sheet. Brush a little water along each edge of the pastry squares and use the reserved pastry trimmings to make a rim around each tart.

3 Cut the red onions into thin wedges and halve and deseed the bell peppers.

4 Place the onions and bell pepper in a roasting pan. Cook under a preheated broiler for 15 minutes or until charred.

5 Place the roasted bell pepper halves in a plastic bag and leave to sweat for 10 minutes. Peel off the skin from the bell peppers and cut the flesh into strips.

6 Line the pastry squares with squares of foil. Bake in a preheated oven at 400°F for 10 minutes. Remove the foil squares and bake for a further 5 minutes.

7 Place the onions, bell pepper strips, tomatoes, and cheese in each tart and sprinkle with the fresh thyme.

8 Return to the oven for 15 minutes or until the pastry is golden. Serve hot.

Broiled Eggplants

Serve plain as a simple vegetable dish, but for a tasty starter or vegetarian dish, serve it with pesto or minty cucumber sauce.

NUTRITIONAL INFORMATION

Calories	340	Sugars	........3g
Protein	........8g	Fat	..........33g
Carbohydrate	....4g	Saturates	.......7g

 30 MINS   10 MINS

SERVES 4

INGREDIENTS

1 large eggplant

3 tablespoons olive oil

1 teaspoon sesame oil

salt and pepper

PESTO

1 clove garlic

¼ cup pine nuts

½ cup fresh basil leaves

2 tablespoons Parmesan cheese

6 tablespoons olive oil

CUCUMBER SAUCE

⅔ cup plain yogurt

2-inch piece of cucumber

½ teaspoon mint sauce

1 Remove the stalk from the eggplant, then cut it lengthwise into 8 thin slices.

2 Lay the slices on a plate or board and sprinkle them liberally with salt to remove the bitter juices. Leave to stand.

3 Meanwhile, prepare the baste. Combine the olive and sesame oils, season with pepper, and set aside.

4 To make the pesto, put the garlic, pine nuts, basil, and cheese in a food processor until finely chopped. With the machine running, gradually add the oil in a thin stream. Season to taste.

5 To make the minty cucumber sauce, place the yogurt in a mixing bowl. Remove the seeds from the cucumber and dice the flesh finely. Stir into the yogurt with the mint sauce.

6 Rinse the eggplant slices and pat them dry on absorbent paper towels. Baste with the oil mixture and barbecue over hot coals for about 10 minutes, turning once. The eggplant should be golden and just tender.

7 Transfer the eggplant slices to serving plates and serve with either the cucumber sauce or the pesto.

Italian Omelet

A baked omelet of substantial proportions with potatoes, onions, artichokes, and sun-dried tomatoes.

NUTRITIONAL INFORMATION

Calories 481	Sugars 4g	
Protein 22g	Fat 26g	
Carbohydrate . . .42g	Saturates 10g	

10 MINS   45 MINS

SERVES 4

I N G R E D I E N T S

2 pounds potatoes

1 tablespoon oil

1 large onion, sliced

2 garlic cloves, chopped

6 sun-dried tomatoes, cut into strips

14-ounce can artichoke hearts, drained
   and halved

1 cup ricotta cheese

4 large eggs, beaten

2 tablespoons milk

⅔ cup grated Parmesan cheese

3 tablespoons chopped thyme

salt and pepper

1   Peel the potatoes and place them in a bowl of cold water (see Cook's Tip). Cut the potatoes into thin slices.

2   Bring a large pan of water to a boil and add the potato slices. Leave the potatoes to simmer for 5–6 minutes or until just tender.

3   Heat the oil in a large skillet. Add the onions and garlic to the skillet and cook, stirring occasionally, for about 3–4 minutes.

4   Add the sun-dried tomatoes and continue cooking for a further 2 minutes.

5   Place a layer of potatoes at the bottom of a deep, ovenproof dish. Top with a layer of the onion mixture, artichokes, and ricotta cheese. Repeat the layers in the same order, finishing with a layer of potatoes on top.

6   Mix together the eggs, milk, half the Parmesan, thyme, and salt and pepper to taste and pour over the potatoes.

7   Top with the remaining Parmesan cheese and bake in a preheated oven, at 375°F, for 20–25 minutes or until golden brown. Cut the omelet into slices and serve.

COOK'S TIP

Placing the potatoes in a bowl of cold water will prevent them from turning brown while you cut the rest into slices.

Bean & Tomato Casserole

This quick and easy casserole can be eaten as a healthy supper dish or as a side dish to accompany sausages or broiled fish.

NUTRITIONAL INFORMATION

Calories ....273 Sugars 8g
Protein ....15g Fat 7g
Carbohydrate ...40g Saturates 1g

10 MINS   15 MINS

SERVES 4

I N G R E D I E N T S

14-ounce can cannellini beans

14-ounce can borlotti beans (also called broad beans)

2 tablespoons olive oil

1 celery stalk

2 garlic cloves, chopped

6 ounces baby onions, halved

1 pound tomatoes

1 bunch arugula

1 Drain both cans of beans and reserve 6 tablespoons of the liquid.

2 Heat the oil in a large pan. Add the celery, garlic, and onions and sauté for 5 minutes or until the onions are golden.

3 Cut a cross in the base of each tomato and plunge them into a bowl of boiling water for 30 seconds until the skins split. Remove the tomatoes with a perforated spoon and leave until cool enough to handle. Peel off the skin and chop the flesh.

4 Add the tomato flesh and the reserved bean liquid to the pan and cook for 5 minutes.

5 Add the beans to the pan and cook for a further 3–4 minutes or until the beans are hot.

6 Stir in the arugula and allow to wilt slightly before serving. Serve hot.

VARIATION

For a spicier tasting dish, add 1–2 teaspoons of hot pepper sauce with the beans in step 5.

Omelet in Tomato Sauce

These omelet strips are delicious smothered in a tomato and rosemary flavored sauce.

NUTRITIONAL INFORMATION

Calories	198	Sugars	.........6g
Protein	........10g	Fat	..........15g
Carbohydrate	....6g	Saturates	.......8g

10 MINS   35 MINS

SERVES 4

INGREDIENTS

2 tablespoons butter

1 onion, finely chopped

2 garlic cloves, chopped

4 eggs, beaten

⅔ cup milk

2¾ ounces Swiss cheese, diced

14-ounce can tomatoes, chopped

1 tablespoon rosemary, stalks removed

⅔ cup vegetable stock

freshly grated Parmesan cheese,
  for sprinkling

fresh, crusty bread, to serve

1 Melt the butter in a large skillet. Add the onion and garlic and cook for 4–5 minutes, until softened.

2 Beat together the eggs and milk and add the mixture to the skillet.

3 Using a spatula, raise the cooked edges of the omelet and tip any uncooked egg around the edge of the pan.

4 Scatter over the cheese. Cook for 5 minutes, turning once, until golden on both sides. Remove the omelet from the pan and roll up.

5 Add the tomatoes, rosemary and vegetable stock to the skillet, stirring, and bring to a boil.

6 Leave the tomato sauce to simmer for about 10 minutes until reduced and thickened.

7 Slice the omelet into strips and add to the tomato sauce in the skillet. Cook for 3–4 minutes or until piping hot.

8 Sprinkle the freshly grated Parmesan cheese over the omelet strips and serve with fresh, crusty bread.

VARIATION

Try adding ½ cup diced pancetta or unsmoked bacon in step 1 and cooking the meat with the onions.

Baked Fennel

Fennel is used extensively in northern Italy. It is a very versatile vegetable, which is good cooked or used raw in salads.

NUTRITIONAL INFORMATION

Calories 111   Sugars 6g
Protein ....7g   Fat 7g
Carbohydrate ....7g   Saturates 3g

10 MINS   35 MINS

SERVES 4

INGREDIENTS

2 fennel bulbs

2 celery stalks, cut into 3-inch sticks

6 sun-dried tomatoes, halved

1 cup sieved tomatoes

2 teaspoon dried oregano

⅔ cup grated Parmesan cheese

1 Using a sharp knife, trim the fennel, discarding any tough outer leaves, and cut the bulb into quarters.

2 Bring a large pan of water to a boil, add the fennel and celery, and cook for 8–10 minutes or until just tender. Remove with a perforated spoon and drain.

3 Place the fennel pieces, celery, and sun-dried tomatoes in a large ovenproof dish.

4 Mix the sieved tomatoes and oregano and pour the mixture over the fennel.

5 Sprinkle with the Parmesan cheese and bake in a preheated oven at 375°F for 20 minutes or until hot. Serve as a starter with bread or as a vegetable side dish.

Garlic & Pine Nut Tarts

A crisp lining of bread is filled with garlic butter and pine nuts to make a delightful light meal.

NUTRITIONAL INFORMATION

Calories 435   Sugars 1g
Protein ....6g   Fat 39g
Carbohydrate ...17g   Saturates 20g

 20 MINS   15 MINS

SERVES 4

I N G R E D I E N T S

4 slices whole wheat bread

½ cup pine nuts

11 tablespoons butter

5 garlic cloves, peeled and halved

2 tablespoons fresh oregano, chopped,
   plus extra for garnish

4 black olives, halved

oregano leaves, to garnish

1 Using a rolling pin, flatten the bread slightly. Using a cookie cutter, cut out 4 rounds of bread to fit your individual tart pans—they should measure about 4 inches across. Reserve the offcuts of bread and leave them in the refrigerator for 10 minutes or until required.

VARIATION

Puff pastry can be used for the tarts. Use 7 ounces puff pastry to line 4 tart pans. Leave the pastry to chill for 20 minutes. Line the pans with the pastry and foil and bake blind for 10 minutes. Remove the foil and bake for 3–4 minutes or until the pastry is set. Cool, then continue from step 2, adding 2 tablespoons bread crumbs to the mixture.

2 Meanwhile, place the pine nuts on a cookie sheet. Toast the pine nuts under a preheated broiler for 2–3 minutes or until golden.

3 Put the bread offcuts, pine nuts, butter, garlic, and oregano into a food processor and blend for about 20 seconds. Alternatively, pound the ingredients by hand in a mortar and pestle. The mixture should have a rough texture.

4 Spoon the pine nut butter mixture into the lined pan and top with the olives. Bake in a preheated oven at 400°F for 10–15 minutes or until golden.

5 Transfer the tarts to serving plates and serve warm, garnished with the fresh oregano leaves.

Pasta Omelet

This is a superb way of using up any leftover pasta, such as penne, macaroni, or conchiglie.

NUTRITIONAL INFORMATION

Calories 460	Sugars 3g	
Protein 16g	Fat 34g	
Carbohydrate ...23g	Saturates 6g	

10 MINS   30 MINS

SERVES 2

I N G R E D I E N T S

4 tablespoons olive oil

1 small onion, chopped

1 fennel bulb, thinly sliced

½ cup diced potato

1 garlic clove, chopped

4 eggs

1 tablespoon chopped fresh flat-leaf parsley

pinch of chili powder

1 cup short pasta, cooked

2 tablespoons stuffed green olives, halved

salt and pepper

fresh marjoram sprigs, to garnish

tomato salad, to serve

1 Heat half of the oil in a heavy-based skillet over a low heat. Add the onion, fennel, and potato and fry, stirring occasionally, for 8–10 minutes, until the potato is just tender.

2 Stir in the garlic and cook for 1 minute. Remove the skillet from the heat and transfer the vegetables to a plate and set aside.

3 Beat the eggs until they are frothy. Stir in the parsley and season with salt, pepper, and a pinch of chilli powder.

4 Heat 1 tablespoon of the remaining oil in a clean skillet. Add half of the egg mixture to the pan, then add the cooked vegetables, pasta, and half of the olives. Pour in the remaining egg mixture and cook until the sides begin to set.

5 Lift up the edges of the omelet with a spatula to allow the uncooked egg to spread underneath. Cook, shaking the pan occasionally, until the underside is a light golden brown color.

6 Slide the omelet out of the pan onto a plate. Wipe the pan with paper towels and heat the remaining oil. Invert the omelet into the pan and cook until the other side is a golden brown color.

7 Slide the omelet onto a warmed serving dish and garnish with the remaining olives and the sprigs of marjoram. Cut the omelet into wedges and serve with a tomato salad.

Spinach & Ricotta Shells

This is a classic combination in which the smooth, creamy cheese balances the sharper taste of the spinach.

NUTRITIONAL INFORMATION

Calories	672	Sugars	........10g
Protein	........23g	Fat	..........26g
Carbohydrate	...93g	Saturates	.......8g

 5 MINS   40 MINS

SERVES 4

I N G R E D I E N T S

14 ounces dried lumache rigate grande (large shells)

5 tablespoons olive oil

1 cup fresh white bread crumbs

½ cup milk

10 ½ ounces frozen spinach, thawed and drained

1 cup ricotta cheese

pinch of freshly grated nutmeg

14-ounce can diced tomatoes, drained

1 garlic clove, crushed

salt and pepper

1 Bring a large saucepan of lightly salted water to a boil. Add the lumache and 1 tablespoon of the olive oil and cook for 8–10 minutes until just tender, but still firm to the bite. Drain the pasta, refresh under cold water and set aside until required.

2 Put the bread crumbs, milk, and 3 tablespoons of the remaining olive oil in a food processor and work to combine.

3 Add the spinach and ricotta cheese to the food processor and work to a smooth mixture. Transfer to a bowl, stir in the nutmeg, and season with salt and pepper to taste.

4 Mix together the tomatoes, garlic, and remaining oil and spoon the mixture into the base of a large ovenproof dish.

5 Using a teaspoon, fill the lumache with the spinach and ricotta mixture and arrange on top of the tomato mixture in the dish. Cover and bake in a preheated oven at 350°F for 20 minutes. Serve hot.

COOK'S TIP

Ricotta is a creamy Italian cheese traditionally made from ewes' milk whey. It is soft and white, with a smooth texture and a slightly sweet flavor. It should be used within 2–3 days of purchase.

Rotelle with Spicy Sauce

Prepare the sauce well in advance—it is a good idea to freeze batches of the sauce so that you always have some on hand.

NUTRITIONAL INFORMATION

Calories 530	Sugars 4g
Protein 13g	Fat 18g
Carbohydrate . . .78g	Saturates 3g

  8¼ HOURS   40 MINS

SERVES 4

INGREDIENTS

1 cup Italian Red Wine Sauce
  (see page 29)

5 tablespoons olive oil

3 garlic cloves, crushed

2 fresh red chilies, chopped

1 green chili, chopped

3½ cups dried rotelle

salt and pepper

warm Italian bread, to serve

1 Make the Italian Red Wine Sauce (see page 29).

2 Heat 4 tablespoons of the oil in a saucepan. Add the garlic and chilies and fry for 3 minutes.

3 Stir in the Italian Red Wine Sauce, season with salt and pepper to taste, and simmer gently over low heat for 20 minutes.

4 Bring a large saucepan of lightly salted water to a boil. Add the rotelle and the remaining oil and cook for 8 minutes, until just tender, but still firm to the bite. Drain the pasta.

5 Pour the Italian Red Wine Sauce over the rotelle and toss to mix.

6 Transfer to a warm serving dish and serve with warm Italian bread.

COOK'S TIP

Remove chili seeds before chopping the chilies, as they are the hottest part, and shouldn't be allowed to slip into the food.

Tagliarini with Gorgonzola

This simple, creamy pasta sauce is a classic Italian recipe. You could use Danish blue cheese instead of the Gorgonzola, if you prefer.

NUTRITIONAL INFORMATION

Calories 904	Sugars 4g
Protein 27g	Fat 53g
Carbohydrate . . .83g	Saturates 36g

5 MINS   20 MINS

SERVES 4

I N G R E D I E N T S

2 tablespoons butter

8 ounces Gorgonzola cheese, roughly crumbled

⅔ cup heavy cream

2 tablespoons dry white wine

1 teaspoon cornstarch

4 fresh sage sprigs, finely chopped

14 ounces dried tagliarini

2 tablespoons olive oil

salt and white pepper

1 Melt the butter in a heavy-based pan. Stir in 6 ounces of the cheese and melt, over low heat, for about 2 minutes.

2 Add the cream, wine and cornstarch and beat with a whisk until fully incorporated.

COOK'S TIP

Gorgonzola is one of the world's oldest veined cheeses and, arguably, its finest. When buying, always check that it is creamy yellow with delicate green veining. Avoid hard or discolored cheese. It should have a rich, piquant aroma, not a bitter smell.

3 Stir in the sage and season to taste with salt and white pepper. Bring to a boil over low heat, whisking constantly, until the sauce thickens. Remove from the heat and set aside while you cook the pasta.

4 Bring a large saucepan of lightly salted water to a boil. Add the tagliarini and 1 tablespoon of the olive oil. Cook the pasta for 8–10 minutes or until

just tender, drain thoroughly and toss in the remaining olive oil. Transfer the pasta to a serving dish and keep warm.

5 Reheat the sauce over a low heat, whisking constantly. Spoon the Gorgonzola sauce over the tagliarini, generously sprinkle over the remaining cheese and serve immediately.

Spaghetti with Ricotta

This light pasta dish has a delicate flavor ideally suited for a summer lunch.

NUTRITIONAL INFORMATION

Calories	701	Sugars	........12g
Protein	........17g	Fat	..........40g
Carbohydrate	...73g	Saturates	......15g

   5 MINS   25 MINS

SERVES 4

INGREDIENTS

12 ounces dried spaghetti

3 tablespoons olive oil

3 tablespoons butter

2 tablespoons chopped flat-leaf parsley

1 cup freshly ground almonds

½ cup ricotta cheese

pinch of grated nutmeg

pinch of ground cinnamon

⅔ cup crème fraîche (see page 472)
   or plain yogurt

½ cup hot chicken stock

1 tablespoon pine nuts

salt and pepper

fresh flat-leaf parsley sprigs, to garnish

1 Bring a pan of lightly salted water to a boil. Add the spaghetti and 1 tablespoon of the oil and cook for 8–10 minutes until tender, but still firm to the bite.

2 Drain the pasta, return to the pan, and toss with the butter and chopped parsley. Set aside and keep warm.

3 To make the sauce, mix together the ground almonds, ricotta cheese, nutmeg, cinnamon and crème fraîche or unsweetened yogurt over low heat to form a thick paste. Gradually stir in the remaining oil. When the oil has been fully incorporated, gradually stir in the hot chicken stock, until smooth. Season to taste with black pepper.

4 Transfer the spaghetti to a warm serving dish, pour over the sauce and toss together well. Sprinkle over the pine nuts, garnish with the sprigs of flat leaf parsley, and serve warm.

COOK'S TIP

Use two large forks to toss spaghetti or other long pasta, so that it is thoroughly coated with the sauce. Special spaghetti forks are available from some cookware departments and kitchen shops.

Three-Cheese Bake

Serve this dish while the cheese is still hot and melted, as cooked cheese turns very rubbery if it is allowed to cool down.

NUTRITIONAL INFORMATION

Calories	710	Sugars	. . . . .6g
Protein	. . . . .34g	Fat	. . . . .30g
Carbohydrate	. . .80g	Saturates	. . . . . .16g

  5 MINS   1 HOUR

SERVES 4

I N G R E D I E N T S

butter, for greasing

14 ounces dried penne

1 tablespoon olive oil

2 eggs, beaten

1½ cups ricotta cheese

4 fresh basil sprigs

1 cup grated mozzarella cheese

4 tablespoons freshly grated Parmesan cheese

salt and pepper

fresh basil leaves (optional), to garnish

1 Lightly grease a large ovenproof dish with butter.

2 Bring a large pan of lightly salted water to a boil. Add the penne and olive oil and cook for 8–10 minutes until just tender, but still firm to the bite. Drain the pasta, set aside and keep warm.

3 Beat the eggs into the ricotta cheese and season to taste.

4 Spoon half of the penne into the base of the dish and cover with half of the basil leaves.

5 Spoon over half of the ricotta cheese mixture. Sprinkle over the mozzarella or halloumi cheese and top with the remaining basil leaves. Cover with the remaining penne and then spoon over the remaining ricotta cheese mixture. Lightly sprinkle over the freshly grated Parmesan cheese.

6 Bake in a preheated oven at 375°F for 30–40 minutes, until golden brown and the cheese topping is hot and bubbling. Garnish with fresh basil leaves, if liked, and serve hot.

VARIATION

Try substituting smoked Bavarian cheese for the mozzarella and grated Cheddar cheese for the Parmesan, for a slightly different but just as delicious flavor.

Eggplant & Pasta

Prepare the marinated eggplants well in advance so that all you have to do is cook the pasta.

NUTRITIONAL INFORMATION

Calories . . . . . . .378 Sugars 3g
Protein . . . . .12g Fat 30g
Carbohydrate . . .16g Saturates 3g

12¼ HOURS   15 MINS

SERVES 4

I N G R E D I E N T S

⅔ cup vegetable stock

⅔ cup white wine vinegar

2 teaspoons balsamic vinegar

3 tablespoons olive oil

fresh oregano sprig

1 pound eggplants, peeled and thinly sliced

14 ounces dried linguine

M A R I N A D E

2 tablespoons extra virgin oil

2 garlic cloves, crushed

2 tablespoons chopped fresh oregano

2 tablespoons finely chopped roasted almonds

2 tablespoons diced red bell pepper

2 tablespoons lime juice

grated rind and juice of 1 orange

salt and pepper

1 Put the vegetable stock, wine vinegar, and balsamic vinegar into a saucepan and bring to a boil over low heat. Add 2 teaspoons of the olive oil and the sprig of oregano and simmer gently for about 1 minute.

2 Add the eggplant slices to the pan, remove from the heat and set aside for 10 minutes.

3 Meanwhile make the marinade. Combine the oil, garlic, fresh oregano, almonds, bell pepper, lime juice, orange rind, and juice together in a large bowl and season to taste.

4 Carefully remove the eggplant from the saucepan with a slotted spoon, and drain well. Add the eggplant slices to the marinade, mixing well, and set aside in the refrigerator for about 12 hours.

5 Bring a large pan of lightly salted water to a boil. Add half of the remaining oil and the linguine and cook for 8–10 minutes until just tender. Drain the pasta thoroughly and toss with the remaining oil while still warm. Arrange the pasta on a serving plate with the eggplant slices and the marinade and serve.

Tricolor Timballini

An unusual way of serving pasta, these cheese molds are excellent with a crunchy salad for a light lunch.

NUTRITIONAL INFORMATION

Calories 529   Sugars 7g
Protein . . . . .18g   Fat 29g
Carbohydrate . . .46g   Saturates 12g

 30 MINS   🕐 1 HOUR

SERVES 4

I N G R E D I E N T S

1 tablespoon butter, softened

1 cup dried white
   bread crumbs

6 ounces dried tricolor spaghetti, broken
   into 2-inch lengths

3 tablespoons olive oil

1¼ cups Béchamel Sauce
   (see page 28)

1 egg yolk

1 cup grated Swiss cheese

1 onion, finely chopped

1 bay leaf

⅔ cup dry white wine

⅔ cup sieved tomatoes

1 tablespoon tomato paste

salt and pepper

fresh basil leaves,
   to garnish

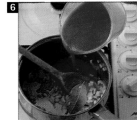

1   Grease four ¾ cup molds or ramekins with the butter. Evenly coat the insides with half of the bread crumbs.

2   Bring a pan of lightly salted water to a boil. Add the spaghetti and 1 tablespoon oil and cook for 8–10 minutes or until just tender. Drain and transfer to a mixing bowl. Add the egg yolk and cheese to the pasta and season.

3   Pour the Béchamel Sauce into the bowl containing the pasta and mix. Spoon the mixture into the ramekins and sprinkle over the remaining bread crumbs.

4   Stand the ramekins on a cookie sheet and bake in a preheated oven at 425°F for 20 minutes. Set aside for 10 minutes.

5   Meanwhile, make the sauce. Heat the remaining oil in a pan and gently fry the onion and bay leaf for 2-3 minutes.

6   Stir in the wine, sieved tomatoes and tomato paste and season with salt and pepper to taste. Simmer for 20 minutes, until thickened. Remove and discard the bay leaf.

7   Turn the timballini out onto serving plates, garnish with the basil leaves, and serve with the tomato sauce.

Baked Tuna & Ricotta Rigatoni

Ribbed tubes of pasta are filled with tuna and ricotta cheese and then baked in a creamy sauce.

NUTRITIONAL INFORMATION

Calories	949	Sugars	.........5g
Protein	........51g	Fat	..........48g
Carbohydrate	...85g	Saturates	......26g

🍲 10 MINS   🕐 45 MINS

SERVES 4

I N G R E D I E N T S

butter, for greasing

1 pound dried rigatoni

1 tablespoon olive oil

7-ounce can flaked tuna, drained

1 cup ricotta cheese

½ cup heavy cream

2 ⅔ cups grated
  Parmesan cheese

4 ounces sun-dried tomatoes, drained
  and sliced

salt and pepper

1 Lightly grease a large ovenproof dish with butter.

2 Bring a large saucepan of lightly salted water to a boil. Add the rigatoni and olive oil and cook for 8–10 minutes until just tender, but still firm to the bite. Drain the pasta and set aside until cool enough to handle.

3 Meanwhile, in a bowl, mix together the tuna and ricotta cheese to form a soft paste. Spoon the mixture into a pastry bag and use to fill the rigatoni. Arrange the filled pasta tubes side by side in the prepared ovenproof dish.

4 To make the sauce, mix the cream and Parmesan cheese and season with salt and pepper to taste. Spoon the sauce over the rigatoni and top with the sun-dried tomatoes, arranged in a criss-cross pattern. Bake in a preheated oven at 400°F for 20 minutes. Serve hot straight from the dish.

VARIATION

For a vegetarian version of this recipe, simply substitute a mixture of pitted and chopped black olives and chopped walnuts for the tuna. Follow exactly the same cooking method.

Pancakes with Smoked Fish

These are delicious as a starter or light supper dish and you can vary the filling with whichever fish you prefer.

NUTRITIONAL INFORMATION

Calories	.399	Sugars	.6g
Protein	36g	Fat	18g
Carbohydrate	25g	Saturates	10g

  15 MINS 1 HR 20 MINS

Makes 12 pancakes

INGREDIENTS

PANCAKES

¾ cup all-purpose flour

½ teaspoon salt

1 egg, beaten

1 ¼ cups milk

1 tablespoon oil, for frying

SAUCE

1 pound smoked haddock or cod, skinned

1¼ cups milk

3 tablespoons butter or margarine

⅓ cup all-purpose flour

1¼ cups fish stock

1 cup grated Parmesan cheese

1 cup frozen peas, thawed

3½ ounces shrimp, cooked and peeled

½ cup grated Swiss cheese

salt and pepper

1 To make the pancake batter, sift the flour and salt into a large bowl and make a well in the center. Add the egg and, using a wooden spoon, begin to draw in the flour. Slowly add the milk and beat together to form a smooth batter. Set aside until required.

2 Place the fish in a large skillet, add the milk, and bring to a boil. Simmer for 10 minutes or until the fish begins to flake. Drain thoroughly, reserving the milk.

3 Melt the butter in a saucepan. Add the flour, mix to a paste, and cook for 2–3 minutes. Remove the pan from the heat and add the reserved milk a little at a time, stirring to make a smooth sauce. Repeat with the fish stock. Return to the heat and bring to a boil, stirring. Stir in the Parmesan and season with salt and pepper to taste.

4 Grease a skillet with oil. Add 2 tablespoons of the pancake batter, swirling it around the skillet and cook for 2–3 minutes. Loosen the sides with a spatula and flip over the pancake. Cook for 2–3 minutes until golden; repeat. Stack the pancakes with sheets of baking parchment between them and keep warm in the oven.

5 Stir the flaked fish, peas and shrimp into half of the sauce and use to fill each pancake. Pour over the remaining sauce, top with the Swiss cheese, and bake for 20 minutes until golden.

Pasta & Anchovy Sauce

This is an ideal dish for cooks in a hurry, as it is prepared in minutes from pantry ingredients.

NUTRITIONAL INFORMATION

Calories 712	Sugars 4g
Protein 25g	Fat 34g
Carbohydrate . . .81g	Saturates 8g

 10 MINS   25 MINS

SERVES 4

I N G R E D I E N T S

⅓ cup olive oil

2 garlic cloves, crushed

2 ounces can anchovy fillets, drained

1 pound dried spaghetti

2 ounces pesto sauce (see page 39)

2 tablespoons finely chopped fresh oregano

1 cup grated Parmesan cheese,
  plus extra for serving (optional)

salt and pepper

2 fresh oregano sprigs, to garnish

1 Reserve 1 tablespoon of the oil and heat the remainder in a small saucepan. Add the garlic and fry for 3 minutes.

2 Lower the heat, stir in the anchovies, and cook, stirring occasionally, until the anchovies have disintegrated.

3 Bring a large saucepan of lightly salted water to a boil. Add the spaghetti and the remaining olive oil and cook for 8–10 minutes or until just tender, but still firm to the bite.

4 Add the pesto sauce (see page 39) and chopped fresh oregano to the anchovy mixture and then season with pepper to taste.

5 Drain the spaghetti, using a slotted spoon, and transfer to a warm serving dish. Pour the pesto sauce over the spaghetti and then sprinkle over the grated Parmesan cheese.

6 Garnish with oregano sprigs and serve with extra cheese, if using.

COOK'S TIP

If you find canned anchovies too salty, soak them in a saucer of cold milk for 5 minutes, drain, and pat dry with paper towels before using. The milk absorbs the salt.

Roasted Seafood

Vegetables become deliciously sweet and juicy when they are roasted, and they go particularly well with fish and seafood.

NUTRITIONAL INFORMATION

Calories 280   Sugars 5g
Protein . . . . .15g   Fat 12g
Carbohydrate . . .28g   Saturates 2g

15 MINS   50 MINS

SERVES 4

I N G R E D I E N T S

1 pound 5 ounces new potatoes

3 red onions, cut into wedges

2 zucchini, sliced into chunks

8 garlic cloves, peeled

2 lemons, cut into wedges

4 sprigs rosemary

4 tablespoons olive oil

12 ounces unpeeled, raw shrimp

2 small squid, chopped
   into rings

4 tomatoes, quartered

1 Scrub the potatoes to remove any excess dirt. Cut any large potatoes in half. Place the potatoes in a large roasting pan, together with the onions, zucchini, garlic, lemon, and rosemary sprigs.

2 Pour over the oil and toss to coat all of the vegetables in the oil. Cook in a preheated oven, at 400°F, for 40 minutes, turning occasionally, until the potatoes are tender.

3 Once the potatoes are tender, add the shrimp, squid, and tomatoes, tossing to coat them in the oil, and roast for 10 minutes. All of the vegetables should be cooked through and slightly charred for full flavor.

4 Transfer the roasted seafood and vegetables to warm serving plates and serve hot.

VARIATION

Most vegetables are suitable for roasting in the oven. Try adding 1 pound pumpkin, squash, or eggplant, if you prefer.

Penne with Fried Mussels

This is quick and simple, but one of the nicest of Italian fried fish dishes, served with penne.

NUTRITIONAL INFORMATION

Calories	537	Sugars 2g
Protein	........22g	Fat 24g
Carbohydrate	...62g	Saturates 3g

 10 MINS   🕐 25 MINS

SERVES 6

I N G R E D I E N T S

3 ½ cups dried penne

½ cup olive oil

1 pound mussels, cooked and shelled

1 teaspoon sea salt

⅔ cup all-purpose flour

3 ½ ounces sun-dried tomatoes, sliced

2 tablespoons chopped, fresh basil leaves

salt and pepper

1 lemon, thinly sliced, to garnish

1 Bring a large saucepan of lightly salted water to a boil. Add the penne and 1 tablespoon of the olive oil and cook for 8–10 minutes or until the pasta is just tender, but still firm to the bite.

2 Drain the pasta thoroughly and place in a large, warm serving dish. Set aside and keep warm while you cook the mussels.

3 Lightly sprinkle the mussels with the sea salt. Season the flour with salt and pepper to taste, sprinkle into a bowl and toss the mussels in the flour until well coated.

4 Heat the remaining oil in a large skillet. Add the mussels and fry, stirring frequently, until a light golden brown color.

5 Toss the mussels with the penne and sprinkle with the sun-dried tomatoes and basil leaves. Garnish with slices of lemon and serve immediately.

COOK'S TIP

Sun-dried tomatoes, used in Italy for a long time, have become popular elsewhere only quite recently. They are dried and then preserved in oil. They have a concentrated, roasted flavor and a dense texture. They should be drained and chopped or sliced before using.

Potatoes, Olives, & Anchovies

This side dish makes a delicious accompaniment for broiled fish or for lamb chops. The fennel adds a subtle aniseed flavor.

NUTRITIONAL INFORMATION

Calories	202	Sugars	.........2g
Protein	.........7g	Fat	..........12g
Carbohydrate	...19g	Saturates	.......1g

 10 MINS   30 MINS

SERVES 4

I N G R E D I E N T S

1 pound baby new potatoes, scrubbed

2 tablespoons olive oil

2 fennel bulbs, trimmed and sliced

2 sprigs rosemary, stalks removed

½ cup mixed olives

8 canned anchovy fillets, drained and
  chopped

1 Bring a large saucepan of water to a boil and cook the potatoes for 8–10 minutes or until tender. Remove the potatoes from the saucepan using a perforated spoon and set aside to cool slightly.

2 Once the potatoes are just cool enough to handle, cut them into wedges, using a sharp knife.

3 Pit the mixed olives and cut them in half, using a sharp knife.

4 Using a sharp knife, chop the anchovy fillets into smaller strips.

5 Heat the oil in a large skillet. Add the potato wedges, sliced fennel, and rosemary. Cook for 7–8 minutes or until the potatoes are golden.

6 Stir in the olives and anchovies and cook for 1 minute or until completely warmed through.

7 Transfer to serving plates and serve at once.

COOK'S TIP

Fresh rosemary is a particular favorite with Italians, but you can experiment with your favorite herbs in this recipe, if you prefer.

Mozzarella Snack

These deep-fried mozzarella sandwiches are a tasty snack at any time of the day, or serve smaller triangles as an antipasto with drinks.

NUTRITIONAL INFORMATION

Calories . . . . . . .379 Sugars 4g
Protein . . . . .20g Fat 22g
Carbohydrate . . .28g Saturates 5g

 20 MINS   5–10 MINS

SERVES 4

I N G R E D I E N T S

8 slices bread, preferably slightly stale, crusts removed

3 ½ ounces mozzarella cheese, sliced thickly

½ cup pitted black olives, chopped

8 canned anchovy fillets, drained and chopped

16 fresh basil leaves

4 eggs, beaten

⅔ cup milk

oil, for deep-frying

salt and pepper

1 Cut each slice of bread into 2 triangles. Top 8 of the bread triangles with the mozzarella slices, olives, and chopped anchovies.

2 Place the basil leaves on top and season with salt and pepper to taste.

3 Lay the other 8 triangles of bread over the top and press down round the edges to seal.

4 Mix the eggs and milk and pour into an ovenproof dish. Add the sandwiches and leave to soak for about 5 minutes.

5 Heat the oil in a large saucepan to 350°–375°F or until a cube of bread browns in 30 seconds.

6 Before cooking the sandwiches, squeeze the edges together again.

7 Carefully place the sandwiches in the oil and deep-fry for 2 minutes or until golden, turning once. Remove the sandwiches with a perforated spoon and drain on absorbent paper towels. Serve immediately while still hot.

Spinach & Anchovy Pasta

This colorful light meal can be made with a variety of different pasta, including spaghetti and linguine.

NUTRITIONAL INFORMATION

Calories	.619	Sugars	.5g
Protein	.21g	Fat	.31g
Carbohydrate	.67g	Saturates	.3g

 10 MINS   25 MINS

SERVES 4

I N G R E D I E N T S

2 pounds fresh, young spinach leaves

14 ounces dried fettuccine

6 tablespoons olive oil

3 tablespoons pine nuts

3 garlic cloves, crushed

8 canned anchovy fillets, drained and
   chopped

salt

1 Trim off any tough spinach stalks. Rinse the spinach leaves and place them in a large saucepan with only the water that is clinging to them after washing. Cover and cook over high heat, shaking the pan from time, until the spinach has wilted, but retains its color. Drain well, set aside, and keep warm.

COOK'S TIP

If you are in a hurry, you can use frozen spinach. Thaw and drain it thoroughly, pressing out as much moisture as possible. Cut the leaves into strips and add to the dish with the anchovies in step 4.

2 Bring a large saucepan of lightly salted water to a boil. Add the fettuccine and 1 tablespoon of the oil and cook for 8–10 minutes until it is just tender, but still firm to the bite.

3 Heat 4 tablespoons of the remaining oil in a saucepan. Add the pine nuts and fry until golden. Remove the pine nuts from the pan and set aside until required.

4 Add the garlic to the pan and fry until golden. Add the anchovies and stir in the spinach. Cook, stirring, for 2-3 minutes, until heated through. Return the pine nuts to the pan.

5 Drain the fettuccine, toss in the remaining olive oil, and transfer to a warm serving dish. Spoon the anchovy and spinach sauce over the fettuccine, toss lightly, and serve at once.

Ciabatta Rolls

Sandwiches are always a welcome snack, but can be mundane. These crisp rolls filled with roast bell peppers and cheese are irresistible.

NUTRITIONAL INFORMATION

Calories 328	Sugars 6g
Protein 8g	Fat 19g
Carbohydrate . . .34g	Saturates 9g

15 MINS 10 MINS

SERVES 4

I N G R E D I E N T S

4 ciabatta rolls, or other Italian rolls

2 tbsp olive oil

1 garlic clove, crushed

FILLING

1 red bell pepper

1 green bell pepper

1 yellow bell pepper

4 radishes, sliced

1 bunch watercress

3½ ounces cream cheese

1 Slice the ciabatta rolls in half. Heat the olive oil and crushed garlic in a saucepan. Pour the garlic and oil mixture over the cut surfaces of the rolls and leave to stand.

2 Halve the bell peppers and place, skin side uppermost, on a broiler rack. Cook under a hot broiler for 8–10 minutes, until just beginning to char. Remove the bell peppers from the broiler, peel and slice thinly.

3 Arrange the radish slices on one half of each roll with a few watercress leaves. Spoon the cream cheese on top. Pile the bell peppers on top of the cream cheese and top with the other half of the roll. Serve immediately.

Baked Eggplants

This delicious recipe is from Parma. Ensure that you simmer the tomato sauce gently to reduce it slightly before using.

NUTRITIONAL INFORMATION

Calories . . . . . . .578 Sugars 22g
Protein . . . . .17g Fat 43g
Carbohydrate . . .25g Saturates 13g

🍳 15 MINS   🕐 1¼ HOURS

SERVES 4

I N G R E D I E N T S

4 eggplants, trimmed

3 tablespoons olive oil

11 ounces mozzarella cheese,
    thinly sliced

4 slices prosciutto, shredded

1 tablespoon chopped, fresh marjoram

1 tablespoon chopped, fresh basil

½ quantity Béchamel Sauce (see page 28)

⅓ cup Parmesan, grated

salt and pepper

T O M A T O   S A U C E

4 tablespoons olive oil

1 large onion, sliced

4 garlic cloves, crushed

14-ounce can diced tomatoes

1 pound fresh tomatoes, peeled and
    chopped

4 tablespoons chopped, fresh parsley

2½ cups hot vegetable stock

1 tablespoon sugar

2 tablespoons lemon juice

⅔ cup dry white wine

salt and pepper

1 To make the tomato sauce, heat the oil in a large pan. Fry the onion and garlic until just beginning to soften. Add the canned and fresh tomatoes, parsley, stock, sugar, and lemon juice. Cover and simmer for 15 minutes. Stir in the wine and season.

2 Slice the eggplants thinly lengthwise. Bring a large saucepan of water to a boil and cook the eggplant slices for 5 minutes. Drain the eggplant slices on paper towels and pat dry.

3 Pour half of the fresh tomato sauce into a large, greased ovenproof dish. Cover with half of the cooked eggplants and drizzle with a little oil. Cover with half of the mozzarella, prosciutto, and herbs. Season with salt and pepper to taste.

4 Repeat the layers and cover with the Béchamel Sauce. Sprinkle with the Parmesan. Bake in a preheated oven, 375°F, for 35–40 minutes until golden on top. Serve.

 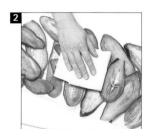 

Chorizo & Mushroom Pasta

Simple and quick to make, this spicy dish is sure to set the taste buds tingling.

NUTRITIONAL INFORMATION

Calories ....495 Sugars 1g
Protein ....15g Fat 35g
Carbohydrate ...33g Saturates 5g

 5 MINS   20 MINS

SERVES 6

I N G R E D I E N T S

1½ pounds dried vermicelli

½ cup olive oil

2 garlic cloves

4½ ounces chorizo, sliced

8 ounces exotic mushrooms

3 fresh red chilies, chopped

2 tablespoons grated Parmesan cheese

salt and pepper

10 anchovy fillets, to garnish

1 Bring a large saucepan of lightly salted water to a boil. Add the vermicelli and 1 tablespoon of the oil and cook for 8–10 minutes or until just tender, but still firm to the bite.

2 Drain the pasta thoroughly, place on a large, warm serving plate and keep warm.

3 Meanwhile, heat the remaining oil in a large skillet. Add the garlic and fry for 1 minute.

4 Add the chorizo and exotic mushrooms and cook for 4 minutes,

5 Add the chopped chilies and cook for 1 further minute.

6 Pour the chorizo and exotic mushroom mixture over the vermicelli and season with a little salt and pepper.

7 Sprinkle with freshly grated Parmesan cheese, garnish with a lattice of anchovy fillets, and serve at once.

COOK'S TIP

Many varieties of mushrooms are now cultivated and most are indistinguishable from the wild varieties. Mixed-color oyster mushrooms have been used here, but you could also use chanterelles. Remember that chanterelles shrink during cooking, so you may need more.

Pan Bagna

This is a deliciously moist picnic dish, lunch dish, or snack. It was originally designed for workers to take to the fields in a box.

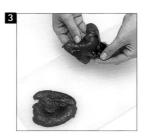

NUTRITIONAL INFORMATION

Calories	377	Sugars	.........3g
Protein	........20g	Fat	..........25g
Carbohydrate	...19g	Saturates	.......6g

  2½ HOURS · 30 MINS

SERVES 4

INGREDIENTS

1 red bell pepper, halved, cored, and
 deseeded

8 ounces sirloin steak, 1-inch thick

1 small white baguette

4 tablespoons olive oil

2 extra-large tomatoes, sliced

10 black olives, halved

½ cucumber, peeled and sliced

6 anchovies, chopped

salt and pepper

1 Cook the bell pepper over a hot barbecue for 15 minutes, turning once. Put the bell pepper into a plastic bag and seal.

2 Meanwhile, sear both sides of the steak first and then broil for 8 minutes, turning once.

VARIATION

Different fillings, such as pâtés, sausages, and other salad items, can be used according to appetite and taste. Mozzarella cheese is good, as it is so moist. Onions give a bit of a zing to the other ingredients.

3 When the bell pepper is cool enough to handle, peel and slice it.

4 Using a sharp knife, cut the steak into thin strips.

5 Cut the loaf of bread lengthwise and hollow out each half, leaving a 1 inch crust. Brush both halves very liberally with olive oil.

6 Lay the tomatoes, olives, cucumber, steak strips, anchovies, and red bell pepper strips on the bottom half. Season with salt and pepper to taste and cover with the top half.

7 Put the Pan Bagna on top of a piece of baking parchment. Squash the whole loaf and its filling down well and wrap tightly in plastic wrap. Secure with adhesive tape if necessary. Chill for at least 2 hours. If made in the morning, by lunchtime it will be ready to eat and all the flavors will have combined.

Pasta with Bacon & Tomatoes

As this dish cooks, the mouthwatering aroma of bacon, sweet tomatoes, and oregano is a feast in itself.

NUTRITIONAL INFORMATION

Calories 431   Sugars 8g
Protein . . . . .10g   Fat 29g
Carbohydrate . . .34g   Saturates 14g

10 MINS   35 MINS

SERVES 4

I N G R E D I E N T S

2 pounds small, sweet tomatoes

6 slices bacon

4 tablespoons butter

1 onion, chopped

1 garlic clove, crushed

4 fresh oregano sprigs, finely chopped

4 cups dried orecchiette pasta

1 tablespoon olive oil

salt and pepper

freshly grated Romano cheese, to serve

1 Blanch the tomatoes in boiling water. Drain, peel, and seed the tomatoes, then roughly chop the flesh.

2 Using a sharp knife, chop the bacon into small dice.

3 Melt the butter in a saucepan. Add the bacon and fry until it is golden.

4 Add the onion and garlic and fry over medium heat for 5-7 minutes, until just softened.

5 Add the tomatoes and oregano to the pan and then season to taste with salt and pepper. Lower the heat and simmer for 10-12 minutes.

6 Bring a large pan of lightly salted water to a boil. Add the orecchiette and oil and cook for 12 minutes, until just tender, but still firm to the bite. Drain the pasta and transfer to a warm serving dish or bowl.

7 Spoon the bacon and tomato sauce over the pasta, toss to coat, and serve with the cheese.

COOK'S TIP

For an authentic Italian flavor use pancetta, rather than ordinary bacon. This kind of bacon is streaked with fat and adds rich undertones of flavor to many traditional dishes. It is available both smoked and unsmoked from large supermarkets and Italian delicatessens.

Italian Platter

This popular hors d'oeuvre usually consists of vegetables soaked in olive oil and rich, creamy cheeses. Try this great low-fat version.

NUTRITIONAL INFORMATION

Calories	 198	Sugars	.... 12g
Protein	.... 12g	Fat	.... 6g
Carbohydrate	... 25g	Saturates	...... 3g

10 MINS   0 MINS

SERVES 4

I N G R E D I E N T S

4½ oz reduced-fat Mozzarella cheese, drained

2 oz lean Parma ham (prosciutto)

14 oz can artichoke hearts, drained

4 ripe figs

1 small mango

few plain bread sticks, to serve

D R E S S I N G

1 small orange

1 tbsp sieved tomatoes

1 tsp wholegrain mustard

4 tbsp low-fat plain yogurt

fresh basil leaves

salt and pepper

1   Cut the cheese into 12 sticks, 2½ inches long. Remove the fat from the ham and slice the meat into 12 strips. Carefully wrap a strip of ham around each stick of cheese and arrange neatly on a serving platter.

2   Halve the artichoke hearts and cut the figs into quarters. Arrange them on the serving platter in groups.

3   Peel the mango, then slice it down each side of the large, flat central stone. Slice the flesh into strips and arrange them so that they form a fan shape on the serving platter.

4   To make the dressing, pare the rind from half the orange using a vegetable peeler. Cut the rind into small strips and place them in a bowl. Extract the juice from the orange and add it to the bowl containing the rind.

5   Add the sieved tomatoes, mustard, yogurt, and seasoning to the bowl and mix together. Shred the basil leaves and mix them into the dressing.

6   Spoon the dressing into a small dish and serve with the Italian Platter, accompanied with bread sticks.

VARIATION

For a change serve with a French stick or an Italian bread, widely available from supermarkets, and use to mop up the delicious dressing.

Pancetta & Romano Cakes

This makes an excellent light meal when served with a topping of pesto or anchovy sauce.

NUTRITIONAL INFORMATION

Calories 619	Sugars 4g
Protein 22g	Fat 29g
Carbohydrate 71g	Saturates 8g

🍞 🍞 🍞 🍞

🥔 20 MINS   🕐 25 MINS

SERVES 4

INGREDIENTS

2 tablespoons butter, plus extra for
   greasing

3 ½ ounces pancetta, rind removed

2 cups self-rising
   flour

1 cup grated Romano cheese

⅔ cup milk, plus extra
   for glazing

1 tablespoon ketchup

1 teaspoon Worcestershire sauce

3 ½ cups dried farfalle

1 tablespoon olive oil

salt and pepper

3 tablespoons pesto sauce (see page 39)
   or anchovy sauce (optional) to serve

salad greens, to serve

1 Grease a cookie sheet with butter. Broil the pancetta until it is cooked. Allow the pancetta to cool, then chop finely.

2 Sift together the flour and a pinch of salt into a mixing bowl. Add the butter and rub in with your fingertips. When the butter and flour have been thoroughly incorporated, add the pancetta and one-third of the grated cheese.

3 Mix together the milk, ketchup, and Worcestershire sauce and add to the dry ingredients, mixing to make a soft dough.

4 Roll out the dough on a lightly floured board to make a 7-inch round. Brush with a little milk to glaze and cut into 8 wedges.

5 Arrange the dough wedges on the prepared cookie sheet and sprinkle over the remaining cheese. Bake in a preheated oven at 400°F for 20 minutes.

6 Meanwhile, bring a saucepan of lightly salted water to a boil. Add the farfalle and the oil and cook for 8–10 minutes until just tender, but still firm to the bite. Drain and transfer to a large serving dish. Top with the pancetta and Romano cakes. Serve with the sauce of your choice and salad greens.

Mozzarella & Ham Snack

A delicious way of serving mozzarella—the cheese stretches out into melted strings as you cut into the bread.

NUTRITIONAL INFORMATION

Calories 461	Sugars 10g
Protein 19g	Fat 2.8g
Carbohydrate . . .37g	Saturates 7g

15 MINS   40 MINS

SERVES 4

I N G R E D I E N T S

7 ounces mozzarella

4 slices prosciutto,
 (3 ounces)

8 two-day-old slices white bread,
 crusts removed

butter, for spreading

2–3 eggs

3 tablespoons milk

vegetable oil, for deep-frying

salt and pepper

TOMATO & BELL PEPPER SAUCE

1 onion, chopped

2 garlic cloves, crushed

3 tablespoons olive oil

1 red bell pepper, cored, deseeded,
 and chopped

14-ounce can peeled tomatoes

2 tablespoons tomato paste

3 tablespoons water

1 tablespoon lemon juice

salt and pepper

flat-leaf parsley, to garnish (optional)

1 To make the sauce, fry the onion and garlic in the oil until soft. Add the bell pepper and continue to cook for a few minutes. Add the tomatoes, tomato paste, water, lemon juice, and seasoning. Bring to a boil, cover, and simmer for 10–15 minutes or until tender. Cool the sauce a little, then purée or blend until smooth and return to a clean pan.

2 Cut the mozzarella into 4 slices as large as possible; if the cheese is a square piece cut into 8 slices. Trim the prosciutto slices to the same size as the cheese.

3 Lightly butter the bread and use the cheese and ham to make 4 sandwiches, pressing the edges firmly together. If liked, they may be cut in half at this stage. Cover with plastic wrap and chill.

4 Lightly beat the eggs with the milk and seasoning in a shallow dish. Dip the sandwiches in the egg mixture until well coated, and leave to soak for a few minutes.

5 Heat the oil to 350°–375°F, or until a cube of bread browns in 30 seconds. Fry the sandwiches in batches until golden on both sides. Drain and keep warm. Serve with the reheated tomato and bell pepper sauce, and garnish with parsley.

Smoked Ham Linguine

Served with freshly-made Italian bread or tossed with pesto, this makes a mouthwatering light lunch.

NUTRITIONAL INFORMATION

Calories . . . . . . .537 Sugars 4g
Protein . . . . .22g Fat 29g
Carbohydrate . . . .71g Saturates 8g

 25 MINS   15 MINS

SERVES 4

I N G R E D I E N T S

1 pound dried linguine

1 pound green broccoli flowerets

8 ounces Italian smoked ham

⅔ cup Italian Cheese Sauce
  (see page 30)

salt and pepper

Italian bread, such as ciabatta or focaccia,
  to serve

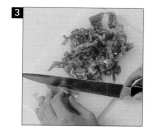

1 Bring a large saucepan pan of lightly salted water to a boil. Add the linguine and broccoli flowerets and cook for about 10 minutes, or until the linguine is tender, but still firm to the bite.

2 Drain the linguine and broccoli thoroughly, set aside, and keep warm until required.

3 Cut the Italian smoked ham into thin strips.

4 Toss the linguine, broccoli, and ham into the Italian Cheese Sauce and gently warm through over very low heat.

5 Transfer the pasta mixture to a warm serving dish. Sprinkle with pepper and serve with Italian bread.

COOK'S TIP

There are many types of Italian bread which would be suitable to serve with this dish. Ciabatta is made with olive oil and is available plain and with different ingredients, such as olives or sun-dried tomatoes.

Fish & Seafood

Italians eat everything that comes out of the sea, from the smallest smelt to the massive tuna fish. Fish markets in Italy are fascinating, with a huge variety of fish on display,

but as most of the fish comes from the Mediterranean it is not always easy to find an equivalent elsewhere. However, fresh or frozen imported fish of all kinds is increasingly appearing in fish stores and supermarkets. After pasta, fish is probably the most important source of food in Italy, and in many recipes fish or seafood are served with one type of pasta or another—a winning combination!

Orange Mackerel

Mackerel can be quite rich, but when it is stuffed with oranges and toasted ground almonds it is tangy and light.

NUTRITIONAL INFORMATION

Calories . . . . . . .623 Sugars 7g
Protein . . . . .42g Fat 47g
Carbohydrate . . . .8g Saturates 8g

  15 MINS   35 MINS

SERVES 4

I N G R E D I E N T S

2 tablespoon oil

4 green onions, chopped

2 oranges

½ cup ground almonds

1 tablespoon rolled oats

½ cup mixed green and black olives,
   pitted and chopped

8 mackerel fillets

salt and pepper

crisp salad, to serve

1 Heat the oil in a skillet. Add the green onions and cook for 2 minutes.

2 Finely grate the rind of the oranges, then, using a sharp knife, cut away the remaining skin and white pith.

3 Using a sharp knife, segment the oranges by cutting down either side of the lines of pith to loosen each segment. Do this over a plate so that you can reserve any juices. Cut each orange segment in half.

4 Lightly toast the almonds, under a preheated broiler, for 2–3 minutes or until golden; watch them carefully as they brown very quickly.

5 Mix the green onions, oranges, ground almonds, oats, and olives together in a bowl and season to taste with salt and pepper.

6 Spoon the orange mixture along the center of each fillet. Roll up each fillet, securing it in place with a toothpick or skewer.

7 Bake in a preheated oven at 375°F for 25 minutes until the fish is tender.

8 Transfer to serving plates and serve warm with a salad.

Marinated Fish

Marinating fish, for even a short period, adds a subtle flavor to the flesh and makes even simply broiled or fried fish delicious.

NUTRITIONAL INFORMATION

Calories 361	Sugars 0g	
Protein 26g	Fat 29g	
Carbohydrate 0g	Saturates 5g	

 45 MINS   15 MINS

SERVES 4

I N G R E D I E N T S

4 whole mackerel

4 tablespoons chopped marjoram

2 tablespoons extra virgin olive oil

finely grated rind and juice of 1 lime

2 garlic cloves, crushed

salt and pepper

1 Under gently running water, scrape the mackerel with the blunt side of a knife to remove any scales.

2 Using a sharp knife, make a slit in the stomach of the fish and cut horizontally along until the knife will go no further very easily. Gut the fish and rinse under water. You may prefer to remove the heads before cooking, but it is not necessary.

3 Using a sharp knife, cut 4–5 diagonal slashes on each side of the fish. Place the fish in a shallow, nonmetallic dish.

4 To make the marinade, mix together the marjoram, olive oil, lime rind and juice, garlic, and salt and pepper in a bowl.

5 Pour the mixture over the fish. Leave to marinate in the refrigerator for about 30 minutes.

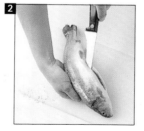

6 Cook the mackerel, under a preheated broiler, for 5–6 minutes on each side, brushing occasionally with the reserved marinade, until golden.

7 Transfer the fish to serving plates. Pour over any remaining marinade before serving.

COOK'S TIP

If the lime is too hard to squeeze, microwave on high power for 30 seconds to release the juice. This dish is also excellent cooked on the barbecue.

Sea Bass with Olive Sauce

A favorite fish for chefs, the delicious sea bass is now becoming increasingly common in supermarkets and fish stores for family meals.

NUTRITIONAL INFORMATION

Calories 877	Sugars 3g	
Protein 50g	Fat 47g	
Carbohydrate ...67g	Saturates 26g	

10 MINS   30 MINS

SERVES 4

I N G R E D I E N T S

1 pound dried macaroni

1 tablespoon olive oil

8 x 4 ounce sea bass
   medallions

S A U C E

2 tablespoons butter

4 shallots, chopped

2 tablespoons capers

1½ cups pitted green
   olives, chopped

4 tablespoons balsamic vinegar

1¼ cups fish stock

1¼ cups heavy cream

juice of 1 lemon

salt and pepper

T O   G A R N I S H

lemon slices

shredded leek

shredded carrot

1 To make the sauce, melt the butter in a skillet. Add the shallots and cook over a low heat for 4 minutes. Add the capers and olives and cook for a further 3 minutes.

2 Stir in the balsamic vinegar and fish stock, bring to a boil, and reduce by half. Add the cream, stirring, and reduce again by half. Season to taste with salt and pepper and stir in the lemon juice. Remove the pan from the heat, set aside and keep warm.

3 Bring a large pan of lightly salted water to a boil. Add the pasta and olive oil and cook for about 12 minutes, until tender but still firm to the bite.

4 Meanwhile, lightly broil the sea bass medallions for 3–4 minutes on each side, until cooked through, but still moist and delicate.

5 Drain the pasta thoroughly and transfer to large individual serving dishes. Top the pasta with the fish medallions and pour over the olive sauce. Garnish with lemon slices, shredded leek, and shredded carrot and serve at once.

Baked Sea Bass

Sea bass is a delicious white-fleshed fish. If cooking two small fish, they can be broiled; if cooking one large fish, bake it in the oven.

NUTRITIONAL INFORMATION

Calories	378	Sugars	.........0g
Protein	........62g	Fat	..........14g
Carbohydrate	....0g	Saturates	.......2g

15-20 MINS   20-55 MINS

SERVES 4

I N G R E D I E N T S

3 pounds fresh sea bass or

  2 x 1 pound 10 ounce sea bass, gutted

2–4 sprigs fresh rosemary

½ lemon, sliced thinly

2 tablespoons olive oil

bay leaves and lemon wedges, to garnish

G A R L I C   S A U C E

2 teaspoons coarse sea salt

2 teaspoons capers

2 garlic cloves, crushed

4 tablespoons water

2 fresh bay leaves

1 teaspoon lemon juice or wine vinegar

2 tablespoons olive oil

pepper

1 Scrape off the scales from the fish and cut off the sharp fins. Make diagonal cuts along both sides. Wash and dry thoroughly. Place a sprig of rosemary in the cavity of each of the smaller fish with half the lemon slices; or two sprigs and all the lemon in the large fish.

2 To broil, place in a foil-lined pan, brush with 1–2 tablespoons oil, and broil under moderate heat for 5 minutes each side or until cooked through.

3 To bake: place the fish in a foil-lined dish or roasting pan brushed with oil, and brush the fish with the rest of the oil. Cook in a preheated oven, 375°F, for 30 minutes for the small fish or 45–50 minutes for the large fish, until the thickest part of the fish is opaque.

4 For the sauce: crush the salt and capers with the garlic in a pestle and mortar and then work in the water. Or, work in a food processor or blender until smooth.

5 Bruise the bay leaves and remaining sprigs of rosemary and put in a bowl. Add the garlic mixture, lemon juice or vinegar, and oil and pound together until the flavors are released. Season with pepper to taste.

6 Place the fish on a serving dish and, if liked, remove the skin. Spoon some of the sauce over the fish and serve the rest separately. Garnish with fresh bay leaves and lemon wedges.

Salt Cod Fritters

These tasty little fried fish cakes make an excellent snack or main course. Prepare in advance as the salt cod needs to be soaked overnight.

NUTRITIONAL INFORMATION

Calories	142	Sugars	.........2g
Protein	........10g	Fat	...........5g
Carbohydrate	...14g	Saturates	.......1g

30 MINS   45 MINS

SERVES 6

INGREDIENTS

¾ cup self-rising flour

1 egg, beaten

⅔ cup milk

9 ounces salt cod, soaked overnight

1 small red onion, finely chopped

1 small fennel bulb, finely chopped

1 red chili, finely chopped

2 tablespoons oil

TO SERVE

crisp salad and chili relish, or cooked rice
   and fresh vegetables

1 Sift the flour into a large bowl. Make a well in the center of the flour and add the egg.

2 Using a wooden spoon, gradually draw in the flour, slowly adding the milk, and mix to form a smooth batter. Leave to stand for 10 minutes.

3 Drain the salt cod and rinse it under cold running water. Drain again thoroughly.

4 Remove and discard the skin and any bones from the fish, then mash the flesh with a fork.

5 Place the fish in a large bowl and combine with the onion, fennel, and chili. Add the mixture to the batter and blend together.

6 Heat the oil in a large skillet and, taking about 1 tablespoon of the mixture at a time, spoon it into the hot oil. Cook the fritters, in batches, for 3–4 minutes on each side until golden and slightly puffed. Keep warm while cooking the remaining mixture.

7 Serve with salad and a chili relish for a light meal or with vegetables and rice.

COOK'S TIP

If you prefer larger fritters, use 2 tablespoons per fritter and cook for slightly longer.

Celery & Salt Cod Casserole

Salt cod is dried and salted in order to preserve it. It has an unusual flavor, which goes particularly well with celery in this dish.

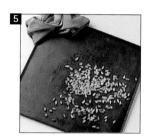

NUTRITIONAL INFORMATION

Calories 173	Sugars 3g
Protein 14g	Fat 12g
Carbohydrate 3g	Saturates 1g

25 MINS   25 MINS

SERVES 4

I N G R E D I E N T S

9 ounces salt cod, soaked overnight

1 tablespoon oil

4 shallots, finely chopped

2 garlic cloves, chopped

3 celery stalks, chopped

14-ounce can tomatoes, chopped

⅔ cup fish stock

½ cup pine nuts

2 tablespoons roughly chopped tarragon

2 tablespoons capers

crusty bread or mashed potatoes, to serve

1 Drain the salt cod, rinse it under plenty of running water, and drain again thoroughly. Remove and discard any skin and bones. Pat the fish dry with paper towels and cut it into chunks.

2 Heat the oil in a large skillet. Add the shallots and garlic and cook for 2–3 minutes. Add the celery and cook for a further 2 minutes, then add the tomatoes and stock.

3 Bring the mixture to a boil, reduce the heat, and leave to simmer for about 5 minutes.

4 Add the fish and cook for 10 minutes or until tender.

5 Meanwhile, place the pine nuts on a cookie sheet. Place under a preheated broiler and toast for 2–3 minutes or until golden.

6 Stir the tarragon, capers, and pine nuts into the fish casserole and heat gently to warm through.

7 Transfer to serving plates and serve with lots of fresh crusty bread or mashed potato.

COOK'S TIP

Salt cod is a useful ingredient to keep in the pantry and, once soaked, can be used in the same way as any other fish. It does, however, have a stronger, saltier flavor than normal. It can be found in fish stores, larger supermarkets, and delicatessens.

Sole Fillets in Marsala

A rich wine and cream sauce makes this an excellent dinner party dish. Make the stock the day before to cut down on the preparation time.

NUTRITIONAL INFORMATION

Calories	474	Sugars	.........3g
Protein	........47g	Fat	..........28g
Carbohydrate	....3g	Saturates	......14g

  1¼ HOURS   1½ HOURS

SERVES 4

INGREDIENTS

1 tablespoon peppercorns, lightly crushed

8 sole fillets

⅓ cup Marsala

⅔ cup heavy cream

STOCK

2½ cups water

bones and skin from the sole fillets

1 onion, halved

1 carrot, halved

3 fresh bay leaves

SAUCE

1 tablespoon olive oil

1 tablespoon butter

4 shallots, finely chopped

3½ ounces mushrooms, wiped and halved

1 To make the stock, place the water, fish bones and skin, onion, carrot, and bay leaves in a large saucepan and bring to a boil.

2 Reduce the heat and leave the mixture to simmer for 1 hour or until the stock has reduced to about ⅔ cup. Drain the stock through a fine strainer, discarding the bones and vegetables, and set aside.

3 To make the sauce, heat the oil and butter in a skillet. Add the shallots and cook, stirring, for 2–3 minutes or until just softened.

4 Add the mushrooms to the skillet and cook, stirring, for a further 2–3 minutes or until they are just beginning to brown.

5 Add the peppercorns and sole fillets to the skillet in batches. Fry the sole fillets for 3–4 minutes on each side or until golden brown. Remove the fish with a perforated spoon, set aside and keep warm while you cook the remainder.

6 When all the fillets have been cooked and removed from the pan, pour the wine and stock into the pan and leave to simmer for 3 minutes. Increase the heat and boil the mixture in the pan for about 5 minutes or until the sauce has reduced and thickened.

7 Pour in the cream and heat through. Pour the sauce over the fish and serve with the cooked vegetables of your choice.

Cannelloni Filetti di Sogliola

This is a lighter dish than the better-known cannelloni stuffed with ground beef.

NUTRITIONAL INFORMATION

Calories 555   Sugars 4g
Protein ....53g   Fat 21g
Carbohydrate ...36g   Saturates 12g

20 MINS   45 MINS

SERVES 6

INGREDIENTS

12 small fillets of sole (4 ounces each)

⅔ cup red wine

6 tablespoons butter

1¾ cups cups sliced
   mushrooms

4 shallots, finely chopped

4 ounces tomatoes, chopped

2 tablespoons tomato paste

½ cup all-purpose
   flour, sifted

⅔ cup warm milk

2 tablespoons heavy cream

6 dried cannelloni tubes

6 ounces cooked, peeled shrimp,

salt and pepper

1 fresh fennel sprig, to garnish

1 Brush the fillets with a little wine, season with salt and pepper, and roll them up, skin side inward. Secure with a skewer or toothpick.

2 Arrange the fish rolls in a single layer in a large skillet, add the remaining red wine and poach for 4 minutes. Remove from the pan; reserve the liquid.

3 Melt the butter in another pan. Fry the mushrooms and shallots for 2 minutes, then add the tomatoes and tomato paste. Season the flour and stir it into the pan. Stir in the reserved cooking liquid and half the milk. Cook over low heat, stirring, for 4 minutes. Remove from the heat and stir in the cream.

4 Bring a large saucepan of lightly salted water to a boil. Add the cannelloni and cook for about 8 minutes, until tender but still firm to the bite. Drain and set aside to cool.

5 Remove the toothpicks from the fish rolls. Put 2 sole fillets into each cannelloni tube with 2–3 shrimp and a little red wine sauce. Arrange the cannelloni in an ovenproof dish, pour over the sauce and bake in a preheated oven at 400°F for 20 minutes.

6 Serve the cannelloni with the red wine sauce, garnished with the remaining shrimp and a fresh sprig of fennel.

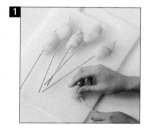  

Spaghetti alla Bucaniera

Brill was once known as poor man's turbot, an unfair description as it is a delicately flavored and delicious fish in its own right.

NUTRITIONAL INFORMATION

Calories	588	Sugars	........5g
Protein	........36g	Fat	..........18g
Carbohydrate	...68g	Saturates	.......9g

25 MINS   50 MINS

SERVES 4

I N G R E D I E N T S

¾ cup all-purpose flour

1 pound brill or sole fillets,
   skinned and chopped

1 pound hake fillets,
   skinned and chopped

6 tablespoons butter

4 shallots, finely chopped

2 garlic cloves, crushed

1 carrot, diced

1 leek, finely chopped

1¼ cups hard cider or apple juice

1¼ cups medium sweet cider or apple juice

2 teaspoon anchovy paste

1 tablespoon tarragon vinegar

1 pound dried spaghetti

1 tablespoon olive oil

salt and pepper

chopped fresh parsley, to garnish

crusty brown bread, to serve

1 Season the flour with salt and pepper. Sprinkle ¼ cup of the seasoned flour onto a shallow plate. Press the fish pieces into the seasoned flour to coat thoroughly.

2 Melt the butter in a flameproof casserole. Add the fish fillets, shallots, garlic, carrot, and leek and cook over low heat, stirring frequently, for about 10 minutes.

3 Sprinkle over the remaining seasoned flour and cook, stirring constantly, for 2 minutes. Gradually stir in the cider, anchovy paste, and tarragon vinegar. Bring to a boil and simmer over low heat for 35 minutes. Alternatively, bake in a preheated oven at 350°F for 30 minutes.

4 About 15 minutes before the end of the cooking time, bring a large pan of lightly salted water to a boil. Add the spaghetti and olive oil and cook for about 12 minutes, until tender but still firm to the bite. Drain the pasta thoroughly and transfer to a large serving dish.

5 Arrange the fish on top of the spaghetti and pour over the sauce. Garnish with chopped parsley and serve at once with warm, crusty brown bread.

Broiled Stuffed Sole

A delicious stuffing of sun-dried tomatoes and fresh lemon thyme is used to stuff whole sole.

NUTRITIONAL INFORMATION

Calories	207	Sugars	.......0.2g
Protein	........24g	Fat	..........10g
Carbohydrate	....8g	Saturates	.......4g

  25 MINS   🕐 20 MINS

SERVES 4

INGREDIENTS

1 tablespoon olive oil

2 tablespoons butter

1 small onion, finely chopped

1 garlic clove, chopped

3 sun-dried tomatoes, chopped

2 tablespoons lemon thyme

¾ cup bread crumbs

1 tablespoon lemon juice

4 small whole sole, gutted and cleaned

salt and pepper

lemon wedges, to garnish

fresh salad greens, to serve

1 Heat the oil and butter in a skillet until it just begins to froth.

2 Add the onion and garlic to the skillet and cook, stirring, for 5 minutes until just softened.

3 To make the stuffing, mix the tomatoes, thyme, bread crumbs, and lemon juice in a bowl, and season.

4 Add the stuffing mixture to the skillet, and stir to mix.

5 Using a sharp knife, pare the skin from the bone inside the gut hole of the fish to make a pocket. Spoon the tomato and herb stuffing into the pocket.

6 Cook the fish, under a preheated broiler, for 6 minutes on each side or until golden brown.

7 Transfer the stuffed fish to serving plates and garnish with lemon wedges. Serve at once with fresh salad greens.

COOK'S TIP

Lemon thyme (*Thymus* x *citriodorus*) has a delicate lemon scent and flavor. Ordinary thyme can be used instead, but mix it with 1 teaspoon of lemon rind to add extra flavor.

Lemon Sole & Haddock Ravioli

This delicate-tasting dish is surprisingly satisfying for even the hungriest appetites. Prepare the Italian Red Wine Sauce well in advance.

NUTRITIONAL INFORMATION

Calories	977	Sugars	.........7g
Protein	........67g	Fat	..........40g
Carbohydrate	...93g	Saturates	......17g

9³/₄ HOURS　　25 MINS

SERVES 4

I N G R E D I E N T S

1 pound lemon sole fillets, skinned

1 pound haddock fillets, skinned

3 eggs beaten

1 pound cooked potato gnocchi
　(see page 410)

3 cups fresh bread crumbs

¼ cup heavy cream

1 pound Basic Pasta Dough
　(see page 24)

1¼ cups Italian Red Wine
Sauce (see page 29)

⅔ cup freshly grated
　Parmesan cheese

salt and pepper

COOK'S TIP

For square ravioli, divide the dough in two. Wrap half in plastic wrap; thinly roll out the other half. Cover; roll out the remaining dough. Pipe the filling at regular intervals and brush the spaces in between with water or beaten egg. Lift the second sheet of dough into position and press between the filling to seal. Cut with a ravioli cutter or a knife.

1　Flake the lemon sole and haddock fillets with a fork and transfer the flesh to a large mixing bowl.

2　Mix the eggs, cooked potato gnocchi, bread crumbs, and cream in a bowl until thoroughly combined. Add the fish to the bowl containing the gnocchi and season the mixture with salt and pepper to taste.

3　Roll out the pasta dough on a lightly floured surface and cut out 3-inch rounds using a plain cutter.

4　Place a spoonful of the fish stuffing on each round. Dampen the edges slightly and fold the pasta rounds over, pressing together to seal.

5　Bring a large saucepan of lightly salted water to a boil. Add the ravioli and cook for 15 minutes.

6　Drain the ravioli, using a slotted spoon, and transfer to a large serving dish. Pour over the Italian Red Wine Sauce, sprinkle over the Parmesan cheese, and serve at once.

Trout in Red Wine

This recipe from Trentino is best when the fish are freshly caught, but it is a good way to cook any trout, giving it an interesting flavor.

NUTRITIONAL INFORMATION

Calories	489	Sugars	.......0.6g
Protein	........48g	Fat	..........27g
Carbohydrate	...0.6g	Saturates	......14g

🕒 20 MINS   🕐 45 MINS

SERVES 4

I N G R E D I E N T S

4 fresh trout, about 10 ounces each

1 cup red or white wine vinegar

1¼ cups red or dry white wine

⅔ cup water

1 carrot, sliced

2–4 bay leaves

thinly pared rind of 1 lemon

1 small onion, sliced very thinly

4 sprigs fresh parsley

4 sprigs fresh thyme

1 teaspoon black peppercorns

6–8 whole cloves

6 tablespoons butter

1 tablespoon chopped fresh mixed herbs

salt and pepper

T O   G A R N I S H

sprigs of herbs

lemon slices

1 Gut the trout but leave their heads on. Dry on paper towels and lay the fish head to tail in a shallow container or baking pan large enough to hold them.

2 Bring the wine vinegar to a boil and pour slowly all over the fish. Leave the fish to marinate in the refrigerator for about 20 minutes.

3 Meanwhile, put the wine, water, carrot, bay leaves, lemon rind, onion, herbs, peppercorns, and cloves into a pan with a good pinch of sea salt and heat gently.

4 Drain the fish thoroughly, discarding the vinegar. Place the fish in a fish kettle or large skillet so they touch. When the wine mixture boils, strain gently over the fish so they are about half covered. Cover the pan and simmer very gently for 15 minutes.

5 Carefully remove the fish from the pan, draining off as much of the liquid as possible, and arrange on a serving dish. Keep warm.

6 Boil the cooking liquid until reduced to about 4–6 tablespoons. Melt the butter in a pan and strain in the cooking liquid. Season and spoon the sauce over the fish. Garnish and serve.

Trout with Smoked Bacon

Most trout available now is farmed rainbow trout, however, if you can, buy wild brown trout for this recipe.

NUTRITIONAL INFORMATION

Calories	802	Sugars	.........8g
Protein	........68g	Fat	..........36g
Carbohydrate	...54g	Saturates	......10g

35 MINS   25 MINS

SERVES 4

INGREDIENTS

butter, for greasing

4 x 9½-ounce trout, gutted and cleaned

12 anchovies in oil, drained and chopped

2 apples, peeled, cored and sliced

4 fresh mint sprigs

juice of 1 lemon

12 slices bacon

1 pound dried tagliatelle

1 tablespoon olive oil

salt and pepper

TO GARNISH

2 apples, cored and sliced

4 fresh mint sprigs

1 Grease a deep cookie sheet with butter.

2 Open up the cavities of each trout and rinse with warm salt water.

3 Season each cavity with salt and pepper. Divide the anchovies, sliced apples, and mint sprigs among each of the cavities. Sprinkle the lemon juice into each cavity.

4 Carefully cover the whole of each trout, except the head and tail, with three slices of bacon in a spiral.

5 Arrange the trout on the cookie sheet with the loose ends of bacon tucked underneath. Season with pepper and bake in a preheated oven at 400°F for 20 minutes, turning the trout over after 10 minutes.

6 Meanwhile, bring a large pan of lightly salted water to a boil. Add the tagliatelle and olive oil and cook for about 12 minutes, until tender but still firm to the bite. Drain the pasta and transfer to a large, warm serving dish.

7 Remove the trout from the oven and arrange on the tagliatelle. Garnish with sliced apples and fresh mint sprigs and serve at once.

Fillets of Red Mullet & Pasta

This simple recipe perfectly complements the sweet flavor and delicate texture of the fish. If you can't find red mullet, use snapper instead.

NUTRITIONAL INFORMATION

Calories	457	Sugars	.........3g
Protein	........39g	Fat	..........12g
Carbohydrate	...44g	Saturates	.......5g

  15 MINS   1 HOUR

SERVES 4

I N G R E D I E N T S

2¼ pounds red mullet or snapper fillets

1¼ cups dry white wine

4 shallots, finely chopped

1 garlic clove, crushed

3 tablespoons finely chopped mixed herbs

finely grated rind and juice of 1 lemon

pinch of freshly grated nutmeg

3 anchovy fillets, roughly chopped

2 tablespoons heavy cream

1 teaspoon cornstarch

1 pound dried vermicelli

1 tablespoon olive oil

salt and pepper

TO GARNISH

1 fresh mint sprig

lemon slices

lemon rind

1 Put the red mullet or snapper fillets in a large casserole. Pour over the wine and add the shallots, garlic, herbs, lemon rind and juice, nutmeg, and anchovies. Season. Cover and bake in a preheated oven at 350°F for 35 minutes.

2 Transfer the mullet or snapper to a warm dish. Set aside and keep warm.

3 Pour the cooking liquid into a pan and bring to a boil. Simmer for about 25 minutes, until reduced by half. Mix the cream and cornstarch and stir into the sauce to thicken.

4 Meanwhile, bring a pan of lightly salted water to a boil. Add the vermicelli and oil and cook for 8–10 minutes, until tender but still firm to the bite. Drain the pasta and transfer to a warm serving dish.

5 Arrange the fillets on top of the vermicelli and pour over the sauce. Garnish with a fresh mint sprig, slices of lemon, and strips of lemon rind and serve at once.

Sardinian Red Mullet

Red mullet has a beautiful pink skin, which is enhanced in this dish by being cooked in red wine and orange juice.

NUTRITIONAL INFORMATION

Calories 287	Sugars 15g
Protein 31g	Fat 9g
Carbohydrate ...15g	Saturates 1g

 2¹/₂ HOURS   25 MINS

SERVES 4

I N G R E D I E N T S

⅓ cup golden raisins

⅔ cup red wine

2 tablespoons olive oil

2 medium onions, sliced

1 zucchini, cut into
  2-inch sticks

2 oranges

2 teaspoon coriander seeds, lightly crushed

4 red mullet, boned and filleted

1 ¾-ounce can anchovy fillets, drained

2 tablespoons chopped, fresh oregano

1 Place the golden raisins in a bowl. Pour over the red wine and leave to soak for about 10 minutes.

COOK'S TIP

Red mullet is usually available all year round—frozen, if not fresh—from your fish store or supermarket. If you cannot get hold of it try using snapper. This dish can also be served warm, if you prefer.

2 Heat the oil in a large skillet. Add the onions and sauté for 2 minutes.

3 Add the zucchini to the pan and fry for a further 3 minutes or until tender.

4 Using a zester, pare long, thin strips from one of the oranges. Using a sharp knife, remove the skin from both of the oranges, then segment the oranges by slicing between the lines of membrane.

5 Add the orange zest to the skillet with the coriander seeds, red wine, golden raisins, red mullet, and anchovies to the pan and leave to simmer for 10–15 minutes or until the fish is cooked through.

6 Stir in the oregano, set aside, and leave to cool. Place the mixture in a large bowl and leave to chill, covered, in the refrigerator for at least 2 hours to allow the flavors to mingle. Transfer to serving plates and serve.

Red Mullet & Amaretto Sauce

This succulent fish and pasta dish is ideal for serving on a warm, summer's evening—preferably *al fresco*. You can use snapper instead.

NUTRITIONAL INFORMATION

Calories ....806 Sugars 6g
Protein ....64g Fat 34g
Carbohydrate ...64g Saturates 16g

 15 MINS   25 MINS

SERVES 4

INGREDIENTS

3¾ cup all-purpose flour

8 red mullet or snapper fillets

2 tablespoons butter

⅔ cup fish stock

1 tablespoon crushed almonds

1 teaspoon pink peppercorns

1 orange, peeled and cut
  into segments

1 tablespoon orange liqueur

grated rind of 1 orange

1 pound dried orecchiette

1 tablespoon olive oil

⅔ cup heavy cream

4 tablespoons amaretto

salt and pepper

TO GARNISH

2 tablespoons snipped fresh chives

1 tablespoon toasted almonds

1 Season the flour with salt and pepper and sprinkle into a shallow bowl. Press the fish fillets into the flour to coat. Melt the butter in a skillet. Add the fish and fry over low heat for 3 minutes, until browned.

2 Add the fish stock to the pan and cook for 4 minutes. Carefully remove the fish, cover with foil, and keep warm.

3 Add the almonds, pink peppercorns, half the orange, the orange liqueur, and orange rind to the pan. Simmer until the liquid has reduced by half.

4 Meanwhile, bring a large pan of lightly salted water to a boil. Add the orecchiette and oil and cook for 15 minutes, until tender but still firm to the bite.

5 Meanwhile, season the sauce with salt and pepper and stir in the cream and amaretto. Cook for 2 minutes. Return the fish to the pan to coat with the sauce.

6 Drain the pasta and transfer to a serving dish. Top with the fish fillets and their sauce. Garnish with the remaining orange segments, the chives, and toasted almonds. Serve at once.

Italian Cod

Cod roasted with herbs and topped with a lemon and rosemary crust is a delicious main course.

NUTRITIONAL INFORMATION

Calories	.313	Sugars	.0.4g
Protein	.29g	Fat	.20g
Carbohydrate	.6g	Saturates	.5g

 10 MINS   🕐 35 MINS

SERVES 4

I N G R E D I E N T S

2 tablespoons butter

1 cup whole wheat bread crumbs

¼ cup chopped walnuts

grated rind and juice of 2 lemons

2 sprigs rosemary, stalks removed

2 tablespoons chopped parsley

4 cod fillets, each about 5½ ounces

1 garlic clove, crushed

3 tablespoons walnut oil

1 small red chili, diced

salad greens, to serve

VARIATION

If preferred, the walnuts may be omitted from the crust. In addition, extra virgin olive oil can be used instead of walnut oil, if you prefer.

1 Melt the butter in a large saucepan, stirring.

2 Remove the pan from the heat and add the bread crumbs, walnuts, the rind and juice of 1 lemon, half of the rosemary, and half of the parsley.

3 Press the bread crumb mixture over the top of the cod fillets. Place the cod fillets in a shallow, foil-lined roasting pan.

4 Bake in a preheated oven at 400°F for 25–30 minutes.

5 Mix the garlic, the remaining lemon rind and juice, rosemary, parsley, and chili in a bowl. Beat in the walnut oil and mix to combine. Drizzle the dressing over the cod steaks as soon as they are cooked.

6 Transfer to serving plates and serve at once.

Smoked Fish Lasagne

Use smoked cod or haddock in this delicious lasagne. It's a great way to make a little go a long way.

NUTRITIONAL INFORMATION

Calories . . . . . . .483 Sugars 8g
Protein . . . . .36g Fat 24g
Carbohydrate . . .32g Saturates 12g

20 MINS   1¼ HOURS

SERVES 4

I N G R E D I E N T S

2 teaspoons olive or vegetable oil

1 garlic clove, crushed

1 small onion, chopped finely

2 cups sliced mushrooms

14-ounce can diced tomatoes

1 small zucchini, sliced

⅔ cup vegetable stock
   or water

2 tablespoons butter or margarine

1¼ cups skim milk

¼ cup all-purpose flour

1 cup grated sharp
   Cheddar cheese

1 tablespoon chopped fresh parsley

4½ ounces (6 sheets) pre-cooked lasagne

12 ounces skinned and boned smoked
   cod or haddock, cut into chunks

salt and pepper

fresh parsley sprigs to garnish

1 Heat the oil in a saucepan and fry the garlic and onion for about 5 minutes. Add the mushrooms and cook for 3 minutes, stirring.

2 Add the tomatoes, zucchini, and stock or water and simmer, uncovered, for 15–20 minutes until the vegetables are soft. Season to taste.

3 Put the butter or margarine, milk, and flour into a small saucepan and heat, whisking constantly, until the sauce boils and thickens. Remove from the heat and add half of the cheese and all of the parsley. Stir gently to melt the cheese and season to taste.

4 Spoon the tomato sauce mixture into a large, shallow ovenproof dish and top with half of the lasagne sheets. Scatter the chunks of fish evenly over the top, then pour over half of the cheese sauce. Top with the remaining lasagne sheets and then spread the rest of the cheese sauce on top. Sprinkle with the remaining cheese.

5 Bake in a preheated oven at 375°F for 40 minutes, until the top is golden brown and bubbling. Garnish with parsley sprigs and serve hot.

Pasta & Fish Pudding

A tasty mixture of creamy fish and pasta cooked in a bowl, unmolded, and drizzled with tomato sauce presents macaroni in a new guise.

NUTRITIONAL INFORMATION

Calories 454	Sugars 1g	
Protein 30g	Fat 30g	
Carbohydrate ...17g	Saturates 16g	

 10 MINS   2 HOURS

SERVES 4

I N G R E D I E N T S

1 cup dried short-cut macaroni
   or other short pasta

1 tablespoon olive oil

1 tablespoon butter,
   plus extra for greasing

1 pound white fish fillets,
   such as cod or haddock

2–3 fresh parsley sprigs

6 black peppercorns

½ cup heavy cream

2 eggs, separated

2 tablespoons chopped fresh dill or parsley

pinch of freshly grated nutmeg

⅔ cup freshly grated Parmesan cheese

salt and pepper

fresh dill or parsley sprigs, to garnish

Tomato Sauce (see page 110),
   to serve

1 Bring a pan of salted water to a boil. Add the pasta and oil and cook for 8–10 minutes until tender, but still firm to the bite. Drain the pasta and return to the pan. Add the butter, cover, and keep warm.

2 Place the fish in a skillet. Add the parsley sprigs, peppercorns, and enough water to cover. Bring to a boil, cover, and simmer for 10 minutes. Lift out the fish and set aside to cool. Reserve the cooking liquid.

3 Skin the fish and cut into bite-size pieces. Put the pasta in a bowl. Mix the cream, egg yolks, chopped dill or parsley, nutmeg, and cheese, pour into the pasta, and mix. Spoon in the fish without breaking it. Add enough of the reserved cooking liquid to make a moist, but firm mixture. Whisk the egg whites until stiff, then fold them into the mixture.

4 Grease a heatproof bowl and spoon in the fish mixture to within 1½ inches of the rim. Cover with greased wax paper and foil and tie securely with string.

5 Stand the bowl on a trivet in a saucepan. Add boiling water to reach halfway up the sides. Cover and steam for 1½ hours.

6 Invert the pudding onto a serving plate. Pour over a little tomato sauce. Garnish and serve with the remaining tomato sauce.

Charred Tuna Steaks

Tuna has a firm flesh, which is ideal for grilling, but it can be a little dry unless it is marinated first.

NUTRITIONAL INFORMATION

Calories	153	Sugars	.........1g
Protein	........29g	Fat	...........3g
Carbohydrate	....1g	Saturates	......1g

 2 HOURS   15 MINS

SERVES 4

I N G R E D I E N T S

4 tuna steaks

3 tablespoons soy sauce

1 tablespoon Worcestershire sauce

1 teaspoon wholegrain mustard

1 teaspoon sugar

1 tablespoon sunflower oil

green salad, to serve

T O   G A R N I S H

flat-leaf parsley

lemon wedges

1 Place the tuna steaks in a shallow dish.

2 Mix together the soy sauce, Worcestershire sauce, mustard, sugar and oil in a small bowl.

3 Pour the marinade over the tuna steaks.

4 Gently turn over the tuna steaks, using your fingers or a fork. Make sure that the fish steaks are well coated with the marinade.

5 Cover and place the tuna steaks in the refrigerator. Leave to chill for between 30 minutes and 2 hours.

6 Grill the marinated fish over hot coals for 10–15 minutes, turning once.

7 Baste frequently with any of the marinade that is left in the dish.

8 Garnish with flat-leaf parsley and lemon wedges. Serve with a fresh green salad.

COOK'S TIP

If a marinade contains soy sauce, the marinating time should be limited, usually to 2 hours. If allowed to marinate for too long, the fish will dry out and become tough.

Mediterranean Fish Stew

Popular in fishing ports around Europe, gentle stewing is an excellent way to maintain the flavour and succulent texture of fish and shellfish.

NUTRITIONAL INFORMATION

Calories	533	Sugars	.......11g
Protein	........71g	Fat	..........10g
Carbohydrate	...30g	Saturates	......2g

1¼ HOURS   25 MINS

SERVES 4

INGREDIENTS

2 teaspoons olive oil

2 red onions, sliced

2 garlic cloves, crushed

2 tablespoons red wine vinegar

2 teaspoons sugar

1¼ cups Fresh Fish Stock (see page 30)

1¼ cups dry red wine

2 × 14 ounce cans diced tomatoes

8 ounces baby eggplant, quartered

8 ounces yellow zucchini, quartered or sliced

1 green bell pepper, sliced

1 tablespoon chopped fresh rosemary

1 pound 2 ounces halibut fillet, skinned and cut into 1 inch cubes

1 pound 10 ounces fresh mussels, prepared

8 ounces baby squid, cleaned, trimmed and sliced into rings

8 ounces fresh tiger prawns, peeled and deveined

salt and pepper

4 slices toasted French bread rubbed with a cut garlic clove

lemon wedges, to serve

1 Heat the oil in a large non-stick saucepan and fry the onions and garlic gently for 3 minutes.

2 Stir in the vinegar and sugar and cook for a further 2 minutes.

3 Stir in the stock, wine, canned tomatoes, eggplant, zucchini, bell pepper and rosemary. Bring to the boil and simmer, uncovered, for 10 minutes.

4 Add the halibut, mussels and squid. Mix well and simmer, covered, for 5 minutes until the fish is opaque.

5 Stir in the shrimp and continue to simmer, covered, for a further 2–3 minutes until the prawns are pink and cooked through.

6 Discard any mussels which haven't opened and season to taste.

7 To serve, put a slice of the prepared garlic bread in the base of each warmed serving bowl and ladle the stew over the top. Serve with lemon wedges.

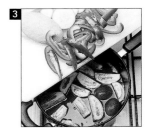

Seafood Pizza

Make a change from the standard pizza toppings—this dish is piled high with seafood baked with a red bell pepper and tomato sauce.

NUTRITIONAL INFORMATION

Calories 248   Sugars 7g
Protein ....27g   Fat 6g
Carbohydrate ...22g   Saturates 2g

25 MINS   55 MINS

SERVES 4

I N G R E D I E N T S

5 ounces standard pizza base mix

4 tablespoons chopped fresh dill or 2 tablespoons dried dill

fresh dill, to garnish

S A U C E

1 large red bell pepper

14-ounce can diced tomatoes with onion and herbs

3 tablespoons tomato paste

salt and pepper

T O P P I N G

12 ounces assorted cooked seafood, thawed if frozen

1 tablespoon capers in brine, drained

1 ounce pitted black olives in brine, drained

1 ounce low-fat Mozzarella cheese, grated

1 tablespoon grated, fresh Parmesan cheese

1 Preheat the oven to 400°F. Place the pizza base mix in a bowl and stir in the dill. Make the dough according to the instructions on the packet.

2 Press the dough into a circle measuring 10 inches across on a baking sheet lined with baking parchment. Set aside to rise.

3 Preheat the broiler to hot. To make the sauce, halve and deseed the bell pepper and arrange on a broiler rack. Cook for 8–10 minutes until softened and charred. Leave to cool slightly, peel off the skin and chop the flesh.

4 Place the tomatoes and bell pepper in a saucepan. Bring to the boil and simmer for 10 minutes. Stir in the tomato paste and season to taste.

5 Spread the sauce over the pizza base and top with the seafood. Sprinkle over the capers and olives, top with the cheeses and bake for 25–30 minutes.

6 Garnish with sprigs of dill and serve hot.

Spaghetti al Tonno

The classic Italian combination of pasta and tuna is enhanced in this recipe with a delicious parsley sauce.

NUTRITIONAL INFORMATION

Calories	1065	Sugars	.........3g
Protein	........27g	Fat	..........85g
Carbohydrate	...52g	Saturates	......18g

10 MINS 15 MINS

SERVES 4

I N G R E D I E N T S

7-ounce can tuna, drained

2-ounce can anchovies, drained

1⅛ cups olive oil

1 cup roughly chopped
   flat-leaf parsley

⅔ cup crème fraîche (see page 472)

1 pound dried spaghetti

2 tablespoons butter

salt and pepper

black olives, to garnish

crusty bread, to serve

1 Remove any bones from the tuna. Put the tuna into a food processor or blender, together with the anchovies, 1 cup of the olive oil, and the flat leaf parsley. Process until the sauce is very smooth.

VARIATION

If liked, you could add 1–2 garlic cloves to the sauce, substitute ½ cup chopped fresh basil for half the parsley and garnish with capers instead of black olives.

2 Spoon the crème fraîche into the food processor or blender and process again for a few seconds to blend thoroughly. Season with salt and pepper to taste.

3 Bring a large pan of lightly salted water to a boil. Add the spaghetti and the remaining olive oil and cook for 8–10 minutes until tender, but still firm to the bite.

4 Drain the spaghetti, return to the pan and place over medium heat. Add the butter and toss well to coat. Spoon in the sauce and quickly toss into the spaghetti, using 2 forks.

5 Remove the pan from the heat and divide the spaghetti among 4 warm individual serving plates. Garnish with the olives and serve at once with warm, crusty bread.

Tuna with Roast Bell Peppers

Fresh tuna will be either a small bonito fish or steaks from a skipjack. The more delicately flavored fish have a paler flesh.

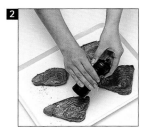  

NUTRITIONAL INFORMATION

Calories 428	Sugars 5g	
Protein 60g	Fat 19g	
Carbohydrate 5g	Saturates 3g	

 20 MINS   30 MINS

SERVES 4

INGREDIENTS

4 tuna steaks, about 9 ounces each

3 tablespoons lemon juice

4 cups water

6 tablespoons olive oil

2 orange bell peppers

2 red bell peppers

12 black olives

1 teaspoon balsamic vinegar

salt and pepper

1 Put the tuna steaks into a bowl with the lemon juice and water. Leave for 15 minutes.

2 Drain and brush the steaks all over with olive oil and season well with salt and pepper.

3 Halve, core and deseed the bell peppers. Put them over a hot barbecue and cook for 12 minutes until they are charred all over. Put them into a plastic bag and seal it.

4 Meanwhile, cook the tuna over a hot barbecue for 12–15 minutes, turning once.

5 When the bell peppers are cool enough to handle, peel them and cut each piece into 4 strips. Toss them with the remaining olive oil, olives, and balsamic vinegar.

6 Serve the tuna steaks piping hot, with the roasted bell pepper salad.

COOK'S TIP

Red, orange, and yellow bell peppers can also be peeled by cooking them in a hot oven for 30 minutes, turning them frequently, or roasting them straight over a naked flame, again turning them frequently. In both methods, deseed the bell peppers after peeling.

Salmon with Caper Sauce

The richness of salmon is beautifully balanced by the tangy capers in this creamy herb sauce.

NUTRITIONAL INFORMATION

Calories	302	Sugars	.........0g
Protein	........21g	Fat	..........24g
Carbohydrate	....1g	Saturates	......9g

5 MINS   25 MINS

SERVES 4

I N G R E D I E N T S

4 salmon fillets, skinned

1 fresh bay leaf

few black peppercorns

1 tsp white wine vinegar

⅔ cup fish stock

3 tablespoons heavy cream

1 tablespoon capers

1 tablespoon chopped fresh dill

1 tablespoon chopped fresh chives

1 teaspoon cornstarch

2 tablespoons skimmed milk

salt and pepper

new potatoes, to serve

T O   G A R N I S H

fresh dill sprigs

chive flowers

1 Lay the salmon fillets in a shallow ovenproof dish. Add the bay leaf, peppercorns, vinegar and stock.

2 Cover with foil and bake in a preheated oven at 350°F for 15–20 minutes until the flesh is opaque and flakes easily when tested with a fork.

3 Transfer the fish to warmed serving plates, cover and keep warm.

4 Strain the cooking liquid into a saucepan. Stir in the cream, capers, dill and chives and seasoning to taste.

5 Blend the cornstarch with the milk. Add to the saucepan and heat, stirring, until thickened slightly. Boil for 1 minute.

6 Spoon the sauce over the salmon, garnish with dill sprigs and chive flowers.

7 Serve with new potatoes.

COOK'S TIP

Ask the fish store to skin the fillets for you. The cooking time for the salmon will depend on the thickness of the fish: the thin tail end of the salmon takes the least time to cook.

Baked Red Snapper

You can substitute other whole fish for the snapper, or use cutlets of cod or halibut.

NUTRITIONAL INFORMATION

Calories 519   Sugars 12g
Protein ....61g   Fat 23g
Carbohydrate ...18g   Saturates 3g

  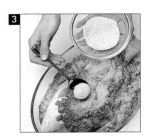

 20 MINS   50 MINS

SERVES 4

INGREDIENTS

1 red snapper, about 2 pounds 12 ounces, cleaned

juice of 2 limes, or 1 lemon

4–5 sprigs of thyme or parsley

3 tablespoons olive oil

1 large onion, chopped

2 garlic cloves, finely chopped

1 x 15 ounce can diced tomatoes

2 tablespoons tomato paste

2 tablespoons red wine vinegar

5 tablespoons low-fat yogurt

2 tablespoons chopped parsley

2 teaspoons dried oregano

6 tablespoons dry breadcrumbs

¼ cup low-fat yogurt

salt and pepper

SALAD

1 small lettuce, thickly sliced

10–12 young spinach leaves, torn

½ small cucumber, sliced and quartered

4 green onions, thickly sliced

3 tablespoons chopped parsley

2 tablespoons olive oil

2 tablespoons plain low-fat yogurt

1 tablespoons red wine vinegar

1 Sprinkle the lime or lemon juice inside and over the fish and season. Place the herbs inside the fish.

2 Heat the oil in a pan and fry the onion until translucent. Stir in the garlic and cook for 1 minute, then add the diced tomatoes, tomato paste and vinegar. Simmer, uncovered, for 5 minutes. Allow the sauce to cool, then stir in the yogurt, parsley, and oregano.

3 Pour half the sauce into an ovenproof dish just large enough for the fish. Add the fish an then pour the remainder of the sauce over it, and sprinkle with breadcrumbs. Bake uncovered for 30–35 minutes. Sprinkle the cheese over the fish and serve with lime wedges and dill sprigs.

4 Arrange the salad ingredients in a bowl. Whisk the oil, yogurt and vinegar and pour over the salad.

Smoky Fish Pie

This flavorsome and colorful fish pie is perfect for a light supper. The addition of smoked salmon gives it a touch of luxury.

NUTRITIONAL INFORMATION

Calories 523   Sugars 15g
Protein . . . . .58g   Fat 6g
Carbohydrate . . .63g   Saturates 2g

15 MINS   1 HOUR

SERVES 4

I N G R E D I E N T S

2 pounds smoked haddock or cod fillets

2½ cups skimmed milk

2 bay leaves

4 ounces mushrooms, quartered

4 ounces frozen peas

4 ounces frozen corn kernels

1½ pounds potatoes, diced

5 tablespoons low-fat yogurt

4 tablespoons chopped fresh parsley

2 ounces smoked salmon, sliced into thin strips

3 tablespoons cornstarch

1 ounce smoked cheese, grated

salt and pepper

1 Preheat the oven to 400°F. Place the fish in a pan and add the milk and bay leaves. Bring to the boil, cover and then simmer for 5 minutes.

2 Add the mushrooms, peas and sweetcorn, bring back to a simmer, cover and cook for 5–7 minutes. Leave to cool.

3 Place the potatoes in a saucepan, cover with water, boil and cook for 8 minutes. Drain well and mash with a fork or a potato masher. Stir in the yogurt, parsley and seasoning. Set aside.

4 Using a slotted spoon, remove the fish from the pan. Flake the cooked fish away from the skin and place in an ovenproof gratin dish. Reserve the cooking liquid.

5 Drain the vegetables, reserving the cooking liquid, and gently stir into the fish with the salmon strips.

6 Blend a little cooking liquid into the cornstarch to make a paste. Transfer the rest of the liquid to a saucepan and add the paste. Heat through, stirring, until thickened. Discard the bay leaves and season to taste. Pour the sauce over the fish and vegetables and mix. Spoon over the mashed potatoes so that the fish is covered, sprinkle with cheese and bake for 25–30 minutes.

COOK'S TIP

If possible, use smoked haddock or cod that has not been dyed bright yellow or artificially flavored to give the illusion of having been smoked.

Salmon Fillet with Herbs

This is a great party dish, as the salmon is cooked in one piece. The combination of the herbs and grill give a great flavor.

NUTRITIONAL INFORMATION

Calories 507	Sugars 0.4g
Protein 46g	Fat 35g
Carbohydrate . . .0.5g	Saturates 6g

5 MINS   30 MINS

SERVES 4

I N G R E D I E N T S

½ large bunch dried thyme

5 fresh rosemary branches, 6–8 inches long

8 bay leaves

2 pound salmon fillet

1 bulb fennel, cut into 8 pieces

2 tablespoons lemon juice

2 tablespoons olive oil

TO SERVE

crusty bread

green salad

1 Make a base on a hot grill with the dried thyme, rosemary branches, and bay leaves, overlapping them so that they cover a slightly bigger area than the salmon.

2 Carefully place the salmon on top of the herbs.

3 Arrange the fennel around the edge of the fish.

4 Combine the lemon juice and oil and brush the salmon with it.

5 Cover the salmon loosely with a piece of foil, to keep it moist.

6 Cook for about 20–30 minutes, basting frequently with the lemon juice mixture.

7 Remove the salmon from the barbecue, cut it into slices and serve with the fennel.

8 Serve with slices of crusty bread and a green salad.

VARIATION

Use whatever combination of herbs you may have on hand—but avoid the stronger tasting herbs, such as sage and marjoram, which are unsuitable for fish.

Smoked Haddock Casserole

This quick, easy, and inexpensive dish would be ideal for a midweek family supper.

NUTRITIONAL INFORMATION

Calories	525	Sugars	.........8g
Protein	........41g	Fat	..........18g
Carbohydrate	...53g	Saturates	......10g

 20 MINS   45 MINS

SERVES 4

I N G R E D I E N T S

2 tablespoons butter, plus extra
    for greasing

1 pound smoked haddock fillets,
    cut into 4 slices

2½ cups milk

¼ cup all-purpose flour

pinch of freshly grated nutmeg

3 tablespoons heavy cream

1 tablespoon chopped fresh parsley

2 eggs, hard-cooked and
    mashed to a pulp

4 cups dried fusilli

1 tablespoon lemon juice

salt and pepper

boiled new potatoes and beet,
    to serve

1 Thoroughly grease a casserole with butter. Put the haddock in the casserole and pour over the milk. Bake in a preheated oven at 400°F for about 15 minutes. Carefully pour the cooking liquid into a pitcher without breaking up the fish.

2 Melt the butter in a saucepan and stir in the flour. Gradually whisk in the reserved cooking liquid. Season to taste with salt, pepper and nutmeg. Stir in the cream, parsley, and mashed egg and cook, stirring constantly, for 2 minutes.

3 Meanwhile, bring a large saucepan of lightly salted water to a boil. Add the fusilli and lemon juice and cook for 8–10 minutes until tender, but still firm to the bite.

4 Drain the pasta and spoon or tip it over the fish. Top with the egg sauce and return the casserole to the oven for 10 minutes.

5 Serve the casserole with boiled new potatoes and beet.

VARIATION

You can use any type of
dried pasta for this casserole.
Try penne, conchiglie, or rigatoni.

Poached Salmon with Penne

Fresh salmon and pasta in a mouthwatering lemon and watercress sauce—a wonderful summer evening treat.

NUTRITIONAL INFORMATION

Calories 968	Sugars 3g
Protein 59g	Fat 58g
Carbohydrate . . .49g	Saturates 19g

10 MINS   30 MINS

SERVES 4

INGREDIENTS

9½ ounces fresh salmon steaks

4 tablespoons butter

¾ cup dry white wine

sea salt

8 peppercorns

fresh dill sprig

fresh tarragon sprig

1 lemon, sliced

1 pound dried penne

2 tablespoons olive oil

lemon slices and fresh watercress,
     to garnish

LEMON & WATERCRESS SAUCE

2 tablespoons butter

¼ cup all-purpose flour

⅔ cup warm milk

juice and finely grated rind of 2 lemons

2 ounces watercress, chopped

salt and pepper

1 Put the salmon in a large, nonstick pan. Add the butter, wine, a pinch of sea salt, the peppercorns, dill, tarragon, and lemon. Cover, bring to a boil, and simmer for 10 minutes.

2 Using a fish slice, carefully remove the salmon. Strain and reserve the cooking liquid. Remove and discard the salmon skin and center bones. Place on a warm dish, cover, and keep warm.

3 Meanwhile, bring a saucepan of salted water to a boil. Add the penne and 1 tablespoon of the oil and cook for 8–10 minutes, until tender but still firm to the bite. Drain and sprinkle over the remaining olive oil. Place on a warm serving dish, top with the salmon steaks, and keep warm.

4 To make the sauce, melt the butter and stir in the flour for 2 minutes. Stir in the milk and about 7 tablespoons of the reserved cooking liquid. Add the lemon juice and rind and cook, stirring, for a further 10 minutes.

5 Add the watercress to the sauce, stir gently, and season to taste with salt and pepper.

6 Pour the sauce over the salmon and penne, garnish with slices of lemon and fresh watercress, and serve.

Salmon Lasagne Rolls

Sheets of green lasagne are filled with a mixture of fresh salmon and oyster mushrooms. This recipe has been adapted for the microwave.

NUTRITIONAL INFORMATION

Calories 352	Sugars 5g	
Protein 19g	Fat 19g	
Carbohydrate ...25g	Saturates 9g	

 20 MINS ⏱ 35 MINS

SERVES 4

I N G R E D I E N T S

8 sheets green lasagne

1 onion, sliced

1 tablespoon butter

½ red bell pepper, chopped

1 zucchini, diced

1 teaspoon chopped ginger

4½ ounces oyster mushrooms, preferably yellow, chopped coarsely

8 ounces fresh salmon fillet, skinned and cut into chunks

2 tablespoons dry sherry

2 teaspoons cornstarch

3 tablespoons all-purpose flour

4½ teaspoons butter

1¼ cups milk

¼ cup grated Cheddar cheese

¼ cup fresh white bread crumbs

salt and pepper

salad greens, to serve

1 Place the lasagne sheets in a large shallow dish. Cover with plenty of boiling water. Cook on HIGH power for 5 minutes. Leave to stand, covered, for a few minutes before draining. Rinse in cold water and lay the sheets out on a clean work surface.

2 Put the onion and butter into a bowl. Cover and cook on HIGH power for 2 minutes. Add the bell pepper, zucchini, and ginger. Cover and cook on HIGH power for 3 minutes.

3 Add the mushrooms and salmon to the bowl. Mix the sherry into the cornstarch, then stir into the bowl. Cover and cook on HIGH power for 4 minutes until the fish flakes when tested with a fork. Season to taste.

4 Whisk the flour, butter, and milk in a bowl. Cook on HIGH power for 3–4 minutes, whisking every minute, to give a sauce of coating consistency. Stir in half the cheese and season with salt and pepper to taste.

5 Spoon the salmon filling in equal quantities along the shorter side of each lasagne sheet. Roll up to enclose the filling. Arrange in a lightly oiled large rectangular dish. Pour over the sauce and sprinkle over the remaining cheese and the bread crumbs.

6 Cook on HIGH power for 3 minutes until heated through. If possible, lightly brown under a preheated broiler before serving. Serve with salad.

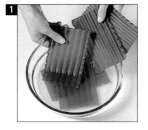

Spaghetti & Smoked Salmon

Made in moments, this is a luxurious dish to astonish and delight unexpected guests.

NUTRITIONAL INFORMATION

Calories	803	Sugars	.........3g
Protein	........21g	Fat	..........49g
Carbohydrate	...52g	Saturates	......27g

 10 MINS   20 MINS

SERVES 4

I N G R E D I E N T S

1 pound dried buckwheat
   spaghetti

2 tablespoons olive oil

½ cup crumbled feta cheese

salt

fresh cilantro or parsley leaves,
   to garnish

S A U C E

1¼ cups heavy cream

⅔ cup whiskey or brandy

4½ ounces smoked salmon

pinch of cayenne pepper

pepper

2 tablespoons chopped fresh cilantro
   or parsley

1 Bring a large pan of lightly salted water to a boil. Add the spaghetti and 1 tablespoon of the olive oil and cook for 8–10 minutes until tender, but still firm to the bite. Drain the spaghetti, return to the pan, and sprinkle over the remaining olive oil. Cover, shake the pan, set aside, and keep warm.

2 Pour the cream into a small saucepan and bring to simmering point, but do not let it boil. Pour the whiskey or brandy into another small saucepan and bring to simmering point, but do not allow it to boil. Remove both saucepans from the heat and mix together the cream and whiskey or brandy.

3 Cut the smoked salmon into thin strips and add to the cream mixture. Season to taste with cayenne and pepper. Just before serving, stir in the fresh cilantro or parsley.

4 Transfer the spaghetti to a warm serving dish, pour over the sauce. and toss thoroughly with 2 large forks. Scatter over the crumbled feta cheese, garnish with the cilantro or parsley leaves, and serve at once.

Squid & Macaroni Stew

This scrumptious seafood dish is quick and easy to make, yet deliciously satisfying to eat.

NUTRITIONAL INFORMATION

Calories 292	Sugars 3g	
Protein 13g	Fat 14g	
Carbohydrate ...24g	Saturates 2g	

15 MINS   35 MINS

SERVES 6

I N G R E D I E N T S

2 cups dried short-cut macaroni or other
   small pasta shapes

7 tablespoons olive oil

2 onions, sliced

12 ounces prepared squid, cut into
   1½-inch strips

1 cup fish stock

⅔ cup cup red wine

12 ounces tomatoes, peeled and
   thinly sliced

2 tablespoons tomato paste

1 teaspoon dried oregano

2 bay leaves

2 tablespoons chopped fresh parsley

salt and pepper

crusty bread, to serve

COOK'S TIP

To prepare squid, peel off the skin, then cut off the head and tentacles. Discard the transparent flat oval bone from the body. Remove the sac of black ink, then turn the body sac inside out. Wash in cold water. Cut off the tentacles; discard the rest. Rinse.

1 Bring a large saucepan of lightly salted water to a boil. Add the pasta and 1 tablespoon of the olive oil and cook for 3 minutes. Drain, return to the pan, cover, and keep warm.

2 Heat the remaining oil in a pan over medium heat. Add the onions and fry until they are translucent. Add the squid and stock and simmer for 5 minutes. Pour in the wine and add the tomatoes, tomato paste, oregano, and bay leaves. Bring the sauce to a boil, season to taste, and cook for 5 minutes.

3 Stir the pasta into the pan, cover, and simmer for about 10 minutes, or until the squid and macaroni are tender and the sauce has thickened. If the sauce remains too liquid, uncover the pan and continue cooking for a few minutes longer.

4 Remove and discard the bay leaves. Reserve a little parsley and stir the remainder into the pan. Transfer to a warm serving dish and sprinkle over the remaining parsley. Serve with crusty bread to soak up the sauce.

Stuffed Squid

Whole squid are stuffed with a mixture of fresh herbs and sun-dried tomatoes and then cooked in a wine sauce.

NUTRITIONAL INFORMATION

Calories 276   Sugars 1g
Protein . . . . .23g   Fat 8g
Carbohydrate . . .20g   Saturates 1g

25 MINS   35 MINS

SERVES 4

I N G R E D I E N T S

8 squid, cleaned and gutted but left whole
   (ask your fish store to do this)

6 canned anchovies, chopped

2 garlic cloves, chopped

2 tablespoons rosemary, stalks removed
   and leaves chopped

2 sun-dried tomatoes, chopped

2¾ cups bread crumbs

1 tablespoon olive oil

1 onion, finely chopped

1 cup white wine

1 cup fish stock

cooked rice, to serve

1 Remove the tentacles from the body of the squid and chop the flesh finely.

2 Grind the anchovies, garlic, rosemary, and tomatoes to a paste in a mortar and pestle.

3 Add the bread crumbs and the chopped squid tentacles and mix. If the mixture is too dry to form a thick paste at this point, add 1 teaspoon of water.

4 Spoon the paste into the body sacs of the squid then tie a length of cotton around the end of each sac to fasten

them. Do not overfill the sacs, because they will expand during cooking.

5 Heat the oil in a skillet. Add the onion and cook, stirring, for 3–4 minutes or until golden.

6 Add the stuffed squid to the pan and cook for 3–4 minutes or until brown all over.

7 Add the wine and stock and bring to a boil. Reduce the heat, cover, and then leave to simmer for 15 minutes.

8 Remove the lid and cook for a further 5 minutes or until the squid is tender and the juices reduced. Serve with plenty of cooked rice.

Squid Casserole

Squid is often served fried in Italy, but here it is casseroled with tomatoes and bell peppers to give a rich sauce.

NUTRITIONAL INFORMATION

Calories 281   Sugars 8g
Protein . . . . .31g   Fat 10g
Carbohydrate . . . .9g   Saturates 1g

25 MINS   1¹/₂ HOURS

SERVES 4

I N G R E D I E N T S

2¼ pounds whole squid, cleaned or
   1 pound 10 ounces squid rings, thawed
   if frozen

3 tablespoons olive oil

1 large onion, sliced thinly

2 garlic cloves, crushed

1 red bell pepper, cored,
   deseeded and sliced

1–2 sprigs fresh rosemary

²/₃ cup dry white wine and 1 cup water, or
   1½ cups water or fish stock

14-ounce can diced tomatoes

2 tablespoons tomato paste

1 teaspoon paprika

salt and pepper

fresh sprigs of rosemary or parsley,
   to garnish

1 Cut the squid pouch into ¹/₂-inch slices; cut the tentacles into lengths of about 2 inches. If using frozen squid rings, make sure they are fully thawed and well drained.

2 Heat the oil in a ovenproof casserole and fry the onion and garlic gently until soft. Add the squid, increase the heat, and continue to cook for about 10 minutes until sealed and beginning to color lightly. Add the red bell pepper, rosemary, wine (if using) and water or stock and bring to a boil. Cover and simmer gently for 45 minutes.

3 Discard the sprigs of rosemary (but don't take out any leaves that have come off). Add the tomatoes, tomato paste, seasonings, and paprika. Continue to simmer gently for 45–60 minutes, or cover the casserole tightly and cook in a moderate oven, 350°F, for 45–60 minutes until tender.

4 Give the sauce a good stir, season, and serve with fresh, crusty bread.

Pasta & Shrimp Parcels

This is the ideal dish when you have unexpected guests because the parcels can be prepared in advance, then put in the oven when you are ready to eat.

 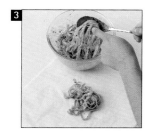 

NUTRITIONAL INFORMATION

Calories	640	Sugars	.........1g
Protein	........50g	Fat	..........29g
Carbohydrate	...42g	Saturates	.......4g

 15 MINS   30 MINS

SERVES 4

INGREDIENTS

1 pound dried fettuccine

⅔ cup Pesto Sauce

  (see page 39)

4 teaspoons extra virgin olive oil

1 pound 10 ounces large raw shrimp,

  peeled and deveined

2 garlic cloves, crushed

½ cup dry white wine

salt and pepper

1 Cut out 4 x 12-inch squares of wax paper.

2 Bring a large saucepan of lightly salted water to a boil. Add the fettuccine and cook for 2–3 minutes, until just softened. Drain and set aside.

3 Mix together the fettuccine and half of the Pesto Sauce. Spread out the paper squares and put 1 teaspoon olive oil in the middle of each. Divide the fettuccine among the the squares, then divide the shrimp and place on top of the fettuccine.

4 Mix together the remaining Pesto Sauce and the garlic and spoon it over the shrimp. Season each parcel with salt and black pepper and sprinkle with the white wine.

5 Dampen the edges of the wax paper and wrap the parcels loosely, twisting the edges to seal.

6 Place the parcels on a cookie sheet and bake in a preheated oven at 400°F for 10–15 minutes. Transfer the parcels to 4 individual serving plates and serve.

COOK'S TIP

Traditionally, these parcels are designed to look like money bags. The resemblance is more effective with waxed paper than with foil.

Pan-Fried Shrimp

A luxurious dish which makes an impressive starter or light meal. Shrimp and garlic are a winning combination.

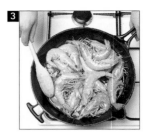

NUTRITIONAL INFORMATION

Calories 455	Sugars 0g
Protein 6g	Fat 37g
Carbohydrate 0g	Saturates 18g

 10 MINS   5 MINS

SERVES 4

INGREDIENTS

4 garlic cloves

20–24 unshelled large raw shrimp

9 tablespoons butter

4 tablespoons olive oil

6 tablespoons brandy

salt and pepper

2 tablespoons chopped fresh parsley

TO SERVE

lemon wedges

ciabatta bread

1 Using a sharp knife, peel and slice the garlic.

2 Wash the shrimp and pat dry using paper towels.

3 Melt the butter with the oil in a large skillet, add the garlic and shrimp, and fry over a high heat, stirring, for 3–4 minutes until the shrimp are pink.

4 Sprinkle with brandy and season with salt and pepper to taste. Sprinkle with parsley and serve at once with lemon wedges and ciabatta bread, if liked.

Macaroni & Seafood Bake

This adaptation of an eighteenth-century Italian dish is baked until it is golden brown and sizzling, then cut into wedges like a cake.

NUTRITIONAL INFORMATION

Calories	478	Sugars	.........6g
Protein	........27g	Fat	..........17g
Carbohydrate	...57g	Saturates	.......7g

30 MINS   50 MINS

SERVES 4

INGREDIENTS

3 cups dried short-cut macaroni

1 tablespoon olive oil, plus
    extra for brushing

6 tablespoons butter, plus
    extra for greasing

2 small fennel bulbs, thinly sliced and
    fronds reserved

2¼ cups thinly sliced mushrooms

6 ounces peeled, cooked shrimp

pinch of cayenne pepper

1¼ cups Béchamel Sauce
    (see page 28)

⅔ cup freshly grated
    Parmesan cheese

2 large tomatoes, sliced

1 teaspoon dried oregano

salt and pepper

1 Bring a saucepan of salted water to a boil. Add the pasta and oil and cook for 8–10 minutes until tender, but still firm to the bite. Drain the pasta and return to the pan.

2 Add 2 tablespoons of the butter to the pasta, cover, shake the pan, and keep warm.

3 Melt the remaining butter in a saucepan. Fry the fennel for 3–4 minutes. Stir in the mushrooms and fry for a further 2 minutes.

4 Stir in the shrimp, then remove the pan from the heat.

5 Stir the cayenne pepper and shrimp mixture into the Béchamel Sauce, mixing well.

6 Pour into a greased ovenproof dish and spread evenly. Sprinkle over the Parmesan cheese and arrange the tomato slices in a ring around the edge. Brush the tomatoes with olive oil and then sprinkle over the oregano.

7 Bake in a preheated oven at 350°F for 25 minutes, until golden brown. Serve at once.

Saffron Mussel Tagliatelle

Saffron is the most expensive spice in the world, but you only ever need a small quantity. Saffron threads or powdered saffron may be used.

NUTRITIONAL INFORMATION

Calories	854	Sugars	.........3g
Protein	........43g	Fat	..........49g
Carbohydrate	...57g	Saturates	......28g

15 MINS   35 MINS

SERVES 4

I N G R E D I E N T S

2¼ pounds mussels

⅔ cup white wine

1 medium onion, finely chopped

2 tablespoons butter

2 garlic cloves, crushed

2 teaspoon cornstarch

1¼ cups heavy cream

pinch of saffron threads or saffron powder

juice of ½ lemon

1 egg yolk

1 pound dried tagliatelle

1 tablespoon olive oil

salt and pepper

3 tablespoons chopped fresh parsley,
   to garnish

1 Scrub and debeard the mussels under cold running water. Discard any that do not close when sharply tapped. Put the mussels in a pan with the wine and onion. Cover and cook over a high heat, shaking the pan, for 5–8 minutes, until the shells open.

2 Drain and reserve the cooking liquid. Discard any mussels that are still closed. Reserve a few mussels for the garnish and remove the remainder from their shells.

3 Strain the cooking liquid into a pan. Bring to a boil and reduce by about half. Remove the pan from the heat.

4 Melt the butter in a saucepan. Add the garlic and cook, stirring frequently, for 2 minutes, until golden brown. Stir in the cornstarch and cook, stirring, for 1 minute. Gradually stir in the cooking liquid and the cream. Crush the saffron threads and add to the pan. Season with salt and pepper to taste and simmer over low heat for 2–3 minutes, until thickened.

5 Stir in the egg yolk, lemon juice, and shelled mussels. Do not allow the mixture to boil.

6 Meanwhile, bring a pan of salted water to a boil. Add the pasta and oil and cook for 8–10 minutes until tender, but still firm to the bite. Drain and transfer to a serving dish. Add the mussel sauce and toss. Garnish with the parsley and reserved mussels and serve.

Mussel Casserole

Mussels are not difficult to cook, just a little messy to eat. Serve this dish with a finger bowl to help keep things clean!

NUTRITIONAL INFORMATION

Calories	299	Sugars	........3g
Protein	........33g	Fat	..........7g
Carbohydrate	....3g	Saturates	.......1g

25 MINS   25 MINS

SERVES 4

I N G R E D I E N T S

2¼ pounds mussels

⅔ cup white wine

1 tablespoon oil

1 onion, finely chopped

3 garlic cloves, chopped

1 red chili, finely chopped

½ cup sieved tomatoes

1 tablespoon chopped marjoram

toast or crusty bread, to serve

1 Scrub the mussels to remove any mud or sand.

2 Remove the beards from the mussels by pulling away the hairy bit between the two shells. Rinse the mussels in a bowl of clean water. Discard any mussels that do not close when they are tapped—they are dead and should not be eaten.

3 Place the mussels in a large saucepan. Pour in the wine and cook for 5 minutes, shaking the pan occasionally until the shells open. Remove and discard any mussels that do not open.

4 Remove the mussels from the saucepan with a slotted spoon. Strain the cooking liquid through a fine strainer set over a bowl, reserving the liquid.

5 Heat the oil in a large skillet. Add the onion, garlic and chili and cook for 4–5 minutes or until just softened.

6 Add the reserved cooking liquid to the pan and cook for 5 minutes or until reduced, stirring.

7 Stir in the sieved tomatoes, marjoram, and mussels and cook until hot, about 3 minutes.

8 Transfer to serving bowls and serve with toast or plenty of crusty bread to mop up the juices.

COOK'S TIP

Finger bowls are individual bowls of warm water with a slice of lemon floating in them. They are used to clean your fingers at the end of a meal.

Pasta Shells with Mussels

Serve this aromatic seafood dish to family and friends who admit to a love of garlic.

NUTRITIONAL INFORMATION

Calories	686	Sugars	.........2g
Protein	........30g	Fat	..........45g
Carbohydrate	...36g	Saturates	......27g

 15 MINS 25 MINS

SERVES 6

INGREDIENTS

2¾ pounds mussels

1 cup dry white wine

2 large onions, chopped

½ cup butter

6 large garlic cloves,
   finely chopped

5 tablespoons chopped fresh parsley

1¼ cups heavy cream

14 ounces dried pasta shells

1 tablespoon olive oil

salt and pepper

crusty bread, to serve

1 Scrub and debeard the mussels under cold running water. Discard any mussels that do not close at once when sharply tapped. Put the mussels into a large saucepan, together with the wine and half of the onions. Cover and cook over medium heat, shaking the pan frequently, for 2–3 minutes, or until the shells open.

2 Remove the pan from the heat. Drain the mussels and reserve the cooking liquid. Discard any mussels that have not opened. Strain the cooking liquid through a clean cloth into a glass pitcher or bowl and reserve.

3 Melt the butter in a pan over medium heat. Add the remaining onion and fry until translucent. Stir in the garlic and cook for 1 minute. Gradually stir in the reserved cooking liquid. Stir in the parsley and cream and season to taste with salt and pepper. Bring to simmering point over low heat.

4 Meanwhile, bring a large pan of lightly salted water to a boil. Add the pasta and oil and cook for 8–10 minutes until just tender, but still firm to the bite. Drain the pasta, return to the pan, cover, and keep warm.

5 Reserve a few mussels for the garnish and remove the remainder from their shells. Stir the shelled mussels into the cream sauce and warm briefly.

6 Transfer the pasta to a serving dish. Pour over the sauce and toss to coat. Garnish with the reserved mussels.

Mussels with Tomato Sauce

This recipe for Mediterranean-style baked mussels, topped with a fresh tomato sauce and bread crumbs, has been adapted for the microwave.

NUTRITIONAL INFORMATION

Calories 254	Sugars 1g	
Protein 37g	Fat 10g	
Carbohydrate 4g	Saturates 3g	

20 MINS   15 MINS

SERVES 4

I N G R E D I E N T S

½ small onion, chopped

1 garlic clove, crushed

1 tablespoon olive oil

3 tomatoes

1 tablespoon chopped fresh parsley

2 pounds live mussels

1 tablespoon freshly grated Parmesan cheese

1 tablespoon fresh white bread crumbs

salt and pepper

chopped fresh parsley, to garnish

1 Place the onion, garlic, and oil in a bowl. Cover and cook on HIGH power for 3 minutes.

2 Cut a cross in the base of each tomato and place them in a small bowl. Pour on boiling water and leave for about 45 seconds. Drain and then plunge into cold water. The skins will slide off easily. Chop the tomatoes, removing any hard cores.

3 Add the tomatoes to the onion mixture, cover, and cook on HIGH power for 3 minutes. Stir in the parsley and season to taste.

4 Scrub the mussels well in several changes of cold water. Remove the

beards and discard any open mussels and those which do not close when tapped sharply with the back of a knife.

5 Place the mussels in a large bowl. Add enough boiling water to cover them. Cover and cook on HIGH power for 2 minutes, stirring halfway through, until the mussels open. Drain well and remove the empty half of each shell. Arrange the mussels in 1 layer on a plate.

6 Spoon the tomato sauce over each mussel. Mix the Parmesan cheese with the bread crumbs and sprinkle on top.

Cook, uncovered, on HIGH power for 2 minutes. Garnish with parsley and serve.

COOK'S TIP

Dry out the bread crumbs in the microwave for an extra crunchy topping. Spread them on a plate and cook on HIGH power for 2 minutes, stirring once. Leave to stand, uncovered.

Vermicelli with Clams

A quickly cooked recipe that transforms pantry ingredients into a dish with style.

NUTRITIONAL INFORMATION

Calories	520	Sugars	........2g
Protein	........26g	Fat	..........13g
Carbohydrate	....71g	Saturates	.......4g

 10 MINS   25 MINS

SERVES 4

I N G R E D I E N T S

14 ounces dried vermicelli, spaghetti, or
   other long pasta

2 tablespoons olive oil

2 tablespoons butter

2 onions, chopped

2 garlic cloves, chopped

2 x 7-ounce jars clams in brine

½ cup white wine

4 tablespoons chopped fresh parsley

½ teaspoon dried oregano

pinch of freshly grated nutmeg

salt and pepper

TO GARNISH

2 tablespoons Parmesan cheese shavings

fresh basil sprigs

COOK'S TIP

There are many different types of clams found along almost every coast in the world. Those traditionally used in this dish are the tiny ones—only 1-2 inches across—known in Italy as vongole.

1 Bring a large pan of lightly salted water to a boil. Add the pasta and half of the olive oil and cook for 8–10 minutes until tender, but still firm to the bite. Drain, return to the pan and add the butter. Cover the pan, shake well, and keep warm.

2 Heat the remaining oil in a pan over medium heat. Add the onions and fry until they are translucent. Stir in the garlic and cook for 1 minute.

3 Strain the liquid from 1 jar of clams and add the liquid to the pan, with the wine. Stir, bring to simmering point, and simmer for 3 minutes. Drain the second jar of clams and discard the liquid.

4 Add the clams, parsley, and oregano to the pan and season with pepper and nutmeg. Lower the heat and cook until the sauce is heated through.

5 Transfer the pasta to a warm serving dish and pour over the sauce. Sprinkle with the Parmesan cheese, garnish with the basil, and serve at once.

Farfallini Buttered Lobster

This is one of those dishes that looks almost too lovely to eat—but you should!

NUTRITIONAL INFORMATION

Calories 686   Sugars 1g
Protein ....45g   Fat 36g
Carbohydrate ...44g   Saturates 19g

30 MINS   25 MINS

SERVES 4

I N G R E D I E N T S

2 x 1 pound 9 ounce lobsters, split
    into halves

juice and grated rind of 1 lemon

½ cup butter

4 tablespoons fresh white bread crumbs

2 tablespoons brandy

5 tablespoons heavy cream or
    crème fraîche (see page 472)

1 pound dried farfallini

1 tablespoon olive oil

⅔ cup freshly grated Parmesan cheese

salt and pepper

TO GARNISH

1 kiwi, sliced

4 unpeeled, cooked jumbo prawns

fresh dill sprigs

1 Carefully discard the stomach sac, vein, and gills from each lobster. Remove all the meat from the tail and chop. Crack the claws and legs, remove the meat and chop. Transfer the meat to a bowl and add the lemon juice and grated lemon rind.

2 Clean the shells thoroughly and place in a warm oven at 325°F to dry out.

3 Melt 2 tablespoons of the butter in a skillet. Add the bread crumbs and fry for about 3 minutes, until crisp and golden brown in color.

4 Melt the remaining butter in a saucepan. Add the lobster meat and heat through gently. Add the brandy and cook for a further 3 minutes, then add the cream or crème fraîche, and season to taste with salt and pepper.

5 Meanwhile, bring a large pan of lightly salted water to a boil. Add the farfallini and olive oil and cook for 8–10 minutes, until tender but still firm to the bite. Drain and spoon the pasta into the clean lobster shells.

6 Top with the buttered lobster and sprinkle with a little grated Parmesan cheese and the bread crumbs. Broil for 2–3 minutes, until golden brown.

7 Transfer the lobster shells to a warm serving dish, garnish with the lemon slices, kiwi, jumbo prawns, and dill sprigs, and serve at once.

Baked Scallops & Pasta

This is another tempting seafood dish where the eye is delighted as much as the tastebuds.

20 MINS   30 MINS

SERVES 4

INGREDIENTS

12 scallops

3 tablespoons olive oil

3 cups small, dried whole wheat
   pasta shells

$2/3$ cup fish stock

1 onion, chopped

juice and finely grated rind of 2 lemons

$2/3$ cup heavy cream

2 cups grated Cheddar cheese

salt and pepper

crusty brown bread, to serve

1 Remove the scallops from their shells. Scrape off the skirt and the black intestinal thread. Reserve the white part (the flesh) and the orange part (the coral or roe). Very carefully ease the flesh and coral from the shell with a short, but very strong knife.

2 Wash the shells thoroughly and dry them well. Put the shells on a cookie sheet, sprinkle lightly with two-thirds of the olive oil and set aside.

3 Meanwhile, bring a large saucepan of lightly salted water to a boil. Add the pasta shells and remaining olive oil and cook for 8–10 minutes or until tender, but still firm to the bite. Drain well and spoon about 1 ounce of pasta into each scallop shell.

4 Put the scallops, fish stock, onion and lemon rind in an ovenproof dish and season to taste with pepper. Cover with foil and bake in a preheated oven at 350°F for 8 minutes.

5 Remove the dish from the oven. Remove the foil and, using a slotted spoon, transfer the scallops to the shells. Add 1 tablespoon of the cooking liquid to each shell, together with a drizzle of lemon juice and a little cream, and top with the grated cheese.

6 Increase the oven temperature to 450°F and return the scallops to the oven for a further 4 minutes.

7 Serve the scallops in their shells with crusty brown bread and butter.

Seafood Lasagne

You can use any fish and any sauce you like in this recipe: try smoked finnan haddock and whiskey sauce or cod with cheese sauce.

NUTRITIONAL INFORMATION

Calories	790	Sugars	. . . . .23g
Protein	. . . . .55g	Fat	. . . . .32g
Carbohydrate	. . .74g	Saturates	. . . . . .19g

30 MINS   45 MINS

SERVES 4

I N G R E D I E N T S

1 pound smoked haddock, filleted, skin
   removed and flesh flaked

4 ounces shrimp

4 ounces sole fillet, skin removed and
   flesh sliced

juice of 1 lemon

4 tablespoons butter

3 leeks, very thinly sliced

½ cup all-purpose flour

2 ⅓ cups milk

2 tablespoons liquid honey

1 ¾ cups grated mozzarella cheese

1 pound pre-cooked lasagne

⅔ cup freshly grated
   Parmesan cheese

pepper

1 Put the haddock fillet, shrimp, and sole fillet into a large bowl and season with pepper and lemon juice according to taste. Set aside while you make the sauce.

2 Melt the butter in a large saucepan. Add the leeks and cook, stirring occasionally, for 8 minutes. Add the flour and cook, stirring constantly, for 1 minute. Gradually stir in enough milk to make a thick, creamy sauce.

3 Blend in the honey and mozzarella cheese and cook for a further 3 minutes. Remove the pan from the heat and mix in the fish and shrimp.

4 Make alternate layers of fish sauce and lasagne in an ovenproof dish, finishing with a layer of fish sauce on top. Generously sprinkle over the grated Parmesan cheese and bake in a preheated oven at 350°F for 30 minutes. Serve at once.

VARIATION

For a cider sauce, substitute 1 finely chopped shallot for the leeks, 1½ cups cider and 1½ cups heavy cream for the milk and 1 teaspoon mustard for the honey. For a Tuscan sauce, substitute 1 chopped fennel bulb for the leeks and omit the honey.

A Seafood Medley

You can use almost any kind of sea fish in this recipe. Red sea bream or bass are good choices.

NUTRITIONAL INFORMATION

Calories	699	Sugars	.........4g
Protein	........56g	Fat	..........35g
Carbohydrate	...35g	Saturates	......20g

20 MINS   30 MINS

SERVES 4

I N G R E D I E N T S

12 raw jumbo prawns

12 raw (small) shrimp

1 pound fillet of sea bream or bass

4 tablespoons butter

12 scallops, shelled

4½ ounces freshwater shrimp

juice and finely grated rind
    of 1 lemon

pinch of saffron powder or threads

4 cups vegetable stock

⅔ cup rose petal vinegar

1 pound dried farfalle

1 tablespoon olive oil

⅔ cup white wine

1 tablespoon pink peppercorns

4 ounces baby carrots

⅔ cup heavy cream

salt and pepper

1 Peel and devein the prawns and (small) shrimp. Thinly slice the fillet. Melt the butter in a skillet, add the fillet, scallops, prawns and (small) shrimp and cook for 1–2 minutes.

2 Season with pepper to taste. Add the lemon juice and grated rind. Very

carefully add a pinch of saffron powder or a few strands of saffron to the cooking juices (not to the seafood).

3 Remove the seafood from the pan, set aside, and keep warm.

4 Return the pan to the heat and add the stock. Bring to a boil and reduce by one-third. Add the rose petal vinegar and cook for 4 minutes, until reduced.

5 Bring a pan of salted water to a boil. Add the farfalle and oil and cook for 8–10 minutes until tender, but still firm to the bite. Drain the pasta, transfer to a serving plate, and top with the seafood.

6 Add the wine, peppercorns, and carrots to the pan and reduce the sauce for 6 minutes. Add the cream and simmer for 2 minutes.

7 Pour the sauce over the seafood and pasta and serve at once.

Spaghetti & Seafood Sauce

Peeled shrimp from the freezer can become the star ingredient in this colorful and tasty dish.

NUTRITIONAL INFORMATION

Calories 498	Sugars 5g
Protein 32g	Fat 23g
Carbohydrate . . .43g	Saturates 11g

  30 MINS   🕐 35 MINS

SERVES 4

I N G R E D I E N T S

8 ounces dried spaghetti, broken into
  6-inch lengths

2 tablespoons olive oil

1 ¼ cups chicken stock

1 teaspoon lemon juice

1 small cauliflower, cut into flowerets

2 carrots, thinly sliced

4 ounces snow peas

4 tablespoons butter

1 onion, sliced

8 ounces zucchini, sliced

1 garlic clove, chopped

12 ounces frozen, cooked, peeled
  shrimp, thawed

2 tablespoons chopped fresh parsley

⅓ cup freshly grated Parmesan cheese

½ teaspoon paprika

salt and pepper

4 unpeeled, cooked shrimp, to garnish

1 Bring a pan of lightly salted water to a boil. Add the spaghetti and 1 tablespoon of the olive oil and cook for 8–10 minutes until tender, but still firm to the bite. Drain the spaghetti and return to the pan. Toss with the remaining olive oil, cover, and keep warm.

2 Bring the chicken stock and lemon juice to a boil. Add the cauliflower and carrots and cook for 3–4 minutes. Remove from the pan and set aside. Add the snow peas to the pan and cook for 1–2 minutes. Set aside with the other vegetables.

3 Melt half of the butter in a skillet over medium heat. Add the onion and zucchini and fry for about 3 minutes. Add the garlic and shrimp and cook for a further 2–3 minutes, until thoroughly heated through.

4 Stir in the reserved vegetables and heat through. Season to taste and stir in the remaining butter.

5 Transfer the spaghetti to a warm serving dish. Pour over the sauce and add the chopped parsley. Toss well with 2 forks until coated. Sprinkle over the Parmesan cheese and paprika, garnish with the unpeeled shrimp, and serve at once.

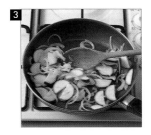

Meat

Italians have their very own special way of butchering meat, producing very different cuts. Most meat is sold ready-boned and often cut straight across the grain. Veal is a great favorite and widely available. Pork is also popular, with roast pig being the traditional dish of Umbria. Suckling pig is roasted with lots of fresh herbs,

especially rosemary, until the skin is crisp and brown. Lamb is often served for special occasions, cooked on a spit or roasted in the oven with wine, garlic, and herbs; and the very small cutlets from young lambs feature widely, especially in Rome. Variety meats play an important role, too, with liver, brains, sweetbreads, tongue, heart, tripe, and kidneys always available. Whatever your favorite Italian meat dish is, it's sure to be included in this chapter.

Beef & Spaghetti Surprise

This delicious Sicilian recipe originated as a handy way of using up leftover cooked pasta.

NUTRITIONAL INFORMATION

Calories	797	Sugars	........7g
Protein	........31g	Fat	.........60g
Carbohydrate	...35g	Saturates	......16g

30 MINS   1 1/2 HOURS

SERVES 4

I N G R E D I E N T S

⅔ cup olive oil, plus extra
   for brushing

2 eggplants

3 cups ground beef

1 onion, chopped

2 garlic cloves, crushed

2 tablespoons tomato paste

14-ounce can diced tomatoes

1 teaspoon Worcestershire sauce

1 teaspoon chopped fresh marjoram or
   oregano or ½ teaspoon dried marjoram or
   oregano

½ cup pitted black olives, sliced

1 green, red, or yellow bell pepper, cored,
   deseeded and chopped

6 ounces dried spaghetti

1 cup freshly grated
   Parmesan cheese

salt and pepper

fresh oregano or parsley sprigs,
   to garnish

1 Brush an 8-inch loose-based round cake pan with oil, line the base with baking parchment and brush with oil.

2 Slice the eggplants. Heat a little oil in a pan and fry the eggplants, in batches, for 3–4 minutes or until browned on both sides. Add more oil, as necessary. Drain on paper towels.

3 Put the ground beef, onion, and garlic in a saucepan and cook over medium heat, stirring occasionally, until browned. Add the tomato paste, tomatoes, Worcestershire sauce, marjoram or oregano, and salt and pepper to taste. Leave to simmer, stirring occasionally, for 10 minutes. Add the olives and bell pepper and cook for a further 10 minutes.

4 Bring a pan of salted water to the boil. Add the spaghetti and 1 tablespoon oil and cook for 8–10 minutes until tender, but still firm to the bite. Drain and turn the spaghetti into a bowl. Add the meat mixture and cheese and toss with 2 forks.

5 Arrange eggplant slices over the base and up the sides of the pan. Add the spaghetti, pressing down firmly, and then cover with the rest of the eggplant slices. Bake in a preheated oven at 400°F for 40 minutes. Leave to stand for 5 minutes, then invert onto a serving dish. Discard the baking parchment. Garnish with the fresh herbs and serve.

Beef in Barolo

Barolo is a famous wine from the Piedmont area of Italy. Its mellow flavor is the key to this dish, so don't stint on the quality of the wine.

NUTRITIONAL INFORMATION

Calories	744	Sugars	.........1g
Protein	........66g	Fat	..........43g
Carbohydrate	....1g	Saturates	......16g

15 MINS   2¼ HOURS

SERVES 4

INGREDIENTS

4 tablespoons oil

2¼-pound piece boned rolled rib of beef, or piece of round

2 garlic cloves, crushed

4 shallots, sliced

1 teaspoon chopped fresh rosemary

1 teaspoon chopped fresh oregano

2 celery stalks, sliced

1 large carrot, diced

2 cloves

1 bottle Barolo wine

freshly grated nutmeg

salt and pepper

cooked vegetables, such as broccoli, carrots, and new potatoes, to serve

1 Heat the oil in a flameproof casserole and brown the meat all over. Remove the meat from the casserole.

2 Add the garlic, shallots, herbs, celery, carrot, and cloves and fry for 5 minutes.

3 Replace the meat on top of the vegetables. Pour in the wine. Cover the casserole and simmer gently for about 2 hours until tender. Remove the meat from the casserole, slice, and keep warm.

4 Rub the contents of the pan through a strainer or purée in a blender, adding a little hot beef stock if necessary. Season with nutmeg, salt, and pepper.

5 Serve the meat with the sauce and accompanied by cooked vegetables, such as broccoli, carrots, and new potatoes, if wished.

Layered Meat Loaf

The cheese-flavored pasta layer comes as a pleasant surprise inside this lightly spiced meat loaf.

NUTRITIONAL INFORMATION

Calories	.412	Sugars	.3g
Protein	.21g	Fat	.30g
Carbohydrate	.15g	Saturates	.13g

 35 MINS   1½ HOURS

SERVES 6

I N G R E D I E N T S

2 tablespoons butter, plus extra
  for greasing

1 small onion, finely chopped

1 small red bell pepper, cored, deseeded,
  and chopped

1 garlic clove, chopped

4 cups ground beef

½ cup white bread crumbs

½ teaspoon cayenne pepper

1 tablespoon lemon juice

½ teaspoon grated lemon rind

2 tablespoons chopped fresh parsley

¾ cup dried short pasta,
  such as fusilli

1 tablespoon olive oil

4 bay leaves

1 cup Italian Cheese Sauce
  (see page 30)

6 ounces bacon, rinds removed

salt and pepper

salad greens, to serve

1 Melt the butter in a pan over a medium heat and fry the onion and bell pepper for about 3 minutes. Stir in the garlic and cook for 1 minute.

  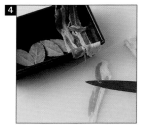

2 Put the meat into a bowl and mash with a wooden spoon until sticky. Add the onion mixture, bread crumbs, cayenne pepper, lemon juice, lemon rind, and parsley. Season and set aside.

3 Bring a pan of salted water to a boil. Add the pasta and oil and cook for 8–10 minutes, until almost tender. Drain and stir into the Italian Cheese Sauce.

4 Grease a 2¼-pound loaf pan and arrange the bay leaves in the base. Stretch the bacon slices with the back of a knife and line the base and sides of the pan with them. Spoon in half the meat mixture and smooth the surface. Cover with the pasta mixed with Italian Cheese Sauce, then spoon in the remaining meat mixture. Level the top and cover with foil.

5 Bake the meat loaf in a preheated oven, at 350°F, for 1 hour or until the juices run clear when a toothpick is inserted into the center and the loaf has shrunk away from the sides. Pour off any fat and turn out the loaf onto a serving dish. Serve with salad greens.

Rich Beef Stew

This slow-cooked beef stew is flavored with oranges, red wine, and porcini mushrooms.

NUTRITIONAL INFORMATION

Calories ....388 Sugars 15g
Protein ....30g Fat 21g
Carbohydrate ...16g Saturates 9g

45 MINS   1¾ HOURS

SERVES 4

INGREDIENTS

1 tablespoon oil

1 tablespoon butter

8 ounces baby onions, peeled and halved

1 pound 5 ounces stewing steak, diced into 1½-inch chunks

1¼ cups beef stock

⅔ cup red wine

4 tablespoons chopped oregano

1 tablespoon sugar

1 orange

1 ounce porcini or other dried mushrooms

8 ounces fresh plum tomatoes

cooked rice or potatoes, to serve

1 Heat the oil and butter in a large skillet. Add the onions and sauté for 5 minutes or until golden. Remove the onions with a perforated spoon, set aside, and keep warm.

2 Add the beef to the pan and cook, stirring, for 5 minutes or until browned all over.

3 Return the onions to the skillet and add the stock, wine, oregano, and sugar, stirring to mix well. Transfer the mixture to an ovenproof casserole dish.

4 Pare the rind from the orange and cut it into strips. Slice the orange flesh into rings. Add the orange rings and the rind to the casserole. Cook in a preheated oven, at 350°F, for 1¼ hours.

5 Soak the porcini mushrooms for 30 minutes in a small bowl containing 4 tablespoons of warm water.

6 Peel and halve the tomatoes. Add the tomatoes, porcini mushrooms, and their soaking liquid to the casserole. Cook for a further 20 minutes until the beef is tender and the juices thickened. Serve with cooked rice or potatoes.

Creamed Strips of Sirloin

This quick and easy dish tastes superb and would make a delicious treat for a special occasion.

NUTRITIONAL INFORMATION

Calories ....796 Sugars 2g
Protein ....29g Fat 63g
Carbohydrate ...26g Saturates 39g

15 MINS   30 MINS

SERVES 4

I N G R E D I E N T S

6 tablespoons butter

1 pound sirloin steak, trimmed
    and cut into thin strips

2¼ cups mushrooms

1 teaspoon mustard

pinch of freshly grated ginger

2 tablespoons dry sherry

⅔ cup heavy cream

salt and pepper

4 slices hot toast, cut into triangles,
    to serve

P A S T A

1 pound dried rigatoni

2 tablespoons olive oil

2 fresh basil sprigs

½ cup butter

COOK'S TIP

Dried pasta will keep for up to 6 months. Keep it in the packet and reseal it once you have opened it, or transfer the pasta to an airtight jar.

1 Melt the butter in a large skillet and gently fry the steak over low heat, stirring frequently, for 6 minutes. Using a slotted spoon, transfer the steak to an ovenproof dish and keep warm.

2 Add the sliced mushrooms to the skillet and cook for 2–3 minutes in the juices remaining in the pan. Add the mustard, ginger, salt, and pepper. Cook for 2 minutes, then add the sherry and cream. Cook for a further 3 minutes, then pour the cream sauce over the steak.

3 Bake the steak and cream mixture in a preheated oven, at 375°F, for 10 minutes.

4 Meanwhile, cook the pasta. Bring a large saucepan of lightly salted water to a boil. Add the rigatoni, olive oil, and 1 of the basil sprigs and boil rapidly for 10 minutes, until tender but still firm to the bite. Drain the pasta and transfer to a warm serving plate. Toss the pasta with the butter and garnish with a sprig of basil.

5 Serve the creamed steak strips with the pasta and triangles of warm toast.

Pizzaiola Steak

This has a Neapolitan sauce, using the delicious red tomatoes so abundant in that area, but canned ones make an excellent alternative.

NUTRITIONAL INFORMATION

Calories 371
Sugars 7g
Protein 43g
Fat 19g
Carbohydrate 7g
Saturates 5g

 25 MINS   30 MINS

SERVES 4

I N G R E D I E N T S

2 x 14-ounce cans peeled tomatoes or
1 pound 10 ounces fresh tomatoes

4 tablespoons olive oil

2–3 garlic cloves, crushed

1 onion, chopped finely

1 tablespoon tomato paste

1½ teaspoons chopped fresh marjoram or
¾ teaspoon dried marjoram

4 thin sirloin or rump steaks

2 tablespoons chopped fresh parsley

1 teaspoon sugar

salt and pepper

fresh herbs, to garnish (optional)

pan-fried potatoes, to serve

1 If using canned tomatoes, purée them in a food processor, then strain to remove the seeds. If using fresh tomatoes, peel, remove the seeds, and chop finely.

2 Heat half of the oil in a pan and fry the garlic and onions very gently for about 5 minutes, or until softened.

3 Add the tomatoes, seasoning, tomato paste, and chopped herbs to the pan. If using fresh tomatoes, add 4 tablespoons water too, and then simmer very gently over low heat for 8–10 minutes, giving an occasional stir.

4 Meanwhile, trim the steaks if necessary and season. Heat the remaining oil in a skillet and fry the steaks quickly on both sides to seal, then continue until cooked to your liking—2 minutes for rare, 3–4 minutes for medium, or 5 minutes for well done. Alternatively, cook the steaks under a hot broiler after brushing lightly with oil.

5 When the sauce has thickened a little, adjust the seasoning and stir in the chopped parsley and sugar.

6 Pour off the excess fat from the skillet containing the steaks and add the tomato sauce. Reheat gently and serve at once, with the sauce spooned over and around the steaks. Garnish with sprigs of fresh herbs, if liked. Pan-fried potatoes and a green vegetable make very good accompaniments.

Fresh Spaghetti & Meatballs

This well-loved Italian dish is famous across the world. Make the most of it by using high-quality steak for the meatballs.

NUTRITIONAL INFORMATION

Calories . . . . .665 Sugars 9g
Protein . . . . .39g Fat 24g
Carbohydrate . . .77g Saturates 8g

 45 MINS   1¼ HOURS

SERVES 4

I N G R E D I E N T S

2½ cups brown bread crumbs

⅔ cup milk

2 tablespoons butter

¼ cup whole wheat flour

1 cup beef stock

14-ounce can diced tomatoes

2 tablespoons tomato paste

1 teaspoon sugar

1 tablespoon finely chopped fresh tarragon

1 large onion, chopped

4 cups ground steak

1 teaspoon paprika

4 tablespoons olive oil

1 pound fresh spaghetti

salt and pepper

fresh tarragon sprigs,
   to garnish

1 Place the bread crumbs in a bowl, add the milk, and set aside to soak for about 30 minutes.

2 Melt half of the butter in a pan. Add the flour and cook, stirring constantly, for 2 minutes. Gradually stir in the beef stock and cook, stirring constantly, for a further 5 minutes. Add the tomatoes, tomato paste, sugar, and tarragon. Season well and simmer for 25 minutes.

3 Mix the onion, steak, and paprika into the bread crumbs and season to taste. Shape the mixture into 14 meatballs.

4 Heat the oil and remaining butter in a skillet and fry the meatballs, turning, until brown all over. Place in a deep casserole, pour over the tomato sauce, cover, and bake in a preheated oven, at 350°F, for 25 minutes.

5 Bring a large saucepan of lightly salted water to a boil. Add the fresh spaghetti, bring back to a boil, and cook for about 2–3 minutes or until tender, but still firm to the bite.

6 Meanwhile, remove the meatballs from the oven and allow them to cool for 3 minutes. Serve the meatballs and their sauce with the spaghetti, garnished with tarragon sprigs.

Beef & Potato Ravioli

In this recipe the "pasta" dough is made with potatoes instead of flour.
The small round ravioli are filled with a rich bolognese sauce.

NUTRITIONAL INFORMATION

Calories 618   Sugars 4g
Protein . . . . .16g   Fat 31g
Carbohydrate . . .74g   Saturates 12g

30 MINS   50 MINS

SERVES 4

I N G R E D I E N T S

FILLING

1 tablespoon vegetable oil

1 cup ground beef

1 shallot, diced

1 garlic clove, crushed

1 tablespoon all-purpose flour

1 tablespoon tomato paste

⅔ cup beef stock

1 celery stalk, chopped

2 tomatoes, peeled and diced

2 teaspoon chopped fresh basil

salt and pepper

RAVIOLI

1 pound russet potatoes, diced

3 small egg yolks

3 tablespoons olive oil

1½ cups all-purpose flour

¼ cup butter, for frying

shredded basil leaves, to garnish

1 To make the filling, heat the vegetable oil in a pan and fry the beef for 3–4 minutes, breaking it up with a spoon.

2 Add the shallots and garlic to the pan and cook for 2–3 minutes, or until the shallots have softened.

3 Stir in the flour and tomato paste and cook for 1 minute. Stir in the beef stock, celery, tomatoes, and chopped fresh basil. Season to taste with salt and pepper.

4 Cook the mixture over low heat for 20 minutes. Remove from the heat and leave to cool.

5 To make the ravioli, cook the potatoes in a pan of boiling water for 10 minutes until cooked.

6 Mash the potatoes thoroughly and place them in a mixing bowl. Blend in the egg yolks and oil. Season with salt and pepper, then stir in the flour and mix to form a dough.

7 On a lightly floured surface, divide the dough into 24 pieces and shape into flat rounds. Spoon the filling onto one half of each round and fold the dough over to encase the filling, pressing down to seal the edges.

8 Melt the butter in a skillet and cook the ravioli for 6-8 minutes, turning once, until golden. Serve hot, garnished with shredded basil leaves.

Beef & Pasta Bake

The combination of Italian and Indian ingredients makes a surprisingly delicious recipe. Marinate the steak in advance to save time.

NUTRITIONAL INFORMATION

Calories . . . . . . .1050 Sugars 4g
Protein . . . . .47g Fat 81g
Carbohydrate . . .37g Saturates 34g

6¼ HOURS   1¼ HOURS

SERVES 4

INGREDIENTS

2 pounds steak, cut into cubes

⅔ cup beef stock

1 pound dried macaroni

1¼ cups heavy cream

½ teaspoon garam masala

salt

fresh cilantro and flaked slivered almonds,
    to garnish

KORMA PASTE

½ cup blanched almonds

6 garlic cloves

1-inch piece fresh ginger,
coarsely chopped

6 tablespoons beef stock

1 teaspoon ground cardamom

4 cloves, crushed

1 teaspoon cinnamon

2 large onions, chopped

1 teaspoon coriander seeds

2 teaspoons ground cumin seeds

pinch of cayenne pepper

6 tablespoons sunflower oil

1 To make the korma paste, grind the almonds finely using a pestle and mortar. Put the ground almonds and the rest of the korma paste ingredients into a food processor or blender and process to make a very smooth paste.

2 Put the steak in a shallow dish and spoon over the korma paste, turning to coat the steak well. Leave in the refrigerator to marinate for 6 hours.

3 Transfer the steak and korma paste to a large saucepan, and simmer over low heat, adding a little beef stock if required, for 35 minutes.

4 Meanwhile, bring a large saucepan of lightly salted water to a boil. Add the macaroni and cook for 10 minutes until tender, but still firm to the bite. Drain the pasta thoroughly and transfer to a deep casserole. Add the steak, heavy cream, and garam masala.

5 Bake in a preheated oven at 400°F for 30 minutes. Remove the casserole from the oven and allow to stand for about 10 minutes. Garnish the bake with fresh cilantro and serve.

Beef, Tomato, & Olive Kabobs

These kabobs have a Mediterranean flavor. The sweetness of the tomatoes and the sharpness of the olives makes them rather unique.

NUTRITIONAL INFORMATION

Calories	166	Sugars	.........1g
Protein	........12g	Fat	..........12g
Carbohydrate	....1g	Saturates	.......3g

45 MINS   15 MINS

SERVES 8

INGREDIENTS

1 pound rump or sirloin steak

16 cherry tomatoes

16 large green olives, pitted

focaccia bread, to serve

BASTE

4 tablespoons olive oil

1 tablespoon sherry vinegar

1 clove garlic, crushed

salt and pepper

FRESH TOMATO RELISH

1 tablespoon olive oil

½ red onion, chopped finely

1 clove garlic, chopped

6 plum tomatoes, deseeded, skinned, and chopped

2 pitted green olives, sliced

1 tablespoon chopped, fresh parsley

1 tablespoon lemon juice

1 Using a sharp knife, trim any fat from the beef and cut the meat into about 24 evenly-sized pieces.

2 Thread the pieces of beef onto 8 wooden skewers, alternating the meat with the cherry tomatoes and the green olives.

3 To make the baste, combine the oil, vinegar, garlic, and salt and pepper to taste in a bowl.

4 To make the relish, heat the oil in a small pan and fry the onion and garlic for 3–4 minutes until softened. Add the tomatoes and olives and cook for 2–3 minutes until the tomatoes have softened slightly. Stir in the parsley and lemon juice and season with salt and pepper to taste. Set aside and keep warm or leave to chill.

5 Barbecue the kabobs on an oiled rack over hot coals for 5–10 minutes, basting and turning frequently. Serve with the tomato relish and slices of focaccia.

COOK'S TIP

The kabobs, baste, and relish can be prepared several hours in advance, avoiding the need for any last minute rush. For a simple meal, serve with crusty fresh bread and a mixed salad.

Beef Rolls in Rich Gravy

Wafer-thin slices of tender beef with a rich garlic and bacon stuffing, flavored with the tang of orange.

NUTRITIONAL INFORMATION

Calories 379	Sugars 4g	
Protein 26g	Fat 24g	
Carbohydrate 4g	Saturates 8g	

SERVES 4

INGREDIENTS

8 thin slices of top round beef

4 tablespoons chopped fresh parsley

4 garlic cloves, chopped finely

4½ ounces smoked bacon, rinded
  and chopped finely

grated rind of ½ small orange

2 tablespoons olive oil

1¼ cups dry red wine

1 bay leaf

1 teaspoon sugar

½ cup pitted black olives, drained

salt and pepper

TO GARNISH

orange slices

chopped fresh parsley

1 Flatten out the beef slices as thinly as possible using a meat tenderizer or mallet. Trim the edges to neaten them.

2 Mix together the parsley, garlic, bacon, orange rind, and salt and pepper to taste. Spread this mixture evenly over each beef slice.

3 Roll up each beef slice tightly, then secure with a toothpick. Heat the oil in a skillet and fry the beef on all sides for 10 minutes.

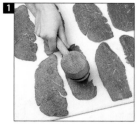

4 Drain the beef rolls, reserving the pan juices, and keep warm. Pour the wine into the juices, add the bay leaf, sugar, and seasoning. Bring to a boil and boil rapidly for 5 minutes to reduce slightly, stirring.

5 Return the cooked beef to the pan along with the black olives and heat

through for a further 2 minutes. Discard the bay leaf and toothpicks.

6 Transfer the beef rolls and gravy to a serving dish, and serve garnished with orange slices and parsley.

Meatballs in Red Wine Sauce

A different twist is given to this traditional pasta dish with a rich but subtle sauce.

NUTRITIONAL INFORMATION

Calories	.811	Sugars	.7g
Protein	.30g	Fat	.43g
Carbohydrate	.76g	Saturates	.12g

45 MINS   1¹/₂ HOURS

SERVES 4

INGREDIENTS

⅔ cup milk

2 cups white bread crumbs

2 tablespoons butter

9 tablespoons olive oil

3 cups sliced
   oyster mushrooms

¼ cup whole wheat flour

1 cup cup beef stock

⅔ cup red wine

4 tomatoes, peeled and chopped

1 tablespoon tomato paste

1 teaspoon brown sugar

1 tablespoon finely chopped fresh basil

12 shallots, chopped

4 cups ground steak

1 teaspoon paprika

1 pound dried egg tagliarini

salt and pepper

fresh basil sprigs, to garnish

1 Pour the milk into a bowl and soak the bread crumbs in the milk for 30 minutes.

2 Heat half of the butter and 4 tablespoons of the oil in a pan. Fry the mushrooms for 4 minutes, then stir in the flour, and cook for 2 minutes. Add the stock and wine and simmer for 15 minutes. Add the tomatoes, tomato paste, sugar, and basil. Season and simmer for 30 minutes.

3 Mix the shallots, steak, and paprika with the bread crumbs and season to taste. Shape the mixture into 14 meatballs.

4 Heat 4 tablespoons of the remaining oil and the remaining butter in a large skillet. Fry the meatballs, turning frequently, until brown all over. Transfer to a deep casserole, pour over the red wine and the mushroom sauce, cover, and bake in a preheated oven, at 350°F, for 30 minutes.

5 Bring a pan of salted water to a boil. Add the pasta and the remaining oil and cook for 8–10 minutes or until tender. Drain and transfer to a serving dish. Remove the casserole from the oven and cool for 3 minutes. Pour the meatballs and sauce onto the pasta, garnish, and serve.

Neapolitan Pork Steaks

An Italian version of broiled pork steaks, this dish is easy to make and delicious to eat.

NUTRITIONAL INFORMATION

Calories	353	Sugars	.........3g
Protein	........39g	Fat	..........20g
Carbohydrate	....4g	Saturates	.......5g

10 MINS   25 MINS

SERVES 4

INGREDIENTS

2 tablespoons olive oil

1 garlic clove, chopped

1 large onion, sliced

14-ounce can tomatoes

4 pork loin steaks, each about 4½ ounces

¾ cup black olives, pitted

2 tablespoons fresh basil, shredded

freshly grated Parmesan cheese, to serve

1 Heat the oil in a large skillet. Add the onions and garlic and cook, stirring, for 3–4 minutes or until they just begin to soften.

2 Add the tomatoes to the skillet and leave to simmer for about 5 minutes or until the sauce starts to thicken.

3 Cook the pork steaks, under a preheated broiler, for 5 minutes on

COOK'S TIP

Parmesan is a mature and exceptionally hard cheese produced in Italy. You only need to add a little as it has a very strong flavor.

both sides, until the the meat is cooked through. Set the pork aside and keep warm.

4 Add the olives and fresh shredded basil to the sauce in the skillet and stir quickly to combine.

5 Transfer the steaks to warm serving plates. Top the steaks with the sauce, sprinkle with freshly grated Parmesan cheese and serve immediately.

Pork Chops with Sage

The fresh taste of sage is the perfect ingredient to counteract the richness of pork.

NUTRITIONAL INFORMATION

Calories 364	Sugars 5g
Protein 34g	Fat 19g
Carbohydrate ...14g	Saturates 7g

 10 MINS   15 MINS

SERVES 4

INGREDIENTS

2 tablespoons flour

1 tablespoon chopped fresh sage or
   1 teaspoon dried

4 lean boneless pork chops, trimmed

2 tablespoons olive oil

1 tablespoon butter

2 red onions, sliced into rings

1 tablespoon lemon juice

2 teaspoons sugar

4 plum tomatoes, quartered

salt and pepper

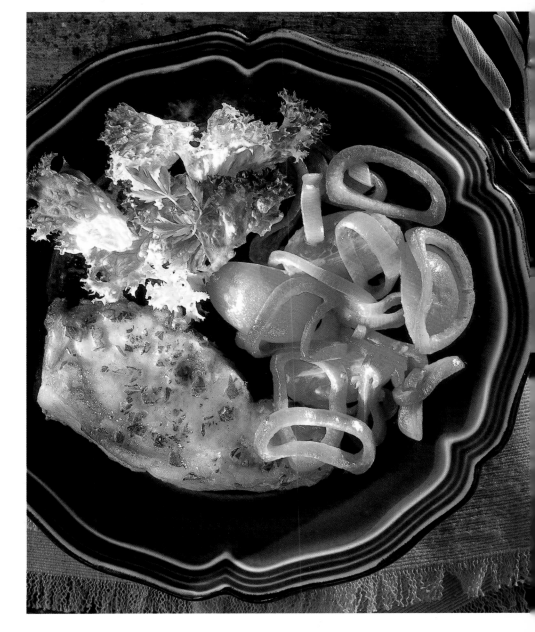

1 Mix the flour, sage, and salt and pepper to taste on a plate. Lightly dust the pork chops on both sides with the seasoned flour.

2 Heat the oil and butter in a skillet, add the chops and cook them for 6–7 minutes on each side until cooked through. Drain the chops, reserving the pan juices, and keep warm.

3 Toss the onion in the lemon juice and fry along with the sugar and tomatoes for 5 minutes until tender.

4 Serve the pork with the tomato and onion mixture and salad greens.

Pork with Fennel & Juniper

The addition of juniper and fennel to the pork chops gives an unusual and delicate flavor to this dish.

NUTRITIONAL INFORMATION

Calories	277	Sugars	.......0.4g
Protein	........32g	Fat	..........16g
Carbohydrate	...0.4g	Saturates	.......5g

2¼ HOURS   15 MINS

SERVES 4

I N G R E D I E N T S

½ fennel bulb

1 tablespoon juniper berries

2 tablespoons olive oil

finely grated rind and juice of 1 orange

4 pork chops, each about 5½ ounces

fresh bread and a crisp salad, to serve

1 Finely chop the fennel bulb, discarding the green parts.

2 Grind the juniper berries in a pestle and mortar. Mix the crushed juniper berries with the fennel flesh, olive oil, and orange rind.

3 Using a sharp knife, score a few cuts all over each chop.

COOK'S TIP

Juniper berries are most commonly associated with gin, but they are often added to meat dishes in Italy for a delicate citrus flavor. They can be bought dried from most health food shops and some larger supermarkets.

4 Place the pork chops in a roasting pan or an ovenproof dish. Spoon the fennel and juniper mixture over the chops.

5 Pour the orange juice over the top of each chop, cover, and marinate in the refrigerator for about 2 hours.

6 Cook the pork chops, under a preheated broiler, for 10–15 minutes, depending on the thickness of the meat, or until the meat is tender and cooked through, turning occasionally.

7 Transfer the pork chops to serving plates and serve with a crisp, fresh salad and plenty of fresh bread to mop up the cooking juices.

Pasta & Pork in Cream Sauce

This unusual and attractive dish is extremely delicious. Make the Italian Red Wine Sauce well in advance to reduce the preparation time.

NUTRITIONAL INFORMATION

Calories 735   Sugars 4g
Protein ....31g   Fat 52g
Carbohydrate ...37g   Saturates 19g

8³/₄ HOURS   35 MINS

SERVES 4

INGREDIENTS

1 pound pork tenderloin,
    thinly sliced

4 tablespoons olive oil

8 ounces mushrooms, sliced

1 cup Italian Red Wine Sauce
    (see page 29)

1 tablespoon lemon juice

pinch of saffron

3 cups dried orecchioni pasta

4 tablespoons heavy cream

12 quail eggs (see Cook's Tip)

salt

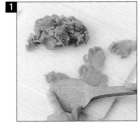

1 Pound the slices of pork between 2 sheets of plastic wrap until wafer thin, then cut into strips.

2 Heat the olive oil in a large skillet, add the pork, and stir-fry for 5 minutes. Add the mushrooms to the pan and stir-fry for a further 2 minutes.

3 Pour over the Italian Red Wine Sauce, lower the heat, and simmer gently for 20 minutes.

4 Meanwhile, bring a large saucepan of lightly salted water to a boil. Add the lemon juice, saffron, and orecchioni and cook for 8–10 minutes, until tender but still firm to the bite. Drain the pasta and keep warm.

5 Stir the cream into the pan with the pork and heat gently for a few minutes.

6 Boil the quail eggs for 3 minutes, cool them in cold water, and remove the shells.

7 Transfer the pasta to a large, warm serving plate, top with the pork, and the sauce and garnish with the eggs. Serve at once.

COOK'S TIP

In this recipe, the quail eggs are soft-cooked. As they are extremely difficult to shell when warm, it is important that they are thoroughly cooled first. Otherwise, they will break up very unattractively.

Pork Cooked in Milk

This traditional dish of boneless pork cooked with garlic and milk can be served hot or cold.

NUTRITIONAL INFORMATION

Calories	.498	Sugars	.15g
Protein	.50g	Fat	.27g
Carbohydrate	.15g	Saturates	.9g

 20 MINS   1³/₄ HOURS

SERVES 4

I N G R E D I E N T S

1 pound 12 ounces leg of pork, boned

1 tablespoon oil

2 tablespoons butter

1 onion, chopped

2 garlic cloves, chopped

½ cup diced pancetta

5 cups milk

1 tablespoon green peppercorns, crushed

2 fresh bay leaves

2 tablespoons marjoram

2 tablespoons thyme

1 Using a sharp knife, remove the fat from the pork. Shape the meat into a neat form, tying it in place with a length of string.

2 Heat the oil and butter in a large pan. Add the onion, garlic, and pancetta to the pan and cook for 2–3 minutes.

3 Add the pork to the pan and cook, turning occasionally, until it is browned all over.

4 Pour over the milk, add the peppercorns, bay leaves, marjoram, and thyme and cook over low heat for 1¼–1½ hours or until tender. Watch the

liquid carefully for the last 15 minutes of cooking time because it tends to reduce very quickly and will then burn. If the liquid reduces and the pork is still not tender, add another ¹/₂ cup milk and continue cooking. Reserve the cooking liquid (as the milk reduces naturally in this dish, it forms a thick and creamy sauce, which curdles slightly but tastes very delicious).

5 Remove the pork from the saucepan. Using a sharp knife, cut the meat into slices. Transfer the pork slices to serving plates and serve immediately with the reserved cooking liquid.

Pork with Lemon & Garlic

This is a simplified version of a traditional dish from the Marche region of Italy. Pork fillet pockets are stuffed with prosciutto and herbs.

NUTRITIONAL INFORMATION

Calories 428   Sugars 2g
Protein . . . . .31g   Fat 32g
Carbohydrate . . . .4g   Saturates 4g

25 MINS   1 HOUR

SERVES 4

INGREDIENTS

1 pound pork fillet

½ cup chopped almonds

2 tablespoons olive oil

3½ ounces raw prosciutto,
   finely chopped

2 garlic cloves, chopped

1 tablespoon fresh oregano, chopped

finely grated rind of 2 lemons

4 shallots, finely chopped

1 cup ham or chicken stock

1 teaspoon sugar

1 Using a sharp knife, cut the pork fillet into 4 equal pieces. Place the pork between sheets of wax paper and pound each piece with a meat mallet or the end of a rolling pin to flatten it.

2 Cut a horizontal slit in each piece of pork to make a pocket.

3 Place the almonds on a cookie sheet. Lightly toast the almonds under a medium hot broiler for 2–3 minutes or until golden.

4 Mix the almonds with 1 tablespoon oil, the prosciutto, garlic, oregano, and the finely grated rind from 1 lemon. Spoon the mixture into the pockets of the pork.

5 Heat the remaining oil in a large skillet. Add the shallots and cook for 2 minutes.

6 Add the pork to the skillet and cook for 2 minutes on each side or until browned all over.

7 Add the ham or chicken stock to the pan, bring to a boil, cover, and leave to simmer for 45 minutes or until the pork is tender. Remove the meat from the pan, set aside and keep warm.

8 Add the lemon rind and sugar to the pan, boil for 3–4 minutes or until reduced and syrupy. Pour the lemon sauce over the pork fillets and serve at once.

Stuffed Cannelloni

Cannelloni, the thick, round pasta tubes, make perfect containers for dense sauces of all kinds.

NUTRITIONAL INFORMATION

Calories	.520	Sugars	.5g
Protein	.21g	Fat	.39g
Carbohydrate	.23g	Saturates	.18g

30 MINS   1¼ HOURS

SERVES 4

INGREDIENTS

8 dried cannelloni tubes

1 tablespoon olive oil

⅓ cup freshly grated
   Parmesan cheese

fresh herb sprigs, to garnish

FILLING

2 tablespoons butter

10½ ounces frozen spinach, thawed
   and chopped

½ cup ricotta cheese

⅓ cup freshly grated Parmesan cheese

¼ cup chopped ham

pinch of freshly grated nutmeg

2 tablespoons heavy cream

2 eggs, lightly beaten

salt and pepper

SAUCE

2 tablespoons butter

¼ cup all-purpose flour

1¼ cups milk

2 bay leaves

pinch of freshly grated nutmeg

1 To make the filling, melt the butter in a pan and stir-fry the spinach for 2–3 minutes. Remove from the heat and stir in the ricotta and Parmesan cheeses and the ham. Season to taste with nutmeg, salt, and pepper. Beat in the cream and eggs to make a thick paste.

2 Bring a pan of lightly salted water to a boil. Add the pasta and the oil and cook for 10–12 minutes, or until almost tender. Drain and set aside to cool.

3 To make the sauce, melt the butter in a pan. Stir in the flour and cook, stirring, for 1 minute. Gradually stir in the milk. Add the bay leaves and simmer, stirring, for 5 minutes. Add the nutmeg and salt and pepper to taste. Remove from the heat and discard the bay leaves.

4 Spoon the filling into a pastry bag and fill the cannelloni.

5 Spoon a little sauce into the base of an ovenproof dish. Arrange the cannelloni in the dish in a single layer and pour over the remaining sauce. Sprinkle over the Parmesan cheese and bake in a preheated oven at 375°F for about 40–45 minutes. Garnish with fresh herb sprigs and serve.

Pork Stuffed with Prosciutto

This sophisticated roast with Mediterranean flavors is ideal served with a pungent olive paste.

NUTRITIONAL INFORMATION

Calories	427	Sugars	.........0g
Protein	........31g	Fat	..........34g
Carbohydrate	...0.2g	Saturates	.......7g

🕐 25 MINS 　 🕐 55 MINS

SERVES 4

INGREDIENTS

1 pound 2 ounces lean pork tenderloin

small bunch fresh of basil leaves

2 tablespoons freshly grated Parmesan

2 tablespoons sun-dried tomato paste

6 thin slices prosciutto

1 tablespoon olive oil

salt and pepper

OLIVE PASTE

¾ cup pitted black olives

4 tablespoons olive oil

2 garlic cloves, peeled

1 Trim away excess fat and membrane from the pork. Slice the pork lengthwise down the middle, taking care not to cut all the way through.

2 Open out the pork and season the inside. Lay the basil leaves down the center. Mix the cheese and sun-dried tomato paste and spread over the basil.

3 Press the pork back together. Wrap the ham around the pork, overlapping, to cover. Place on a rack in a roasting pan, seamside down, and brush with oil. Bake in a preheated oven at 375°F, for about 30–40 minutes depending on thickness until cooked through. Allow to stand for 10 minutes.

4 For the olive paste, place all the ingredients in a blender or food processor and blend until smooth. Alternatively, for a coarser paste, finely chop the olives and garlic and mix with the oil.

5 Drain the cooked pork and slice thinly. Serve with the olive paste and a salad.

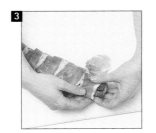

Pot Roasted Leg of Lamb

This dish from the Abruzzi uses a slow-cooking method which ensures that the meat absorbs the flavorings and becomes very tender.

NUTRITIONAL INFORMATION

Calories ....734 Sugars 6g
Protein ....71g Fat .... .42g
Carbohydrate ....7g Saturates 15g

35 MINS   3 HOURS

SERVES 4

INGREDIENTS

3½ pounds leg of lamb

3–4 sprigs fresh rosemary

4½ ounces bacon slices

4 tablespoons olive oil

2–3 garlic cloves, crushed

2 onions, sliced

2 carrots, sliced

2 celery stalks, sliced

1¼ cups dry white wine

1 tablespoon tomato paste

1¼ cups stock

12 ounces tomatoes, peeled, quartered, and deseeded

1 tablespoon chopped fresh parsley

1 tablespoon chopped fresh oregano

salt and pepper

fresh rosemary sprigs, to garnish

1 Wipe the joint of lamb all over, trimming off any excess fat, then season well with salt and pepper, rubbing well in. Lay the sprigs of rosemary over the lamb, cover evenly with the bacon slices, and tie in place with string.

2 Heat the oil in a skillet and fry the lamb for about 10 minutes or until browned all over, turning several times. Remove from the pan.

3 Transfer the oil from the skillet to a large ovenproof casserole and fry the garlic and onion together for 3–4 minutes until beginning to soften. Add the carrots and celery and continue to cook for a few minutes longer.

4 Lay the lamb on top of the vegetables and press down to partly submerge. Pour the wine over the lamb, add the tomato paste, and simmer for about 3–4 minutes. Add the stock, tomatoes, and herbs and seasoning and bring back to a boil for a further 3–4 minutes.

5 Cover the casserole tightly and cook in a moderate oven, 350°F, for 2–2½ hours until very tender.

6 Remove the lamb from the casserole and if preferred, take off the bacon and herbs along with the string. Keep warm. Strain the juices, skimming off any excess fat, and serve in a pitcher. The vegetables may be put around the meat or in a serving dish. Garnish with fresh sprigs of rosemary.

Roman Pan-fried Lamb

Chunks of tender lamb pan-fried with garlic and stewed in red wine are a real Roman dish.

NUTRITIONAL INFORMATION

Calories	299	Sugars	.........1g
Protein	........31g	Fat	..........16g
Carbohydrate	....1g	Saturates	.......7g

 15 MINS   50 MINS

SERVES 4

I N G R E D I E N T S

1 tablespoon oil

1 tablespoon butter

1 pound 5 ounces lamb (shoulder or leg),
  cut into 1-inch chunks

4 garlic cloves, peeled

3 sprigs thyme, stalks removed

6 canned anchovy fillets

⅔ cup red wine

⅔ cup lamb or
  vegetable stock

1 teaspoon sugar

½ cup black olives, pitted and halved

2 tablespoons chopped parsley, to garnish

mashed potato, to serve

1 Heat the oil and butter in a large skillet. Add the lamb and cook for 4–5 minutes, stirring, until the meat is browned all over.

2 Using a pestle and mortar, grind together the garlic, thyme, and anchovies to make a smooth paste.

3 Add the wine and lamb or vegetable stock to the skillet. Stir in the garlic and anchovy paste together with the sugar.

4 Bring the mixture to a boil, reduce the heat, cover, and simmer for 30–40 minutes or until the lamb is tender. For the last 10 minutes of the cooking time, remove the lid to allow the sauce to reduce slightly.

5 Stir the olives into the sauce and mix to combine.

6 Transfer the lamb and the sauce to a serving bowl and garnish. Serve with creamy mashed potatoes.

COOK'S TIP

Rome is the capital of both the region of Lazio and Italy and thus has become a focal point for specialties from all over Italy. Food from this region tends to be fairly simple and quick to prepare, all with plenty of herbs and seasonings, giving really robust flavors.

Pasta & Lamb Loaf

Any dried pasta shapes can be used for this delicious recipe. It has been adapted for microwave cooking for convenience.

NUTRITIONAL INFORMATION

Calories	245	Sugars	.........2g
Protein	........15g	Fat	..........18g
Carbohydrate	....6g	Saturates	.......7g

35 MINS   35 MINS

SERVES 4

I N G R E D I E N T S

1 tablespoon butter

½ small eggplant, diced

½ cup multicolored fusilli

2 teaspoons olive oil

1 cup ground lamb

½ small onion, chopped

½ red bell pepper, chopped

1 garlic clove, crushed

1 teaspoon dried mixed herbs

2 eggs, beaten

2 tablespoons light cream

salt and pepper

TO SERVE

salad

pasta sauce of your choice

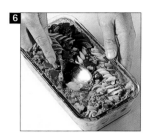

1 Place the butter in a 1 pound loaf pan. Cook on HIGH power for 30 seconds until melted. Brush over the base and sides of the dish.

2 Sprinkle the eggplant with salt, put in a colander, and leave for 20 minutes. Rinse the eggplant well and pat dry with paper towels.

3 Place the pasta in a bowl, add a little salt and enough boiling water to cover by 1 inch. Cover and cook on HIGH power for 8 minutes, stirring halfway through. Leave to stand, covered, for a few minutes.

4 Place the oil, lamb, and onion in a bowl. Cover and cook on HIGH power for 2 minutes.

5 Break up any lumps of meat using a fork. Add the bell pepper, garlic, herbs, and eggplant. Cover and cook on HIGH power for 5 minutes, stirring about halfway through.

6 Drain the pasta and add to the lamb with the eggs and cream. Season well. Turn into the loaf pan and pat down using the back of a spoon.

7 Cook on MEDIUM power for 10 minutes until firm to the touch. Leave to stand for 5 minutes before turning out. Serve in slices with a salad and a pasta sauce.

Lamb Cutlets with Rosemary

A classic combination of flavors, this dish would make a perfect Sunday lunch. Serve with tomato and onion salad and baked potatoes.

NUTRITIONAL INFORMATION

Calories ....560 Sugars 1g
Protein ....48g Fat 40g
Carbohydrate ....1g Saturates 13g

 1¼ HOURS 15 MINS

SERVES 4

INGREDIENTS

8 lamb cutlets

5 tablespoons olive oil

2 tablespoons lemon juice

1 clove garlic, crushed

½ teaspoon lemon pepper

salt

8 sprigs rosemary

jacket potatoes, to serve

SALAD

4 tomatoes, sliced

4 green onions, sliced diagonally

DRESSING

2 tablespoons olive oil

1 tablespoon lemon juice

1 clove garlic, chopped

¼ teaspoon fresh rosemary, chopped finely

1 Trim the lamb chops by cutting away the flesh with a sharp knife to expose the tips of the bones.

2 Place the oil, lemon juice, garlic, lemon pepper, and salt in a shallow, nonmetallic dish and whisk with a fork to combine.

3 Lay the sprigs of rosemary in the dish and place the lamb on top. Leave to marinate for at least 1 hour, turning the lamb cutlets once.

4 Remove the chops from the marinade and wrap a little kitchen foil around the bones to stop them from burning.

5 Place the rosemary sprigs on the rack and place the lamb on top. Barbecue for 10–15 minutes, turning once.

6 Meanwhile make the salad and dressing. Arrange the tomatoes on a serving dish and scatter the green onions on top. Place all the ingredients for the dressing in a screw-top jar, shake well, and pour over the salad. Serve with the lamb cutlets and baked potatoes.

COOK'S TIP

Choose medium to small baking potatoes if you want to cook potatoes on the barbecue. Scrub them well, prick with a fork, and wrap in buttered aluminum foil. Bury them in the hot coals and barbecue for 50–60 minutes.

Lamb with Bay & Lemon

These lamb chops quickly become more elegant when the bone is removed to make noisettes.

NUTRITIONAL INFORMATION

Calories 268	Sugars 0.2g
Protein 24g	Fat 16g
Carbohydrate ...0.2g	Saturates 7g

🥩 10 MINS 🕐 35 MINS

SERVES 4

INGREDIENTS

4 lamb chops

1 tablespoon oil

1 tablespoon butter

⅔ cup white wine

⅔ cup lamb or
    vegetable stock

2 bay leaves

pared rind of 1 lemon

salt and pepper

1 Using a sharp knife, carefully remove the bone from each lamb chop, keeping the meat intact. Alternatively, ask the butcher to prepare the lamb noisettes for you.

2 Shape the meat into rounds and secure with a length of string.

3 In a large skillet, heat together the oil and butter until the mixture starts to froth.

4 Add the lamb noisettes to the skillet and cook for 2–3 minutes on each side or until browned all over.

5 Remove the skillet from the heat, drain off all of the excess fat, and discard.

6 Return the skillet to the heat. Add the wine, stock, bay leaves, and lemon rind to the skillet and cook for about 20–25 minutes or until the lamb is tender. Season the lamb noisettes and sauce to taste with a little salt and pepper.

7 Transfer to serving plates. Remove the string from each noisette and serve with the sauce.

COOK'S TIP

Your local butcher will offer you good advice on how to prepare the lamb noisettes, if you are wary of preparing them yourself.

Lamb with Olives

This is a very simple dish, and the chili adds a bit of spiciness. It is quick to prepare and makes an ideal supper dish.

NUTRITIONAL INFORMATION

Calories	577	Sugars	.........1g
Protein	........62g	Fat	..........33g
Carbohydrate	....1g	Saturates	......10g

15 MINS   1½ HOURS

SERVES 4

I N G R E D I E N T S

2¾ pounds boned leg of lamb

⅓ cup olive oil

2 garlic cloves, crushed

1 onion, sliced

1 small red chili, cored, deseeded, and
    chopped finely

¾ cup dry white wine

1½ cups pitted black olives

salt

chopped fresh parsley, to garnish

1 Using a sharp knife, cut the lamb into
1-inch cubes.

2 Heat the oil in a skillet and fry the
garlic, onion, and chili for 5 minutes.

3 Add the meat and wine and cook for a
further 5 minutes.

4 Stir in the olives, then transfer the
mixture to a casserole. Place in a
preheated oven, 350°F, and cook for
1 hour 20 minutes or until the meat is
tender. Season with salt to taste, and
serve garnished with a little chopped
fresh parsley.

Eggplant Cake

Layers of toasty-brown eggplant, meat sauce, and cheese-flavored pasta make this a popular family supper dish.

NUTRITIONAL INFORMATION

Calories	.859	Sugars	.39g
Protein	.36g	Fat	.58g
Carbohydrate	.51g	Saturates	.19g

1½ HOURS   1½ HOURS

SERVES 4

I N G R E D I E N T S

1 eggplant, thinly sliced

5 tablespoons olive oil

2 cups dried fusilli

2½ cups Béchamel Sauce (see page 28)

¾ cup grated Cheddar cheese

butter, for greasing

⅓ cup freshly grated
    Parmesan cheese

salt and pepper

L A M B   S A U C E

2 tablespoons olive oil

1 large onion, sliced

2 celery stalks,
    thinly sliced

1 pound ground lamb

3 tablespoons tomato paste

5½ ounces bottled sun-dried
    tomatoes, drained and chopped

1 teaspoon dried oregano

1 tablespoon red wine vinegar

⅔ cup chicken stock

salt and pepper

1 Put the eggplant slices in a colander, sprinkle with salt, and set aside for 45 minutes.

2 To make the lamb sauce, heat the oil in a pan. Fry the onion and celery for 3–4 minutes. Add the lamb and fry, stirring frequently, until browned. Stir in the remaining sauce ingredients, bring to a boil, and cook for 20 minutes.

3 Rinse the eggplant slices, drain and pat dry. Heat 4 tablespoons of the oil in a skillet. Fry the eggplant slices for about 4 minutes on each side. Remove from the pan and drain well.

4 Bring a large pan of lightly salted water to a boil. Add the fusilli and the remaining oil and cook for about 8–10 minutes until almost tender, but still firm to the bite. Drain well.

5 Gently heat the Béchamel Sauce, stirring constantly. Stir in the Cheddar cheese. Stir half of the cheese sauce into the fusilli.

6 Make layers of fusilli, lamb sauce, and eggplant slices in a greased dish. Spread the remaining cheese sauce over the top. Sprinkle over the Parmesan and bake in a preheated oven, at 375°F, for 25 minutes. Serve hot or cold.

Barbecued Butterfly Lamb

The appearance of the lamb as it is opened out to cook on the barbecue gives this dish its name. Marinate the lamb in advance if possible.

NUTRITIONAL INFORMATION

Calories	733	Sugars	.........6g
Protein	........69g	Fat	..........48g
Carbohydrate	....6g	Saturates	......13g

6¼ HOURS   1 HOUR

SERVES 4

I N G R E D I E N T S

boned leg of lamb, about 4 pounds

8 tablespoons balsamic vinegar

grated rind and juice of 1 lemon

⅔ cup sunflower oil

4 tablespoons chopped, fresh mint

2 cloves garlic, crushed

2 tablespoons brown sugar

salt and pepper

T O   S E R V E

broiled vegetables

salad greens

1 Open out the boned leg of lamb so that its shape resembles a butterfly. Thread 2–3 skewers through the meat in order to make it easier to turn on the barbecue.

2 Combine the balsamic vinegar, lemon rind and juice, oil, mint, garlic, sugar, and salt and pepper to taste in a nonmetallic dish that is large enough to hold the lamb.

3 Place the lamb in the dish and turn it over a few times so that the meat is coated on both sides with the marinade. Leave to marinate for at least 6 hours or preferably overnight, turning occasionally.

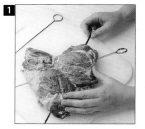  

4 Remove the lamb from the marinade and reserve the liquid for basting.

5 Place the rack about 6 inches above the coals and barbecue the lamb for about 30 minutes on each side, turning once and basting frequently with the marinade.

6 Transfer the lamb to a chopping board and remove the skewers. Cut the lamb into slices across the grain and serve.

COOK'S TIP

If you prefer, cook the lamb for half the cooking time in a preheated oven at 350°F, then finish off on the barbecue.

Saltimbocca

The Italian name for this dish, *saltimbocca*, means "jump into the mouth". The stuffed rolls are quick and easy to make and taste delicious.

NUTRITIONAL INFORMATION

Calories	303	Sugars 0.3g
Protein	........29g	Fat 17g
Carbohydrate	....1g	Saturates 1g

15 MINS   20 MINS

SERVES 4

I N G R E D I E N T S

4 turkey fillets or 4 veal escalopes, about
  1 pound in total

3½ ounces prosciutto

8 sage leaves

1 tablespoon olive oil

1 onion, finely chopped

1 cup cup white wine

1 cup chicken stock

1   Place the turkey or veal between sheets of waxed paper. Pound the meat with a meat mallet or the end of a rolling pin to flatten it slightly. Cut each escalope in half.

2   Trim the prosciutto to fit each piece of turkey or veal and place over the meat. Lay a sage leaf on top. Roll up the escalopes and secure with a toothpick.

3   Heat the oil in a heavy-based skillet and cook the onion for 3–4 minutes. Add the turkey or veal rolls to the skillet and cook for 5 minutes until they are browned all over.

4   Pour the white wine and chicken stock into the pan and leave to simmer for 15 minutes if using turkey, and 20 minutes if using veal, or until tender. Serve at once.

VARIATION

Try a similar recipe called *bocconcini*, meaning "little mouthfuls". Follow the same method as given here, but replace the sage leaf with a piece of Swiss cheese.

Veal in a Rose Petal Sauce

This truly spectacular dish is equally delicious whether you use veal or pork tenderloin. Make sure the roses are free of blemishes.

NUTRITIONAL INFORMATION

Calories 810   Sugars 2g
Protein . . . . .31g   Fat 56g
Carbohydrate . . .49g   Saturates 28g

 10 MINS   35 MINS

SERVES 4

I N G R E D I E N T S

1 pound dried fettuccine

7 tablespoons olive oil

1 teaspoon chopped fresh oregano

1 teaspoon chopped
   fresh marjoram

¾ cup butter

1 pound veal fillet, thinly sliced

⅔ cup rose petal vinegar
   (see Cook's Tip)

⅔ cup fish stock

¼ cup grapefruit juice

¼ cup heavy cream

salt

TO GARNISH

12 pink grapefruit segments

12 pink peppercorns

rose petals

fresh herb leaves

1 Bring a large saucepan of lightly salted water to a boil. Add the fettuccine and 1 tablespoon of the oil and cook for 8–10 minutes or until tender, but still firm to the bite. Drain and transfer to a warm serving dish, sprinkle over 2 tablespoons of the olive oil, the oregano, and marjoram.

2 Heat 4 tablespoons of the butter with the remaining oil in a large skillet. Add the veal and cook over low heat for 6 minutes. Remove the veal from the pan and place on top of the pasta.

3 Add the vinegar and fish stock to the skillet and bring to a boil. Boil vigorously until reduced by two-thirds. Add the grapefruit juice and cream and simmer over low heat for 4 minutes. Dice the remaining butter and add to the pan, one piece at a time, whisking constantly until it has been completely incorporated.

4 Pour the sauce around the veal, garnish with grapefruit segments, pink peppercorns, the rose petals (washed), and your favorite herb leaves.

COOK'S TIP

To make rose petal vinegar, infuse the petals of 8 pesticide-free roses in ⅔ cup white wine vinegar for 48 hours. Prepare well in advance to reduce the preparation time.

Vitello Tonnato

Veal dishes are the specialty of Lombardy, with this dish being one of the more sophisticated. Serve cold with seasonal salads.

NUTRITIONAL INFORMATION

Calories 654   Sugars 1g
Protein ....49g   Fat 47g
Carbohydrate ....1g   Saturates 8g

30 MINS   1¼ HOURS

SERVES 4

I N G R E D I E N T S

1 pound 10 ounces boned leg of veal, rolled

2 bay leaves

10 black peppercorns

2–3 cloves

½ teaspoon salt

2 carrots, sliced

1 onion, sliced

2 celery stalks, sliced

3 cups stock or water

⅔ cup dry white wine (optional)

3 ounces canned tuna, well drained

1½ ounces canned anchovy fillets, drained

⅔ cup olive oil

2 teaspoon bottled capers, drained

2 egg yolks

1 tablespoon lemon juice

salt and pepper

T O   G A R N I S H

capers

lemon wedges

fresh herbs

1 Put the veal in a saucepan with the bay leaves, peppercorns, cloves, salt, and vegetables. Add sufficient stock or water and the wine (if using) to barely cover the veal. Bring to a boil, remove any scum from the surface, then cover the pan, and simmer gently for about 1 hour or until tender. Leave in the water until cold, then drain thoroughly. If time allows, chill the veal to make it easier to carve.

2 For the tuna sauce: thoroughly mash the tuna with 4 anchovy fillets, 1 tablespoon of oil, and the capers. Add the egg yolks and press through a strainer or purée in a food processor or blender until smooth.

3 Stir in the lemon juice then gradually whisk in the rest of the oil a few drops at a time until the sauce is smooth and has the consistency of thick cream. Season with salt and pepper to taste.

4 Slice the veal thinly and arrange on a platter in overlapping slices. Spoon the sauce over the veal to cover. Then cover the dish and chill overnight.

5 Before serving, uncover the veal carefully. Arrange the remaining anchovy fillets and the capers in a decorative pattern on top, and then garnish with lemon wedges and sprigs of fresh herbs.

Neapolitan Veal Cutlets

The delicious combination of apple, onion, and mushrooms perfectly complements the delicate flavor of veal.

NUTRITIONAL INFORMATION

Calories	1071	Sugars	........13g
Protein	........74g	Fat	..........59g
Carbohydrate	...66g	Saturates	......16g

🍳 20 MINS   🕐 45 MINS

SERVES 4

I N G R E D I E N T S

2 cups butter

9 ounces veal cutlets, trimmed

1 large onion, sliced

2 apples, peeled, cored, and sliced

6 ounces mushrooms

1 tablespoon chopped fresh tarragon

8 black peppercorns

1 tablespoon sesame seeds

14 ounces dried marille pasta

½ cup extra virgin olive oil

¾ cup mascarpone cheese,
    broken into small pieces

2 large tomatoes, cut in half

leaves of 1 fresh basil sprig

salt and pepper

fresh basil leaves, to garnish

1 Melt 4 tablespoons of the butter in a skillet. Fry the veal over low heat for 5 minutes on each side. Transfer to a dish and keep warm.

2 Fry the onion and apples until lightly browned. Transfer to a dish, place the veal on top, and keep warm.

3 Melt the remaining butter in the skillet. Gently fry the mushrooms, tarragon, and peppercorns over low heat for 3 minutes. Sprinkle over the sesame seeds.

4 Bring a pan of salted water to a boil. Add the pasta and 1 tablespoon of oil. Cook for 8–10 minutes or until tender, but still firm . Drain and transfer to a plate.

5 Broil or fry the tomatoes and basil for 2–3 minutes.

6 Top the pasta with the mascarpone cheese and sprinkle over the remaining olive oil. Place the onions, apples and veal cutlets on top of the pasta. Spoon the mushrooms, peppercorns, and pan juices onto the cutlets, place the tomatoes and basil leaves around the edge, and place in a preheated oven at 300°F for 5 minutes.

7 Season to taste with salt and pepper, garnish with fresh basil leaves, and serve at once.

Veal Italienne

This dish is really superb if made with tender veal. However, if veal is unavailable, use pork or turkey escalopes instead.

NUTRITIONAL INFORMATION

Calories	592	Sugars	.........5g
Protein	........44g	Fat	..........23g
Carbohydrate	...48g	Saturates	.......9g

25 MINS   1 HR 20 MINS

SERVES 4

INGREDIENTS

¼ cup butter

1 tablespoon olive oil

1½ pounds potatoes, cubed

4 veal escalopes, weighing 6 ounces each

1 onion, cut into 8 wedges

2 garlic cloves, crushed

2 tablespoons all-purpose flour

2 tablespoons tomato paste

⅔ cup red wine

1¼ cups chicken stock

8 ripe tomatoes, peeled, deseeded, and diced

¼ cup pitted black olives, halved

2 tablespoons chopped fresh basil

salt and pepper

fresh basil leaves, to garnish

1 Heat the butter and oil in a large skillet. Add the potato cubes and cook for 5–7 minutes, stirring frequently, until they begin to brown.

2 Remove the potatoes from the skillet with a perforated spoon and set aside.

3 Place the veal in the skillet and cook for 2–3 minutes on each side until sealed. Remove from the skillet and set aside.

4 Stir the onion and garlic into the skillet and cook for 2–3 minutes.

5 Add the flour and tomato paste and cook for 1 minute, stirring. Gradually blend in the red wine and chicken stock, stirring to make a smooth sauce.

6 Return the potatoes and veal to the skillet. Stir in the tomatoes, olives, and chopped basil and season with salt and pepper.

7 Transfer to a casserole dish and cook in a preheated oven, 350°F, for 1 hour or until the potatoes and veal are cooked through. Garnish with basil leaves and serve.

COOK'S TIP

For a quicker cooking time and really tender meat, pound the meat with a meat mallet to flatten it slightly before cooking.

Escalopes & Italian Sausage

Anchovies are often used to enhance flavor, particularly in meat dishes. Either veal or turkey escalopes can be used for this pan-fried dish.

NUTRITIONAL INFORMATION

Calories ....233 Sugars 1g
Protein ....28g Fat 13g
Carbohydrate ....1g Saturates 1g

 10 MINS   20 MINS

SERVES 4

INGREDIENTS

1 tablespoon olive oil

6 canned anchovy fillets, drained

1 tablespoon capers, drained

1 tablespoon fresh rosemary

finely grated rind and juice of 1 orange

2¾ ounces Italian sausage, diced

3 tomatoes, peeled and chopped

4 turkey or veal escalopes, each about
   4½ ounces

salt and pepper

crusty bread or cooked polenta, to serve

1 Heat the oil in a large skillet. Add the anchovies, capers, fresh rosemary, orange rind and juice, Italian sausage, and tomatoes to the pan and cook for 5–6 minutes, stirring occasionally.

2 Meanwhile, place the turkey or veal escalopes between sheets of wax paper. Pound the meat with a meat mallet or the end of a rolling pin to flatten it.

3 Add the meat to the mixture in the skillet. Season to taste with salt and pepper, cover, and cook for 3–5 minutes on each side, slightly longer if the meat is thicker.

4 Transfer to serving plates and serve with fresh crusty bread or cooked polenta, if you prefer.

VARIATION

Try using 4-minute steaks, slightly flattened, instead of the turkey or veal. Cook them for 4–5 minutes on top of the sauce in the pan.

Sausage & Bean Casserole

In this traditional Tuscan dish, Italian sausages are cooked with cannellini beans and tomatoes.

NUTRITIONAL INFORMATION

Calories 609	Sugars 7g
Protein 27g	Fat 47g
Carbohydrate ...20g	Saturates 16g

 15 MINS   🕐 35 MINS

SERVES 4

INGREDIENTS

8 Italian sausages

1 tablespoon olive oil

1 large onion, chopped

2 garlic cloves, chopped

1 green bell pepper

8 ounces fresh tomatoes, peeled and
   chopped or 14-ounce can tomatoes,
   chopped

2 tablespoons sun-dried tomato paste

14-ounce can cannellini beans

mashed potato or rice, to serve

1 Using a sharp knife, deseed the bell pepper and cut it into thin strips.

2 Prick the Italian sausages all over with a fork. Cook the sausages, under a preheated broiler, for 10–12 minutes, turning occasionally, until brown all over. Set aside and keep warm.

3 Heat the oil in a large skillet. Add the onion, garlic, and bell pepper to the skillet and cook for 5 minutes, stirring occasionally, or until softened.

4 Add the tomatoes to the skillet and leave the mixture to simmer for about 5 minutes, stirring occasionally, or until slightly reduced and thickened.

5 Stir the sun-dried tomato paste, cannellini beans, and Italian sausages into the mixture in the skillet. Cook for 4–5 minutes or until the mixture is piping hot. Add 4–5 tablespoons of water, if the mixture becomes too dry during cooking.

6 Transfer the Italian sausage and bean casserole to serving plates and serve with mashed potatoes or cooked rice.

COOK'S TIP

Italian sausages are coarse in texture and have quite a strong flavor. They can be bought in speciality sausage shops, Italian delicatessens, and some larger supermarkets. They are replaceable in this recipe only by game sausages.

Liver with Wine Sauce

Liver is popular in Italy and is served in many ways. Tender calf's liver is the best type to use for this recipe, but you could use lamb's liver.

NUTRITIONAL INFORMATION

Calories 435	Sugars 2g	
Protein 30g	Fat 31g	
Carbohydrate 4g	Saturates 12g	

 25 MINS   🕐 20 MINS

SERVES 4

INGREDIENTS

4 slices calf's liver or 8 slices lamb's liver, about 1 pound 2 ounces

flour, for coating

1 tablespoon olive oil

2 tablespoons butter

4½ ounces lean bacon slices, rinded and cut into narrow strips

1 garlic clove, crushed

1 onion, chopped

1 celery stalk, sliced thinly

⅔ cup red wine

⅔ cup beef stock

pinch of ground allspice

1 teaspoon Worcestershire sauce

1 teaspoon chopped fresh sage or ½ teaspoon dried sage

3–4 tomatoes, peeled, quartered, and deseeded

salt and pepper

fresh sage leaves, to garnish

new potatoes or pan-fried potatoes, to serve

1 Wipe the liver with paper towels, season with salt and pepper to taste, and then coat lightly in flour, shaking off any excess.

2 Heat the oil and butter in a pan and fry the liver until well sealed on both sides and just cooked through—take care not to overcook. Remove the liver from the pan, cover, and keep warm, but do not allow to dry out.

3 Add the bacon to the fat left in the pan, with the garlic, onion and celery. Fry gently until soft.

4 Add the red wine, beef stock, allspice, Worcestershire sauce, sage, and salt and pepper to taste. Bring to a boil and simmer for 3–4 minutes.

5 Cut each tomato segment in half. Add to the sauce and continue to cook for 2–3 minutes.

6 Serve the liver on a little of the sauce, with the remainder spooned over. Garnish with fresh sage leaves and serve with tiny new potatoes or pan-fried potatoes.

Poultry & Game

Poultry dishes provide some of Italy's finest food. Every part of the chicken is used, including the feet and innards for making soup. Spit-roasted chicken, flavored strongly

with aromatic rosemary, has become almost a national dish. Turkey, capon, duck, goose, and guinea fowl are also popular, as is game. Wild rabbit, hare, wild boar, and deer are available, especially in Sardinia. This chapter contains a superb collection of mouthwatering recipes. You will be astonished at how quickly and easily you can prepare some of these gourmet dishes.

Italian Chicken Spirals

These little foil parcels retain all the natural juices of the chicken while cooking conveniently over the pasta while it boils.

NUTRITIONAL INFORMATION

Calories 367	Sugars 1g
Protein 33g	Fat 12g
Carbohydrate ...35g	Saturates 2g

20 MINS   20 MINS

SERVES 4

I N G R E D I E N T S

4 skinless, boneless chicken breasts

1 cup fresh basil leaves

2 tablespoons hazelnuts

1 garlic clove, crushed

2 cups whole wheat pasta spirals

1 tablespoon lemon juice

1 tablespoon olive oil

1 tablespoon capers

2 sun-dried tomatoes, diced

½ cup black olives

1 Beat the chicken breasts with a rolling pin to flatten evenly.

2 Place the basil and hazelnuts in a food processor and process until finely chopped. Mix with the garlic and salt and pepper to taste.

3 Spread the basil mixture over the chicken breasts and roll up from one short end to enclose the filling. Wrap the chicken roll tightly in foil so that they hold their shape, then seal the ends well.

4 Bring a pan of salted water to a boil and cook the pasta for 8–10 minutes until tender, but firm to the bite. Place the chicken parcels in a steamer set over the pan in which the pasta is cooking, cover , and steam for 10 minutes.

5 Drain the pasta and return to the pan with the lemon juice, olive oil, tomatoes, capers, and olives. Heat through.

6 Pierce the chicken with a skewer to make sure that the juices run clear and not pink (this shows that the chicken is cooked through). Slice the chicken, arrange over the pasta and serve.

COOK'S TIP

Sun-dried tomatoes have a wonderful, rich flavor but if they're unavailable, use fresh tomatoes instead.

Chicken Marengo

Napoleon's chef was ordered to cook a sumptuous meal on the eve of the battle of Marengo—this feast of flavors was the result.

NUTRITIONAL INFORMATION

Calories	521	Sugars	.........6g
Protein	........47g	Fat	..........19g
Carbohydrate	...34g	Saturates	.......8g

🥘 20 MINS   🕐 50 MINS

SERVES 4

I N G R E D I E N T S

2 tablespoon olive oil

8 chicken pieces

10½ oz sieved tomatoes

1 cup white wine

2 teaspoon dried mixed herbs

8 slices white bread

3 tablespoons butter, melted

2 garlic cloves, crushed

3½ oz mixed mushrooms
(such as button, oyster and porcini)

½ cup black olives, chopped

1 teaspoon sugar

fresh basil, to garnish

1 Using a sharp knife, remove the bone from each of the chicken pieces.

2 Heat 1 tbsp of oil in a large skillet. Add the chicken pieces and cook for 4–5 minutes, turning occasionally, or until browned all over.

3 Add the sieved tomatoes, wine, and mixed herbs to the skillet. Bring to a boil and then leave to simmer for 30 minutes or until the chicken is tender and the juices run clear when a skewer is inserted into the thickest part of the meat.

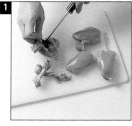  

4 Mix the melted butter and crushed garlic together. Lightly toast the slices of bread and brush with the garlic butter.

5 Add the remaining oil to a separate skillet and cook the mushrooms for 2–3 minutes or until just browned.

6 Add the olives and sugar to the chicken mixture and warm through.

7 Transfer the chicken and sauce to serving plates. Serve with the bruschetta (fried bread) and fried mushrooms.

Mustard Baked Chicken

Chicken pieces are cooked in a succulent, mild mustard sauce, then coated in poppy seeds and served on a bed of fresh pasta shells.

NUTRITIONAL INFORMATION

Calories	652	Sugars	........5g
Protein	........51g	Fat	..........31g
Carbohydrate	...46g	Saturates	......12g

10 MINS   35 MINS

SERVES 4

I N G R E D I E N T S

8 chicken pieces (about 4 ounces each)

4 tablespoons butter, melted

4 tablespoons mild mustard (see Cook's Tip)

2 tablespoons lemon juice

1 tablespoon brown sugar

1 teaspoon paprika

3 tablespoons poppy seeds

14 ounces fresh pasta shells

1 tablespoon olive oil

salt and pepper

1 Arrange the chicken pieces in a single layer in a large ovenproof dish.

2 Mix together the butter, mustard, lemon juice, sugar, and paprika in a bowl and season with salt and pepper to taste. Brush the mixture over the upper

COOK'S TIP

Dijon is the type of mustard most often used in cooking, as it has a clean and only mildly spicy flavor. German mustard has a sweet-sour taste, with Bavarian mustard being slightly sweeter.

surfaces of the chicken pieces and bake in a preheated oven at 400°F for 15 minutes.

3 Remove the dish from the oven and carefully turn over the chicken pieces. Coat the upper surfaces of the chicken with the remaining mustard mixture, sprinkle the chicken pieces with poppy seeds, and return to the oven for a further 15 minutes.

4 Meanwhile, bring a large saucepan of lightly salted water to a boil. Add the pasta shells and olive oil and cook for 8–10 minutes or until tender, but still firm to the bite.

5 Drain the pasta thoroughly and arrange on a warm serving dish. Top the pasta with the chicken, pour over the sauce, and serve at once.

Pan-Cooked Chicken

Artichokes are a familiar ingredient in Italian cookery. In this dish, they are used to delicately flavor chicken.

NUTRITIONAL INFORMATION

Calories	296	Sugars	........2g
Protein	........27g	Fat	..........15g
Carbohydrate	....7g	Saturates	.......6g

🍗 🍗 🍗

15 MINS • 55 MINS

SERVES 4

I N G R E D I E N T S

4 chicken breasts, part boned

2 tablespoons butter

2 tablespoons olive oil

2 red onions, cut into wedges

2 tablespoons lemon juice

⅔ cup dry white wine

⅔ cup chicken stock

2 teaspoons all-purpose flour

14-ounce can artichoke halves,
    drained and halved

salt and pepper

chopped fresh parsley, to garnish

1 Season the chicken with salt and pepper to taste. Heat the oil and 1 tablespoon of the butter in a large skillet. Add the chicken and fry for 4–5 minutes on each side until lightly golden. Remove from the skillet using a slotted spoon.

2 Toss the onion in the lemon juice, and add to the skillet. Gently fry, stirring, for 3–4 minutes until just beginning to soften.

3 Return the chicken to the pan. Pour in the wine and stock, bring to a boil, cover, and simmer gently for 30 minutes.

4 Remove the chicken from the skillet, reserving the cooking juices, and keep warm. Bring the juices to a boil, and boil rapidly for 5 minutes.

5 Blend the remaining butter with the flour to form a smooth paste. Reduce the juices to a simmer and spoon the paste into the skillet, stirring until thickened and fully incorporated.

6 Adjust the seasoning according to taste, stir in the artichoke hearts, and cook for a further 2 minutes. Pour the mixture over the chicken and garnish with chopped parsley.

Boned Chicken & Parmesan

It's really very easy to bone a whole chicken, but if you prefer, you can ask your butcher to do this for you.

NUTRITIONAL INFORMATION

Calories ....578 Sugars 0.4g
Protein ....42g Fat 42g
Carbohydrate ....9g Saturates 15g

35 MINS   1¹/₂ HOURS

SERVES 6

I N G R E D I E N T S

1 chicken, weighing about 5 pounds

8 slices mortadella or salami

2 cups fresh white or
  brown bread crumbs

1 cup freshly grated
  Parmesan cheese

2 garlic cloves, crushed

6 tablespoons chopped fresh basil or

parsley

1 egg, beaten

pepper

fresh spring vegetables, to serve

1 Bone the chicken, keeping the skin intact. Dislocate each leg by breaking it at the thigh joint. Cut down each side of the backbone, taking care not to pierce the breast skin.

VARIATION

Replace the mortadella with slices of bacon, if preferred.

2 Pull the backbone clear of the flesh and discard. Remove the ribs, severing any attached flesh with a sharp knife.

3 Scrape the flesh from each leg and cut away the bone at the joint with a knife or shears.

4 Use the bones for stock. Lay out the boned chicken on a board, skin side down. Arrange the mortadella slices over the chicken, overlapping slightly.

5 Put the bread crumbs, Parmesan, garlic, and basil or parsley in a bowl.

Season with pepper to taste, and mix together well. Stir in the beaten egg to bind the mixture together. Spoon the mixture down the middle of the boned chicken, roll the meat around it and then tie securely with string.

6 Place in a roasting pan and brush lightly with olive oil. Roast in a preheated oven, 400°F, for 1¹/₂ hours or until the juices run clear when pierced.

7 Serve hot or cold, in slices, with fresh spring vegetables.

Chicken Cacciatora

This is a popular Italian classic in which browned chicken quarters are cooked in a tomato and bell pepper sauce.

NUTRITIONAL INFORMATION

Calories	397	Sugars	.........4g
Protein	........37g	Fat	..........17g
Carbohydrate	...22g	Saturates	.......4g

 20 MINS   1 HOUR

SERVES 4

I N G R E D I E N T S

1 roasting chicken, about 3 pound
   5 ounces, cut into 6 or 8 serving pieces

1 cup all-purpose flour

3 tablespoons olive oil

⅔ cup dry white wine

1 green bell pepper, deseeded and sliced

1 red bell pepper, deseeded and sliced

1 carrot, chopped finely

1 celery stalk, chopped finely

1 garlic clove, crushed

7-ounce can diced tomatoes

salt and pepper

1 Rinse and pat dry the chicken pieces with paper towels. Lightly dust them with seasoned flour.

2 Heat the oil in a large skillet. Add the chicken and fry over medium heat until browned all over. Remove from the pan and set aside.

3 Drain off all but 2 tablespoons of the fat in the pan. Add the wine and stir for a few minutes. Then add the bell peppers, carrots, celery, and garlic, season with salt and pepper to taste, and simmer together for about 15 minutes.

4 Add the diced tomatoes to the pan. Cover and simmer for 30 minutes, stirring often, until the chicken is completely cooked through.

5 Check the seasoning before serving piping hot.

Chicken Lasagne

You can use your favorite mushrooms, such as chanterelles or oyster mushrooms, for this delicately flavored dish.

NUTRITIONAL INFORMATION

Calories	708	Sugars	17g
Protein	35g	Fat	35g
Carbohydrate	57g	Saturates	14g

40 MINS   1³/₄ HOURS

SERVES 4

INGREDIENTS

butter, for greasing

14 sheets pre-cooked lasagne

3¾ cups Béchamel Sauce (see page 28)

1 cup grated Parmesan cheese

EXOTIC MUSHROOM SAUCE

2 tablespoons olive oil

2 garlic cloves, crushed

1 large onion, finely chopped

8 ounces exotic mushrooms, sliced

2½ cups minced ground chicken

3 ounces chicken livers,
    finely chopped

4 ounces prosciutto, diced

²/₃ cup Marsala

10-ounce can diced tomatoes

1 tablespoon chopped fresh
    basil leaves

2 tablespoons tomato paste

salt and pepper

1 To make the chicken and exotic mushroom sauce, heat the olive oil in a large saucepan. Add the garlic, onion, and mushrooms and cook, stirring frequently, for 6 minutes.

2 Add the ground chicken, chicken livers, and prosciutto and cook over low heat for 12 minutes, or until the meat has browned.

3 Stir the Marsala, tomatoes, basil, and tomato paste into the mixture in the pan and cook for 4 minutes. Season with salt and pepper to taste, cover, and leave to simmer for 30 minutes. Uncover the pan, stir, and leave to simmer for a further 15 minutes.

4 Lightly grease an ovenproof dish with butter. Arrange sheets of lasagne over the base of the dish, spoon over a layer of exotic mushroom sauce, then spoon over a layer of Béchamel Sauce. Place another layer of lasagne on top and repeat the process twice, finishing with a layer of Béchamel Sauce. Sprinkle over the grated cheese and bake in a preheated oven at 375°F for 35 minutes until golden brown and bubbling. Serve at once.

Barbecued Chicken

You need a bit of brute force to prepare the chicken, but once marinated it's an easy and tasty candidate for the barbecue.

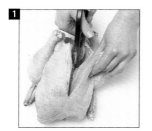
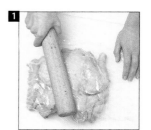
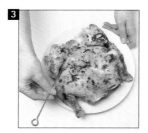

NUTRITIONAL INFORMATION

Calories 129	Sugars 0g	
Protein 22g	Fat 5g	
Carbohydrate 0g	Saturates 1g	

2¹/₂ HOURS   30 MINS

SERVES 4

I N G R E D I E N T S

3 pounds 5 ounces chicken

grated rind of 1 lemon

4 tablespoons lemon juice

2 sprigs rosemary

1 small red chili, chopped finely

²/₃ cup olive oil

1 Split the chicken down the breast bone and open it out. Trim off excess fat, and remove the parson's nose, wings, and leg tips. Break the leg and wing joints to enable you to pound it flat. This ensures that it cooks evenly. Cover the split chicken with plastic wrap and pound it as flat as possible with a rolling pin.

2 Mix the lemon rind and juice, rosemary sprigs, chili, and olive oil together in a small bowl. Place the chicken in a large dish and pour over the marinade, turning the chicken to coat it evenly. Cover the dish and leave the chicken to marinate for at least 2 hours.

3 Cook the chicken over a hot barbecue (the coals should be white, and red when fanned) for about 30 minutes, turning it regularly until the skin is golden and crisp. To test if it is cooked, pierce one of the chicken thighs; the juices will run clear, not pink, when it is ready. Serve.

Broiled Chicken

This Italian-style dish is richly flavored with pesto, which is a mixture of basil, olive oil, pine nuts, and Parmesan cheese.

NUTRITIONAL INFORMATION

Calories	787	Sugars	.........6g
Protein	........45g	Fat	..........38g
Carbohydrate	...70g	Saturates	.......9g

10 MINS   25 MINS

SERVES 4

I N G R E D I E N T S

8 part-boned chicken thighs

olive oil, for brushing

1⅔ cups sieved tomatoes

½ cup green or
   red pesto sauce

12 slices French bread

1 cup freshly grated
   Parmesan cheese

½ cup pine nuts or
   slivered almonds

salad greens,
   to serve

1 Arrange the chicken in a single layer in a wide flameproof dish and brush lightly with oil. Place under a preheated broiler for about 15 minutes, turning occasionally, until golden brown.

COOK'S TIP

Although leaving the skin on the chicken means that it will have a higher fat content, many people like the rich taste and crispy skin especially when it is blackened by the barbecue. The skin also keeps in the cooking juices.

2 Pierce the chicken with a skewer to test if it is cooked through—the juices will run clear, not pink, when it is ready.

3 Pour off any excess fat. Warm the sieved tomatoes and half the pesto sauce in a small pan and pour over the chicken, broil for a few more minutes, turning until coated.

4 Meanwhile, spread the remaining pesto onto the slices of bread. Arrange the bread over the chicken and sprinkle with the Parmesan cheese. Scatter the pine nuts over the cheese, broil for 2–3 minutes, or until browned and bubbling. Serve with salad greens.

Chicken with Green Olives

Olives are a popular flavoring for poultry and game in the Apulia region of Italy, where this recipe originates.

NUTRITIONAL INFORMATION

Calories	614	Sugars	.........6g
Protein	........34g	Fat	..........30g
Carbohydrate	...49g	Saturates	......11g

🍖 15 MINS   🕐 1½ HOURS

SERVES 4

I N G R E D I E N T S

3 tablespoons olive oil

2 tablespoons butter

4 chicken breasts, part boned

1 large onion, finely chopped

2 garlic cloves, crushed

2 red, yellow, or green bell peppers, cored,
    deseeded, and cut into large pieces

9 ounces mushrooms, sliced
    or quartered

6 ounces tomatoes, peeled and halved

⅔ cup dry white wine

1½ cups pitted
    green olives

4–6 tablespoons heavy cream

14 ounces dried pasta

salt and pepper

chopped flat-leaf parsley, to garnish

1 Heat 2 tablespoons of the oil and the butter in a skillet. Add the chicken breasts and fry until golden brown all over. Remove the chicken from the pan.

2 Add the onion and garlic to the pan and fry over medium heat until beginning to soften. Add the bell peppers and mushrooms and cook for 2–3 minutes.

3 Add the tomatoes and season to taste with salt and pepper. Transfer the vegetables to a casserole and arrange the chicken on top.

4 Add the wine to the pan and bring to a boil. Pour the wine over the chicken. Cover and cook in a preheated oven at 350°F for 50 minutes.

5 Add the olives to the casserole and mix in. Pour in the cream, cover, and return to the oven for 10–20 minutes.

6 Meanwhile, bring a large pan of lightly salted water to a boil. Add the pasta and the remaining oil and cook for 8–10 minutes or until tender, but still firm to the bite. Drain the pasta well and transfer to a serving dish.

7 Arrange the chicken on top of the pasta, spoon over the sauce, garnish with the parsley, and serve at once. Alternatively, place the pasta in a large serving bowl and serve separately.

Chicken & Balsamic Vinegar

A rich caramelized sauce, flavored with balsamic vinegar and wine, adds a piquant flavor. The chicken needs to be marinated overnight.

NUTRITIONAL INFORMATION

Calories 148   Sugars 0.2g
Protein . . . . .11g   Fat 8g
Carbohydrate . . .0.2g   Saturates 3g

🥔 10 MINS   🕐 35 MINS

SERVES 4

I N G R E D I E N T S

4 chicken thighs, boned

2 garlic cloves, crushed

1 cup red wine

3 tablespoons white wine vinegar

1 tablespoon oil

1 tablespoon butter

6 shallots

3 tablespoons balsamic vinegar

2 tablespoons fresh thyme

salt and pepper

cooked polenta or rice, to serve

1 Using a sharp knife, make a few slashes in the skin of the chicken. Brush the chicken with the crushed garlic and place in a nonmetallic dish.

2 Pour the wine and white wine vinegar over the chicken and season with salt and pepper to taste. Cover and leave to marinate in the refrigerator overnight.

3 Remove the chicken pieces with a perforated spoon, draining well, and reserve the marinade.

4 Heat the oil and butter in a skillet. Add the shallots and cook for 2–3 minutes or until they begin to soften.

5 Add the chicken pieces to the pan and cook for 3-4 minutes, turning, until browned all over. Reduce the heat and add half of the reserved marinade. Cover and cook for 15–20 minutes, adding more marinade when necessary.

6 Once the chicken is tender, add the balsamic vinegar and thyme and cook for a further 4 minutes.

7 Transfer the chicken and marinade to serving plates and serve with polenta or rice.

COOK'S TIP

To make the chicken pieces look a little neater, use wooden skewers to hold them together or secure them with a length of string.

Chicken Scallops

Served in scallop shells, this makes a stylish presentation for an appetizer or a light lunch.

NUTRITIONAL INFORMATION

Calories ....532 Sugars 3g
Protein ....25g Fat 34g
Carbohydrate ...33g Saturates 14g

20 MINS   25 MINS

SERVES 4

INGREDIENTS

6 oz short-cut macaroni, or other
    short pasta shapes

3 tbsp vegetable oil, plus extra for brushing

1 onion, chopped finely

3 rashers unsmoked collar or back bacon,
    rind removed, chopped

4½ oz button mushrooms, sliced
    thinly or chopped

¾ cup cooked chicken, diced

¾ cup crème fraîche

4 tbsp dry bread crumbs

½ cup sharp Cheddar, grated

salt and pepper

flat-leaf parsley sprigs, to garnish

1 Cook the pasta in a large pan of boiling salted water, to which you have added 1 tablespoon of the oil, for 8–10 minutes or until tender. Drain the pasta, return to the pan, and cover.

2 Heat the broiler to medium. Heat the remaining oil in a pan over medium heat and fry the onion until it is translucent. Add the chopped bacon and mushrooms and cook for 3–4 minutes, stirring once or twice.

3 Stir in the pasta, chicken, and crème fraîche and season to taste with salt and pepper.

4 Brush four large scallop shells with oil. Spoon in the chicken mixture and smooth to make neat mounds.

5 Mix together the bread crumbs and cheese, and sprinkle over the top of the shells. Press the topping lightly into the chicken mixture, and broil for 4–5 minutes, until golden brown and bubbling. Garnish with sprigs of flat-leaf parsley, and serve hot.

Chicken & Lobster on Penne

While this is certainly a treat to get the taste buds tingling, it is not so extravagant as it sounds.

NUTRITIONAL INFORMATION

Calories 696	Sugars 4g
Protein 59g	Fat 32g
Carbohydrate . . .45g	Saturates 9g

20 MINS   30 MINS

SERVES 6

INGREDIENTS

butter, for greasing

6 chicken suprêmes

1 pound dried penne rigate

6 tablespoons extra virgin olive oil

1 cup freshly grated
   Parmesan cheese

salt

FILLING

4 ounces lobster meat, chopped

2 shallots, very finely chopped

2 figs, chopped

1 tablespoon Marsala

2 tablespoons bread crumbs

1 large egg, beaten

salt and pepper

COOK'S TIP

The cut of chicken known as suprême consists of the breast and wing. It is always skinned.

1 Grease 6 pieces of foil large enough to enclose each chicken suprême and lightly grease a cookie sheet.

2 Place all of the filling ingredients into a mixing bowl and blend together thoroughly with a spoon.

3 Cut a pocket in each chicken suprême with a sharp knife and fill with the lobster mixture. Wrap each chicken suprême in foil, place the parcels on the greased cookie sheet, and bake in a preheated oven at 400°F for 30 minutes.

4 Meanwhile, bring a large pan of lightly salted water to a boil. Add the pasta and 1 tablespoon of the olive oil and cook for about 10 minutes, or until tender but still firm to the bite. Drain the pasta thoroughly and transfer to a large serving plate. Sprinkle over the remaining olive oil and the grated Parmesan cheese, set aside, and keep warm.

5 Carefully remove the foil from around the chicken suprêmes. Slice the suprêmes very thinly, arrange over the pasta, and serve at once.

Skewered Chicken Spirals

These unusual chicken kabobs have a wonderful Italian flavor, and the bacon helps keep them moist during cooking.

NUTRITIONAL INFORMATION

Calories 231	Sugars 1g	
Protein 29g	Fat 13g	
Carbohydrate 1g	Saturates 5g	

  15 MINS   10 MINS

SERVES 4

INGREDIENTS

4 skinless, boneless chicken breasts

1 garlic clove, crushed

2 tablespoons tomato paste

4 slices smoked back bacon

large handful of fresh basil leaves

oil, for brushing

salt and pepper

 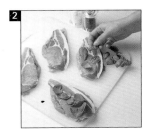 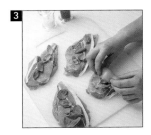

1 Spread out a piece of chicken between two sheets of plastic wrap and beat firmly with a rolling pin to flatten the chicken to an even thickness. Repeat with the remaining chicken breasts.

2 Mix the garlic and tomato paste and spread over the chicken. Lay a bacon slice over each, then scatter with the basil. Season with salt and pepper.

3 Roll up each piece of chicken firmly, then cut into thick slices.

4 Thread the slices onto 4 skewers, making sure the skewer holds the chicken in a spiral shape.

5 Brush lightly with oil and cook on a preheated hot barbecue or broiler for about 10 minutes, turning once. Serve hot with a salad greens.

Chicken with Orange Sauce

The refreshing combination of chicken and orange sauce makes this a perfect dish for a warm summer evening.

NUTRITIONAL INFORMATION

Calories	797	Sugars	........28g
Protein	........59g	Fat	..........25g
Carbohydrate	...77g	Saturates	.......6g

15 MINS   25 MINS

SERVES 4

I N G R E D I E N T S

⅛ cup canola oil

3 tablespoons olive oil

4 x 8 ounces chicken suprêmes

⅔ cup orange brandy

2 tablespoons all-purpose flour

⅔ cup freshly squeezed
    orange juice

1 ounce zucchini, cut into
    matchstick strips

1 ounce red bell pepper, cut into
    matchstick strips

1 ounce leek, finely shredded

14 ounces dried whole-wheat spaghetti

3 large oranges, peeled and cut into
    segments

rind of 1 orange, cut into very fine strips

2 tablespoons chopped fresh tarragon

⅔ cup ricotta cheese

salt and pepper

fresh tarragon leaves, to garnish

1 Heat the rapeseed oil and 1 tablespoon of the olive oil in a skillet. Add the chicken and cook quickly until golden brown. Add the orange brandy and cook for 3 minutes. Sprinkle over the flour and cook for 2 minutes.

2 Lower the heat and add the orange juice, zucchini, bell pepper and leek and season. Simmer for 5 minutes until the sauce has thickened.

3 Meanwhile, bring a pan of salted water to a boil. Add the spaghetti and

1 tablespoon of the olive oil and cook for 10 minutes. Drain the spaghetti, transfer to a serving dish, and drizzle over the remaining oil.

4 Add half of the orange segments, half of the orange rind, the tarragon, and ricotta cheese to the sauce in the pan and cook for 3 minutes.

5 Place the chicken on top of the pasta, pour over a little sauce, garnish with orange segments, rind, and tarragon. Serve at once.

Chicken Pepperonata

All the sunshine colors and flavors of Italy are combined in this easy dish.

NUTRITIONAL INFORMATION

Calories 328	Sugars 7g
Protein 35g	Fat 15g
Carbohydrate . . .13g	Saturates 4g

15 MINS   40 MINS

SERVES 4

I N G R E D I E N T S

8 skinless chicken thighs

2 tablespoons whole wheat flour

2 tablespoons olive oil

1 small onion, sliced thinly

1 garlic clove, crushed

1 each large red, yellow, and green bell
    peppers, sliced thinly

14-ounce can diced tomatoes

1 tablespoon chopped oregano

salt and pepper

fresh oregano, to garnish

crusty whole wheat bread,
    to serve

1 Remove the skin from the chicken thighs and toss in the flour.

2 Heat the oil in a wide skillet and fry the chicken quickly until sealed and lightly browned, then remove from the pan.

3 Add the onion to the pan and gently fry until soft. Add the garlic, bell peppers, tomatoes, and oregano, then bring to a boil, stirring.

4 Arrange the chicken over the vegetables, season well with salt and pepper, then cover the pan tightly and simmer for 20–25 minutes or until the chicken is completely cooked and tender.

5 Season with salt and pepper to taste, garnish with oregano and serve with crusty whole wheat bread.

COOK'S TIP

For extra flavor, halve the bell peppers and broil under a preheated broiler until the skins are charred. Leave to cool then remove the skins and seeds. Slice the bell peppers thinly and use in the recipe.

Roman Chicken

This classic Roman dish makes an ideal light meal. It is equally good cold and could be taken on a picnic—serve with bread to mop up the juices.

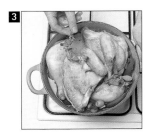

NUTRITIONAL INFORMATION

Calories . . . . .317 Sugars 8g
Protein . . . . .22g Fat 22g
Carbohydrate . . . .9g Saturates 4g

35 MINS   1 HOUR

SERVES 4

INGREDIENTS

4 tablespoons olive oil

6 chicken pieces

2 garlic cloves, crushed with 1 teaspoon salt

1 large red onion, sliced

4 large mixed red, green, and yellow
    bell peppers, cored, deseeded, and
    cut into strips

1 cup pitted green olives

½ quantity Tomato Sauce (see page 120)

1¼ cups hot chicken stock

2 sprigs fresh marjoram

salt and pepper

1 Heat half of the oil in a flameproof casserole and brown the chicken pieces on all sides. Remove the chicken and set aside.

2 Add the remaining oil to the casserole and fry the garlic and onion until softened. Stir in the bell peppers, olives, and tomato sauce.

3 Return the chicken to the casserole with the stock and marjoram. Cover the casserole and simmer for about 45 minutes or until the chicken is tender. Season with salt and pepper to taste and serve with crusty bread.

Pasta with Chicken Sauce

Spinach ribbon noodles, topped with a rich tomato sauce and creamy chicken, make a very appetizing dish.

NUTRITIONAL INFORMATION

Calories .... .995   Sugars 8g
Protein ....36g   Fat .... .74g
Carbohydrate ...50g   Saturates ..... .34g

15 MINS   45 MINS

SERVES 4

INGREDIENTS

9 ounces fresh green tagliatelle

1 tablespoon olive oil

salt

fresh basil leaves, to garnish

TOMATO SAUCE

2 tablespoons olive oil

1 small onion, chopped

1 garlic clove, chopped

14-ounce can diced tomatoes

2 tablespoons chopped fresh parsley

1 teaspoon dried oregano

2 bay leaves

2 tablespoons tomato paste

1 teaspoon sugar

salt and pepper

CHICKEN SAUCE

4 tablespoons butter

14 ounces boned chicken breasts,
    skinned and cut into thin strips

¾ cup blanched almonds

1¼ cups heavy cream

salt and pepper

1 To make the tomato sauce, heat the oil in a pan over medium heat. Add the onion and fry until translucent. Add the garlic and fry for 1 minute. Stir in the tomatoes, parsley, oregano, bay leaves, tomato paste, sugar, and salt and pepper to taste, bring to a boil, and simmer, uncovered, for 15–20 minutes, until reduced by half. Remove the pan from the heat and discard the bay leaves.

2 To make the chicken sauce, melt the butter in a skillet over medium heat. Add the chicken and almonds and stir-fry for 5–6 minutes, or until the chicken is cooked through.

3 Meanwhile, bring the cream to a boil in a small pan over low heat and boil for about 10 minutes, until reduced by almost half. Pour the cream over the chicken and almonds, stir, and season to taste with salt and pepper. Set aside and keep warm.

4 Bring a large pan of lightly salted water to a boil. Add the tagliatelle and olive oil and cook for 8–10 minutes until tender, but still firm to the bite. Drain and transfer to a warm serving dish. Spoon over the tomato sauce and arrange the chicken sauce down the center. Garnish with the basil leaves and serve at once.

Italian Chicken Parcels

This cooking method makes the chicken aromatic and succulent, and reduces the oil needed as the chicken and vegetables cook in their own juices.

NUTRITIONAL INFORMATION

Calories 234	Sugars 5g	
Protein 28g	Fat 12g	
Carbohydrate 5g	Saturates 5g	

25 MINS   30 MINS

SERVES 6

I N G R E D I E N T S

1 tablespoon olive oil

6 skinless chicken breast fillets

9 ounces mozzarella cheese

3½ cups sliced zucchini

6 large tomatoes, sliced

1 small bunch fresh basil or oregano

pepper

rice or pasta,
  to serve

1 Cut 6 pieces of foil, each measuring about 10 inches square. Brush the foil squares lightly with oil and set aside until required.

2 With a sharp knife, slash each chicken breast at regular intervals. Slice the mozzarella cheese and place between the cuts in the chicken.

COOK'S TIP

To aid cooking, place the vegetables and chicken on the shiny side of the foil so that once the parcel is wrapped up the dull surface of the foil is facing outward. This ensures that the heat is absorbed into the parcel and not reflected away from it.

3 Divide the zucchini and tomatoes between the pieces of foil and sprinkle with pepper to taste. Tear or roughly chop the basil or oregano and scatter over the vegetables in each parcel.

4 Place the chicken on top of each pile of vegetables then wrap in the foil to enclose the chicken and vegetables, tucking in the ends.

5 Place on a cookie sheet and bake in a preheated oven, 400°F, for about 30 minutes.

6 To serve, unwrap each foil parcel and serve with rice or pasta.

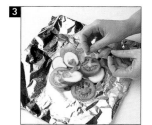

Pasta & Chicken Medley

Strips of cooked chicken are tossed with colored pasta, grapes, and carrot sticks in a pesto-flavored dressing.

NUTRITIONAL INFORMATION

Calories ....609 Sugars 11g
Protein ....26g Fat 38g
Carbohydrate ...45g Saturates 6g

30 MINS   10 MINS

SERVES 2

I N G R E D I E N T S

1¼–1½ cups dried pasta shapes,
     such as twists or bows

1 tablespoon oil

2 tablespoons mayonnaise

2 teaspoons ready-made pesto sauce

1 tablespoon sour cream

6 ounces cooked skinless, boneless
     chicken meat

1–2 celery stalks

1 cup black grapes
     (preferably seedless)

1 large carrot, trimmed

salt and pepper

celery leaves, to garnish

F R E N C H   D R E S S I N G

1 tablespoon wine vinegar

3 tablespoons extra virgin olive oil

salt and pepper

1 To make the French dressing, whisk all the ingredients together until smooth.

2 Cook the pasta with the oil for 8–10 minutes in plenty of boiling salted water until just tender. Drain thoroughly, rinse and drain again. Transfer to a bowl and mix in 1 tablespoon of the French dressing while hot. Set aside until cold.

3 Combine the mayonnaise, pesto sauce, and sour cream or fromage frais in a bowl, and season to taste.

4 Cut the chicken into narrow strips. Cut the celery diagonally into narrow slices. Reserve a few grapes for the garnish, halve the remainder and remove any seeds. Cut the carrot into narrow julienne strips.

5 Add the chicken, the celery, the halved grapes, the carrot, and the mayonnaise mixture to the pasta, and toss thoroughly. Check the seasoning, adding more salt and pepper if necessary.

6 Arrange the pasta mixture on two plates and garnish with the reserved black grapes and the celery leaves.

Prosciutto-wrapped Chicken

Stuffed with ricotta, nutmeg, and spinach, then wrapped with wafer-thin slices of prosciutto and gently cooked in white wine.

NUTRITIONAL INFORMATION

Calories 426	Sugars 4g	
Protein 44g	Fat 21g	
Carbohydrate 9g	Saturates 8g	

🍲 30 MINS   🕐 45 MINS

SERVES 4

I N G R E D I E N T S

½ cup frozen spinach,
   thawed

½ cup ricotta cheese

pinch of grated nutmeg

4 skinless, boneless chicken breasts, each
   weighing 6 ounces

4 prosciutto slices

2 tablespoons butter

1 tablespoon olive oil

12 small onions or shallots

1½ cups
   mushrooms, sliced

1 tablespoon all-purpose flour

⅔ cup dry white
   or red wine

1¼ cups chicken stock

salt and pepper

1 Put the spinach into a strainer and press out the water with a spoon. Mix with the ricotta and nutmeg and season with salt and pepper to taste.

2 Using a sharp knife, slit each chicken breast through the side and enlarge each cut to form a pocket. Fill with the spinach mixture, reshape the chicken breasts, wrap each breast tightly in a slice

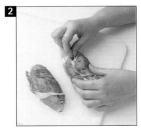  

of ham, and secure with toothpicks. Cover and chill in the refrigerator.

3 Heat the butter and oil in a skillet and brown the chicken breasts for 2 minutes on each side. Transfer the chicken to a large, shallow ovenproof dish and keep warm until required.

4 Fry the onions and mushrooms for 2–3 minutes until lightly browned. Stir in the all-purpose flour, then gradually

add the wine and stock. Bring to a boil, stirring constantly. Season with salt and pepper and spoon the mixture around the chicken.

5 Cook the chicken uncovered in a preheated oven, 400°F, for 20 minutes. Turn the breasts over and cook for a further 10 minutes. Remove the toothpicks and serve with the sauce, together with carrot purée and green beans, if wished.

Chicken Tortellini

Tortellini were said to have been created in the image of the goddess Venus's navel. Whatever the story, they are a delicious blend of Italian flavors.

NUTRITIONAL INFORMATION

Calories 635	Sugars 4g
Protein 31g	Fat 36g
Carbohydrate ...50g	Saturates 16g

🍲 1 HOUR ⏱ 35 MINS

SERVES 4

INGREDIENTS

4 ounces boned chicken breast, skinned

2 ounces prosciutto

1½ ounces cooked spinach, well drained

1 tablespoon finely chopped onion

2 tablespoons freshly grated Parmesan

pinch of ground allspice

1 egg, beaten

1 pound Basic Pasta Dough (see page 24)

salt and pepper

2 tablespoons chopped parsley, to garnish

SAUCE

1¼ cups light cream

2 garlic cloves, crushed

4 ounces mushrooms, thinly sliced

4 tablespoons freshly grated Parmesan

 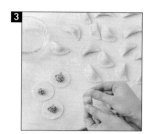 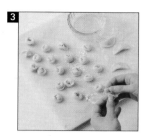

1 Bring a saucepan of seasoned water to a boil. Add the chicken and poach for about 10 minutes. Leave to cool slightly, then put in a food processor with the prosciutto, spinach, and onion and process until finely chopped. Stir in the Parmesan cheese, allspice, and egg and season with salt and pepper to taste.

2 Thinly roll out the pasta dough and cut into 1½–2 inch rounds.

3 Place ½ teaspoon of the filling in the center of each round. Fold the pieces in half and press the edges to seal. Then wrap each piece around your index finger, cross over the ends, and curl the rest of the dough backward to make a navel shape. Re-roll the trimmings and repeat until all of the dough is used up.

4 Bring a saucepan of salted water to a boil. Add the tortellini, in batches, bring back to a boil, and cook for

5 minutes. Drain well and transfer to a serving dish.

5 To make the sauce, bring the cream and garlic to a boil in a small pan, then simmer for 3 minutes. Add the mushrooms and half of the cheese, season with salt and pepper to taste, and simmer for 2–3 minutes. Pour the sauce over the chicken tortellini. Sprinkle over the remaining Parmesan cheese, garnish and serve.

Rich Chicken Casserole

This casserole is packed with the sunshine flavors of Italy. Sun-dried tomatoes add a wonderful richness.

NUTRITIONAL INFORMATION

Calories	320	Sugars	.........8g
Protein	........34g	Fat	..........17g
Carbohydrate	....8g	Saturates	.......4g

  15 MINS 1¹/₄ HOURS

SERVES 4

I N G R E D I E N T S

8 chicken thighs

2 tablespoons olive oil

1 medium red onion, sliced

2 garlic cloves, crushed

1 large red bell pepper, sliced thickly

thinly pared rind and juice of 1 small orange

¹/₂ cup chicken stock

14-ounce can diced tomatoes

¹/₂ cup sun-dried tomatoes,
   thinly sliced

1 tablespoon chopped fresh thyme

¹/₂ cup pitted black olives

salt and pepper

orange rind and thyme sprigs, to garnish

crusty fresh bread, to serve

1 In a heavy or nonstick large skillet, fry the chicken without fat over a fairly high heat, turning occasionally until golden brown. Using a slotted spoon, drain off any excess fat from the chicken, and transfer to a flameproof casserole.

2 Add the oil to the skillet and fry the onion, garlic, and bell pepper in the pan over a moderate heat for 3–4 minutes. Transfer the vegetables to the casserole.

3 Add the orange rind and juice, chicken stock, canned tomatoes, and sun-dried tomatoes to the casserole and stir to combine.

4 Bring to a boil, then cover the casserole with a lid and simmer very gently over low heat for about 1 hour, stirring occasionally. Add the chopped fresh thyme and pitted black olives, then adjust the seasoning with salt and pepper to taste.

5 Scatter orange rind and thyme over the casserole to garnish, and serve with crusty bread.

COOK'S TIP

Sun-dried tomatoes have a dense texture and concentrated taste, and add intense flavor to slow-cooking casseroles.

Chicken with Vegetables

This dish combines succulent chicken with tasty vegetables, flavored with wine and olives.

NUTRITIONAL INFORMATION

Calories	470	Sugars	.........7g
Protein	........29g	Fat	..........34g
Carbohydrate	....7g	Saturates	......16g

20 MINS   1½ HOURS

SERVES 4

I N G R E D I E N T S

4 chicken breasts, part boned

2 tablespoons butter

2 tablespoons olive oil

1 large onion, chopped finely

2 garlic cloves, crushed

2 bell peppers, red, yellow, or green, cored, deseeded,and cut into large pieces

8 ounces large mushrooms, sliced or quartered

6 ounces tomatoes, peeled and halved

⅔ cup dry white wine

4–6 ounces green olives, pitted

4–6 tablespoons heavy cream

salt and pepper

chopped flat-leaf parsley, to garnish

1 Season the chicken with salt and pepper to taste. Heat the oil and butter in a skillet, add the chicken, and fry until browned all over. Remove the chicken from the pan.

2 Add the onion and garlic to the skillet and fry gently until just beginning to soften. Add the bell peppers to the pan with the mushrooms and continue to cook for a few minutes longer, stirring occasionally.

3 Add the tomatoes and plenty of seasoning to the pan and then transfer the vegetable mixture to an ovenproof casserole. Place the chicken on the bed of vegetables.

4 Add the wine to the skillet and bring to a boil. Pour the wine over the chicken and cover the casserole tightly. Cook in a preheated oven, 350°F, for 50 minutes.

5 Add the olives to the chicken, mix lightly, then pour on the cream. Re-cover the casserole and return to the oven for 10–20 minutes or until the chicken is very tender.

6 Adjust the seasoning and serve the pieces of chicken, surrounded by the vegetables and sauce, with pasta or tiny new potatoes. Sprinkle with chopped parsley to garnish.

Chicken & Seafood Parcels

These mouthwatering mini-parcels of chicken and shrimp on a bed of pasta will delight your guests.

NUTRITIONAL INFORMATION

Calories ....799 Sugars 5g
Protein ....50g Fat 45g
Carbohydrate ...51g Saturates 13g

45 MINS   25 MINS

SERVES 4

I N G R E D I E N T S

4 tablespoons butter, plus extra
   for greasing

4 x 7 ounces chicken suprêmes (see page
230), trimmed

4 ounces large spinach leaves, trimmed
   and blanched in hot salted water

4 slices of prosciutto

12–16 raw jumbo shrimp, shelled
   and deveined

1 pound dried tagliatelle

1 tablespoon olive oil

3 leeks, shredded

1 large carrot, grated

⅔ cup thick mayonnaise

2 large cooked beet

salt

1 Grease 4 large pieces of foil and set aside. Place each suprême between 2 pieces of baking parchment and pound with a rolling pin to flatten.

2 Divide half of the spinach between the suprêmes, add a slice of ham to each, and top with more spinach. Place 3–4 shrimp on top of the spinach. Fold the pointed end of the suprême over the shrimp, then fold over again to form a parcel. Wrap in foil, place on a cookie sheet and bake in a preheated oven at 400°F for 20 minutes.

3 Meanwhile, bring a saucepan of salted water to a boil. Add the pasta and oil and cook for 8–10 minutes or until tender. Drain and transfer to a serving dish.

4 Melt the butter in a skillet. Fry the leeks and carrots for 3 minutes. Transfer the vegetables to the center of the pasta.

5 Work the mayonnaise and 1 beet in a food processor or blender until smooth. Rub through a strainer and pour around the pasta and vegetables.

6 Cut the remaining beet into diamond shapes and place them neatly around the mayonnaise. Remove the foil from the chicken and, using a sharp knife, cut the suprêmes into thin slices. Arrange the chicken and shrimp slices on top of the vegetables and pasta, and serve.

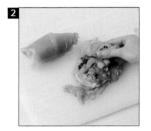

Garlic & Herb Chicken

There is a delicious surprise of creamy herb and garlic soft cheese hidden inside these chicken parcels!

NUTRITIONAL INFORMATION

Calories 272   Sugars 4g
Protein ....29g   Fat 13g
Carbohydrate ....4g   Saturates 6g

 20 MINS   25 MINS

SERVES 4

INGREDIENTS

4 chicken breasts, skin removed

3½ ounces cream cheese, flavored with herbs and garlic

8 slices prosciutto

⅔ cup red wine

⅔ cup chicken stock

1 tablespoon brown sugar

1 Using a sharp knife, make a horizontal slit along the length of each chicken breast to form a pocket.

2 Beat the cheese with a wooden spoon to soften it. Spoon the cheese into the pocket of the chicken breasts.

3 Wrap 2 slices of prosciutto around each chicken breast and secure firmly in place with a length of string.

4 Pour the red wine and chicken stock into a large skillet and bring to a boil over medium heat. When the mixture is just starting to boil, add the brown sugar and stir well. Keep stirring until the sugar has completely dissolved.

5 Add the chicken breasts to the mixture in the skillet. Leave to simmer for 12–15 minutes or until the chicken is tender and the juices run clear when a

skewer is inserted into the thickest part of the meat.

6 Remove the chicken from the pan, set aside and keep warm.

7 Reheat the sauce and boil until reduced and thickened. Remove the string from the chicken and cut into slices. Pour the sauce over the chicken to serve.

VARIATION

Try adding 2 finely chopped sun-dried tomatoes to the soft cheese in step 2, if you prefer.

Italian-style Sunday Roast

A mixture of cheese, rosemary, and sun-dried tomatoes is stuffed under the chicken skin, then roasted with garlic, potatoes, and vegetables.

NUTRITIONAL INFORMATION

Calories	488	Sugars	.........6g
Protein	........37g	Fat	..........23g
Carbohydrate	...34g	Saturates	......11g

🍲 35 MINS   🕐 1½ HOURS

SERVES 6

I N G R E D I E N T S

5½ pounds chicken

sprigs of fresh rosemary

¾ cup feta cheese,
   coarsely grated

2 tablespoons sun-dried tomato paste

4 tablespoons butter, softened

1 bulb garlic

2¼ pounds new potatoes, halved if large

1 each red, green, and yellow bell pepper,
   cut into chunks

3 zucchini, sliced thinly

2 tablespoons olive oil

2 tablespoons all-purpose flour

2½ cups chicken stock

salt and pepper

1 Rinse the chicken inside and out with cold water and drain well. Carefully cut between the skin and the top of the breast meat using a small pointed knife. Slide a finger into the slit and carefully enlarge it to form a pocket. Continue until the skin is completely lifted away from both breasts and the top of the legs.

2 Chop the leaves from 3 rosemary stems. Mix with the feta cheese, sun-dried tomato paste, butter, and pepper to taste, then spoon under the skin. Put the chicken in a large roasting pan, cover with foil, and cook in a preheated oven, 375°F, for 20 minutes per 1 pound 2 ounces, plus 20 minutes.

3 Break the garlic bulb into cloves but do not peel. Add the vegetables to the chicken after 40 minutes.

4 Drizzle with oil, tuck in a few stems of rosemary, and season with salt and pepper. Cook for the remaining calculated time, removing the foil for the last 40 minutes to brown the chicken.

5 Transfer the chicken to a serving platter. Place some of the vegetables around the chicken and transfer the remainder to a warm serving dish. Pour the fat out of the roasting pan and stir the flour into the remaining pan juices. Cook for 2 minutes, then gradually stir in the stock. Bring to a boil, stirring until thickened. Strain into a sauce boat and serve with the chicken.

Slices of Duckling with Pasta

A raspberry and honey sauce superbly counterbalances the richness of the duckling.

NUTRITIONAL INFORMATION

Calories	686	Sugars	........15g
Protein	........62g	Fat	..........20g
Carbohydrate	...70g	Saturates	.......7g

 15 MINS   25 MINS

SERVES 4

INGREDIENTS

4 x 9 ounces boned breasts of duckling

2 tablespoons butter

3 tablespoons finely chopped carrots

4 tablespoons finely chopped shallots

1 tablespoon lemon juice

⅔ cup meat stock

4 tablespoons liquid honey

¾ cup fresh or thawed
   frozen raspberries

¼ cup all-purpose flour

1 tablespoon Worcestershire sauce

14 ounces fresh linguine

1 tablespoon olive oil

salt and pepper

TO GARNISH

fresh raspberries

fresh sprig of flat-leaf parsley

1 Trim and score the duck breasts with a sharp knife and season well all over. Melt the butter in a skillet, add the duck breasts, and fry all over until lightly colored.

2 Add the carrots, shallots, lemon juice, and half the meat stock and simmer over low heat for 1 minute. Stir in half of the honey and half of the raspberries.

Sprinkle over half of the flour and cook, stirring constantly for 3 minutes. Season with pepper to taste and add the Worcestershire sauce.

3 Stir in the remaining stock and cook for 1 minute. Stir in the remaining honey and remaining raspberries and sprinkle over the remaining flour. Cook for a further 3 minutes.

4 Remove the duck breasts from the pan, but leave the sauce to continue simmering over very low heat.

5 Meanwhile, bring a large saucepan of lightly salted water to a boil. Add the linguine and olive oil and cook for 8–10 minutes or until tender, but still firm to the bite. Drain and divide between 4 individual plates.

6 Slice the duck breast lengthwise into ¼-inch thick pieces. Pour a little sauce over the pasta and arrange the sliced duck in a fan shape on top of it. Garnish with raspberries and flat-leaf parsley and serve at once.

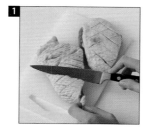

Pheasant Lasagne

This scrumptious and unusual baked lasagne is virtually a meal in itself. It is served with baby onions and green peas.

NUTRITIONAL INFORMATION

Calories 1038   Sugars 13g
Protein . . . . .65g   Fat 64g
Carbohydrate . . .54g   Saturates 27g

 40 MINS   1¼ HOURS

SERVES 4

I N G R E D I E N T S

butter, for greasing

14 sheets pre-cooked lasagne

3¾ cups Béchamel Sauce
    (see page 28)

¾ cup grated mozzarella cheese

F I L L I N G

8 ounces pork fat, diced

2 tablespoons butter

16 small onions

8 large pheasant breasts,
    thinly sliced

¼ cup all-purpose flour

2½ cups chicken stock

bouquet garni

1 pound fresh peas, shelled

salt and pepper

1 To make the filling, put the pork fat into a saucepan of boiling, salted water and simmer for 3 minutes, then drain and pat dry.

2 Melt the butter in a large skillet. Add the pork fat and onions to the pan and cook for about 3 minutes, or until lightly browned.

3 Remove the pork fat and onions from the pan and set aside. Add the slices of pheasant and cook over low heat for 12 minutes, until browned all over. Transfer to an ovenproof dish.

4 Stir the flour into the pan and cook until just brown, then blend in the stock. Pour the mixture over the pheasant, add the bouquet garni and cook in a preheated oven, at 400°F, for 5 minutes. Remove the bouquet garni. Add the

onions, pork fat, and peas and return to the oven for 10 minutes.

5 Put the pheasant and pork fat in a food processor and grind finely.

6 Lower the oven temperature to 375°F. Grease an ovenproof dish with butter. Make layers of lasagne, pheasant sauce, and Béchamel Sauce in the dish, ending with Béchamel Sauce. Sprinkle over the cheese and bake for 30 minutes.

Pesto Baked Partridge

Partridge has a more delicate flavor than many game birds and this subtle sauce perfectly complements it.

NUTRITIONAL INFORMATION

Calories	895	Sugars	........5g
Protein	........79g	Fat	.........45g
Carbohydrate	...45g	Saturates	......18g

 15 MINS 40 MINS

SERVES 4

I N G R E D I E N T S

8 partridge pieces (about 4 ounces each)

4 tablespoons butter, melted

4 tablespoons Dijon mustard

2 tablespoons lime juice

1 tablespoon brown sugar

6 tablespoons Pesto Sauce (see page 39)

1 pound dried rigatoni

1 tablespoon olive oil

1⅓ cups freshly grated Parmesan cheese

salt and pepper

1 Arrange the partridge pieces, smooth side down, in a single layer in a large, ovenproof dish.

2 Mix together the butter, Dijon mustard, lime juice, and brown sugar in a bowl. Season to taste. Brush this mixture over the partridge pieces and bake in a preheated oven at 400°F for 15 minutes.

3 Remove the dish from the oven and coat the partridge pieces with 3 tablespoons of the Pesto Sauce. Return to the oven and bake for a further 12 minutes.

4 Remove the dish from the oven and carefully turn over the partridge pieces. Coat the top of the partridges with the remaining mustard mixture and return to the oven for a further 10 minutes.

5 Meanwhile, bring a large pan of lightly salted water to a boil. Add the rigatoni and olive oil and cook for 8–10 minutes until tender, but still firm to the bite. Drain and transfer to a serving dish. Toss the pasta with the remaining Pesto Sauce and the Parmesan cheese.

6 Serve the partridge with the pasta, pouring over the cooking juices.

VARIATION

You could also prepare young pheasant in the same way.

Vegetables

Vegetables are a staple ingredient in Italian cooking. The different areas supply a prolific amount of fresh and succulent vegetables, including globe artichokes, which grow wild on Sicily, sweet bell peppers, which are sun-ripened in Italy, as are the universally popular sun-ripened tomatoes. Vegetables work well with a variety of different

ingredients, including pasta, rice, grains, and beans to make a selection of delicious dishes. However, vegetables can make a tasty meal in themselves. Try vegetables barbecued on rosemary skewers—the aromatic flavor of this wonderful herb is imparted during the cooking process to make a quintessentially Italian dish. Vegetables have so much potential—experiment and enjoy!

Vegetable Ravioli

It is important not to overcook the vegetable filling or it will become sloppy and unexciting, instead of firm to the bite and delicious.

NUTRITIONAL INFORMATION

Calories 622	Sugars 10g
Protein 12g	Fat 40g
Carbohydrate . . .58g	Saturates 6g

🍤 🍤 🍤 🍤

🧈 1½ HOURS   🕐 55 MINS

SERVES 4

I N G R E D I E N T S

1 pound Basic Pasta Dough (see page 24)

1 tablespoon olive oil

6 tablespoons butter

⅔ cup light cream

1 cup freshly grated
 Parmesan cheese

fresh basil sprigs, to garnish

S T U F F I N G

2 large eggplants

3 large zucchini

6 large tomatoes

1 large green bell pepper

1 large red bell pepper

3 garlic cloves

1 large onion

½ cup olive oil

2 ounces tomato paste

½ teaspoon chopped fresh basil

salt and pepper

1 To make the stuffing, cut the eggplants and zucchini into 1-inch chunks. Put the eggplant pieces in a colander, sprinkle with salt, and set aside for 20 minutes. Rinse and drain.

2 Blanch the tomatoes in boiling water for 2 minutes. Drain, peel. and chop the flesh. Core and seed the bell peppers and cut into 1-inch dice. Chop the garlic and onion.

3 Heat the oil in a saucepan. Add the garlic and onion and fry for 3 minutes.

4 Stir in the eggplants, zucchini, tomatoes, bell peppers, tomato paste, and basil. Season with salt and pepper to taste, cover, and simmer for 20 minutes, stirring frequently.

5 Roll out the pasta dough and cut out 3-inch rounds with a plain cutter. Put a spoonful of the vegetable stuffing on each round. Dampen the edges slightly and fold the pasta rounds over, pressing together to seal.

6 Bring a saucepan of salted water to the boil. Add the ravioli and the oil and cook for 3–4 minutes. Drain and transfer to a greased ovenproof dish, dotting each layer with butter. Pour over the cream and sprinkle over the Parmesan cheese. Bake in a preheated oven at 400°F for 20 minutes. Serve hot.

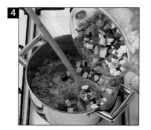

Braised Fennel & Linguine

This aniseed-flavored vegetable gives that extra punch to this delicious creamy pasta dish.

NUTRITIONAL INFORMATION

Calories 650   Sugars 6g
Protein . . . . .14g   Fat 39g
Carbohydrate . . .62g   Saturates 22g

20 MINS   50 MINS

SERVES 4

I N G R E D I E N T S

6 fennel bulbs

⅔ cup vegetable stock

2 tablespoons butter

6 slices bacon, diced

6 shallots, quartered

¼ cup all-purpose flour

7 tablespoons heavy cream

1 tablespoon Madeira

1 pound dried linguine

1 tablespoon olive oil

salt and pepper

1 Trim the fennel bulbs, then gently peel off and reserve the first layer of the bulbs. Cut the bulbs into quarters and put them in a large saucepan, together with the vegetable stock and the reserved outer layers. Bring to a boil, lower the heat, and simmer for 5 minutes.

2 Using a slotted spoon, transfer the fennel to a large dish. Discard the outer layers of the fennel bulb. Bring the vegetable stock to a boil and allow to reduce by half. Set aside.

3 Melt the butter in a skillet. Add the bacon and shallots and fry for 4 minutes. Add the flour, reduced stock, cream, and Madeira and cook, stirring constantly, for 3 minutes, or until the sauce is smooth. Season to taste and pour over the fennel.

4 Bring a large saucepan of lightly salted water to a boil. Add the linguine and olive oil and cook for 8–10 minutes, or until tender but still firm to the bite. Drain and transfer to a deep ovenproof dish.

5 Add the fennel and sauce and braise in a preheated oven at 350°F for 20 minutes. Serve at once.

COOK'S TIP

Fennel will keep in the produce drawer of the refrigerator for 2–3 days, but it is best eaten as fresh as possible. Cut surfaces turn brown quickly, so do not prepare it too much in advance of cooking.

Stuffed Red Bell Peppers

Stuffed bell peppers are a well-known dish, but this is a new version adapted for the barbecue.

NUTRITIONAL INFORMATION

Calories 144	Sugars 4g	
Protein 1g	Fat 12g	
Carbohydrate 9g	Saturates 2g	

40 MINS 10 MINS

SERVES 4

INGREDIENTS

2 red bell peppers, halved lengthwise
    and deseeded

2 tomatoes, halved

2 zucchini, sliced thinly lengthwise

1 red onion, cut into 8 sections,
    each section held together by the root

4 tablespoons olive oil

2 tablespoons fresh thyme leaves

⅓ cup mixed basmati and
    wild rice, cooked

salt and pepper

COOK'S TIP

When charbroiled, red, orange, and yellow bell peppers all take on a remarkable sweet quality. They are often peeled in order to highlight this. Orange bell peppers are worth experimenting with as they do have a different flavor from red and green bell peppers.

1 Put the bell peppers, tomatoes, zucchini, and onion sections onto a cookie sheet.

2 Brush the vegetables with olive oil and sprinkle over the thyme leaves.

3 Cook the bell pepper, onion, and zucchini over medium barbecue for 6 minutes, turning once.

4 When the bell peppers are cooked, put a spoonful of the cooked rice into each one.

5 Add the tomato halves to the grill and cook for 2–3 minutes only. Serve all the vegetables hot, seasoned with plenty of salt and pepper.

Italian Potato Wedges

These oven-cooked potato wedges use classic pizza ingredients and are delicious served with plain meats, such as pork or lamb.

NUTRITIONAL INFORMATION

Calories 115	Sugars 4g
Protein 6g	Fat 5g
Carbohydrate . . .13g	Saturates 3g

 15 MINS   35 MINS

SERVES 4

I N G R E D I E N T S

2 large potatoes, unpeeled

4 large ripe tomatoes, peeled and seeded

⅔ cup vegetable stock

2 tablespoons tomato paste

1 small yellow bell pepper, cut into strips

4½ ounces mushrooms, quartered

1 tablespoon chopped fresh basil

½ cup cheese, grated

salt and pepper

1 Cut each of the potatoes into 8 equal wedges. Parboil the potatoes in a pan of boiling water for 15 minutes. Drain well and place in a shallow ovenproof dish.

2 Chop the tomatoes and add to the dish. Mix together the vegetable stock and tomato paste, then pour the mixture over the potatoes and tomatoes.

3 Add the yellow bell pepper strips, quartered mushrooms, and chopped basil. Season well with salt and pepper.

4 Sprinkle the grated cheese over the top and cook in a preheated oven, 375°F, for 15-20 minutes until the topping is golden brown. Serve at once.

Creamy Pasta & Broccoli

This colorful dish provides a mouthwatering contrast in the crisp *al dente* texture of the broccoli and the creamy cheese sauce.

NUTRITIONAL INFORMATION

Calories	472	Sugars	.........6g
Protein	........15g	Fat	..........24g
Carbohydrate	...52g	Saturates	......14g

 5 MINS   🕐 25 MINS

SERVES 4

INGREDIENTS

4 tablespoons butter

1 large onion, finely chopped

1 pound dried ribbon pasta

1 pound broccoli,
  broken into flowerets

⅔ cup boiling
  vegetable stock

1 tablespoon all-purpose flour

⅔ cup light cream

½ cup grated mozzarella cheese

freshly grated nutmeg

salt and white pepper

fresh apple slices, to garnish

1 Melt half of the butter in a large saucepan over medium heat. Add the onion and fry for 4 minutes.

VARIATION

This dish would also be delicious and look just as colorful made with Cape broccoli, which is actually a purple variety of cauliflower and not broccoli at all.

 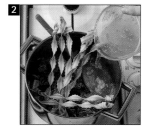 

2 Add the broccoli and pasta to the pan and cook, stirring constantly, for 2 minutes. Add the vegetable stock, bring back to a boil and simmer for a further 12 minutes. Season well with salt and white pepper.

3 Meanwhile, melt the remaining butter in a saucepan over medium heat. Sprinkle over the flour and cook, stirring constantly, for 2 minutes. Gradually stir in the cream and bring to simmering point, but do not boil. Add the grated cheese and season with salt and a little freshly grated nutmeg.

4 Drain the pasta and broccoli mixture and pour over the cheese sauce. Cook, stirring occasionally, for about 2 minutes. Transfer the pasta and broccoli mixture to a warm, large, deep serving dish and serve garnished with slices of fresh apple.

Vegetable Frittata

A frittata is a type of Italian omelet—you can add almost anything to the eggs. It is also delicious eaten cold and makes an ideal picnic dish.

NUTRITIONAL INFORMATION

Calories 310	Sugars 4g
Protein 18g	Fat 17g
Carbohydrate . . .24g	Saturates 4g

 15 MINS   20 MINS

SERVES 4

I N G R E D I E N T S

3 tablespoons olive oil

1 onion, chopped

2 garlic cloves, chopped

8 ounces zucchini,
   sliced thinly

4 eggs

14-ounce can borlotti (broad) beans,
   drained and rinsed

3 tomatoes, peeled and chopped

2 tablespoons chopped
   fresh parsley

1 tablespoon chopped fresh basil

½ cup grated Swiss cheese

salt and pepper

1 Heat 2 tablespoons of the oil in a skillet and fry the onion and garlic, stirring occasionally, for 2–3 minutes or until soft. Add the zucchini and cook for 3–4 minutes, or until softened.

2 Break the eggs into a bowl and add salt and pepper to taste, the fried vegetables, beans, tomatoes, and herbs.

3 Heat the remaining oil in a 9½-inch omelet pan, add the egg mixture, and fry for 5 minutes until the eggs have almost set and the underside is brown.

4 Sprinkle the cheese over the top and place the pan under a preheated moderate broiler for 3–4 minutes or until set on the top but still moist in the middle. Cut into wedges and serve warm or at room temperature.

COOK'S TIP

Swiss cheese is made from unpasteurised cow's milk has a sweet, nutty flavour, which enhances the taste of this frittata. It is firm and close textured and has small holes interspersed throughout.

Spinach & Mushroom Lasagne

Always check the seasoning of vegetables—you can always add a little more to a recipe, but you cannot take it out once it has been added.

NUTRITIONAL INFORMATION

Calories	720	Sugars	.........9g
Protein	........31g	Fat	..........52g
Carbohydrate	...36g	Saturates	......32g

 20 MINS 40 MINS

SERVES 4

I N G R E D I E N T S

8 tablespoons butter, plus extra
    for greasing

2 garlic cloves, finely chopped

4 ounces shallots

8 ounces exotic mushrooms,
    such as chanterelles

1 pound spinach, cooked, drained, and
    finely chopped

2 cups grated Cheddar cheese

¼ teaspoon freshly grated nutmeg

1 teaspoon chopped fresh basil

½ cup all-purpose flour

2½ cups hot milk

½ cup grated Cheshire or Cheddar cheese

salt and pepper

8 sheets pre-cooked lasagne

VARIATION

You could substitute
4 bell peppers for the spinach.
Roast in a preheated oven, at
400°F, for 20 minutes. Rub off the
skins under cold water, deseed, and
chop before using.

1 Lightly grease a large ovenproof dish with a little butter.

2 Melt 4 tablespoons of the butter in a saucepan. Add the garlic, shallots and exotic mushrooms and fry over low heat for 3 minutes. Stir in the spinach, Cheddar cheese, nutmeg, and basil. Season with salt and pepper to taste and set aside.

3 Melt the remaining butter in another saucepan over low heat. Add the flour and cook, stirring constantly, for 1 minute. Gradually stir in the hot milk, whisking constantly until smooth. Stir in ¼ cup of the Cheshire cheese and season to taste with salt and pepper.

4 Spread half of the mushroom and spinach mixture over the base of the prepared dish. Cover with a layer of lasagne and then with half of the cheese sauce. Repeat the process and sprinkle over the remaining Cheshire cheese.

5 Bake in a preheated oven, at 400°F, for 30 minutes, or until golden brown. Serve hot.

Twice Baked Potatoes

The potatoes are baked until fluffy, then the flesh is scooped out and mixed with pesto before being returned to the potato shells and baked again.

NUTRITIONAL INFORMATION

Calories	424	Sugars	.........3g
Protein	.........9g	Fat	..........27g
Carbohydrate	...40g	Saturates	......13g

 10 MINS   1¹/₂ HOURS

SERVES 4

INGREDIENTS

4 baking potatoes, about 8 ounces each

⅔ cup heavy cream

⅓ cup vegetable stock

1 tablespoon lemon juice

2 garlic cloves, crushed

3 tablespoons chopped fresh basil

2 tablespoons pine nuts

2 tablespoons grated Parmesan cheese

salt and pepper

1 Scrub the potatoes and prick the skins with a fork. Rub a little salt into the skins and place the potatoes on a cookie sheet.

2 Cook in a preheated oven, 375˚F, for 1 hour or until the potatoes are cooked through and the skins crisp.

3 Remove the potatoes from the oven and cut them in half lengthwise. Using a spoon, scoop the potato flesh into a mixing bowl, leaving a thin shell of potato inside the skins. Mash the potato flesh with a fork.

4 Meanwhile, mix the cream and stock in a saucepan and simmer for 8–10 minutes or until reduced by half.

5 Stir in the lemon juice, garlic, and chopped basil and season to taste with salt and pepper. Stir the mixture into the potato flesh with the pine nuts.

6 Spoon the mixture back into the potato shells and sprinkle the Parmesan cheese on top. Return the potatoes to the oven for 10 minutes or until the cheese has browned. Serve with salad.

VARIATION

Add cream cheese or thinly sliced mushrooms to the mashed potato in step 5, if you prefer.

Vermicelli & Vegetable Flan

Lightly cooked vermicelli is pressed into a flan ring and baked with a creamy mushroom filling.

NUTRITIONAL INFORMATION

Calories ....528 Sugars 6g
Protein ....15g Fat 32g
Carbohydrate ...47g Saturates 17g

15 MINS   1 HOUR

SERVES 4

INGREDIENTS

6 tablespoons butter, plus extra
  for greasing

8 ounces dried vermicelli or spaghetti

1 tablespoon olive oil

1 onion, chopped

5 ounces button mushrooms

1 green bell pepper, cored, seeded, and
  sliced into thin rings

⅔ cup milk

3 eggs, lightly beaten

2 tablespoons heavy cream

1 teaspoon dried oregano

freshly grated nutmeg

1 tablespoon freshly grated Parmesan

salt and pepper

tomato and basil salad, to serve

1 Generously grease an 8-inch loose-based flan pan with butter.

2 Bring a large pan of lightly salted water to a boil. Add the vermicelli and olive oil and cook for 8–10 minutes until tender, but still firm to the bite. Drain, return to the pan, 2 tablespoons of the butter and shake the pan to coat the pasta.

3 Press the pasta onto the base and around the sides of the flan pan to make a flan case.

4 Melt the remaining butter in a skillet over medium heat. Add the onion and fry until it is translucent.

5 Add the mushrooms and bell pepper rings to the skillet and cook, stirring, for 2–3 minutes. Spoon the onion, mushroom and bell pepper mixture into the flan case and press it evenly into the base.

6 Beat together the milk, eggs, and cream, stir in the oregano and season to taste with nutmeg and pepper. Carefully pour this mixture over the vegetables and then sprinkle with the Parmesan cheese.

7 Bake the flan in a preheated oven at 350°F for 40–45 minutes, or until the filling has set.

8 Slide the flan out of the pan and serve warm with a tomato and basil salad, if wished.

Marinated Tofu

Tofu is full of protein, vitamins, and minerals, and although it is bland on its own, it develops a fabulous flavor when it is marinated.

NUTRITIONAL INFORMATION

Calories	 105	Sugars	. . . . 3g
Protein	. . . . 8g	Fat	. . . . 7g
Carbohydrate	. . . . 4g	Saturates	. . . . 1g

 50 MINS 10 MINS

SERVES 4

I N G R E D I E N T S

12 ounces tofu

1 red bell pepper

1 yellow bell pepper

2 zucchini

8 mushrooms

slices of lemon, to garnish

M A R I N A D E

grated rind and juice of ½ lemon

1 clove garlic, crushed

½ teaspoon fresh rosemary, chopped

½ teaspoon chopped, fresh thyme

1 tablespoon walnut oil

1 To make the marinade, combine the lemon rind and juice, garlic, rosemary, thyme, and oil in a shallow dish.

2 Drain the tofu, pat it dry on paper towels, and cut it into squares. Add to the marinade and toss to coat. Leave to marinate for 20–30 minutes.

3 Meanwhile, deseed and cut the bell peppers into 1-inch pieces. Blanch in boiling water for 4 minutes, refresh in cold water, and drain.

4 Using a canelle knife (or potato peeler), remove strips of peel from the zucchini. Cut the zucchini into 1-inch chunks.

5 Remove the tofu from the marinade, reserving the liquid for basting. Thread the tofu onto 8 skewers, alternating with the bell peppers, zucchini, and button mushrooms.

6 Barbecue the skewers over medium hot coals for about 6 minutes, turning and basting with the marinade.

7 Transfer the skewers to warm serving plates, garnish with slices of lemon and serve.

VARIATION

For a spicy kabob, make a marinade from 1 tablespoon of curry paste, 2 tablespoons of oil, and the juice of ½ lemon.

Pepperonata

A delicious mixture of bell peppers and onions, cooked with tomatoes and herbs for a rich side dish.

NUTRITIONAL INFORMATION

Calories	180	Sugars 14g
Protein	.........3g	Fat 12g
Carbohydrate	...15g	Saturates 2g

 15 MINS 40 MINS

SERVES 4

I N G R E D I E N T S

4 tablespoons olive oil

1 onion, halved and finely sliced

2 red bell peppers, cut into strips

2 green bell peppers, cut into strips

2 yellow bell peppers, cut into strips

2 garlic cloves, crushed

2 x 14-ounce cans diced
   tomatoes, drained

2 tablespoons chopped cilantro

2 tablespoons chopped pitted black olives

salt and pepper

VARIATION

If you don't like the distinctive flavor of fresh cilantro, you can substitute it with 2 tablespoons chopped fresh flat-leaf parsley. Use green olives instead of black ones, if you prefer.

1 Heat the oil in a large skillet. Add the onion and sauté for 5 minutes, stirring until just beginning to color.

2 Add the bell peppers and garlic to the skillet and cook for a further 3–4 minutes.

3 Stir in the tomatoes and cilantro and season with salt and pepper. Cover the skillet and cook the vegetables gently for about 30 minutes or until the mixture is dry.

4 Stir in the pitted black olives and serve the pepperonata at once.

Ricotta & Spinach Parcels

Ricotta and spinach make a great flavor combination, especially when encased in light puff-pastry parcels.

NUTRITIONAL INFORMATION

Calories	639	Sugars	........4g
Protein	........13g	Fat	.........48g
Carbohydrate	...41g	Saturates	......21g

🕒 25 MINS 🕒 30 MINS

SERVES 4

INGREDIENTS

3 cups spinach, trimmed and
   washed thoroughly

2 tablespoons butter

1 small onion, chopped finely

1 teaspoon green peppercorns

1 pound 2 ounces puff pastry

1 cup ricotta cheese

1 egg, beaten

salt

sprigs of fresh herbs, to garnish

fresh vegetables, to serve

1 Pack the spinach into a large saucepan. Add a little salt and a very small amount of water and cook until wilted. Drain well, cool, and then squeeze out any excess moisture with the back of a spoon. Chop roughly.

2 Melt the butter in a small saucepan and fry the onion gently for 2 minutes or until softened, but not browned. Add the green peppercorns and cook for 2 minutes. Remove from the heat, add the spinach and mix together.

3 Roll out the puff pastry thinly on a lightly floured counter and cut into 4 squares, each 7 inches across. Place a

quarter of the spinach mixture in the center of each square and top with a quarter of the cheese.

4 Brush a little beaten egg around the edges of the pastry squares and bring the corners together to form parcels. Press the edges together firmly to seal. Lift the parcels onto a greased cookie sheet, brush with beaten egg, and bake in a preheated oven, at 400°F, for 20–25 minutes, or until risen and golden brown.

5 Serve hot, garnished with sprigs of fresh herbs and accompanied by fresh vegetables.

Garlic Potato Wedges

This is a great recipe for the barbecue. Serve this tasty potato dish with broiled meat or fish.

NUTRITIONAL INFORMATION

Calories	.259	Sugars	.1g
Protein	.3g	Fat	.17g
Carbohydrate	.26g	Saturates	.5g

10 MINS   35 MINS

SERVES 4

I N G R E D I E N T S

3 large baking potatoes, scrubbed

4 tablespoons olive oil

2 tablespoons butter

2 garlic cloves, chopped

1 tablespoon chopped, fresh rosemary

1 tablespoon chopped, fresh parsley

1 tablespoon chopped, fresh thyme

salt and pepper

1 Bring a large saucepan of water to a boil, add the potatoes, and par-boil them for 10 minutes. Drain the potatoes, refresh under cold water, and drain them again thoroughly.

2 Transfer the potatoes to a chopping board. When the potatoes are cold enough to handle, cut them into thick wedges, but do not remove the skins.

COOK'S TIP

You may find it easier to barbecue these potatoes in a hinged rack or in a specially designed barbecue roasting tray.

3 Heat the oil and butter in a small pan together with the garlic. Cook gently until the garlic begins to brown, then remove the pan from the heat.

4 Stir the herbs and salt and pepper to taste into the mixture in the pan.

5 Brush the herb mixture all over the potatoes.

6 Barbecue the potatoes over hot coals for 10–15 minutes, brushing liberally with any of the remaining herb and butter mixture, or until the potatoes are just tender.

7 Transfer the barbecued garlic potatoes to a warm serving plate and serve as a starter or as a side dish.

Spinach Frittata

This Italian dish may be made with many flavorings. Spinach is used as the main ingredient in this recipe for color and flavor.

NUTRITIONAL INFORMATION

Calories 307	Sugars 4g	
Protein 15g	Fat 25g	
Carbohydrate 6g	Saturates 8g	

20 MINS

20 MINS

SERVES 4

I N G R E D I E N T S

1 pound spinach

2 teaspoon water

4 eggs, beaten

2 tablespoons light cream

2 garlic cloves, crushed

¾ cup canned corn, drained

1 celery stalk, chopped

1 red chili, chopped

2 tomatoes, deseeded and diced

2 tablespoons olive oil

2 tablespoons butter

¼ cup pecan nut halves

2 tablespoons grated Romano cheese

¼ cup fontina cheese, cubed

a pinch of paprika

1 Cook the spinach in 2 teaspoons of water in a covered saucepan for 5 minutes. Drain thoroughly and pat dry on absorbent paper towels.

2 Beat the eggs in a bowl and stir in the spinach, light cream, garlic, corn, celery, chili, and tomatoes until the ingredients are well mixed.

3 Heat the oil and butter in an 8-inch heavy-based skillet.

4 Spoon the egg mixture into the skillet and sprinkle with the pecan nut halves, Romano and fontina cheeses, and paprika. Cook, without stirring, over medium heat for 5–7 minutes or until the underside of the frittata is brown.

5 Put a large plate over the pan and invert to turn out the frittata. Slide it back into the skillet and cook the other side for a further 2–3 minutes. Serve the frittata straight from the skillet or transfer to a serving plate.

COOK'S TIP

Be careful not to burn the underside of the frittata during the initial cooking stage—this is why it is important to use a heavy-based skillet. Add a little extra oil to the skillet when you turn the frittata over, if required.

Bell Peppers & Rosemary

The flavor of broiled or roasted bell peppers is very different from when they are eaten raw, so do try them cooked in this way.

NUTRITIONAL INFORMATION

Calories 201   Sugars 6g
Protein . . . . .2g   Fat 19g
Carbohydrate . . . .6g   Saturates 2g

  20 MINS   10 MINS

SERVES 4

INGREDIENTS

4 tablespoons olive oil

finely grated rind of 1 lemon

4 tablespoons lemon juice

1 tablespoon balsamic vinegar

1 tablespoon crushed fresh rosemary, or
   1 teaspoon dried rosemary

2 garlic cloves, crushed

2 red bell peppers, halved, cored,
   and deseeded

2 yellow bell peppers, halved, cored,
   and deseeded

2 tablespoons pine nuts

salt and pepper

sprigs of fresh rosemary, to garnish

1 Mix together the olive oil, lemon rind, lemon juice, vinegar, rosemary and garlic. Season with salt and pepper.

2 Place the bell peppers, skin-side up, on the rack of a broiler pan, lined with foil. Brush with olive oil.

3 Broil the bell peppers for 3–4 minutes or until the skin begins to char, basting frequently with the lemon juice mixture. Remove from the heat, cover with foil to trap the steam, and leave for 5 minutes.

4 Meanwhile, scatter the pine nuts onto the broiler rack and toast them lightly for 2–3 minutes. Keep a close eye on the pine nuts as they tend to burn very quickly.

5 Peel the bell peppers, slice them into strips, and place them in a warm serving dish. Sprinkle with the pine nuts and drizzle any remaining lemon juice mixture over them. Garnish with sprigs of fresh rosemary and serve at once.

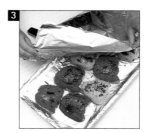

Pasta-stuffed Tomatoes

This unusual and inexpensive dish would make a good starter for eight people or a delicious lunch for four.

NUTRITIONAL INFORMATION

Calories ....298 Sugars 4g
Protein ....10g Fat 20g
Carbohydrate ...20g Saturates 5g

 15 MINS   35 MINS

SERVES 4

I N G R E D I E N T S

5 tablespoons extra virgin olive oil, plus
   extra for greasing

8 large round tomatoes

1 cup dried ditalini or other very
   small pasta shapes

8 black olives, pitted and
   finely chopped

2 tablespoons finely chopped fresh basil

1 tablespoon finely chopped fresh parsley

⅔ cup freshly grated Parmesan cheese

salt and pepper

fresh basil sprigs, to garnish

1 Brush a cookie sheet with olive oil.

2 Slice the tops off the tomatoes and reserve to make "lids." If the tomatoes will not stand up, cut a thin slice off the bottom of each tomato.

3 Using a teaspoon, scoop out the tomato pulp into a strainer, but do not pierce the tomato shells. Invert the tomato shells onto paper towels, pat dry, and then set aside to drain.

4 Bring a large saucepan of lightly salted water to a boil. Add the ditalini or other pasta and 1 tablespoon of the remaining olive oil and cook for 8–10 minutes or until tender, but still firm to the bite. Drain the pasta and set aside.

5 Put the olives, basil, parsley, and Parmesan cheese into a large mixing bowl and stir in the drained tomato pulp. Add the pasta to the bowl. Stir in the remaining olive oil, mix together well, and season to taste with salt and pepper.

6 Spoon the pasta mixture into the tomato shells and replace the lids. Arrange the tomatoes on the cookie sheet and bake in a preheated oven, at 375°F, for 15–20 minutes.

7 Remove the tomatoes from the oven and allow to cool until just warm.

8 Arrange the pasta-stuffed tomatoes on a serving dish, garnish with the basil sprigs, and serve.

Roasted Vegetables

Rosemary branches can be used as brushes for basting and as skewers. Soak the rosemary skewers well in advance to cut down preparation time.

NUTRITIONAL INFORMATION

Calories	16	Sugars	.........3g
Protein	.........1g	Fat	..........0.3g
Carbohydrate	....3g	Saturates	.......0g

 8½ HOURS   10 MINS

SERVES 6

I N G R E D I E N T S

1 small red cabbage

1 head fennel

1 orange bell pepper, cut into
    1½-inch diced pieces

1 eggplant, halved and sliced
    into ½-inch pieces

2 zucchini, sliced thickly
    diagonally

olive oil, for brushing

6 rosemary twigs, about 6 inches
    long, soaked in water for 8 hours

salt and pepper

1 Put the red cabbage on its side on a chopping board and cut through the middle of its stem and heart. Divide each piece into four, each time including a bit of the stem in the slice to hold it together.

VARIATION

Fruit skewers are a deliciously quick and easy dessert. Thread pieces of banana, mango, peach, strawberry, apple, and pear onto soaked wooden skewers and cook over the dying embers. Brush with sugar syrup toward the end of cooking.

2 Prepare the fennel in the same way as the red cabbage.

3 Blanch the red cabbage and fennel in boiling water for 3 minutes, then drain well.

4 With a wooden skewer, pierce a hole through the middle of each piece of vegetable.

5 On to each rosemary twig, thread a piece of orange bell pepper, fennel, red cabbage, eggplant, and zucchini, pushing the rosemary through the holes.

6 Brush liberally with olive oil and season with plenty of salt and pepper.

7 Cook over a hot barbecue for 8–10 minutes, turning occasionally. Serve at once.

Italian Stuffed Bell Peppers

Halved bell peppers are stuffed with the flavors of Italy in this sunshine-bright dish.

NUTRITIONAL INFORMATION

Calories 193   Sugars 8g
Protein . . . . .2g   Fat 17g
Carbohydrate . . . .9g   Saturates 2g

  20 MINS   25 MINS

SERVES 4

I N G R E D I E N T S

1 red bell pepper

1 green bell pepper

1 yellow bell pepper

1 orange bell pepper

6 tablespoons olive oil

1 small red onion, sliced

1 small eggplant,
    chopped roughly

4½ ounces mushrooms, wiped

4½ ounces cherry tomatoes, halved

handful of fresh basil leaves,
    torn into pieces

2 tablespoons lemon juice

salt and pepper

sprigs of fresh basil, to garnish

lemon wedges, to serve

1 Halve the bell peppers, remove the cores, and deseed them. Sprinkle over a few drops of olive oil and season.

2 Heat the remaining olive oil in a skillet. Add the onion, eggplant, and mushrooms, and fry for 3–4 minutes, stirring frequently. Remove from the heat and transfer to a mixing bowl.

3 Add the cherry tomatoes, basil leaves, and lemon juice to the eggplant mixture. Season well with salt and pepper.

4 Spoon the eggplant mixture into the bell pepper halves. Enclose in foil parcels and barbecue over the hot coals for about 15–20 minutes, turning once.

5 Unwrap carefully and serve garnished with sprigs of fresh basil. Serve with lemon wedges.

VARIATION

Dried herbs can be used instead of fresh ones if they are unavailable. Substitute 1 teaspoon dried basil or use mixed dried Italian herbs as an alternative. If you wish, top these stuffed bell peppers with grated mozzarella or Cheddar cheese—¾ cup will be sufficient.

Vegetable Lasagne

This rich, baked pasta dish is packed full of vegetables, tomatoes, and Italian mozzarella cheese.

NUTRITIONAL INFORMATION

Calories	.510	Sugars	.14g
Protein	.17g	Fat	.38g
Carbohydrate	...28g	Saturates	.14g

50 MINS   50 MINS

SERVES 6

I N G R E D I E N T S

2¼ pounds eggplant

8 tablespoons olive oil

2 tablespoons garlic and
  herb butter

1 pound zucchini, sliced

2 cups grated mozzarella cheese

2½ cups sieved tomatoes

6 sheets pre-cooked green lasagne

2½ cups Béchamel Sauce
  (see page 28)

⅔ cup freshly grated
  Parmesan cheese

1 teaspoon dried oregano

salt and pepper

1 Thinly slice the eggplants and place in a colander. Sprinkle with salt and set aside for 20 minutes. Rinse and pat dry with paper towels.

2 Heat 4 tablespoons of the oil in a large skillet. Fry half of the eggplant slices over low heat for 6–7 minutes, or until golden. Drain thoroughly on paper towels. Repeat with the remaining oil and eggplant slices.

3 Melt the garlic and herb butter in the skillet. Add the zucchini and fry for 5–6 minutes, until golden brown all over. Drain thoroughly on paper towels.

4 Place half of the eggplant and zucchini slices in a large ovenproof dish. Season to taste with pepper and sprinkle over half of the mozzarella cheese. Spoon over half of the sieved tomatoes and top with 3 sheets of lasagne. Repeat the process, ending with a layer of lasagne.

5 Spoon over the Béchamel Sauce and sprinkle over the Parmesan cheese and oregano. Put the dish on a cookie sheet and bake in a preheated oven, at 425°F, for 30–35 minutes, or until golden brown. Serve at once.

Macaroni Bake

This satisfying dish would make an excellent supper for a midweek family meal.

NUTRITIONAL INFORMATION

Calories ....728 Sugars 11g
Protein ....17g Fat 42g
Carbohydrate ...75g Saturates 23g

 15 MINS   45 MINS

SERVES 4

I N G R E D I E N T S

4 cups dried short-cut macaroni

1 tablespoon olive oil

4 tablespoons beef drippings

1 pound potatoes, thinly sliced

1 pound onions, sliced

2 cups grated mozzarella cheese

⅔ cup heavy cream

salt and pepper

crusty brown bread and butter,
    to serve

1 Bring a large saucepan of lightly salted water to a boil. Add the macaroni and olive oil and cook for about 12 minutes, or until tender but still firm to the bite. Drain the macaroni thoroughly and set aside.

2 Melt the drippings in a large flame-proof casserole, then remove from the heat.

3 Make alternate layers of potatoes, onions, macaroni, and grated cheese in the dish, seasoning well with salt and pepper between each layer and finishing with a layer of cheese on top. Finally, pour the cream over the top layer of cheese.

4 Bake in a preheated oven at 400°F for 25 minutes. Remove the dish from the oven and carefully brown the top of the bake under a hot broiler.

5 Serve the bake straight from the dish with crusty brown bread and butter as a main course. Alternatively, serve as a vegetable accompaniment with your favorite main course.

VARIATION

For a stronger flavor, use mozzarella affumicata, a smoked version of this cheese, or Swiss cheese instead of the mozzarella.

Filled Eggplants

Combined with tomatoes and mozzarella cheese, pasta makes a tasty filling for baked eggplant shells.

NUTRITIONAL INFORMATION

Calories 342	Sugars 6g	
Protein 11g	Fat 16g	
Carbohydrate ...40g	Saturates 4g	

25 MINS   55 MINS

SERVES 4

I N G R E D I E N T S

2 cups dried penne or other short
   pasta shapes

4 tablespoons olive oil, plus extra for
   brushing

2 eggplants

1 large onion, chopped

2 garlic cloves, crushed

14-ounce can diced tomatoes

2 teaspoon dried oregano

2 ounces mozzarella cheese, thinly sliced

⅓ cup grated Parmesan cheese

2 tablespoons dry bread crumbs

salt and pepper

salad greens, to serve

1 Bring a saucepan of lightly salted water to a boil. Add the pasta and 1 tablespoon of the olive oil and cook for 8–10 minutes or until tender, but still firm to the bite. Drain, return to the pan, cover, and keep warm.

2 Cut the eggplants in half lengthwise and score around the inside with a sharp knife, being careful not to pierce the shells. Scoop out the flesh with a spoon. Brush the insides of the shells with olive oil. Chop the flesh and set aside.

3 Heat the remaining oil in a skillet. Fry the onion until translucent. Add the garlic and fry for 1 minute. Add the chopped eggplant and fry, stirring frequently, for 5 minutes. Add the tomatoes and oregano and season to taste with salt and pepper. Bring to a boil and simmer for 10 minutes, or until thickened. Remove the skillet from the heat and stir in the pasta.

4 Brush a cookie sheet with oil and arrange the eggplant shells in a single layer. Divide half of the tomato and pasta mixture among them. Sprinkle over the mozzarella, then pile the remaining tomato and pasta mixture on top. Mix the Parmesan cheese and bread crumbs and sprinkle over the top, patting it lightly into the mixture.

5 Bake in a preheated oven, at 400°F for about 25 minutes, or until the topping is golden brown. Serve hot with a selection of salad greens.

Spinach & Ricotta Tart

Frozen phyllo pastry is used to line a flan pan, which is then filled with spinach, red bell peppers, cream, eggs, and ricotta cheese.

NUTRITIONAL INFORMATION

Calories	375	Sugars	.........3g
Protein	.........8g	Fat	..........32g
Carbohydrate	...14g	Saturates	......18g

30 MINS　　30 MINS

SERVES 8

INGREDIENTS

8 ounces frozen phyllo pastry, thawed

4½ ounces butter, melted

12 ounces frozen spinach, thawed

2 eggs

⅔ cup light cream

1 cup ricotta cheese

1 red bell pepper, deseeded and
　　sliced into strips

½ cup pine nuts

salt and pepper

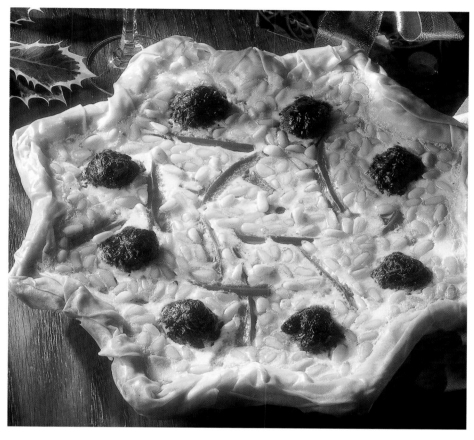

1 Use the sheets of phyllo pastry to line an 8-inch flan pan, brushing each layer with melted butter. Work rapidly, as the phyllo quickly dries out.

2 Put the spinach into a strainer or colander and squeeze out the excess moisture with the back of a spoon or your hand. Form into small balls and arrange in the prepared flan pan.

3 Beat the eggs, cream, and ricotta cheese together until thoroughly blended. Season with salt and pepper to taste and pour over the spinach.

4 Put the remaining butter into a saucepan and melt over low heat. Add the red bell pepper strips and sauté until

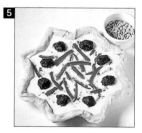

softened, about 4–5 minutes. Arrange the strips in the filling in the flan pan.

5 Scatter the pine nuts over the surface and bake in a preheated oven, at 375°F, for 20–25 minutes, or until the filling has set and the pastry is golden brown. Serve.

VARIATION

If you're not fond of bell peppers, substitute mushrooms instead. Add a few sliced sun-dried tomatoes for extra color and flavor. This recipe makes an ideal dish for vegetarians, although everyone else is sure to enjoy it too.

Patriotic Pasta

The ingredients of this dish have the same bright colors as the Italian flag—hence its name.

NUTRITIONAL INFORMATION

Calories	325	Sugars	.........5g
Protein	.........8g	Fat	..........13g
Carbohydrate	...48g	Saturates	.......2g

 5 MINS   15 MINS

SERVES 4

I N G R E D I E N T S

4 cups dried farfalle

4 tablespoons olive oil

1 pound cherry tomatoes

3 ounces arugula

salt and pepper

Romano cheese, to garnish

1 Bring a large saucepan of lightly salted water to a boil. Add the farfalle and 1 tablespoon of the olive oil and cook for 8–10 minutes or until tender, but still firm to the bite. Drain the farfalle thoroughly and return to the pan.

2 Cut the cherry tomatoes in half and trim the arugula.

COOK'S TIP

Romano cheese is a hard sheep's milk cheese which resembles Parmesan and is often used for grating over a variety of dishes. It has a sharp flavor and is only used in small quantities.

3 Heat the remaining olive oil in a large saucepan. Add the tomatoes to the pan and cook for 1 minute. Add the farfalle and the arugula to the pan and stir gently to mix. Heat through and then season to taste with salt and pepper.

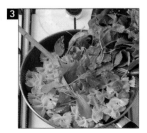

4 Meanwhile, using a vegetable peeler, shave thin slices of Romano cheese.

5 Transfer the farfalle and vegetables to a warm serving dish. Garnish with the Romano cheese shavings and serve at once.

Potatoes in Italian Dressing

The warm potatoes quickly absorb the wonderful flavors of olives, tomatoes, and olive oil. This salad is good warm and cold.

NUTRITIONAL INFORMATION

Calories	239	Sugars	.........2g
Protein	.........4g	Fat	..........10g
Carbohydrate	...36g	Saturates	.......1g

 15 MINS 15 MINS

SERVES 4

INGREDIENTS

1 pound 10 ounces potatoes

1 shallot

2 tomatoes

1 tablespoon chopped fresh basil

salt

ITALIAN DRESSING

1 tomato, peeled and chopped finely

4 black olives, pitted and chopped finely

4 tablespoons olive oil

1 tablespoon wine vinegar

1 garlic clove, crushed

salt and pepper

1 Cook the potatoes in a saucepan of boiling salted water for 15 minutes or until they are tender.

2 Drain the potatoes well, chop roughly, and put into a bowl.

3 Chop the shallot. Cut the tomatoes into wedges and add the shallot and tomatoes to the potatoes.

4 To make the dressing, put all the ingredients into a screw-top jar and mix together thoroughly.

5 Pour the dressing over the potato mixture and toss thoroughly.

6 Transfer the salad to a serving dish and sprinkle with the basil.

COOK'S TIP

This recipe works well with russet potatoes. It doesn't look so attractive, as the potatoes break up when they are cooked, but they absorb the dressing wonderfully. Be sure to use an extra virgin olive oil for the dressing to give a really fruity flavor to the potatoes.

Green Tagliatelle with Garlic

A rich pasta dish for garlic-lovers everywhere. It is quick and easy to prepare and full of flavor.

 20 MINS   15 MINS

SERVES 4

I N G R E D I E N T S

2 tablespoons walnut oil

1 bunch green onions, sliced

2 garlic cloves, thinly sliced

3¼ cups sliced mushrooms

1 pound fresh green and white tagliatelle

1 tablespoon olive oil

8 ounces frozen spinach, thawed
    and drained

½ cup full-fat soft cheese with
    garlic and herbs

4 tablespoons light cream

½ cup chopped, unsalted
    pistachio nuts

salt and pepper

Italian bread, to serve

TO GARNISH

2 tablespoons shredded fresh basil

fresh basil sprigs

1 Heat the walnut oil in a large skillet. Add the green onions and garlic and fry for 1 minute, until just softened.

2 Add the mushrooms to the skillet, stir well, cover, and cook over low heat for about 5 minutes, until softened.

3 Meanwhile, bring a large saucepan of lightly salted water to a boil. Add the tagliatelle and olive oil and cook for 3–5 minutes, or until tender but still firm to the bite. Drain the tagliatelle thoroughly and return to the saucepan.

4 Add the spinach to the skillet and heat through for 1–2 minutes. Add the cheese to the skillet and allow to melt slightly. Stir in the cream and cook, without allowing the mixture to come to a boil, until warmed through.

5 Pour the sauce over the pasta, season to taste with salt and pepper, and mix well. Heat through gently, stirring constantly, for 2–3 minutes.

6 Transfer the pasta to a serving dish and sprinkle with the pistachio nuts and shredded basil. Garnish with the basil sprigs and serve at once with the Italian bread of your choice.

Roasted Bell Pepper Terrine

This delicious terrine is ideal for Sunday lunch. It goes particularly well with Italian bread and salad greens.

NUTRITIONAL INFORMATION

Calories ....196 Sugars 6g
Protein ....6g Fat 14g
Carbohydrate ...13g Saturates 3g

 30 MINS   30 MINS

SERVES 8

I N G R E D I E N T S

3 cups lima beans

6 red bell peppers, halved and deseeded

3 small zucchini, sliced lengthwise

1 eggplant, sliced lengthwise

3 leeks, halved lengthwise

6 tablespoons olive oil, plus extra
   for greasing

6 tablespoons light cream

2 tablespoons chopped fresh basil

salt and pepper

1 Grease a 5-cup terrine. Blanch the lima beans in boiling water for 1–2 minutes and pop them out of their skins. It is not essential to do this, but the effort is worthwhile as the beans taste a lot sweeter.

2 Roast the red bell peppers over a hot barbecue until the skin is black—about 10–15 minutes. Remove and put into a plastic bag. Seal and set aside.

3 Brush the zucchini, eggplant, and leeks with 5 tablespoons of the olive oil, and season with salt and pepper to taste. Cook over the hot barbecue until tender, about 8–10 minutes, turning once.

4 Meanwhile, purée the lima beans in a blender or food processor with 1 tablespoon of the olive oil, the cream, and seasoning. Alternatively, chop and then press through a strainer.

5 Remove the red bell peppers from the bag and peel.

6 Put a layer of red bell pepper along the bottom and up the sides of the terrine.

7 Spread a third of the bean purée over the bell pepper. Cover with the eggplant slices and spread over half of the remaining bean purée.

8 Sprinkle over the basil. Top with zucchini and the remaining bean purée. Lay the leeks on top. Add any remaining pieces of red bell pepper. Put a piece of foil, folded 4 times, on the top and weigh down with cans.

9 Chill until required. Turn out onto a serving platter, slice, and serve with Italian bread and salad greens.

Roast Leeks

Use a good-quality Italian olive oil for this deliciously simple yet sophisticated vegetable accompaniment.

NUTRITIONAL INFORMATION

Calories	52	Sugars	.......0.4g
Protein	........0.3g	Fat	...........5g
Carbohydrate	....1g	Saturates	.......1g

 5 MINS  7 MINS

SERVES 6

I N G R E D I E N T S

4 leeks

3 tablespoons olive oil

2 teaspoon balsamic vinegar

sea salt and pepper

1 Halve the leeks lengthwise, making sure that your knife goes straight, so that the leek is held together by the root.

2 Brush each leek liberally with the olive oil.

3 Cook over a hot barbecue for 6–7 minutes, turning once.

4 Remove the leeks from the barbecue and brush with balsamic vinegar.

5 Sprinkle with salt and pepper and serve hot or warm.

VARIATION

If in season, 8 baby leeks may be used instead of 4 standard-sized ones. Sherry vinegar makes a good substitute for the expensive balsamic vinegar and would work as well in this recipe.

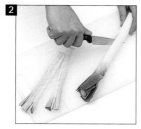

Pesto Potatoes

Pesto sauce is more commonly used as a pasta sauce but is delicious served over potatoes as well.

NUTRITIONAL INFORMATION

Calories	.531	Sugars	.3g
Protein	.13g	Fat	.38g
Carbohydrate	.36g	Saturates	.8g

 15 MINS   15 MINS

SERVES 4

I N G R E D I E N T S

2 pounds small new potatoes

2¾ cups fresh basil

2 tablespoons pine nuts

3 garlic cloves, crushed

½ cup olive oil

1 cup freshly grated Parmesan
    cheese and Romano cheese, mixed

salt and pepper

fresh basil sprigs, to garnish

1 Cook the potatoes in a saucepan of boiling salted water for 15 minutes or until tender. Drain well, transfer to a warm serving dish, and keep warm until required.

2 Meanwhile, put the basil, pine nuts, garlic, and a little salt and pepper to taste in a food processor. Blend for 30 seconds, adding the oil gradually, until smooth.

3 Remove the mixture from the food processor and place in a mixing bowl. Stir in the grated Parmesan and Romano cheeses.

4 Spoon the pesto sauce over the potatoes and mix well. Garnish with fresh basil sprigs and serve at once.

Italian Vegetable Tart

A rich tomato pastry base topped with a mouthwatering selection of vegetables and cheese makes a tart that's tasty as well as attractive.

NUTRITIONAL INFORMATION

Calories	438	Sugars	.........8g
Protein	.........9g	Fat	..........28g
Carbohydrate	...40g	Saturates	......15g

1¾ HOURS   40 MINS

SERVES 6

I N G R E D I E N T S

1 eggplant, sliced

2 tablespoons salt

4 tablespoons olive oil

1 garlic clove, crushed

1 large yellow bell pepper, deseeded
    and sliced

1¼ cups ready-made
    tomato pasta sauce

⅔ cup sun-dried tomatoes in oil, drained
    and halved if necessary

6 ounces mozzarella cheese,
    drained and sliced thinly

P A S T R Y

2 cups all-purpose flour

pinch of celery salt

½ cup butter or margarine

2 tablespoons tomato paste

2–3 tablespoons milk

1 To make the pastry, sift the flour and celery salt into a bowl and rub in the butter or margarine until the mixture resembles fine bread crumbs.

2 Mix together the tomato paste and milk and stir into the mixture to form a firm dough. Knead gently on a lightly

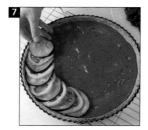

floured counter until smooth. Wrap and chill for 30 minutes.

3 Grease an 11-inch loose-based flan pan. Roll out the pastry on a lightly floured surface and use to line the pan. Trim and prick all over with a fork. Chill for 30 minutes.

4 Meanwhile, layer the eggplant in a dish, sprinkling with the salt. Leave for 30 minutes.

5 Bake the pie shell in a preheated oven, 400°F, for 20–25 minutes until cooked

and lightly golden. Set aside. Increase the oven temperature to 450°F.

6 Rinse the eggplant and pat dry. Heat 3 tablespoons of oil in a skillet and fry the garlic, eggplant, and bell pepper for 5–6 minutes until just softened. Drain on paper towels.

7 Spread the pie shell with pasta sauce and arrange the cooked vegetables, sun-dried tomatoes, and mozzarella on top. Brush with the remaining oil and bake for 5 minutes until the cheese is just melting.

Spinach & Ricotta Pie

This puff pastry pie looks impressive and is actually fairly easy to make. Serve it hot or cold.

NUTRITIONAL INFORMATION

Calories 545   Sugars 3g
Protein . . . . .19g   Fat 42g
Carbohydrate . . .25g   Saturates 13g

🍳 25 MINS   🕐 50 MINS

SERVES 4

I N G R E D I E N T S

8 ounces spinach

¼ cup pine nuts

½ cup ricotta cheese

2 large eggs, beaten

½ cup ground almonds

⅔ cup grated Parmesan cheese

9 ounces puff pastry, thawed if frozen

1 small egg, beaten

1 Rinse the spinach, place in a large saucepan and cook for 4–5 minutes until wilted. Drain thoroughly. When the spinach is cool enough to handle, squeeze out the excess liquid.

2 Place the pine nuts on a cookie sheet and lightly toast under a preheated broiler for 2–3 minutes or until golden.

3 Place the ricotta, spinach, and eggs in a bowl and mix together. Add the pine nuts, beat well, then stir in the ground almonds and Parmesan cheese.

4 Roll out the puff pastry and make 2 x 8-inch squares. Trim the edges, reserving the pastry trimmings.

5 Place 1 pastry square on a cookie sheet. Spoon over the spinach mixture, keeping within ½ inch of the

 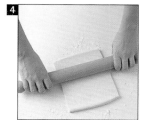 

edge of the pastry. Brush the edges with beaten egg and place the second square over the top.

6 Using a round-bladed knife, press the pastry edges together by tapping along the sealed edge. Use the pastry trimmings to make a few leaves to decorate the pie.

7 Brush the pie with the beaten egg and bake in a preheated oven, at 425°F, for 10 minutes. Reduce the oven temperature to 375°F and bake for a further 25–30 minutes. Serve hot.

COOK'S TIP

Spinach is very nutritious as it is full of iron—this is particularly important for women and elderly people who may lack this in their diet.

Parmesan Potatoes

This is a very simple way to jazz up roast potatoes. Serve them in the same way as roasted potatoes with roasted meats or fish.

NUTRITIONAL INFORMATION

Calories 307	Sugars 2g	
Protein 11g	Fat 14g	
Carbohydrate . . .37g	Saturates 6g	

 15 MINS   1 HR 5 MINS

SERVES 4

INGREDIENTS

6 potatoes

⅔ cup grated Parmesan cheese

pinch of grated nutmeg

1 tablespoon chopped fresh parsley

4 smoked bacon slices, cut into strips

oil, for roasting

salt

1 Cut the potatoes in half lengthwise and cook them in a saucepan of boiling salted water for 10 minutes. Drain thoroughly.

2 Mix the grated Parmesan cheese, nutmeg, and parsley together in a shallow bowl.

3 Roll the potato pieces in the cheese mixture to coat them completely. Shake off any excess.

VARIATION

If you prefer, use slices of salami or prosciutto instead of the bacon, adding it to the dish 5 minutes before the end of the cooking time.

4 Pour a little oil into a roasting pan and heat it in a preheated oven, 400°F, for 10 minutes. Remove from the oven and place the potatoes into the pan. Return the pan to the oven and cook for 30 minutes, turning once.

5 Remove from the oven and sprinkle the bacon on top of the potatoes. Return to the oven for 15 minutes or until the potatoes and bacon are cooked. Drain off any excess fat and serve.

Spaghetti & Mushroom Sauce

This easy vegetarian dish is ideal for busy people with little time, but good taste!

NUTRITIONAL INFORMATION

Calories 604   Sugars 5g
Protein . . . . .11g   Fat 39g
Carbohydrate . . .54g   Saturates 21g

20 MINS   35 MINS

SERVES 4

INGREDIENTS

4 tablespoons butter

2 tablespoons olive oil

6 shallots, sliced

6 cups sliced mushrooms

1 teaspoon all-purpose flour

⅔ cup heavy cream

2 tablespoons port

4 ounces sun-dried tomatoes, chopped

freshly grated nutmeg

1 pound dried spaghetti

1 tablespoon freshly chopped parsley

salt and pepper

6 triangles of fried white bread, to serve

  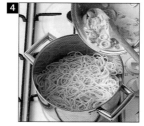

1 Heat the butter and 1 tablespoon of the oil in a large pan. Add the shallots and cook over medium heat for 3 minutes. Add the mushrooms and cook over low heat for 2 minutes. Season with salt and pepper, sprinkle over the flour, and cook, stirring constantly, for 1 minute.

2 Gradually stir in the cream and port, add the sun-dried tomatoes and a pinch of grated nutmeg, and cook over low heat for 8 minutes.

3 Meanwhile, bring a large saucepan of lightly salted water to a boil. Add the spaghetti and remaining olive oil and cook for 12–14 minutes, until tender but still firm to the bite.

4 Drain the spaghetti and return to the pan. Pour over the mushroom sauce and cook for 3 minutes. Transfer the spaghetti and mushroom sauce to a large serving plate and sprinkle over the chopped parsley. Serve with crispy triangles of fried bread.

VARIATION

Non-vegetarians could add 4 ounces prosciutto, cut into thin strips and heated gently in 2 tablespoons butter, to the pasta along with the mushroom sauce.

Pasta & Bean Casserole

A satisfying winter dish, this is a slow-cooked, one-pot meal. The beans need to be soaked overnight so prepare well in advance.

NUTRITIONAL INFORMATION

Calories ....377 Sugars 5g
Protein ....10g Fat 18g
Carbohydrate ...43g Saturates 5g

30 MINS   3¹/₂ HOURS

SERVES 6

I N G R E D I E N T S

1¼ cups dried navy beans, soaked
   overnight and drained

8 ounces dried penne

6 tablespoons olive oil

3½ cups vegetable stock

2 large onions, sliced

2 garlic cloves, chopped

2 bay leaves

1 teaspoon dried oregano

1 teaspoon dried thyme

5 tablespoons red wine

2 tablespoons tomato paste

2 celery stalks, sliced

1 fennel bulb, sliced

2 cups sliced mushrooms

8 ounces tomatoes, sliced

1 teaspoon brown sugar

4 tablespoons dry white bread crumbs

salt and pepper

salad greens and crusty bread,
   to serve

1 Put the navy beans in a large saucepan and add sufficient cold water to cover. Bring to a boil and continue to boil vigorously for 20 minutes. Drain, set aside and keep warm.

2 Bring a large saucepan of lightly salted water to a boil. Add the penne and 1 tablespoon of the olive oil and cook for about 3 minutes. Drain the pasta thoroughly, set aside, and keep warm.

3 Put the beans in a large, flameproof casserole. Add the vegetable stock and stir in the remaining olive oil, the onions, garlic, bay leaves, oregano, thyme, wine, and tomato paste. Bring to a boil, then cover, and cook in a preheated oven at 350°F for 2 hours.

4 Add the penne, celery, fennel, mushrooms, and tomatoes to the casserole and season to taste with salt and pepper. Stir in the sugar and sprinkle over the bread crumbs. Cover the dish and cook in the oven for 1 hour.

5 Serve the pasta and bean casserole hot with salad greens and crusty bread.

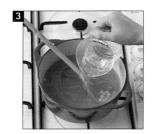

Macaroni & Corn Pancakes

This vegetable pancake can be filled with your favorite vegetables—a favorite alternative is shredded parsnips with 1 tablespoon mustard.

NUTRITIONAL INFORMATION

Calories	702	Sugars	. . . . .4g
Protein	. . . . .13g	Fat	. . . . .50g
Carbohydrate	. . .55g	Saturates	. . . . . .23g

 15 MINS   40 MINS

SERVES 4

I N G R E D I E N T S

2 corn cobs

4 tablespoons butter

4 ounces red bell peppers, cored, deseeded, and finely diced

2½ cups dried short-cut macaroni

⅔ cup heavy cream

¼ cup all-purpose flour

4 egg yolks

4 tablespoons olive oil

salt and pepper

TO SERVE

oyster mushrooms

fried leeks

1 Bring a saucepan of water to a boil, add the corn cobs, and cook for about 8 minutes. Drain thoroughly and refresh under cold running water for 3 minutes. Carefully cut away the kernels onto paper towels and set aside to dry.

2 Melt 2 tablespoons of the butter in a skillet. Add the bell peppers and cook over low heat for 4 minutes. Drain and pat dry with paper towels.

3 Bring a large saucepan of lightly salted water to a boil. Add the macaroni and cook for about 12 minutes, or until tender but still firm to the bite. Drain the macaroni thoroughly and leave to cool in cold water until required.

4 Beat together the cream, flour, a pinch of salt, and the egg yolks in a bowl until smooth. Add the corn and bell peppers to the cream and egg mixture. Drain the macaroni and then toss into the corn and cream mixture. Season with pepper to taste.

5 Heat the remaining butter with the oil in a large skillet. Drop spoonfuls of the mixture into the skillet and press down until the mixture forms a flat pancake. Fry until golden on both sides, and all the mixture is used up. Serve at once with oyster mushrooms and fried leeks.

Fettuccine & Walnut Sauce

This mouthwatering dish would make an excellent light, vegetarian lunch for four or a good starter for six.

NUTRITIONAL INFORMATION

Calories 833   Sugars 5g
Protein . . . . .20g   Fat 66g
Carbohydrate . . .44g   Saturates 15g

  15 MINS   10 MINS

SERVES 6

INGREDIENTS

2 thick slices whole wheat
   bread, crusts removed

1¼ cups milk

2½ cups shelled walnuts

2 garlic cloves, crushed

1 cup pitted black olives

⅔ cup freshly grated
   Parmesan cheese

8 tablespoons extra virgin olive oil

⅔ cup heavy cream

1 pound fresh fettuccine

salt and pepper

2–3 tablespoons chopped fresh parsley

1 Put the bread in a shallow dish, pour over the milk, and set aside to soak until the liquid has been absorbed.

2 Spread the walnuts out on a cookie sheet and toast in a preheated oven, at 375°F, for about 5 minutes, or until golden. Set aside to cool.

3 Put the soaked bread, walnuts, garlic, olives, Parmesan cheese, and 6 tablespoons of the olive oil in a food processor and work to make a purée. Season to taste with salt and pepper and stir in the cream.

4 Bring a large pan of lightly salted water to a boil. Add the fettuccine and 1 tablespoon of the remaining oil and cook for 2–3 minutes, or until tender but still firm to the bite. Drain the fettuccine thoroughly and toss with the remaining olive oil.

5 Divide the fettuccine among individual serving plates and spoon the olive, garlic, and walnut sauce on top. Sprinkle over the fresh parsley and serve.

COOK'S TIP

Parmesan quickly loses its pungency and "bite". It is better to buy small quantities and grate it yourself. Wrapped in foil, it will keep in the refrigerator for several months.

Pasta with Garlic & Broccoli

Broccoli coated in a garlic-flavored cream sauce, served on herb tagliatelle. Try sprinkling with toasted pine nuts to add extra crunch.

NUTRITIONAL INFORMATION

Calories	538	Sugars	.........4g
Protein	........23g	Fat	..........29g
Carbohydrate	...50g	Saturates	......17g

 5 MINS 5 MINS

SERVES 4

I N G R E D I E N T S

1 pound 2 ounces broccoli

1¼ cups garlic & herb
   cream cheese

4 tablespoons milk

12 ounces fresh herb tagliatelle

⅓ cup grated Parmesan cheese

chopped fresh chives, to garnish

1 Cut the broccoli into even-sized flowerets. Cook the broccoli in a saucepan of boiling salted water for 3 minutes and drain thoroughly.

2 Put the soft cheese into a saucepan and heat gently, stirring, until melted. Add the milk and stir until well combined.

3 Add the broccoli to the cheese mixture and stir to coat.

4 Meanwhile, bring a large saucepan of salted water to a boil and add the tagliatelle. Stir and bring back to a boil. Reduce the heat slightly and cook the tagliatelle, uncovered, for 3–4 minutes until just tender.

5 Drain the tagliatelle thoroughly and divide among 4 warm serving plates. Spoon the broccoli and cheese sauce on top. Sprinkle with grated Parmesan cheese, garnish with chopped chives, and serve at once.

COOK'S TIP

An herb flavored pasta goes particularly well with the broccoli sauce, but failing this, a tagliatelle verde or "paglia e fieno" (literally "straw and hay"—thin green and yellow noodles) will fill the bill.

Fettuccine all'Alfredo

This simple, traditional dish can be made with any long pasta, but is especially good with flat noodles, such as fettuccine or tagliatelle.

NUTRITIONAL INFORMATION

Calories	627	Sugars	........2g
Protein	........18g	Fat	..........41g
Carbohydrate	...51g	Saturates	......23g

5 MINS   10 MINS

SERVES 4

INGREDIENTS

2 tablespoons butter

1 cup heavy cream

1 pound fresh fettuccine

1 tablespoon olive oil

1 cup freshly grated Parmesan
  cheese, plus extra to serve

pinch of freshly grated nutmeg

salt and pepper

fresh parsley sprigs, to garnish

1 Put the butter and ²⁄₃ cup of the cream in a large saucepan and bring the mixture to a boil over medium heat. Reduce the heat and then simmer gently for about 1½ minutes, or until slightly thickened.

2 Meanwhile, bring a large pan of lightly salted water to a boil. Add the

VARIATION

This classic Roman dish is often served with the addition of strips of ham and fresh peas. Add 2 cups shelled cooked peas and 6 ounces ham strips with the Parmesan cheese in step 4.

fettuccine and olive oil and cook for 2–3 minutes, until tender but still firm to the bite. Drain the fettuccine thoroughly and then pour over the cream sauce.

3 Toss the fettuccine in the sauce over low heat until thoroughly coated.

4 Add the remaining cream, the Parmesan cheese, and nutmeg to the fettuccine mixture and season to taste

with salt and pepper. Toss thoroughly to coat while gently heating through.

5 Transfer the fettucine mixture to a warm serving plate and garnish with the fresh sprig of parsley. Serve at once, handing extra grated Parmesan cheese separately.

Italian Spaghetti

Delicious vegetables, cooked in a rich tomato sauce, make an ideal topping for nutty whole wheat pasta.

NUTRITIONAL INFORMATION

Calories 381   Sugars 9g
Protein . . . . .11g   Fat 16g
Carbohydrate . . .53g   Saturates 5g

 20 MINS   35 MINS

SERVES 4

I N G R E D I E N T S

2 tablespoons olive oil

1 large red onion, chopped

2 garlic cloves, crushed

1 tablespoon lemon juice

4 baby eggplants, quartered

2½ cups sieved tomatoes

2 teaspoons sugar

2 tablespoons tomato paste

14-ounce can artichoke hearts, drained
    and halved

1 cup pitted black olives

12 ounces dried spaghetti

2 tablespoons butter

salt and pepper

fresh basil sprigs, to garnish

olive bread, to serve

1 Heat 1 tablespoon of the olive oil in a large skillet. Add the onion, garlic, lemon juice, and eggplants and cook over low heat for 4–5 minutes, or until the onion and eggplants are lightly golden brown.

2 Pour in the sieved tomatoes, season to taste with salt and pepper, and stir in the sugar, and tomato paste. Bring to a boil, lower the heat, and then simmer, stirring occasionally, for 20 minutes.

3 Gently stir in the artichoke hearts and black olives and cook for 5 minutes.

4 Meanwhile, bring a large saucepan of lightly salted water to a boil. Add the spaghetti and the remaining oil and cook for 7–8 minutes, or until tender but still firm to the bite.

5 Drain the spaghetti thoroughly and toss with the butter. Transfer the spaghetti to a large serving dish.

6 Pour the vegetable sauce over the spaghetti, garnish with the sprigs of fresh basil, and serve at once with olive bread.

Pasta & Vegetable Sauce

The different shapes and textures of the vegetables make a mouthwatering presentation in this light and summery dish.

NUTRITIONAL INFORMATION

Calories	389	Sugars	........4g
Protein	........16g	Fat	.........20g
Carbohydrate	...38g	Saturates	......11g

 10 MINS 30 MINS

SERVES 4

I N G R E D I E N T S

2 cups dried gemelli or other pasta shapes

1 tablespoon olive oil

1 head green broccoli, cut into flowerets

2 zucchini, sliced

8 ounces asparagus spears

4 ounces snow peas

1 cup frozen peas

2 tablespoons butter

3 tablespoons vegetable stock

4 tablespoons heavy cream

freshly grated nutmeg

2 tablespoons chopped fresh parsley

2 tablespoons freshly grated
Parmesan cheese

salt and pepper

1 Bring a large saucepan of lightly salted water to a boil. Add the pasta and olive oil and cook for 8–10 minutes or until tender, but still firm to the bite. Drain the pasta, return to the pan, cover, and keep warm.

2 Steam the broccoli flowerets, zucchini slices, asparagus spears, and snow peas over a pan of boiling salted water until they are just beginning to soften. Remove the vegetables from the heat and immediately refresh in cold water. Drain and set aside.

3 Bring a small pan of lightly salted water to a boil. Add the frozen peas and cook for 3 minutes. Drain the peas, refresh in cold water, and then drain again. Set aside with the other vegetables.

4 Put the butter and vegetable stock in a pan over medium heat. Add all of the vegetables, reserving a few of the asparagus spears, and toss carefully with a wooden spoon until they have heated through, taking care not to break them up.

5 Stir in the cream and heat through without bringing to a boil. Season to taste with salt, pepper, and nutmeg.

6 Transfer the pasta to a warm serving dish and stir in the chopped parsley. Spoon over the vegetable sauce and sprinkle over the Parmesan cheese. Arrange the reserved asparagus spears in a pattern on top and serve.

Paglia e Fieno

The name of this dish—"straw and hay"—refers to the colors of the pasta when mixed together.

NUTRITIONAL INFORMATION

Calories	699	Sugars	.........7g
Protein	........26g	Fat	.........39g
Carbohydrate	...65g	Saturates	......23g

  10 MINS   10 MINS

SERVES 4

I N G R E D I E N T S

4 tablespoons butter

1 pound fresh peas, shelled

1 cup heavy cream

1 pound mixed fresh green and white

spaghetti or tagliatelle

1 tablespoon olive oil

²⁄₃ cup freshly grated Parmesan

   cheese, plus extra to serve

pinch of freshly grated nutmeg

salt and pepper

1 Melt the butter in a large saucepan. Add the peas and cook, over low heat, for 2–3 minutes.

2 Using a measuring cup, pour ²⁄₃ cup of the cream into the pan, bring to a boil, and simmer for 1–1½ minutes, or until slightly thickened. Remove the pan from the heat.

3 Meanwhile, bring a large pan of lightly salted water to a boil. Add the spaghetti or tagliatelle and olive oil and cook for 2–3 minutes, or until just tender but still firm to the bite. Remove the pan from the heat, drain the pasta thoroughly, and return to the pan.

4 Add the peas and cream sauce to the pasta. Return the pan to the heat and add the remaining cream and the Parmesan cheese, and season to taste with salt, pepper, and grated nutmeg.

5 Using 2 forks, gently toss the pasta to coat with the peas and cream sauce, while heating through.

6 Transfer the pasta to a serving dish and serve at once, with extra Parmesan cheese.

VARIATION

Fry 2 cups sliced button or oyster mushrooms in 4 tablespoons butter over low heat for 4–5 minutes. Stir into the peas and cream sauce just before adding to the pasta in step 4.

Spaghetti Olio e Aglio

This easy and satisfying Roman dish originated as a cheap meal for poor people, but has now become a favorite in restaurants and trattorias.

NUTRITIONAL INFORMATION

Calories	.515	Sugars	.1g
Protein	.8g	Fat	.33g
Carbohydrate	.50g	Saturates	.5g

 5 MINS   5 MINS

SERVES 4

INGREDIENTS

½ cup olive oil

3 garlic cloves, crushed

1 pound fresh spaghetti

3 tablespoons chopped fresh parsley

salt and pepper

1 Reserve 1 tablespoon of the olive oil and heat the remainder in a medium saucepan. Add the garlic and a pinch of salt and cook over low heat, stirring constantly, until golden brown, then remove the pan from the heat. Do not allow the garlic to burn as it will taint its flavor. (If it does burn, you will have to start all over again!)

2 Meanwhile, bring a large saucepan of lightly salted water to a boil. Add the spaghetti and remaining olive oil to the pan and cook for 2–3 minutes, or until tender, but still firm to the bite. Drain the spaghetti thoroughly and return to the pan.

3 Add the oil and garlic mixture to the spaghetti and toss to coat thoroughly. Season with pepper, add the chopped fresh parsley and toss to coat again.

4 Transfer the spaghetti to a warm serving dish and serve at once.

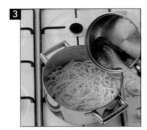

COOK'S TIP

Oils produced by different countries, mainly Italy, Spain, and Greece, have their own characteristic flavors. Some produce an oil which has a hot, peppery taste while others have a "green" flavor.

Vegetables & Tofu

This is a simple, clean-tasting dish of green vegetables, bean curd, and pasta, lightly tossed in olive oil.

NUTRITIONAL INFORMATION

Calories	....	.400
Protein	....	.19g
Carbohydrate	...	.46g

Sugars	....	.5g
Fat	....	.17g
Saturates	....	.5g

25 MINS   20 MINS

SERVES 4

I N G R E D I E N T S

8 ounces asparagus

4½ ounces snow peas

8 ounces green beans

1 leek

8 ounces shelled small lima beans

10½ ounces dried fusilli

2 tablespoons olive oil

2 tablespoons butter or margarine

1 garlic clove, crushed

8 ounces tofu, cut into
   1-inch cubes

½ cup pitted green olives in
   brine, drained

salt and pepper

freshly grated Parmesan, to serve

1 Cut the asparagus into 2-inch lengths. Finely slice the snow peas diagonally and slice the green beans into 1-inch pieces. Finely slice the leek.

2 Bring a large saucepan of water to a boil and add the asparagus, green beans and lima beans. Bring back to a boil and cook for 4 minutes until just tender. Drain well and rinse in cold water. Set aside.

3 Bring a large saucepan of salted water to a boil and cook the fusilli for 8–9 minutes until just tender. Drain well. Toss in 1 tablespoon of the oil and season well with salt and pepper.

4 Meanwhile, in a wok or large skillet, heat the remaining oil and the butter or margarine and gently fry the leek, garlic, and tofu for 1–2 minutes until the vegetables have just softened.

5 Stir in the snow peas and cook for 1 minute.

6 Add the boiled vegetables and olives to the pan and heat through for 1 minute. Carefully stir in the pasta and seasoning. Cook for 1 minute and pile into a warm serving dish. Serve sprinkled with Parmesan cheese.

Salads

If you need inspiration for salads to accompany your main courses, look no further than this chapter. All of the salads complement a wide variety of dishes, and many make ideal starters. You could even serve a proportion of these salads as main courses as they are often quite filling. Use plenty of colorful, fresh ingredients in your salad—choose from a

wide range of bell peppers, snow peas, and baby corn cobs as they are all readily available. If possible, use Italian staple ingredients, such as extra virgin olive oil and balsamic vinegar, for salad dressings, and sprinkle over some Italian cheeses, such as Parmesan and Romano, for extra taste. All of the salads in this chapter are refreshing and full of flavor, and are sure to get the tastebuds tingling.

Yellow Bell Pepper Salad

A colorful combination of yellow bell peppers, red radishes, and celery combine to give a wonderfully crunchy texture and fresh taste.

NUTRITIONAL INFORMATION

Calories 176	Sugars 4g
Protein 4g	Fat 16g
Carbohydrate 4g	Saturates 4g

  25 MINS   5 MINS

SERVES 4

INGREDIENTS

4 slices bacon, chopped

2 yellow bell peppers

8 radishes, washed and trimmed

1 celery stalk, finely chopped

3 plum tomatoes, cut into wedges

3 tablespoons olive oil

1 tablespoon fresh thyme

1 Dry fry the chopped bacon in a skillet for 4–5 minutes or until crispy. Remove the bacon from the skillet, set aside, and leave to cool until required.

2 Using a sharp knife, halve and deseed the bell peppers. Slice the bell peppers into long strips.

3 Using a sharp knife, halve the radishes and cut them into wedges.

COOK'S TIP

Tomatoes are actually berries and are related to potatoes. There are many different shapes and sizes of this versatile fruit. The one most used in Italian cooking is the plum tomato, or Roma, which is very flavorsome.

4 Mix together the bell peppers, radishes, celery, and tomatoes and toss the mixture in the olive oil and fresh thyme. Season to taste with a little salt and pepper.

5 Transfer the salad to serving plates and garnish with the reserved crispy bacon pieces.

Pasta & Garlic Mayo Salad

This crisp salad would make an excellent accompaniment to broiled meat and is ideal for summer barbecues.

NUTRITIONAL INFORMATION

Calories 858   Sugars 35g
Protein . . . . .11g   Fat 64g
Carbohydrate . . .64g   Saturates 8g

 1½ HOURS   10 MINS

SERVES 4

INGREDIENTS

2 large lettuces

9 oz dried penne

1 tablespoon olive oil

8 red apples

juice of 4 lemons

1 head of celery, sliced

¾ cup shelled, halved walnuts

1 cup fresh garlic
    mayonnaise (see Cook's Tip)

salt

1 Wash, drain, and pat dry the lettuce leaves with paper towels. Transfer them to the refrigerator for 1 hour or until crisp.

2 Meanwhile, bring a large saucepan of lightly salted water to the boil. Add the pasta and olive oil and cook for 8–10 minutes or until tender, but still firm to the bite. Drain the pasta and refresh under cold running water. Drain thoroughly again and set aside.

3 Core and dice the apples, place them in a small bowl and sprinkle with the lemon juice.

4 Mix together the pasta, celery, apples, and walnuts and toss the mixture in the garlic mayonnaise (see Cook's Tip, right). Add more mayonnaise, if liked.

5 Line a salad bowl with the lettuce leaves and spoon the pasta salad into the lined bowl. Serve when required.

COOK'S TIP

To make garlic mayo, beat 2 egg yolks with salt and 6 crushed garlic cloves. Start beating in 1½ cups oil, 1–2 teaspoons at a time. When ¼ of the oil has been incorporated, beat in 1–2 tablespoons white wine vinegar. Continue beating in the oil. Stir in 1 teaspoon Dijon mustard and season.

Eggplant Salad

A starter with a difference from Sicily. It has a real bite, both from the sweet-sour sauce, and from the texture of the celery.

NUTRITIONAL INFORMATION

Calories	390	Sugars	.......15g
Protein	.........8g	Fat	..........33g
Carbohydrate	...16g	Saturates	.......5g

1½ HOURS   25 MINS

SERVES 4

I N G R E D I E N T S

2 large eggplants, about 2¼ pounds

6 tablespoons olive oil

1 small onion, chopped finely

2 garlic cloves, crushed

6–8 celery stalks, cut into ½-inch slices

2 tablespoons capers

12–16 green olives, pitted
   and sliced

2 tablespoons pine nuts

1 ounce bitter or dark
   chocolate, grated

4 tablespoons wine vinegar

1 tablespoon brown sugar

salt and pepper

2 hard-cooked eggs,
   sliced, to serve

celery leaves or curly endive,
   to garnish

1 Cut the eggplants into 1-inch cubes and sprinkle liberally with 2–3 tablespoons of salt. Leave to stand for 1 hour to extract the bitter juices, then rinse off the salt thoroughly under cold water, drain and dry on paper towels.

2 Heat most of the oil in a skillet and fry the eggplant cubes until golden brown all over. Drain on paper towels then put in a large bowl.

3 Add the onion and garlic to the skillet with the remaining oil and fry very gently until just soft. Add the celery to the skillet and fry for a few minutes, stirring frequently, until lightly colored but still crisp.

4 Add the celery to the eggplants with the capers, olives, and pine nuts and mix lightly.

5 Add the chocolate, vinegar, and sugar to the residue in the pan. Heat gently until melted, then bring to a boil. Season with salt and pepper to taste. Pour over the salad and mix lightly. Cover, leave until cold, and then chill thoroughly.

6 Serve with sliced hard-cooked eggs and garnish with celery leaves or curly endive.

Green Salad

Herb-flavored croutons are topped with peppery arugula, red chard, green olives, and pistachios to make an elegant combination.

NUTRITIONAL INFORMATION

Calories	256	Sugars	. . . . .3g
Protein	. . . . .4g	Fat	. . . . .17g
Carbohydrate	. . .23g	Saturates	. . . . . . .3g

 25 MINS   10 MINS

SERVES 4

I N G R E D I E N T S

¼ cup pistachio nuts

5 tablespoons extra virgin olive oil

1 tablespoon rosemary, chopped

2 garlic cloves, chopped

4 slices rustic bread

1 tablespoon red wine vinegar

1 teaspoon wholegrain mustard

1 teaspoon sugar

1 ounce arugula

1 ounce red chard

½ cup pitted green olives

2 tablespoons fresh basil, shredded

1 Shell the pistachios and roughly chop them, using a sharp knife.

2 Place 2 tablespoons of the extra virgin olive oil in a skillet. Add the rosemary and garlic and cook for 2 minutes.

3 Add the slices of bread to the skillet and fry for 2–3 minutes on both sides until golden. Remove the bread from the pan and drain on absorbent paper towels.

4 To make the dressing, mix together the remaining olive oil with the red wine vinegar, mustard, and sugar.

5 Place a slice of bread onto a serving plate and top with the arugula and red chard. Sprinkle with the olives.

6 Drizzle the dressing over the top of the salad greens. Sprinkle with the chopped pistachios and shredded basil leaves and serve the salad at once.

COOK'S TIP

If you cannot find red chard, try slicing a tomato into very thin wedges to add a splash of vibrant red color to the salad.

Niçoise with Pasta Shells

This is an Italian variation of the traditional Niçoise salad from southern France.

NUTRITIONAL INFORMATION

Calories 484	Sugars 5g
Protein 28g	Fat 26g
Carbohydrate ...35g	Saturates 4g

 45 MINS   30 MINS

SERVES 4

INGREDIENTS

3 cups dried small pasta shells

1 tablespoon olive oil

4 ounces green beans

1¾ ounces canned anchovies, drained

5 teaspoons milk

2 small crisp lettuces

1 pound or 3 large tomatoes

4 hard-cooked eggs

8-ounce can tuna, drained

1 cup pitted black olives

salt and pepper

VINAIGRETTE DRESSING

¼ cup extra virgin olive oil

5 teaspoons white wine vinegar

1 teaspoon wholegrain mustard

salt and pepper

COOK'S TIP

It is very convenient to make salad dressings in a screw-top jar. Put all the ingredients in the jar, cover securely, and shake well to mix and emulsify the oil.

1 Bring a large saucepan of lightly salted water to a boil. Add the pasta and the olive oil and cook for 8–10 minutes or until tender, but still firm to the bite. Drain and refresh in cold water.

2 Bring a small saucepan of lightly salted water to a boil. Add the beans and cook for 10–12 minutes, until tender but still firm to the bite. Drain, refresh in cold water, drain thoroughly once more, and then set aside.

3 Put the anchovies in a shallow bowl, pour over the milk, and set aside for 10 minutes. Meanwhile, tear the lettuces into large pieces. Blanch the tomatoes in boiling water for 1–2 minutes, then drain, peel, and roughly chop the flesh. Shell the eggs and cut into quarters. Cut the tuna into large chunks.

4 Drain the anchovies and the pasta. Put all of the salad ingredients, the beans and the olives into a large bowl and gently mix together.

5 To make the vinaigrette dressing, beat together all of the dressing ingredients and keep in the refrigerator until required. Just before serving, pour the vinaigrette dressing over the salad.

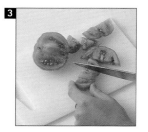

Tuscan Bean & Tuna Salad

The combination of beans and tuna is a favorite in Tuscany. The hint of honey and lemon in the dressing makes this salad very refreshing.

NUTRITIONAL INFORMATION

Calories . . . . . . .224 Sugars 4g
Protein . . . . .19g Fat 10g
Carbohydrate . . .16g Saturates 2g

30 MINS   0 MINS

SERVES 4

INGREDIENTS

1 small white onion or 2 green onions,
   finely chopped

2 x 14-ounce cans lima beans, drained

2 medium tomatoes

6½-ounce can tuna, drained

2 tablespoons flat-leaf parsley, chopped

2 tablespoons olive oil

1 tablespoon lemon juice

2 teaspoons liquid honey

1 garlic clove, crushed

1 Place the chopped onions or green onions and lima beans in a bowl and mix well to combine.

2 Using a sharp knife, cut the tomatoes into wedges.

3 Add the tomatoes to the onion and bean mixture.

4 Flake the tuna with a fork and add it to the onion and bean mixture, together with the parsley.

5 In a screw-top jar, mix together the olive oil, lemon juice, honey, and garlic. Shake the jar until the dressing emulsifies and thickens.

6 Pour the dressing over the bean salad. Toss the ingredients together using 2 spoons and serve.

VARIATION

Substitute fresh salmon for the tuna if you wish to create a luxurious version of this recipe for a special occasion.

Chargrilled Chicken Salad

This is a quick starter to serve at a barbecue—if the bread is bent in half, the chicken salad can be put in the middle and eaten as finger food.

NUTRITIONAL INFORMATION

Calories 225	Sugars 5g	
Protein 16g	Fat 12g	
Carbohydrate . . .15g	Saturates 2g	

10 MINS   15 MINS

SERVES 4

INGREDIENTS

2 skinless, boneless chicken breasts

1 red onion

oil for brushing

1 avocado, peeled and pitted

1 tbsp lemon juice

½ cup low-fat mayonnaise

¼ tsp chilli powder

½ tsp pepper

¼ tsp salt

4 tomatoes, quartered

½ loaf sun-dried tomato-flavored focaccia bread

green salad, to serve

1 Using a sharp knife, cut the chicken breasts into ½ inch strips.

VARIATION

Instead of focaccia, serve the salad in pita bread which have been warmed through on the barbecue.

2 Cut the onion into eight pieces, held together at the root. Rinse under cold running water and then brush with oil.

3 Purée or mash the avocado and lemon juice together. Whisk in the mayonnaise. Add the chilli powder, pepper and salt.

4 Put the chicken and onion over a hot barbecue and grill for 3–4 minutes

on each side. Combine the chicken, onion, tomatoes and avocado mixture together.

5 Cut the bread in half twice, so that you have quarter-circle-shaped pieces, then in half horizontally. Toast on the hot barbecue (grill) for about 2 minutes on each side.

6 Spoon the chicken mixture on to the toasts and serve with a green salad.

Roast Bell Pepper Salad

Serve chilled as an antipasto with cold meats, or warm as a side dish. Garlic bread makes a delicious accompaniment.

NUTRITIONAL INFORMATION

Calories 141	Sugars 8g
Protein 1g	Fat 11g
Carbohydrate 9g	Saturates 2g

20 MINS   20 MINS

SERVES 4

I N G R E D I E N T S

4 large mixed red, green, and yellow bell peppers

4 tablespoons olive oil

1 large red onion, sliced

2 garlic cloves, crushed

4 tomatoes, peeled and chopped

pinch of sugar

1 teaspoon lemon juice

salt and pepper

1 Trim and halve the bell peppers and remove the seeds.

2 Place the bell peppers, skin-side up, under a preheated hot broiler. Cook until the skins char. Rinse under cold water and remove the skins.

3 Trim off any thick membranes and slice thinly.

4 Heat the oil and fry the onion and garlic until softened. Then add the bell peppers and tomatoes and fry over low heat for 10 minutes.

5 Remove from the heat, add the sugar and lemon juice, and season to taste. Serve at once or leave to cool (the flavors will develop as the salad cools).

Spinach Salad

Fresh baby spinach is tasty and light, and it makes an excellent salad to go with the chicken and creamy dressing.

NUTRITIONAL INFORMATION

Calories 145	Sugars 3g	
Protein 10g	Fat 10g	
Carbohydrate 4g	Saturates 1g	

🥗 30 MINS   🕐 0 MINS

SERVES 4

INGREDIENTS

3½ ounces baby spinach, washed

2¾ ounces radicchio leaves, shredded

1¾ ounces mushrooms

3½ ounces cooked chicken,
  preferably breast

1¾ ounces prosciutto

2 tablespoons olive oil

finely grated rind of ½ orange and juice
  of 1 orange

1 tablespoon yogurt

1 Wipe the mushrooms with a damp cloth to remove any excess dirt.

2 Gently mix together the spinach and radicchio in a large salad bowl.

3 Using a sharp knife, thinly slice the wiped mushrooms and add them to the bowl containing the spinach and radicchio.

4 Tear the cooked chicken breast and prosciutto into strips and mix them into the spinach salad.

5 To make the dressing, place the olive oil, orange rind, juice, and yogurt into a screw-top jar. Shake the jar until the mixture is well combined. Season to taste with salt and pepper.

6 Drizzle the dressing over the spinach salad and toss to mix well. Serve.

VARIATION

Spinach is delicious when served raw. Try raw spinach in a salad garnished with bacon or garlicky croûtons. The young leaves have a wonderfully sharp flavor.

Goat Cheese & Penne Salad

This superb salad is delicious when served with strongly flavored meat dishes, such as venison.

NUTRITIONAL INFORMATION

Calories 634	Sugars 13g	
Protein 18g	Fat 51g	
Carbohydrate . . .27g	Saturates 13g	

1½ HOURS   15 MINS

SERVES 4

INGREDIENTS

9 ounces dried penne

5 tablespoons olive oil

1 head radicchio, torn into pieces

1 lettuce, torn into pieces

7 tablespoons chopped walnuts

2 ripe pears, cored and diced

1 fresh basil sprig

1 bunch of watercress, trimmed

2 tablespoons lemon juice

3 tablespoons garlic vinegar

4 tomatoes, quartered

1 small onion, sliced

1 large carrot, grated

1 cup diced goat cheese

salt and pepper

1 Bring a large saucepan of lightly salted water to a boil. Add the penne and 1 tablespoon of the olive oil and cook for 8–10 minutes or until tender, but still firm to the bite. Drain the pasta, refresh under cold running water, drain thoroughly again, and set aside to cool.

2 Place the radicchio and lettuce in a large salad bowl and mix together well. Top with the pasta, walnuts, pears, basil, and watercress.

3 Mix together the lemon juice, the remaining olive oil and the vinegar in a pitcher. Pour the mixture over the salad ingredients and toss to coat the salad greens well.

4 Add the tomato quarters, onion slices, grated carrot, and diced goat cheese and toss together, using 2 forks, until well mixed. Leave the salad to chill in the refrigerator for about 1 hour before serving.

COOK'S TIP

Radicchio is a variety of chicory originating in Italy. It has a slightly bitter flavor.

Potato & Sausage Salad

Sliced Italian sausage blends well with the other Mediterranean flavors of sun-dried tomato and basil in this salad.

NUTRITIONAL INFORMATION

Calories	450	Sugars	.........6g
Protein	........13g	Fat	..........28g
Carbohydrate	...38g	Saturates	.......1g

25 MINS   25 MINS

SERVES 4

INGREDIENTS

1 pound potatoes

1 radicchio

1 green bell pepper, sliced

6 ounces Italian sausage, sliced

1 red onion, halved and sliced

2 cups sun-dried tomatoes, sliced

2 tablespoons shredded fresh basil

DRESSING

1 tablespoon balsamic vinegar

1 teaspoon tomato paste

2 tablespoons olive oil

salt and pepper

COOK'S TIP

Any sliced Italian sausage or salami can be used in this salad. Italy is home of the salami and there are numerous varieties to choose from—those from the south tend to be more highly spiced than those from the north of the country.

1 Cook the potatoes in a saucepan of boiling water for 20 minutes or until cooked through. Drain and leave to cool.

2 Line a large serving platter with the radicchio leaves.

3 Slice the cooled potatoes and arrange them in layers on the lettuce-lined serving platter, together with the sliced green bell pepper, sliced Italian sausage, red onion, sun-dried tomatoes, and shredded fresh basil.

4 In a small bowl, whisk the balsamic vinegar, tomato paste, and olive oil together and season to taste with salt and pepper. Pour the dressing over the potato salad and serve at once.

Minted Fennel Salad

This is a very refreshing salad. The subtle licorice flavor of fennel combines well with the cucumber and mint.

NUTRITIONAL INFORMATION

Calories	90	Sugars	.........7g
Protein	.........4g	Fat	...........5g
Carbohydrate	....7g	Saturates	.......1g

 25 MINS   0 MINS

SERVES 4

INGREDIENTS

1 bulb fennel

2 small oranges

1 small or ½ a large cucumber

1 tablespoon chopped mint

1 tablespoon virgin olive oil

2 eggs, hard-cooked

1 Using a sharp knife, trim the outer leaves from the fennel. Slice the fennel bulb thinly into a bowl of water and sprinkle with lemon juice (see Cook's Tip).

2 Grate the rind of the oranges over a bowl. Using a sharp knife, pare away the orange peel, then segment the orange by carefully slicing between each line of membrane. Do this over the bowl in order to retain the juice.

3 Using a sharp knife, cut the cucumber into ½-inch rounds and then cut each round into quarters.

4 Add the cucumber to the fennel and orange mixture, together with the mint.

5 Pour the olive oil over the fennel and cucumber salad and toss well.

6 Peel and quarter the eggs and use these to decorate the top of the salad. Serve at once.

COOK'S TIP

Fennel will discolor if it is left for any length of time without a dressing. To prevent any discoloration, place it in a bowl of water and sprinkle with lemon juice.

Pasta Salad & Basil Vinaigrette

All the ingredients of pesto sauce are included in this salad, which has a fabulous summery taste, perfect for *al fresco* eating.

NUTRITIONAL INFORMATION

Calories	432	Sugars 3g
Protein	........14g	Fat .... .29g
Carbohydrate	...30g	Saturates 6g

 25 MINS   15 MINS

SERVES 4

I N G R E D I E N T S

2 cups fusilli

4 tomatoes

½ cup black olives

½ cup sun-dried tomatoes in oil

2 tablespoons pine nuts

2 tablespoons grated Parmesan cheese

fresh basil, to garnish

V I N A I G R E T T E

½ cup basil leaves

1 clove garlic

2 tablespoons grated Parmesan cheese

4 tablespoons extra virgin olive oil

2 tablespoons lemon juice

salt and pepper

COOK'S TIP

Sun-dried tomatoes have a strong, intense flavor. They are most frequently found packed in oil with herbs and garlic. Do not waste the oil, which has an excellent flavor, instead use it in salad dressings.

1 Cook the pasta in a saucepan of lightly salted boiling water for 8–10 minutes or until just tender. Drain the pasta, rinse under cold water, then drain again thoroughly. Place the pasta in a large bowl.

2 To make the vinaigrette, place the basil leaves, garlic, cheese, oil, and lemon juice in a food processor. Season with salt and pepper to taste. Process until the leaves are well chopped and the ingredients are combined. Alternatively, finely chop the basil leaves by hand and combine with the other vinaigrette ingredients. Pour the vinaigrette over the pasta and toss to coat.

3 Cut the tomatoes into wedges. Pit and halve the olives. Slice the sun-dried tomatoes. Place the pine nuts on a cookie sheet and toast under the broiler until golden.

4 Add the tomatoes (fresh and sun-dried) and the olives to the pasta and mix.

5 Transfer the pasta to a serving dish, scatter over the Parmesan and pine nuts, and garnish with a few basil leaves.

Seafood Salad

Seafood is plentiful in Italy and each region has its own seafood salad. The dressing needs to be chilled for several hours so prepare in advance.

NUTRITIONAL INFORMATION

Calories 471   Sugars 2g
Protein . . . . .34g   Fat 33g
Carbohydrate . . . .4g   Saturates 5g

45-55 MINS   40 MINS

SERVES 4

INGREDIENTS

6 ounces squid rings, thawed if frozen

2½ cups water

⅔ cup dry white wine

8 ounces hake or monkfish, cut into cubes

16–20 mussels, scrubbed and debearded

20 clams in shells, scrubbed, if available

   (otherwise use extra mussels)

4½–6 ounces peeled jumbo shrimp)

3–4 green onions, trimmed and

   sliced (optional)

radicchio and curly endive leaves, to serve

lemon wedges, to garnish

DRESSING

6 tablespoons olive oil

1 tablespoon wine vinegar

2 tablespoons chopped fresh parsley

1–2 garlic cloves, crushed

salt and pepper

GARLIC MAYONNAISE

5 tablespoons thick mayonnaise

2–3 tablespoons plain yogurt

2 garlic cloves, crushed

1 tablespoon capers

2 tablespoons chopped fresh parsley or

   mixed herbs

1 Poach the squid in the water and wine for 20 minutes or until nearly tender. Add the fish and continue to cook gently for 7–8 minutes or until tender. Strain, reserving the fish. Pour the stock into a clean pan.

2 Bring the fish stock to a boil and add the mussels and clams. Cover the pan and simmer gently for about 5 minutes or until the shells open. Discard any that remain closed.

3 Drain the shellfish and remove from their shells. Put into a bowl with the cooked fish and add the shrimp and green onions, if using.

4 For the dressing, whisk together the oil, vinegar, parsley, garlic, salt and pepper to taste. Pour over the fish, mixing well. Cover and chill for several hours.

5 Arrange small leaves of radicchio and curly endive on 4 plates and spoon the fish salad into the center. Garnish with lemon wedges. Combine all the ingredients for the garlic mayonnaise and serve with the salad.

Rare Beef Pasta Salad

This salad is a meal in itself and would be perfect for an *al fresco* lunch, perhaps with a bottle of red wine.

NUTRITIONAL INFORMATION

Calories	575	Sugars	. . . . .4g
Protein	. . . . .31g	Fat	. . . . .33g
Carbohydrate	. . .44g	Saturates	. . . . . . .9g

15 MINS   30 MINS

SERVES 4

INGREDIENTS

1 pound rump or sirloin steak in
   one piece

1 pound dried fusilli

5 tablespoons olive oil

2 tablespoons lime juice

2 tablespoons Thai fish sauce
   (see Cook's Tip)

2 teaspoon liquid honey

4 green onions, sliced

1 cucumber, peeled and cut into
   1-inch chunks

3 tomatoes, cut into wedges

1 tablespoon finely chopped fresh mint

salt and pepper

1 Season the steak with salt and pepper. Broil or pan-fry the steak for 4 minutes on each side. Allow to rest for 5 minutes, then slice thinly across the grain.

2 Meanwhile, bring a large saucepan of lightly salted water to a boil. Add the fusilli and 1 tablespoon of the olive oil and cook for 8–10 minutes or until tender, but still firm to the bite. Drain the fusilli, refresh in cold water. and drain again thoroughly. Toss the fusilli in the remaining olive oil.

3 Combine the lime juice, fish sauce, and honey in a small saucepan and cook over medium heat for 2 minutes.

4 Add the grren onions, cucumber, tomatoes, and mint to the pan, then add the steak, and mix well. Season to taste with salt.

5 Transfer the fusilli to a large, warm serving dish and top with the steak and salad mixture. Serve just warm or allow to cool completely.

COOK'S TIP

Thai fish sauce, also known as nam pla, is made from salted anchovies and has quite a strong flavor, so it should be used with discretion. It is available from some supermarkets and from Chinese food stores.

Mushroom Salad

Raw mushrooms are a great favorite in Italian dishes—they have a fresh, almost creamy flavor.

NUTRITIONAL INFORMATION

Calories 121	Sugars 0.1g	
Protein 2g	Fat 13g	
Carbohydrate . . .0.1g	Saturates 2g	

20 MINS   0 MINS

SERVES 4

I N G R E D I E N T S

5½ ounces firm white mushrooms

4 tablespoons virgin olive oil

1 tablespoon lemon juice

5 anchovy fillets, drained and chopped

1 tablespoon fresh marjoram

salt and pepper

1 Gently wipe each mushroom with a damp cloth in order to remove any excess dirt.

2 Slice the mushrooms thinly, using a sharp knife.

3 To make the dressing, mix together the olive oil and lemon juice.

4 Pour the dressing mixture over the mushrooms. Toss together so that the mushrooms are completely coated with the lemon juice and oil.

5 Stir the chopped anchovy fillets into the mushrooms.

6 Season the mushroom mixture with pepper to taste and garnish with the fresh marjoram.

7 Leave the mushroom salad to stand for about 5 minutes before serving in order for all the flavors to be absorbed.

8 Season the mushroom salad with a little salt (see Cook's Tip) and then serve.

COOK'S TIP

Do not season the mushroom salad with salt until the very last minute as it will cause the mushrooms to blacken and the juices to leak. The result will not be as tasty as it should be as the full flavors won't be absorbed and it will also look very unattractive.

Pasta Salad & Mixed Cabbage

This crunchy, colorful salad would be a good accompaniment for broiled meat or fish.

NUTRITIONAL INFORMATION

Calories 388   Sugars 17g
Protein . . . . .18g   Fat 18g
Carbohydrate . . .41g   Saturates 3g

 25 MINS   🕐 30 MINS

SERVES 4

I N G R E D I E N T S

2 ¼ cups dried
   short-cut macaroni

5 tablespoons olive oil

1 large red cabbage, shredded

1 large white cabbage, shredded

2 large apples, diced

9 ounces cooked smoked bacon or
   ham, diced

8 tablespoons wine vinegar

1 tablespoon sugar

salt and pepper

1 Bring a pan of lightly salted water to a boil. Add the macaroni and 1 tablespoon of the oil and cook for 8–10 minutes or until tender, but still firm to the bite. Drain the pasta, then refresh in cold water. Drain again and set aside.

VARIATION

Alternative dressings can be made with 4 tablespoons olive oil, 4 tablespoons red wine, 4 tablespoons red wine vinegar and 1 tablespoon sugar. Or use 3 tablespoons olive oil and 1 tablespoon walnut or hazelnut oil.

2 Bring a large saucepan of lightly salted water to a boil. Add the shredded red cabbage and cook for 5 minutes. Drain the cabbage thoroughly and set aside to cool.

3 Bring a large saucepan of lightly salted water to a boil. Add the white cabbage and cook for 5 minutes. Drain the cabbage thoroughly and set aside to cool.

4 In a large bowl, mix together the pasta, red cabbage, and apple. In a separate bowl, mix together the white cabbage and bacon or ham.

5 In a small bowl, mix together the remaining oil, the vinegar, and sugar and season to taste with salt and pepper. Pour the dressing over each of the 2 cabbage mixtures and, finally, mix them all together. Serve at once.

Italian Potato Salad

Potato salad is always a favorite, but it is even more delicious with the addition of sun-dried tomatoes and fresh parsley.

NUTRITIONAL INFORMATION

Calories 425   Sugars 6g
Protein . . . . .6g   Fat 27g
Carbohydrate . . .43g   Saturates 5g

  40 MINS   15 MINS

SERVES 4

I N G R E D I E N T S

1 pound baby potatoes, unpeeled, or
  larger potatoes, halved

4 tablespoons plain yogurt

4 tablespoons mayonnaise

8 sun-dried tomatoes

2 tablespoons flat leaf parsley, chopped

salt and pepper

1 Rinse and clean the potatoes and place them in a large pan of water. Bring to a boil and cook for 8–12 minutes or until just tender. (The cooking time will vary according to the size of the potatoes.)

2 Using a sharp knife, cut the sun-dried tomatoes into thin slices.

3 To make the dressing, mix together the yogurt and mayonnaise in a bowl and season to taste with a little salt and pepper. Stir in the sun-dried tomato slices and the chopped flat leaf parsley.

4 Remove the potatoes with a perforated spoon, drain them thoroughly, and then set them aside to cool. If you are using larger potatoes, cut them into 2-inch chunks.

5 Pour the dressing over the potatoes and toss to mix.

6 Leave the potato salad to chill in the refrigerator for about 20 minutes, then serve as a starter or as an accompaniment.

COOK'S TIP

It is easier to cut the larger potatoes once they are cooked. Although smaller pieces of potato will cook more quickly, they tend to disintegrate and become mushy.

Italian Bell Pepper Salad

This salad goes well with all barbecued foods, especially meats. Alternatively, serve it with a selection of Italian bread for a simple starter.

NUTRITIONAL INFORMATION

Calories ....150 Sugars 6g
Protein ....4g Fat 12g
Carbohydrate ....7g Saturates 1g

30 MINS   30 MINS

SERVES 4

I N G R E D I E N T S

2 red bell peppers, halved and
  deseeded

2 yellow bell peppers, halved and
  deseeded

3 tablespoons extra virgin olive oil

1 onion, cut into wedges

2 large zucchini, sliced

2 garlic cloves, sliced

1 tablespoon balsamic vinegar

1¾ ounces anchovy fillets, chopped

¼ cup pitted black olives, quartered

fresh basil leaves

1 Place the bell pepper halves, cut side down, on a broiler pan and cook until the skin blackens and chars. Leave to cool slightly, then pop them into a plastic bag for about 10 minutes.

2 Peel away the skin from the bell peppers and discard. Cut the flesh into thick strips.

3 Heat the oil in a large skillet, add the onion, and cook gently for 10 minutes or until softened. Add the zucchini slices, garlic, and bell pepper strips to the skillet and cook, stirring occasionally, for a further 10 minutes.

4 Add the vinegar, anchovies, and olives to the skillet. Season with salt and pepper to taste. Mix well and leave to cool.

5 Reserve a few basil leaves for garnishing, then tear the remainder into small pieces. Stir them into the salad.

6 Transfer the salad to a serving dish and garnish with a few whole basil leaves.

COOK'S TIP

Balsamic vinegar is made in and around Modena in Italy. Its rich, mellow flavor is perfect for Mediterranean-style salads, but if it is unavailable, use sherry vinegar or white wine vinegar instead.

Lentil & Tuna Salad

In this recipe, lentils, combined with spices, lemon juice, and tuna, make a wonderfully tasty and filling salad.

NUTRITIONAL INFORMATION

Calories 227   Sugars 2g
Protein . . . . .19g   Fat 9g
Carbohydrate . . .19g   Saturates 1g

25 MINS   0 MINS

SERVES 4

INGREDIENTS

3 tablespoons virgin olive oil

1 tablespoon lemon juice

1 teaspoon wholegrain mustard

1 garlic clove, crushed

½ teaspoon cumin powder

½ teaspoon ground coriander

1 small red onion

2 ripe tomatoes

14-ounce can lentils, drained

6½ oz can tuna, drained

2 tablespoons fresh cilantro, chopped

pepper

1 Using a sharp knife, deseed the tomatoes and then chop them into finely diced pieces.

2 Using a sharp knife, finely chop the red onion.

3 To make the dressing, whisk together the virgin olive oil, lemon juice, mustard, garlic, cumin powder, and ground coriander in a small bowl. Set aside until required.

4 Mix together the chopped onion, diced tomatoes, and drained lentils in a large bowl.

5 Flake the tuna and stir it into the onion, tomato, and lentil mixture.

6 Stir in the chopped fresh cilantro.

7 Pour the dressing over the lentil and tuna salad and season with pepper to taste. Serve at once.

COOK'S TIP

Lentils are a good source of protein and contain important vitamins and minerals. Buy them dried for soaking and cooking yourself, or buy canned varieties for speed and convenience.

Spicy Sausage Salad

A warm sausage and pasta dressing spooned over chilled salad greens makes a refreshing combination to start a meal.

NUTRITIONAL INFORMATION

Calories 383	Sugars 2g
Protein 11g	Fat 28g
Carbohydrate ...20g	Saturates 1g

15 MINS   25 MINS

SERVES 4

I N G R E D I E N T S

1 cup small pasta shapes, such as
   elbow tubetti

3 tablespoons olive oil

1 medium onion, chopped

2 cloves garlic, crushed

1 small yellow bell pepper, cored, seeded,
   and cut into matchstick strips

6 ounces spicy pork sausage such as
   chorizo, skinned and sliced

2 tablespoons red wine

1 tablespoon red wine vinegar

mixed salad greens, chilled

salt

VARIATION

Other sausages to use are the Italian pepperoni, flavored with chili peppers, fennel, and spices, and one of the many varieties of salami, usually flavored with garlic and pepper.

1 Cook the pasta in a pan of boiling salted water, adding 1 tablespoon of the oil, for 8–10 minutes or until tender. Drain in a colander and set aside.

2 Heat the remaining oil in a saucepan over medium heat. Fry the onion until it is translucent, stir in the garlic, bell pepper, and sliced sausage and cook for 3–4 minutes, stirring once or twice.

3 Add the wine, wine vinegar, and reserved pasta to the pan, stir to blend well, and bring the mixture just to a boil.

4 Arrange the chilled salad green on 4 individual serving plates and spoon on the warm sausage and pasta mixture. Serve at once.

Capri Salad

This tomato, olive, and mozzarella salad, dressed with balsamic vinegar and olive oil, makes a delicious starter on its own.

NUTRITIONAL INFORMATION

Calories 95   Sugars 3g
Protein ....3g   Fat 8g
Carbohydrate ....3g   Saturates 3g

20 MINS   3–5 MINS

SERVES 4

INGREDIENTS

2 large tomatoes

4½ ounces mozzarella cheese

12 black olives

8 basil leaves

1 tablespoon balsamic vinegar

1 tablespoon olive oil

salt and pepper

basil leaves, to garnish

1 Using a sharp knife, cut the tomatoes into thin slices.

2 Using a sharp knife, cut the mozzarella into slices.

3 Pit the olives and slice them into rings.

4 Layer the tomato, mozzarella cheese, and olives in a stack, finishing with a layer of cheese on top.

5 Place each stack under a preheated hot broiler for 2–3 minutes or just long enough to melt the mozzarella.

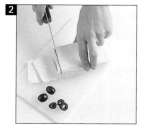

6 Drizzle over the vinegar and olive oil, and season to taste with a little salt and pepper.

7 Transfer to serving plates and garnish with basil leaves. Serve at once.

COOK'S TIP

Buffalo mozzarella cheese, although it is usually more expensive because of the comparative rarity of buffalo, does have a better flavor than the cow's milk variety. It is popular in salads, but also provides a tangy layer in baked dishes.

Neapolitan Seafood Salad

This delicious mix of seafood, salad greens, and ripe tomatoes conjures up all the warmth and sunshine of Naples.

NUTRITIONAL INFORMATION

Calories	1152	Sugars	.........3g
Protein	........67g	Fat	..........81g
Carbohydrate	...35g	Saturates	......12g

  6¹/₂ HOURS   25 MINS

SERVES 4

INGREDIENTS

1 pound prepared squid,
   cut into strips

1 pound 10 ounces cooked mussels

1 pound cooked clams in brine

²/₃ cup white wine

1¼ cups olive oil

2 cups dried campanelle or
   other small pasta shapes

juice of 1 lemon

1 bunch chives, snipped

1 bunch fresh parsley,
   finely chopped

4 large tomatoes

mixed salad greens

salt and pepper

sprig of fresh basil, to garnish

VARIATION

You can substitute cooked scallops for the mussels, if you prefer. The seafood needs to be marinated for 6 hours, so prepare well in advance.

1 Put all of the seafood into a large bowl, pour over the wine and half of the olive oil, and set aside for 6 hours.

2 Put the seafood mixture into a saucepan and simmer over low heat for 10 minutes. Set aside to cool.

3 Bring a large saucepan of lightly salted water to a boil. Add the pasta and 1 tablespoon of the remaining olive oil and cook for 8–10 minutes or until tender, but still firm to the bite. Drain thoroughly and refresh in cold water.

4 Strain off about half of the cooking liquid from the seafood and discard the rest. Mix in the lemon juice, chives, parsley, and the remaining olive oil. Season to taste with salt and pepper. Drain the pasta and add to the seafood.

5 Cut the tomatoes into quarters. Shred the salad greens and arrange them at the base of a salad bowl. Spoon in the seafood salad and garnish with the tomatoes and a sprig of basil. Serve.

Sweet & Sour Salad

This delicious sweet and sour eggplant salad from Sicily was first brought to Italy by the Moors.

NUTRITIONAL INFORMATION

Calories 217	Sugars 12g
Protein 2g	Fat 18g
Carbohydrate . . .13g	Saturates 3g

 25 MINS 30 MINS

SERVES 4

I N G R E D I E N T S

6 tablespoons olive oil

1 onion, chopped

2 garlic cloves, chopped

2 celery stalks, chopped

1 pound eggplant

14-ounce can tomatoes, chopped

½ cup pitted green olives, chopped

2 tablespoons sugar

2⅓ cups red wine vinegar

1 ounce capers, drained

salt and pepper

1 tablespoon flat leaf parsley, roughly chopped, to garnish

1 Heat 2 tablespoons of the oil in a large skillet. Add the prepared onions, garlic, and celery to the skillet and cook, stirring, for 3–4 minutes.

2 Using a sharp knife, slice the eggplants into thick rounds, then cut each round into 4 pieces.

3 Add the eggplant pieces to the skillet with the remaining olive oil and fry for 5 minutes or until golden.

4 Add the tomatoes, olives and sugar to the skillet, stirring until the sugar has completely dissolved.

5 Add the red wine vinegar, reduce the heat, and leave to simmer for 10–15 minutes or until the sauce is thick and the eggplants are tender.

6 While the skillet is still on the heat, stir in the capers. Season to taste with salt and pepper.

7 Transfer to serving plates and garnish with the chopped fresh parsley.

COOK'S TIP

This salad is best served cold the day after it is made, which allows the flavors to mingle and be fully absorbed.

Goat Cheese Salad

The black olive vinaigrette and bitter salad greens give a real tang to this quick snack.

NUTRITIONAL INFORMATION

Calories	362	Sugars	.........3g
Protein	........14g	Fat	..........22g
Carbohydrate	...29g	Saturates	......10g

🥪 30 MINS   🕐 5-6 MINS

SERVES 4

I N G R E D I E N T S

3 tablespoons olive oil

1 tablespoon white wine vinegar

1 teaspoon black olive paste

1 garlic clove, crushed

1 teaspoon chopped fresh thyme

1 ciabatta loaf, or other Italian bread

4 small tomatoes, sliced

12 fresh basil leaves

9 ounces goat cheese

fresh basil sprigs, to garnish

salad greens, to serve

1 Put the oil, vinegar, olive paste, garlic, and thyme in a small bowl and whisk together.

2 Cut the ciabatta in half horizontally, then in half vertically to make 4 pieces.

3 Drizzle some of the dressing over the pieces of ciabatta bread, then arrange the tomato slices and fresh basil leaves on top.

4 Cut the goat cheese into 12 slices and lay 3 slices on each piece of ciabatta.

5 Brush the cheese with some of the dressing and place in a preheated oven, at 450°F, for 5-6 minutes or until just turning brown at the edges.

6 Cut each piece of bread in half. Arrange the salad greens on serving plates and top with the baked bread. Pour over the remaining dressing, garnish with the fresh basil sprigs, and serve with salad greens.

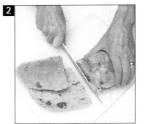

COOK'S TIP

Goat cheeses range in flavor from fresh and creamy to strong and tangy, developing flavor as they mature. Fresh goat cheese must be eaten within about 2 days but the mature cheeses, which have a firmer, drier texture, will keep for longer.

Cheese, Nut, & Pasta Salad

Use colorful salad greens to provide visual contrast to match the contrasts of taste and texture.

NUTRITIONAL INFORMATION

Calories	694	Sugars	.........1g
Protein	........22g	Fat	..........57g
Carbohydrate	...24g	Saturates	......15g

🍲 15 MINS 🕐 15–20 MINS

SERVES 4

INGREDIENTS

2 cups dried pasta shells

1 tablespoon olive oil

1 cup shelled and halved walnuts

mixed salad greens, such as
   radicchio, escarole, arugula

8 ounces dolcelatte or roquefort cheese,
   crumbled

salt

DRESSING

2 tablespoons walnut oil

4 tablespoons extra virgin olive oil

2 tablespoons red wine vinegar

salt and pepper

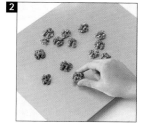

1. Bring a large saucepan of lightly salted water to a boil. Add the pasta shells and olive oil and cook for 8–10 minutes or until just tender, but still firm to the bite. Drain the pasta, refresh under cold running water, drain thoroughly again, and set aside.

2. Spread out the shelled walnut halves on a cookie sheet and toast under a preheated broiler for 2–3 minutes. Set aside to cool while you make the dressing.

3. To make the dressing, whisk together the walnut oil, olive oil, and vinegar in a small bowl, and season to taste.

4. Arrange the salad greens in a large serving bowl. Pile the cooled pasta in the middle of the salad greens and sprinkle over the cheese. Pour the dressing over the pasta salad, scatter over the walnut halves. and toss together to mix. Serve at once.

COOK'S TIP

Dolcelatte is a semisoft, blue-veined cheese from Italy. Its texture is creamy and smooth and the flavor is delicate, but piquant. You could use Roquefort instead. It is essential that whatever cheese you choose, it is of the best quality and in peak condition.

Artichoke & Ham Salad

This elegant starter would make a good first course. Serve it with a little fresh bread for mopping up the juices.

NUTRITIONAL INFORMATION

Calories 124	Sugars 2g	
Protein 2g	Fat 11g	
Carbohydrate 4g	Saturates 1g	

 25 MINS   0 MINS

SERVES 4

I N G R E D I E N T S

9½ ounces marinated artichoke hearts
drained

4 small tomatoes

½ cup sun-dried tomatoes in oil

1½ ounces prosciutto

¼ cup pitted black olives, halved

a few basil leaves

D R E S S I N G

3 tablespoons olive oil

1 tablespoon white wine vinegar

1 clove garlic, crushed

½ teaspoon mustard

1 teaspoon liquid honey

salt and pepper

COOK'S TIP

Use bottled artichokes in oil if you can find them as they have a better flavor. If only canned artichokes are available, rinse them carefully to remove the salty liquid.

1 Make sure the artichokes hearts are thoroughly drained, then cut them into quarters, and place in a bowl.

2 Cut each fresh tomato into wedges. Slice the sun-dried tomatoes into thin strips. Cut the prosciutto into thin strips and add to the bowl with the tomatoes and olive halves.

3 Keeping a few basil leaves whole for garnishing, tear the remainder of the leaves into small pieces and add to the bowl containing the other salad ingredients.

4 To make the dressing, put the oil, wine vinegar, garlic, mustard, honey, and salt and pepper to taste in a screw-top jar and shake vigorously until the ingredients are well blended.

5 Pour the dressing over the salad and toss together.

6 Serve the salad garnished with a few whole basil leaves.

Tuna, Bean, & Anchovy Salad

Serve as part of a selection of *antipasti*, or for a summer lunch with hot garlic bread.

NUTRITIONAL INFORMATION

Calories 397   Sugars 8g
Protein ....23g   Fat 30g
Carbohydrate ...10g   Saturates 4g

35 MINS   0 MINS

SERVES 4

INGREDIENTS

1 pound 2 ounces tomatoes

7-ounce can tuna fish, drained

2 tablespoons chopped fresh parsley

½ cucumber

1 small red onion, sliced

8 ounces cooked green beans

1 small red bell pepper, cored and
  deseeded

1 small crisp lettuce

6 tablespoons Italian-style dressing

3 hard-cooked eggs

2 ounces can anchovies, drained

12 black olives, pitted

1 Cut the tomatoes into wedges, flake the tuna, and put both into the bowl with the parsley.

2 Cut the cucumber in half lengthwise, then cut into slices. Slice the onion. Add the cucumber and onion to the bowl.

3 Cut the beans in half, chop the bell pepper, and add both to the bowl with the lettuce leaves. Pour over the dressing and toss to mix, then spoon into a salad bowl. Cut the eggs into quarters, arrange over the top with the anchovies, and scatter with the olives.

Italian Pasta Salad

Tomatoes and mozzarella cheese are a classic Italian combination. Here they are joined with pasta and avocado for an extra touch of luxury.

NUTRITIONAL INFORMATION

Calories 541	Sugars 5g	
Protein 12g	Fat 43g	
Carbohydrate . . .29g	Saturates 10g	

15 MINS   15 MINS

SERVES 4

I N G R E D I E N T S

2 tablespoons pine nuts

1½ cups dried fusilli

1 tablespoon olive oil

6 tomatoes

8 ounces mozzarella cheese

1 large avocado

2 tablespoons lemon juice

3 tablespoons chopped fresh basil

salt and pepper

fresh basil sprigs, to garnish

D R E S S I N G

6 tablespoons extra virgin olive oil

2 tablespoons white wine vinegar

1 teaspoon wholegrain mustard

pinch of sugar

1 Spread the pine nuts out on a cookie sheet and toast them under a preheated broiler for 1–2 minutes. Remove and set aside to cool.

2 Bring a large saucepan of lightly salted water to a boil. Add the fusilli and olive oil and cook for 8–10 minutes or until tender, but still firm to the bite. Drain the pasta and refresh in cold water. Drain again and set aside to cool.

3 Thinly slice the tomatoes and the mozzarella cheese.

4 Cut the avocado in half, then carefully remove the pit and skin. Cut into thin slices lengthwise and sprinkle with lemon juice to prevent discoloration.

5 To make the dressing, whisk together the oil, vinegar, mustard, and sugar in a small bowl, and season to taste with salt and pepper.

6 Arrange the tomatoes, mozzarella cheese, and avocado alternately in overlapping slices on a large serving platter.

7 Toss the pasta with half of the dressing and the chopped basil and season to taste with salt and pepper. Spoon the pasta into the center of the platter and pour over the remaining dressing. Sprinkle over the pine nuts, garnish with fresh basil sprigs, and serve at once.

Pasta with Pesto Vinaigrette

Sun-dried tomatoes and olives enhance this delicious pesto-inspired salad, which is just as tasty served cold.

NUTRITIONAL INFORMATION

Calories	275	Sugars	.........2g
Protein	.........9g	Fat	..........19g
Carbohydrate	...17g	Saturates	.......4g

35–40 MINS   15 MINS

SERVES 6

I N G R E D I E N T S

2 cups pasta spirals

4 tomatoes, peeled

½ cup black olives

½ cup sun-dried tomatoes

2 tablespoons pine nuts, toasted

2 tablespoons Parmesan shavings

sprig of fresh basil, to garnish

P E S T O   V I N A I G R E T T E

4 tablespoons chopped fresh basil

1 garlic clove, crushed

2 tablespoons freshly grated Parmesan

4 tablespoons olive oil

2 tablespoons lemon juice

pepper

1 Cook the pasta in a saucepan of boiling salted water for 8–10 minutes or until al dente. Drain the pasta and rinse well in hot water, then drain again thoroughly.

2 To make the vinaigrette, whisk the basil, garlic, Parmesan, olive oil, lemon juice, and pepper until well blended.

3 Put the pasta into a bowl, pour over the basil vinaigrette, and toss thoroughly.

4 Cut the tomatoes into wedges. Halve and pit the olives and slice the sun-dried tomatoes.

5 Add the tomatoes, olives, and sun-dried tomatoes to the pasta and mix.

6 Transfer to a salad bowl and scatter the nuts and Parmesan shavings over the top. Serve warm, garnished with a sprig of basil.

Vegetable & Pasta Salad

Roasted vegetables and pasta make a delicious, colorful salad, ideal as a starter or to serve with a platter of cold meats.

NUTRITIONAL INFORMATION

Calories 462	Sugars 9g	
Protein 11g	Fat 32g	
Carbohydrate ...33g	Saturates 7g	

🐷 🐷 🐷

🥔 1½ HOURS 🕐 1 HOUR

SERVES 4

INGREDIENTS

2 small eggplants, thinly sliced

1 large onion, sliced

2 large tomatoes, peeled and
    cut into wedges

1 red bell pepper, cored, seeded, and sliced

1 fennel bulb, thinly sliced

2 garlic cloves, sliced

4 tablespoons olive oil

1½ cups small pasta shapes

½ cup feta cheese, crumbled

a few basil leaves, torn

salt and pepper

salad greens, to serve

DRESSING

5 tablespoons olive oil

juice of 1 orange

1 teaspoon grated orange zest

¼ teaspoon paprika

4 canned anchovies, finely chopped

1 Place the sliced eggplants in a colander, sprinkle with salt, and set them aside for about 1 hour to draw out some of the bitter juices. Rinse under cold, running water to remove the salt, then drain. Toss on paper towels to dry.

2 Arrange the eggplants, onion, tomatoes, bell pepper, fennel, and garlic in a single layer in an ovenproof dish, sprinkle on 3 tablespoons of the oil, and season. Bake uncovered in a preheated oven, at 450°F, for 45 minutes, or until the vegetables begin to turn brown. Remove from the oven and set aside to cool.

3 Cook the pasta in a large pan of boiling salted water, to which you have added the remaining olive oil, for 8–10 minutes or until tender. Drain the pasta, then transfer to a bowl.

4 To make the dressing, mix together the olive oil, orange juice, orange zest, and paprika. Stir in the finely chopped anchovies and season with pepper to taste. Pour the dressing over the pasta while it is still hot, and toss well. Set the pasta aside to cool.

5 To assemble the salad, line a shallow serving dish with the salad greens and arrange the cold roasted vegetables in the center. Spoon the pasta in a ring around the vegetables and scatter over the feta cheese and basil leaves. Serve the salad at once.

Tomato & Basil Salad

These extra-large tomatoes make an excellent salad, especially when combined with basil, garlic, kiwi fruit, onion rings, and new potatoes.

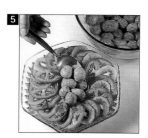

NUTRITIONAL INFORMATION

Calories 167	Sugars 4g	
Protein 2g	Fat 11g	
Carbohydrate ...16g	Saturates 2g	

  35 MINS   15 MINS

SERVES 8

I N G R E D I E N T S

1 pound 2 ounces tiny new potatoes, scrubbed

4–5 extra-large tomatoes

2 kiwi fruit

1 onion, sliced very thinly

2 tablespoons chopped fresh basil leaves

fresh basil leaves, to garnish

D R E S S I N G

4 tablespoons virgin olive oil

2 tablespoons balsamic vinegar

1 garlic clove, crushed

2 tablespoons mayonnaise or sour cream

salt and pepper

1 Cook the potatoes in their skins in a saucepan of salted water for about 10–15 minutes or until just tender. Drain the potatoes thoroughly.

2 To make the dressing, whisk together the oil, vinegar, garlic, and salt and pepper to taste until completely emulsified. Transfer half of the dressing to another bowl and whisk in the mayonnaise or sour cream.

3 Add the creamy dressing to the warm potatoes and toss thoroughly, then leave until cold.

4 Wipe the tomatoes and slice thinly. Peel the kiwi fruit and cut into thin slices. Layer the tomatoes with the kiwi fruit, slices of onion, and chopped basil in a fairly shallow dish, leaving a space in the center for the potatoes.

5 Spoon the potatoes in their dressing into the center of the tomato salad.

6 Drizzle a little of the dressing over the tomatoes, or serve separately in a bowl or pitcher. Garnish the salad with fresh basil leaves. Cover the dish with plastic wrap and chill until ready to serve.

COOK'S TIP

Ordinary tomatoes can be used for this salad, but make sure they are firm and bright red. You will need 8–10 ordinary-sized tomatoes.

Artichoke Salad

Use bottled artichokes rather than canned ones if possible, as they have a better flavor.

NUTRITIONAL INFORMATION

Calories ....139 Sugars 4g
Protein ....2g Fat 12g
Carbohydrate ....6g Saturates 1g

30 MINS   0 MINS

SERVES 4

I N G R E D I E N T S

9 ounces marinated artichokes, drained

4 small tomatoes

½ cup sun-dried tomatoes,
cut into strips

¼ cup black olives,
 halved and pitted

¼ cup shredded prosciutto

1 tablespoon roughly chopped
 fresh basil

D R E S S I N G

3 tablespoons olive oil

1 tablespoon wine vinegar

1 small garlic clove, crushed

½ teaspoon mustard

1 teaspoon liquid honey

salt and pepper

1 Drain the artichokes thoroughly, then cut them into quarters, and place in a bowl.

2 Cut each tomato into 6 wedges and place in the bowl with the sun-dried tomatoes, olives, and prosciutto.

3 To make the dressing, put the olive oil, wine vinegar, garlic, mustard, and

honey into a screw-top jar and shake vigorously until the ingredients are thoroughly blended. Season to taste.

4 Pour the dressing over the salad and toss well together. Transfer the salad

to individual plates and sprinkle with the chopped basil.

Italian Mozzarella Salad

This colorful salad is packed full of delicious flavors, but is easy to make.

NUTRITIONAL INFORMATION

Calories	79	Sugars	........2g
Protein	.........4g	Fat	......6g
Carbohydrate	....2g	Saturates	.......2g

20 MINS   0 MINS

SERVES 6

I N G R E D I E N T S

7 ounces baby spinach

4 ½ ounces watercress

4 ½ ounces mozzarella cheese

8 ounces cherry tomatoes

2 teaspoons balsamic vinegar

14½ teaspoons extra virgin olive oil

salt and pepper

1 Wash the spinach and watercress and drain thoroughly on absorbent paper towels. Remove any tough stalks. Place the spinach and watercress leaves in a large serving dish.

2 Cut the mozzarella into small pieces and scatter them over the spinach and watercress leaves.

3 Cut the cherry tomatoes in half and scatter them over the salad.

4 Sprinkle over the balsamic vinegar and oil, and season with salt and pepper to taste. Toss the mixture together to coat the leaves. Serve at once or leave to chill in the refrigerator until required.

Cherry Tomato & Pasta Salad

Pasta tastes perfect in this lively salad, dressed with red wine vinegar, lemon juice, basil, and olive oil.

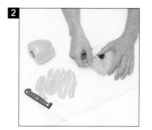

NUTRITIONAL INFORMATION

Calories 228	Sugars 4g	
Protein 5g	Fat 12g	
Carbohydrate ...27g	Saturates 2g	

50 MINS   20 MINS

SERVES 4

I N G R E D I E N T S

1½ cups dried pasta shapes

1 yellow bell pepper, halved,
    cored, and deseeded

2 small zucchini, sliced

1 red onion, sliced thinly

4½ ounces cherry tomatoes, halved

a handful of fresh basil leaves, torn into
    small pieces

salt

sprigs of fresh basil, to garnish

D R E S S I N G

4 tablespoons olive oil

2 tablespoons red wine vinegar

2 teaspoons lemon juice

1 teaspoon mustard

½ teaspoon sugar

salt and pepper

1 Cook the pasta in a pan of boiling, lightly salted water for 8–10 minutes, or until just tender.

2 Meanwhile, place the bell pepper halves, skin-side uppermost, under a preheated broiler until they just begin to char. Leave them to cool, then peel, and slice them into strips.

3 Cook the zucchini in a small amount of boiling, lightly salted water for 3–4 minutes, until cooked, yet still crunchy. Drain and refresh under cold running water to cool quickly.

4 To make the dressing, mix together the olive oil, red wine vinegar, lemon juice, mustard, and sugar. Season well with salt and pepper. Add the basil leaves.

5 Drain the pasta well and tip it into a large serving bowl. Add the dressing and toss well. Add the bell pepper, zucchini, onion and cherry tomatoes, stirring to combine. Cover and leave at room temperature for about 30 minutes to allow the flavors to develop.

6 Serve, garnished with a few sprigs of fresh basil.

Mozzarella with Radicchio

Sliced mozzarella is served with tomatoes and radicchio, which is singed over hot coals and drizzled with pesto dressing.

NUTRITIONAL INFORMATION

Calories 413   Sugars 6g
Protein . . . . .12g   Fat 38g
Carbohydrate . . . .6g   Saturates 14g

 15 MINS   2–3 MINS

SERVES 4

I N G R E D I E N T S

1 pound 2 ounces mozzarella

4 large tomatoes, sliced

2 heads of radicchio

D R E S S I N G

fresh basil leaves, to garnish

1 tablespoon red or green pesto

6 tablespoons virgin olive oil

3 tablespoons red wine vinegar

handful of fresh basil leaves

salt and pepper

1 To make the dressing, mix the pesto, oil and red wine vinegar together.

2 Tear the basil leaves into tiny pieces and add them to the dressing. Season.

3 Slice the mozzarella thinly and arrange on 4 serving plates with the tomatoes.

4 Leaving the root end on the radicchio, slice each one into quarters. Barbecue them quickly, so that the leaves singe on the outside. Place two quarters on each serving plate.

5 Drizzle the dressing over the radicchio, cheese, and tomatoes. Garnish with extra basil leaves and serve.

Sesame Seed Salad

This salad uses sesame seed paste as a flavoring for the dressing, which complements the eggplant.

NUTRITIONAL INFORMATION

Calories	89	Sugars	.........1g
Protein	.........3g	Fat	..........8g
Carbohydrate	....1g	Saturates	.......1g

45 MINS   15 MINS

SERVES 4

I N G R E D I E N T S

1 large eggplant

3 tablespoons tahini

juice and rind of 1 lemon

1 garlic clove, crushed

pinch of paprika

1 tablespoon chopped cilantro

salt and pepper

Little Gem lettuce leaves

GARNISH

strips of pimiento

lemon wedges

toasted sesame seeds

1 Cut the eggplant in half, place in a colander and sprinkle with salt. Leave to stand for 30 minutes, rinse under cold running water, and drain well. Pat dry with paper towels.

2 Place the eggplant halves, skin-side uppermost, on an oiled cookie sheet. Cook in a preheated oven, 450°F, for 10–15 minutes. Remove from the oven and allow to cool.

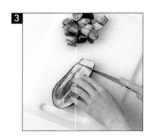

3 Cut the eggplant into cubes and set aside until required. Mix the tahini, lemon juice and rind, garlic, paprika, and cilantro together. Season with salt and pepper to taste and stir in the eggplant.

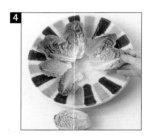

4 Line a serving dish with lettuce leaves and spoon the eggplant into the center. Garnish the salad with pimiento slices, lemon wedges, and toasted sesame seeds and serve at once.

COOK'S TIP

Tahini, a sesame seed paste, is a nutty-flavored sauce available from most health food shops and many delicatessens.

Pink Grapefruit & Cheese Salad

Fresh pink grapefruit segments, ripe avocados, and sliced Italian dolcelatte cheese make a deliciously different salad combination.

NUTRITIONAL INFORMATION

Calories	390	Sugars	.........3g
Protein	........13g	Fat	..........36g
Carbohydrate	....4g	Saturates	......13g

  25 MINS · 0 MINS

SERVES 4

I N G R E D I E N T S

½ romaine lettuce

½ red leaf lettuce

2 pink grapefruit

2 ripe avocados

6 ounces dolcelatte cheese, sliced thinly

sprigs of fresh basil, to garnish

D R E S S I N G

4 tablespoons olive oil

1 tablespoon white wine vinegar

salt and pepper

1 Arrange the lettuce leaves on 4 serving plates or in a salad bowl.

2 Remove the peel and pith from the grapefruit with a sharp serrated knife, catching the grapefruit juice in a bowl.

3 Segment the grapefruit by cutting down each side of the membrane. Remove all the membrane. Arrange the segments on the serving plates.

4 Peel, pit, and slice the avocados, dipping them in the grapefruit juice to prevent them from going brown. Arrange the slices on the salad with the dolcelatte cheese.

5 To make the dressing, combine any remaining grapefruit juice with the olive oil and wine vinegar. Season with salt and pepper to taste, mixing well to combine.

6 Drizzle the dressing over the salads. Garnish with fresh basil leaves and serve at once.

COOK'S TIP

Pink grapefruit segments make a very attractive color combination with the avocados, but ordinary grapefruit will work just as well. To help avocados to ripen, keep them at room temperature in a brown paper bag.

Pasta

The simplicity and satisfying nature of pasta in all its varieties make it a universal favorite. Easy to cook and economical, pasta is wonderfully versatile. It can be served with sauces made from meat, fish, or vegetables, or baked in the oven. The classic Spaghetti Bolognese needs no introduction, and yet it is said that there are almost as

many versions of this delicious regional dish as there are lovers of Italian food! Fish and seafood are irresistible combined with pasta and need only the briefest of cooking times. Pasta combined with vegetables provides inspiration for countless dishes which will please vegetarians and meat-eaters alike. The delicious pasta dishes in this chapter range from easy, economic mid-week suppers to sophisticated and elegant meals for special occasions.

Pasta Carbonara

Lightly cooked eggs and pancetta are combined with cheese to make this rich, classic sauce.

NUTRITIONAL INFORMATION

Calories 547	Sugars 1g	
Protein 21g	Fat 31g	
Carbohydrate ...49g	Saturates 14g	

15 MINS   20 MINS

SERVES 4

INGREDIENTS

1 tablespoon olive oil

3 tablespoons butter

⅔ cup diced pancetta or
   unsmoked bacon

3 eggs, beaten

2 tablespoons milk

1 tablespoon thyme, stalks removed

1½ pounds fresh or 12 ounces dried
   conchigoni rigati

⅔ cup grated Parmesan cheese

salt and pepper

1 Heat the oil and butter in a skillet until the mixture is just beginning to froth.

2 Add the pancetta or bacon to the skillet and cook for 5 minutes or until browned all over.

3 Mix together the eggs and milk in a small bowl. Stir in the thyme and season to taste with salt and pepper.

4 Cook the pasta in a saucepan of boiling water for 8–10 minutes until tender, but still has bite. Drain thoroughly.

5 Add the cooked, drained pasta to the skillet with the eggs and cook over high heat for about 30 seconds or until the eggs just begin to cook and set. Do not overcook the eggs or they will become rubbery.

6 Add half of the grated Parmesan cheese, stirring to combine well.

7 Transfer the pasta to a serving plate, pour over the sauce, and toss to mix well.

8 Sprinkle the rest of the grated Parmesan over the top and serve at once.

VARIATION

For an extra rich carbonara sauce, stir in 4 tablespoons of heavy cream with the eggs and milk in step 3. Follow exactly the same cooking method.

Spaghetti Bolognese

The original recipe takes about 4 hours to cook and should be left overnight to allow the flavors to mingle. This version is much quicker.

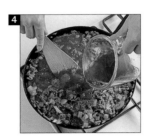

NUTRITIONAL INFORMATION

Calories	.591	Sugars	.7g
Protein	.29g	Fat	.24g
Carbohydrate	.64g	Saturates	.9g

 20 MINS 1 HR 5 MINS

SERVES 4

INGREDIENTS

1 tablespoon olive oil

1 onion, finely chopped

2 garlic cloves, chopped

1 carrot, scraped and chopped

1 celery stalk, chopped

⅓ cup diced pancetta or bacon

12 ounces lean ground beef

14-ounce can diced tomatoes

2 teaspoons dried oregano

½ cup red wine

2 tablespoons tomato paste

salt and pepper

1½ pounds fresh spaghetti or 12 ounces
   dried spaghetti

1 Heat the oil in a large skillet. Add the onions and cook for 3 minutes.

2 Add the garlic, carrot, celery, and pancetta or bacon and sauté for 3–4 minutes or until just beginning to brown.

3 Add the ground beef and cook over high heat for another 3 minutes or until all of the meat is brown.

4 Stir in the tomatoes, oregano, and red wine and bring to a boil. Reduce the heat and leave to simmer for about 45 minutes.

5 Stir in the tomato paste and season with salt and pepper.

6 Cook the spaghetti in a pan of boiling water for 8–10 minutes until tender, but still has bite. Drain thoroughly.

7 Transfer the spaghetti to a serving plate and pour over the bolognese sauce. Toss to mix well and serve hot.

VARIATION

Try adding 1 oz dried porcini, soaked for 10 minutes in 2 tablespoons of warm water, to the bolognese sauce in step 4, if you wish.

Chicken & Tomato Lasagne

This variation of the traditional beef dish has layers of pasta and chicken or turkey baked in red wine, tomatoes, and a delicious cheese sauce.

NUTRITIONAL INFORMATION

Calories . . . . . . .550 Sugars 11g
Protein . . . . .35g Fat 29g
Carbohydrate . . .34g Saturates 12g

20 MINS   1¹/₄ HOURS

SERVES 4

INGREDIENTS

12 ounces fresh lasagne (about 9 sheets)
   or 5½ ounces dried lasagne
   (about 9 sheets)

1 tablespoon olive oil

1 red onion, finely chopped

1 garlic clove, crushed

3½ ounces mushrooms, wiped and sliced

12 ounces chicken or turkey breast, cut
   into chunks

⅔ cup red wine, diluted with
   ⅓ cup water

1 cup sieved tomatoes

1 teaspoon sugar

BECHAMEL SAUCE

5 tablespoons butter

⅓ cup all-purpose flour

2½ cups milk

1 egg, beaten

1 cup grated Parmesan cheese

salt and pepper

1 Cook the lasagne in a pan of boiling water according to the instructions on the packet. Lightly grease a deep ovenproof dish.

2 Heat the oil in a pan. Add the onion and garlic and cook for 3–4 minutes. Add the mushrooms and chicken and stir-fry for 4 minutes or until the meat browns.

3 Add the wine, bring to a boil, then simmer for 5 minutes. Stir in the sieved tomatoes and sugar and cook for 3–5 minutes until the meat is tender and cooked through. The sauce should have thickened, but still be quite runny.

4 To make the Béchamel Sauce, melt the butter in a pan, stir in the flour, and cook for 2 minutes. Remove the pan from the heat and gradually add the milk, mixing to form a smooth sauce. Return the pan to the heat and bring to a boil, stirring until thickened. Leave to cool slightly, then beat in the egg and half of the cheese. Season to taste.

5 Place 3 sheets of lasagne in the base of the dish and spread with half of the chicken mixture. Repeat the layers. Top with the last 3 sheets of lasagne, pour over the Béchamel Sauce and sprinkle with the Parmesan. Bake in a preheated oven, at 375°F, for 30 minutes until golden and the pasta is cooked.

Traditional Cannelloni

You can buy ready-made dried pasta tubes. However, if using fresh pasta (see page 24), you must cut out squares and roll them yourself.

NUTRITIONAL INFORMATION

Calories	342	Sugars	.........6g
Protein	........15g	Fat	..........15g
Carbohydrate	...38g	Saturates	.......8g

50 MINS   30 MINS

SERVES 4

I N G R E D I E N T S

20 tubes dried cannelloni (about 7 ounces)
  or 20 square sheets of fresh pasta
  (about 12 ounces)

1 cup ricotta cheese

5½ ounces frozen spinach, thawed

½ small red bell pepper, diced

2 green onions, chopped

⅔ cup hot vegetable or
  chicken stock

1 portion of Basil & Tomato Sauce
  (see page 364)

⅓ cup grated Parmesan or
  Romano cheese

salt and pepper

1 If you are using dried cannelloni, check the packet instructions; many varieties do not need pre-cooking. If necessary, pre-cook your pasta: bring a large saucepan of water to a boil, add 1 tablespoon of oil, and cook the pasta for 3–4 minutes—it is far easier to do this in batches.

2 In a bowl, mix together the ricotta, spinach, bell pepper, and green onions and season to taste with salt and pepper.

3 Lightly butter an ovenproof dish, large enough to contain all of the pasta tubes in a single layer. Spoon the ricotta mixture into the pasta tubes and place them into the prepared dish. If you are using fresh sheets of pasta, spread the ricotta mixture along one side of each fresh pasta square and roll up to form a tube.

4 Mix together the stock and Basil and Tomato Sauce and pour over the pasta tubes.

5 Sprinkle the Parmesan or Romano cheese over the cannelloni and bake in a preheated oven, 375°F, for 20–25 minutes or until the pasta is cooked through. Serve at once.

VARIATION

If you would prefer a creamier version, omit the stock and the Basil and Tomato sauce and replace with Béchamel Sauce (see page 336).

Tagliatelle & Chicken Sauce

Spinach ribbon noodles covered with a rich tomato sauce and topped with creamy chicken makes a very appetizing dish.

NUTRITIONAL INFORMATION

Calories 853	Sugars 6g	
Protein 32g	Fat 71g	
Carbohydrate ...23g	Saturates 34g	

30 MINS   25 MINS

SERVES 4

INGREDIENTS

Basic Tomato Sauce (see page 28)

8 ounces fresh green ribbon noodles

1 tablespoon olive oil

salt

basil leaves, to garnish

CHICKEN SAUCE

¼ cup butter

14 ounces boneless, skinless chicken
   breast, thinly sliced

¾ cup blanched almonds

1¼ cups heavy cream

salt and pepper

basil leaves,
   to garnish

1 Make the tomato sauce, and keep warm.

2 To make the chicken sauce, melt the butter in a pan over medium heat and fry the chicken strips and almonds for 5–6 minutes, stirring frequently, until the chicken is cooked through.

3 Meanwhile, pour the cream into a small pan over a low heat, bring it to a boil, and boil for about 10 minutes, until reduced by almost half. Pour the cream over the chicken and almonds, stir well, and season with salt and pepper to taste. Set aside and keep warm.

4 Cook the pasta in a pan of boiling salted water, to which you have added the oil, for 8–10 minutes or until tender. Drain, then return to the pan, cover, and keep warm.

5 Turn the pasta into a warmed serving dish and spoon the tomato sauce over it. Spoon the chicken and cream over the center, scatter over the basil leaves, and serve at once.

Meat & Pasta Loaf

The cheesy pasta layer comes as a pleasant surprise inside this lightly spiced meat loaf.

NUTRITIONAL INFORMATION

Calories 497   Sugars 4g
Protein ....26g   Fat 37g
Carbohydrate ...16g   Saturates 16g

45 MINS   1¼ HOURS

SERVES 6

I N G R E D I E N T S

2 tablespoons butter, plus extra
   for greasing

1 onion, chopped finely

1 small red bell pepper, cored, deseeded,
   and chopped

1 garlic clove, chopped

1 pound 2 ounces ground lean beef

½ cup soft white bread crumbs

½ teaspoon cayenne pepper

1 tablespoon lemon juice

½ teaspoon grated lemon rind

2 tablespoons chopped fresh parsley

¾ cup short pasta, such as fusilli

4 bay leaves

1 tablespoon olive oil

Cheese Sauce (see page 29)

6 ounces bacon slices, rind
   removed

salt and pepper

salad greens, to garnish

1 Melt the butter in a pan over medium heat and fry the onion and bell pepper for about 3 minutes, until the onion is translucent. Stir in the garlic and cook for 1 minute.

2 Put the meat into a large bowl and mash it with a wooden spoon until it becomes a sticky paste. Tip in the fried vegetables and stir in the bread crumbs, cayenne, lemon juice, lemon rind, and parsley. Season the mixture with salt and pepper and set aside.

3 Cook the pasta in a large pan of boiling water, to which you have added salt and the olive oil, for 8–10 minutes or until tender. Drain the pasta, then stir it into the cheese sauce.

4 Grease a 2¼-pound loaf pan and arrange the bay leaves in the base. Stretch the bacon slices with the back of a knife blade and arrange them to line the base and the sides of the pan.

5 Spoon in half of the meat mixture, level the surface, and cover it with the pasta. Spoon in the remaining meat mixture, level the top, and cover the pan with foil.

6 Cook the meat loaf in a preheated oven, 350°F, for 1 hour, or until the juices run clear and the loaf has shrunk away from the sides of the pan. Pour off any excess fat from the pan and turn the loaf out on a warm serving dish. Garnish with the salad greens and serve hot.

Tortelloni

These tasty little squares of pasta stuffed with mushrooms and cheese are surprisingly filling. This recipe makes 36 tortelloni.

NUTRITIONAL INFORMATION

Calories 360	Sugars 1g
Protein 9g	Fat 21g
Carbohydrate ...36g	Saturates 12g

1¹/₄ HOURS　　**25 MINS**

SERVES 4

INGREDIENTS

10½ ounces fresh pasta (see
　page 24), rolled out to thin sheets

5 tablespoons butter

1¾ ounces shallots, finely chopped

3 garlic clove, crushed

1¾ ounces mushrooms, wiped and
　finely chopped

½ celery stalk, finely chopped

⅓ cup finely grated Romano cheese,
　plus extra to garnish

1 tablespoon oil

salt and pepper

1 Using a serrated pasta cutter, cut 2-inch squares from the sheets of fresh pasta. To make 36 tortelloni you will need 72 squares. Once the pasta is cut, cover the squares with plastic wrap to keep them from drying out.

2 Heat 2 tablespoons of the butter in a skillet. Add the shallots, 1 crushed garlic clove, the mushrooms, and celery and cook for 4–5 minutes.

3 Remove the skillet from the heat, stir in the cheese, and season with salt and pepper to taste.

4 Spoon ½ teaspoon of the mixture onto the middle of 36 pasta squares. Brush the edges of the squares with water and top with the remaining 36 squares. Press the edges together to seal. Leave to rest for 5 minutes.

5 Bring a large pan of water to a boil, add the oil, and cook the tortelloni, in batches, for 2–3 minutes. The tortelloni will rise to the surface when cooked and the pasta should be tender with a slight bite. Remove from the pan with a perforated spoon and drain thoroughly.

6 Meanwhile, melt the remaining butter in a pan. Add the remaining garlic and plenty of pepper and cook for 1–2 minutes. Transfer the tortelloni to serving plates and pour over the garlic butter. Garnish with grated Romano cheese and serve at once.

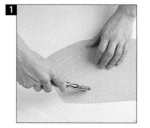

Tagliatelle with Meatballs

There is an appetizing contrast of textures and flavors in this satisfying family dish.

NUTRITIONAL INFORMATION

Calories 910   Sugars 13g
Protein . . . . .40g   Fat 54g
Carbohydrate . . .65g   Saturates 19g

 45 MINS   🕐 1 HR 5 MINS

SERVES 4

I N G R E D I E N T S

1 pound 2 ounces ground lean beef

1 cup soft white bread crumbs

1 garlic clove, crushed

2 tablespoons chopped fresh parsley

1 teaspoon dried oregano

large pinch of freshly grated nutmeg

¼ teaspoon ground coriander

⅔ cup grated Parmesan cheese

2–3 tablespoons milk

flour, for dusting

4 tablespoons olive oil

14 ounces tagliatelle

2 tablespoons butter, diced

salt and pepper

S A U C E

3 tablespoons olive oil

2 large onions, sliced

2 celery stalks, sliced thinly

2 garlic cloves, chopped

14-ounce can diced tomatoes

2¼ ounces chopped sun-dried
    tomatoes packed in oil

2 tablespoons tomato paste

1 tablespoon brown sugar

⅔ cup white wine, or water

1 To make the sauce, heat the oil in a skillet and fry the onions and celery until translucent. Add the garlic and cook for 1 minute. Stir in the tomatoes, tomato paste, sugar, and wine, and season. Bring to a boil and simmer for 10 minutes.

2 Meanwhile, break up the meat in a bowl with a wooden spoon until it becomes a sticky paste. Stir in the bread crumbs, garlic, herbs, and spices. Stir in the cheese and enough milk to make a firm paste. Flour your hands, take large spoonfuls of the mixture, and shape it into 12 balls. Heat 3 tbsp of the oil in a skillet and fry the meatballs for 5–6 minutes until browned.

3 Pour the tomato sauce over the meatballs. Lower the heat, cover the pan, and simmer for 30 minutes, turning once or twice. Add a little extra water if the sauce begins to dry.

4 Cook the pasta in a large saucepan of boiling salted water, adding the remaining oil, for 8–10 minutes or until tender. Drain the pasta, then turn into a warm serving dish, dot with the butter, and toss with two forks. Spoon the meatballs and sauce over the pasta and serve.

Cheese & Spinach Cannelloni

The delicious filling of Ricotta and Parmesan cheeses with spinach and ham make this Italian classic hard to resist!

NUTRITIONAL INFORMATION

Calories	.575	Sugars	.6g
Protein	.22g	Fat	.42g
Carbohydrate	.28g	Saturates	.21g

🄶 🄶 🄶

🍴 30 MINS   🕐 1¼ HOURS

SERVES 4

INGREDIENTS

8 cannelloni tubes

1 tablespoon olive oil

fresh herb sprigs, to garnish

FILLING

2 tablespoons butter

10½ ounces frozen spinach, thawed and chopped

½ cup ricotta cheese

⅓ cup grated Parmesan cheese

¼ cup chopped ham

¼ teaspoon freshly grated nutmeg

2 tablespoons heavy cream

2 eggs, lightly beaten

salt and pepper

SAUCE

2 tablespoons butter

¼ cup all-purpose flour

1¼ cups milk

2 bay leaves

large pinch of grated nutmeg

⅓ cup grated Parmesan cheese

1 To prepare the filling, melt the butter in a pan and stir in the spinach. Cook for 2–3 minutes, stirring, to allow the moisture to evaporate, then remove the pan from the heat. Stir in the cheeses and the ham. Season with nutmeg and salt and pepper. Beat in the cream and eggs to make a thick paste. Set aside to cool.

2 Cook the cannelloni in a large pan of boiling salted water, adding the olive oil, for 8–10 minutes, or until tender. Drain the cannelloni in a colander and set aside to cool.

3 To make the sauce, melt the butter in a pan, stir in the flour and, when it has formed a roux, gradually pour on the milk, stirring all the time. Add the bay leaves, bring to simmering point, and cook for 5 minutes. Season with nutmeg, salt and pepper. Remove the pan from the heat and discard the bay leaves.

4 To assemble the dish, spoon the filling into a pastry bag and pipe it into each of the cannelloni tubes.

5 Spoon a little of the sauce into a shallow ovenproof dish. Arrange the cannelloni in a single layer, then pour over the remaining sauce. Sprinkle on the remaining Parmesan cheese and bake in a preheated oven, 375°F, for 40–45 minutes or until the sauce is golden brown and bubbling. Serve garnished with fresh herb sprigs.

Pasticcio

A recipe that has both Italian and Greek origins, this dish may be served hot or cold, cut into thick, satisfying squares.

NUTRITIONAL INFORMATION

Calories 590   Sugars 8g
Protein ....34g   Fat 39g
Carbohydrate ...23g   Saturates 16g

 35 MINS   1¼ HOURS

SERVES 6

I N G R E D I E N T S

2 cups fusilli, or other short
    pasta shapes

1 tablespoon olive oil

4 tablespoons heavy cream

salt

rosemary sprigs, to garnish

S A U C E

2 tablespoons olive oil, plus extra
    for brushing

1 onion, sliced thinly

1 red bell pepper, cored, deseeded,
    and chopped

2 cloves garlic, chopped

1 pound 6 ounces ground lean beef

14-ounce can diced tomatoes

½ cup dry white wine

2 tablespoons chopped fresh parsley

1¾-ounce can anchovies, drained
    and chopped

salt and pepper

T O P P I N G

1¼ cups plain yogurt

3 eggs

pinch of freshly grated nutmeg

½ cup grated Parmesan cheese

1 To make the sauce, heat the oil in a large skillet and fry the onion and red bell pepper for 3 minutes. Stir in the garlic and cook for 1 minute more. Stir in the beef and cook, stirring frequently, until no longer pink.

2 Add the tomatoes and wine, stir well and bring to a boil. Simmer, uncovered, for 20 minutes, or until the sauce is fairly thick. Stir in the parsley and anchovies, and season to taste.

3 Cook the pasta in a large pan of boiling salted water, adding the oil, for 8–10 minutes or until tender. Drain the pasta in a colander, then transfer to a bowl. Stir in the cream and set aside.

4 To make the topping, beat together the yogurt and eggs and season with nutmeg, and salt and pepper to taste.

5 Brush a shallow ovenproof dish with oil. Spoon in half of the pasta and cover with half of the meat sauce. Repeat these layers, then spread the topping evenly over the final layer. Sprinkle the cheese on top.

6 Bake in a preheated oven, 375°F, for 25 minutes, or until the topping is golden brown and bubbling. Garnish with sprigs of rosemary and serve with a selection of raw vegetable crudités.

Lasagne Verde

The sauce in this delicious baked pasta dish can be used as an alternative sauce for Spaghetti Bolognese (see page 335).

NUTRITIONAL INFORMATION

Calories	.619	Sugars	.7g
Protein	.29g	Fat	.45g
Carbohydrate	.21g	Saturates	.19g

1³/4 HOURS   55 MINS

SERVES 6

I N G R E D I E N T S

Ragù Sauce (see page 12)

1 tablespoon olive oil

8 ounces green lasagne

Béchamel Sauce (see page 28)

⅔ cup grated Parmesan cheese

salt and pepper

salad greens, tomato salad, or black olives,
    to serve

1 Begin by making the Ragù Sauce as described on page 12, but cook for 10–12 minutes longer than the time given, in an uncovered pan, to allow the excess liquid to evaporate. To layer the sauce with lasagne, it needs to be reduced to the consistency of a thick paste.

2 Have ready a large saucepan of boiling, salted water and add the olive oil. Drop the pasta sheets into the boiling water a few at a time, and return the water to a boil before adding further pasta sheets. If you are using fresh lasagne, cook the sheets for a total of 8 minutes. If you are using dried or partly precooked pasta, cook it according to the directions given on the packet.

3 Remove the pasta sheets from the saucepan of boiling water with a slotted spoon. Spread them in a single layer on damp dish cloths.

4 Grease a rectangular ovenproof dish, about 10–11 inches long. To assemble the dish, spoon a little of the meat sauce into the prepared dish, cover with a layer of lasagne, then spoon over a little Béchamel Sauce, and sprinkle with some of the cheese. Continue making layers in this way, covering the final layer of lasagne with the remaining Béchamel Sauce.

5 Sprinkle on the remaining cheese and bake in a preheated oven, 375°F, for 40 minutes or until the sauce is golden brown and bubbling. Serve with a salad greens, a tomato salad, or a bowl of black olives.

Vegetable Pasta Nests

These large pasta nests look impressive when presented filled with broiled mixed vegetables, and taste delicious.

NUTRITIONAL INFORMATION

Calories	392	Sugars	.........1g
Protein	.........6g	Fat	..........28g
Carbohydrate	...32g	Saturates	.......9g

25 MINS   40 MINS

SERVES 4

I N G R E D I E N T S

6 ounces spaghetti

1 eggplant, halved and sliced

1 zucchini, diced

1 red bell pepper, seeded and chopped
diagonally

6 tablespoons olive oil

2 garlic cloves, crushed

4 tablespoons butter or margarine,
melted

1 tablespoon dry white bread crumbs

salt and pepper

fresh parsley sprigs,
to garnish

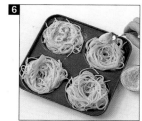

1 Bring a large saucepan of water to a boil and cook the spaghetti for 8–10 minutes or until al dente. Drain the spaghetti in a colander and set aside until required.

2 Place the eggplant, zucchini, and bell pepper on a cookie sheet.

3 Mix the oil and garlic together and pour over the vegetables, tossing to coat all over.

4 Cook under a preheated hot broiler for about 10 minutes, turning, until tender and lightly charred. Set aside and keep warm.

5 Divide the spaghetti among 4 lightly greased muffin pans. Using 2 forks, curl the spaghetti to form nests.

6 Brush the pasta nests with melted butter or margarine and sprinkle with the bread crumbs. Bake in a preheated oven, at 400°F, for 15 minutes or until lightly golden. Remove the pasta nests from the pans and transfer to serving plates. Divide the broiled vegetables among the pasta nests, season to taste and garnish with parsley.

COOK'S TIP

"Al dente" means "to the bite" and describes cooked pasta that is not too soft, but still has a "bite" to it.

Eggplant Layers

Layers of toasty-brown eggplant, meat sauce, and cheese-flavored pasta make this a popular family supper dish.

NUTRITIONAL INFORMATION

Calories 900   Sugars 10g
Protein . . . . .43g   Fat 62g
Carbohydrate . . .44g   Saturates 27g

1½ HOURS   50 MINS

SERVES 4

I N G R E D I E N T S

1 eggplant, sliced thinly

5 tablespoons olive oil

2 cups short pasta shapes, such as
   fusilli

¼ cup butter, plus extra
   for greasing

6 tablespoons all-purpose flour

1¼ cups milk

⅔ cup light cream

⅔ cup chicken stock

large pinch of freshly grated nutmeg

¾ cup grated sharp Cheddar cheese

⅓ cup grated Parmesan cheese

Lamb Sauce (see page 28)

salt and pepper

artichoke heart and tomato salad,
   to serve

1 Put the eggplant slices in a colander, sprinkle with salt, and leave for about 45 minutes. Rinse under cold, running water and drain. Pat dry with paper towels.

2 Heat 4 tablespoons of the oil in a skillet over medium heat. Fry the eggplant slices for about 4 minutes on each side, until golden brown. Remove with a slotted spoon and drain thoroughly on paper towels.

3 Meanwhile, cook the pasta in a large pan of boiling salted water, adding 1 tablespoon of olive oil, for 8–10 minutes or until tender. Drain the pasta in a colander and return to the pan. Cover and keep warm.

4 Melt the butter in a small pan, stir in the flour, and cook for 1 minute. Gradually pour in the milk, stirring all the time, then stir in the cream and chicken stock. Season with nutmeg and salt and pepper to taste, bring to a boil, and simmer for 5 minutes. Stir in the Cheddar and remove from the heat. Pour half of the sauce over the pasta and mix well. Reserve the remaining sauce.

5 Grease a shallow ovenproof dish. Spoon in half of the pasta, cover with half of the Lamb Sauce, and then with the eggplant in a single layer. Repeat the layers of pasta and Lamb Sauce and spread the remaining cheese sauce over the top. Sprinkle with Parmesan. Bake in the preheated oven, 375°F, for 25 minutes, until golden brown. Serve hot or cold, with an artichoke heart and tomato salad.

Sicilian Spaghetti Cake

Any variety of long pasta could be used for this very tasty dish from Sicily.

NUTRITIONAL INFORMATION

Calories ....876 Sugars 10g
Protein ....37g Fat 65g
Carbohydrate ...39g Saturates 18g

30 MINS   50 MINS

SERVES 4

INGREDIENTS

2 eggplants, about 1 pound 7 ounces

⅔ cup olive oil

12 ounces finely ground
    lean beef

1 onion, chopped

2 garlic cloves, crushed

2 tablespoons tomato paste

14-ounce can diced tomatoes

1 teaspoon Worcestershire sauce

1 teaspoon chopped fresh oregano or
    ½ teaspoon dried oregano

½ cup pitted black olives, sliced

1 green, red, or yellow bell pepper, cored,
    deseeded, and chopped

6 ounces spaghetti

1⅔ cups grated Parmesan cheese

salt and pepper

1 Brush an 8-inch loose-based round cake pan with olive oil, place a disc of baking parchment in the base, and brush with oil. Trim the eggplants and cut into slanting slices, 5¼ inch thick. Heat some of the oil in a skillet. Fry a few slices of eggplant at a time until lightly browned, turning once, and adding more oil as necessary. Drain on paper towels.

2 Put the ground beef, onion, and garlic into a saucepan and cook, stirring frequently, until browned all over. Add the tomato paste, tomatoes, Worcestershire sauce, herbs, and seasoning. Simmer for 10 minutes, stirring occasionally, then add the olives and bell pepper, and cook for 10 minutes.

3 Bring a large saucepan of salted water to a boil. Cook the spaghetti for 8–10 minutes or until just tender. Drain the spaghetti thoroughly. Turn the spaghetti into a bowl and mix in the meat mixture and Parmesan, tossing together with 2 forks.

4 Lay overlapping slices of eggplant over the base of the cake pan and up the sides. Add the meat mixture, pressing it down, and cover with the remaining eggplant slices.

5 Stand the cake pan in a baking pan and cook in a preheated oven, 400°F, for 40 minutes. Leave to stand for 5 minutes, then loosen around the edges and invert onto a warm serving dish, releasing the clip. Remove the baking parchment. Serve at once.

Penne & Butternut Squash

The creamy, nutty flavor of squash complements the al dente texture of the pasta perfectly. This recipe has been adapted for the microwave.

NUTRITIONAL INFORMATION

Calories ....499 Sugars 4g
Protein ....20g Fat 26g
Carbohydrate ...49g Saturates 13g

 15 MINS   30 MINS

SERVES 4

INGREDIENTS

2 tablespoons olive oil

1 garlic clove, crushed

1 cup fresh white bread crumbs

1 pound 2 ounces peeled and deseeded
   butternut squash

8 tablespoon water

1 pound 2 ounces fresh penne,
   or other pasta shape

1 tablespoon butter

1 onion, sliced

½ cup ham, cut into strips

1 cup light cream

½ cup grated Cheddar cheese

2 tablespoons chopped fresh parsley

salt and pepper

1 Mix together the oil, garlic, and bread crumbs and spread out on a large plate. Cook on HIGH power for 4–5 minutes, stirring every minute, until crisp and beginning to brown. Set aside.

2 Dice the squash. Place in a large bowl with half of the water. Cover and cook on HIGH power for 8–9 minutes, stirring occasionally. Leave to stand for 2 minutes.

3 Place the pasta in a large bowl, add a little salt, and pour over boiling water to cover by 1 inch. Cover and cook on HIGH power for 5 minutes, stirring once, until the pasta is just tender but still firm to the bite. Leave to stand, covered, for 1 minute before draining.

4 Place the butter and onion in a large bowl. Cover and cook on HIGH power for 3 minutes.

5 Coarsely mash the squash, using a fork. Add to the onion with the pasta, ham, cream, cheese, parsley, and remaining water. Season generously and mix well. Cover and cook on HIGH power for 4 minutes until heated through.

6 Serve the pasta sprinkled with the crisp garlic crumbs.

COOK'S TIP

If the squash weighs more than is needed for this recipe, blanch the excess for 3–4 minutes in the microwave on HIGH power in a covered bowl with a little water. Drain, cool, and place in a freezer bag. Store in the freezer for up to 3 months.

Spaghetti, Tuna, & Parsley

This is a recipe to look forward to when parsley is at its most prolific, in the growing season.

NUTRITIONAL INFORMATION

Calories	970	Sugars	.........2g
Protein	........23g	Fat	..........80g
Carbohydrate	...42g	Saturates	......18g

 10 MINS   15 MINS

SERVES 4

I N G R E D I E N T S

1 pound 2 ounces spaghetti

1 tablespoon olive oil

2 tablespoons butter

black olives, to serve (optional)

S A U C E

7-ounce can tuna, drained

2-ounce can anchovies, drained

1 cup olive oil

1 cup roughly chopped fresh, flat-
   leaf parsley

⅔ cup crème fraîche (see page 472)

salt and pepper

1 Cook the spaghetti in a large saucepan of salted boiling water, adding the olive oil, for 8–10 minutes or until tender. Drain the spaghetti in a colander and return to the pan. Add the butter, toss thoroughly to coat, and keep warm until required.

2 Remove any bones from the tuna and flake into smaller pieces, using 2 forks. Put the tuna in a blender or food processor with the anchovies, olive oil, and parsley and process until the sauce is smooth. Pour in the crème fraîche and process for a few seconds to blend. Taste the sauce and season with salt and pepper.

3 Warm 4 plates. Shake the saucepan of spaghetti over medium heat for a few minutes or until it is thoroughly warmed through.

4 Pour the sauce over the spaghetti and toss quickly, using 2 forks. Serve at once with a small dish of black olives, if liked.

Pasta Vongole

Fresh clams are available from most good fish stores. If you prefer, use canned clams, which are less messy to eat but not as attractive.

NUTRITIONAL INFORMATION

Calories	.410	Sugars	.1g
Protein	.39g	Fat	.9g
Carbohydrate	.39g	Saturates	.1g

20 MINS   20 MINS

SERVES 4

INGREDIENTS

1½ pounds fresh clams or 10-ounce can clams, drained

14 ounces mixed seafood, such as shrimp, squid, and mussels, thawed if frozen

2 tablespoons olive oil

2 cloves garlic, finely chopped

⅔ cup white wine

⅔ cup fish stock

2 tablespoons chopped tarragon

salt and pepper

1½ pounds fresh pasta or 12 ounces dried pasta

1 If you are using fresh clams, scrub them clean, and discard any that are already open.

2 Heat the oil in a large skillet. Add the garlic and the clams to the pan and cook for 2 minutes, shaking the pan to ensure that all of the clams are coated in the oil.

3 Add the remaining seafood mixture to the pan and cook for a further 2 minutes.

4 Pour the wine and stock over the mixed seafood and garlic and bring to a boil. Cover the pan, reduce the heat, and leave to simmer for 8–10 minutes or until the shells open. Discard any clams or mussels that do not open.

5 Meanwhile, cook the pasta in a saucepan of boiling water for 8–10 minutes or until it is cooked through, but still has bite. Drain the pasta thoroughly.

6 Stir the tarragon into the sauce and season with salt and pepper to taste.

7 Transfer the pasta to a serving plate and pour over the sauce. Serve at once.

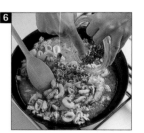

VARIATION

Red clam sauce can be made by adding 8 tablespoons of sieved tomatoes to the sauce along with the stock in step 4. Follow the same cooking method.

Spaghetti & Shellfish

Frozen shelled shrimp from the freezer can become the star ingredient in this colorful and tasty dish.

35 MINS   30 MINS

SERVES 4

I N G R E D I E N T S

8 ounces short-cut spaghetti, or
    long spaghetti broken into
    6-inch lengths

2 tablespoons olive oil

1¼ cups chicken stock

1 teaspoon lemon juice

1 small cauliflower, cut
    into flowerets

2 carrots, sliced thinly

4½ ounces snow peas

¼ cup butter

1 onion, sliced

8 ounces zucchini, sliced thinly

1 garlic clove, chopped

12 ounces frozen shelled
    shrimp, thawed

2 tablespoons chopped fresh parsley

⅓ cup grated Parmesan cheese

salt and pepper

½ teaspoon paprika,
    to sprinkle

4 unshelled shrimp,
    to garnish (optional)

1 Cook the spaghetti in a large pan of boiling salted water, adding 1 tablespoon of the oil, for 8–10 minutes or until tender. Drain, then return to the pan, and stir in the remaining oil. Cover and keep warm.

2 Bring the chicken stock and lemon juice to a boil. Add the cauliflower and carrots and cook for 3–4 minutes until they are barely tender. Remove with a slotted spoon and set aside. Add the snow peas and cook for 1–2 minutes, until they begin to soften. Remove with a slotted spoon and add to the other vegetables. Reserve the stock for future use.

3 Melt half of the butter in a skillet over medium heat and fry the onion and zucchini for about 3 minutes. Add the garlic and shrimp and cook for a further 2–3 minutes until thoroughly heated through.

4 Stir in the reserved vegetables and heat through. Season with salt and pepper, then stir in the remaining butter.

5 Transfer the spaghetti to a warm serving dish. Pour on the sauce and parsley. Toss well using 2 forks, until thoroughly coated. Sprinkle on the grated cheese and paprika, and garnish with unshelled shrimp, if using. Serve at once.

Pasta Pudding

A tasty mixture of creamy fish and pasta cooked in a bowl, unmolded and drizzled with tomato sauce presents macaroni in a new guise.

NUTRITIONAL INFORMATION

Calories ...... .536 Sugars 4g
Protein .... .35g Fat .... .35g
Carbohydrate ...21g Saturates ..... .17g

35 MINS   2 HOURS

SERVES 4

I N G R E D I E N T S

1 cup short-cut macaroni, or other
   short pasta shapes

1 tablespoon olive oil

1 tablespoon butter, plus extra for
   greasing

1 pound 2 ounces white fish fillets, such as
   cod or haddock

a few parsley stalks

6 black peppercorns

½ cup heavy cream

2 eggs, separated

2 tablespoons chopped dill, or parsley

pinch of grated nutmeg

½ cup Parmesan, grated

Basic Tomato Sauce (see page 28), to serve

pepper

dill or parsley sprigs, to garnish

1 Cook the pasta in a pan of salted boiling water, adding the oil, for 8–10 minutes. Drain, return to the pan, add the butter, and cover. Keep warm.

2 Place the fish in a skillet with the parsley stalks and peppercorns and pour on just enough water to cover. Bring to a boil, cover, and simmer for 10 minutes. Lift out the fish with a fish slice, reserving the liquor. When the fish is cool enough to handle, skin, and remove any bones. Cut into bite-size pieces.

3 Transfer the pasta to a large bowl and stir in the cream, egg yolks, and dill. Stir in the fish, taking care not to break it up, and enough liquid to make a moist but firm mixture. It should fall easily from a spoon, but not be too runny. Whisk the egg whites until stiff but not dry, then fold into the mixture.

4 Grease a heatproof bowl and spoon in the mixture to within 1½ inches of the rim. Cover the top with greased wax paper and a cloth, or with foil, and tie firmly around the rim. Do not use foil if you cook the pudding in a microwave.

5 Stand the pudding on a trivet in a large pan of boiling water to come halfway up the sides. Cover and steam for 1½ hours, topping up the boiling water as needed, or cook in a microwave on maximum power for 7 minutes.

6 Run a knife around the inside of the bowl and invert onto a warm serving dish. Pour some tomato sauce over the top; serve the rest separately. Garnish and serve.

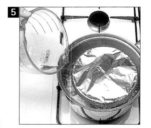

Macaroni & Shrimp Bake

This adaptation of an 18th-century Italian dish is baked until it is golden brown and sizzling, then cut into wedges, like a cake.

NUTRITIONAL INFORMATION

Calories ....576 Sugars 6g
Protein ....25g Fat 35g
Carbohydrate ...42g Saturates 19g

20 MINS

1 HR 5 MINS

SERVES 4

INGREDIENTS

3 cups short pasta, such as

short-cut macaroni

1 tablespoon olive oil, plus extra for brushing

6 tablespoons butter, plus extra

for greasing

2 small fennel bulbs, sliced thinly,

leaves reserved

6 ounces mushrooms, sliced thinly

6 ounces peeled shrimp

½ cup Parmesan, grated

2 large tomatoes, sliced

1 teaspoon dried oregano

salt and pepper

pinch of cayenne

Béchamel Sauce (see page 28)

1 Cook the pasta in a large saucepan of boiling, salted water, with 1 tablespoon of olive oil, for 8–10 minutes or until tender. Drain the pasta in a colander, return to the pan and dot with 2 tablespoons of the butter. Shake the pan well, cover, and keep warm.

2 Melt the remaining butter in a pan over medium heat and fry the fennel for 3–4 minutes, until it begins to soften. Stir in the mushrooms and fry for 2 minutes. Stir in the shrimp, remove the pan from the heat, and set aside until required.

3 Make the Béchamel Sauce and add the cayenne. Remove the pan from the heat and stir in the reserved vegetables, shrimp, and the pasta.

4 Grease a round, shallow ovenproof dish. Pour in the pasta mixture and spread evenly. Sprinkle with the Parmesan and arrange the tomato slices in a ring around the edge of the dish. Brush the tomato with olive oil and sprinkle with the dried oregano.

5 Bake in a preheated oven, 350°F, for 25 minutes, or until golden brown. Serve hot.

Pasta & Sicilian Sauce

This Sicilian recipe of anchovies mixed with pine nuts and golden raisins in a tomato sauce is delicious with all types of pasta.

NUTRITIONAL INFORMATION

Calories 286	Sugars 14g
Protein 11g	Fat 8g
Carbohydrate ...46g	Saturates 1g

25 MINS 　　 30 MINS

SERVES 4

I N G R E D I E N T S

1 pound tomatoes, halved

¼ cup pine nuts

⅓ cup golden raisins

1¾-ounce can anchovies, drained and
　halved lengthwise

2 tablespoons tomato paste

1½ pounds fresh or
　12 ounces dried penne

1 Cook the tomatoes under a preheated broiler for about 10 minutes. Leave to cool slightly, then once cool enough to handle, peel off the skin and dice the flesh.

2 Place the pine nuts on a cookie sheet and lightly toast under the broiler for 2–3 minutes or until golden brown.

VARIATION

3½ ounces bacon, broiled for 5 minutes until crispy, then chopped, instead of the anchovies, if you prefer.

3 Soak the golden raisins in a bowl of warm water for about 20 minutes. Drain the golden raisins thoroughly.

4 Place the tomatoes, pine nuts, and golden raisins in a small saucepan and gently heat.

5 Add the anchovies and tomato paste, heating the sauce for a further 2–3 minutes or until hot.

6 Cook the pasta in a saucepan of boiling water for 8–10 minutes or until it is cooked through, but still has bite. Drain thoroughly.

7 Transfer the pasta to a serving plate and serve with the hot Sicilian sauce.

Pasta & Mussel Sauce

Serve this aromatic seafood dish with plenty of fresh, crusty bread to soak up the delicious sauce.

NUTRITIONAL INFORMATION

Calories	735	Sugars	.........3g
Protein	........37g	Fat	..........46g
Carbohydrate	...41g	Saturates	......26g

 25 MINS   25 MINS

SERVES 6

INGREDIENTS

3½ cups pasta shells

1 tablespoon olive oil

SAUCE

2½ pounds mussels, scrubbed

1 cup dry white wine

2 large onions, chopped

½ cup butter

6 large garlic cloves, chopped finely

5 tablespoons chopped fresh parsley

1¼ cups heavy cream

salt and pepper

crusty bread, to serve

1 Pull off the beards from the mussels and rinse well in several changes of water. Discard any mussels that refuse to close when tapped. Put the mussels in a large pan with the white wine and half of the onions. Cover the pan, shake, and cook over medium heat for 2–3 minutes until the mussels open.

2 Remove the pan from the heat, lift out the mussels with a slotted spoon, reserving the liquor, and set aside until they are cool enough to handle. Discard any mussels that have not opened.

3 Melt the butter in a pan over medium heat and fry the remaining onion for 3–4 minutes or until translucent. Stir in the garlic and cook for 1 minute. Gradually pour on the reserved cooking liquid, stirring to blend thoroughly. Stir in the parsley and cream. Season to taste and bring to simmering point. Taste and adjust the seasoning if necessary.

4 Cook the pasta in a large pan of salted boiling water, adding the oil, for 8–10 minutes or until tender. Drain the pasta in a colander, return to the pan, cover, and keep warm.

5 Remove the mussels from their shells, reserving a few shells for garnish. Stir the mussels into the cream sauce. Tip the pasta into a warm serving dish, pour on the sauce and, using 2 large spoons, toss it together well. Garnish with a few of the reserved mussel shells. Serve hot, with warm, crusty bread.

Spaghetti & Salmon Sauce

The smoked salmon ideally complements the spaghetti to give a very luxurious dish.

NUTRITIONAL INFORMATION

Calories 782   Sugars 3g
Protein ....20g   Fat 48g
Carbohydrate ...48g   Saturates 27g

10 MINS   15 MINS

SERVES 4

INGREDIENTS

1 pound 2 ounces buckwheat
   spaghetti

2 tablespoons olive oil

½ cup feta cheese, crumbled

cilantro or parsley, to garnish

SAUCE

1¼ cups heavy cream

⅔ cup whiskey or brandy

4½ ounces smoked salmon

large pinch of cayenne pepper

2 tablespoons chopped cilantro or
   parsley

salt and pepper

1 Cook the spaghetti in a large saucepan of salted boiling water, adding 1 tablespoon of the olive oil, for 8–10 minutes or until tender. Drain the pasta in a colander. Return the pasta to the pan, sprinkle over the remaining oil, cover, and shake the pan. Set aside and keep warm until required.

2 In separate small saucepans, heat the cream and the whiskey or brandy to simmering point. Do not let them boil.

3 Combine the cream with the whiskey or brandy.

4 Cut the smoked salmon into thin strips and add to the cream mixture. Season with a little black pepper and cayenne pepper to taste, and then stir in the chopped cilantro or parsley.

5 Transfer the spaghetti to a warm serving dish, pour on the sauce, and toss thoroughly using 2 large forks. Scatter the crumbled cheese over the pasta and garnish with the cilantro or parsley. Serve at once.

Seafood Pasta

This attractive seafood salad platter is full of different flavors, textures, and colors.

NUTRITIONAL INFORMATION

Calories 188   Sugars 2g
Protein ....16g   Fat 7g
Carbohydrate ...13g   Saturates 1g

30 MINS   30 MINS

SERVES 8

I N G R E D I E N T S

1½ cups dried pasta shapes

1 tablespoon oil

4 tablespoons Italian dressing

2 garlic cloves, crushed

6 tablespoon white wine

4½ ounces baby button
    mushrooms, trimmed

3 carrots

2½ cups fresh mussels in shells

4½–6 ounces frozen squid or
    octopus rings, thawed

1 cup peeled jumbo shrimp, thawed
    if frozen

6 sun-dried tomatoes, drained
    and sliced

3 tablespoon chives, cut into 1-inch pieces

salt and pepper

TO GARNISH

24 snow peas, trimmed

12 baby corn cobs

12 shrimp in shells

1 Cook the pasta in a pan of boiling salted water, with the oil added, for 8–10 minutes or until just tender. Drain the pasta thoroughly.

2 Combine the dressing, garlic, and 2 tablespoons of wine. Mix in the mushrooms and leave to marinate.

3 Slice the carrots about ½ inch thick and using a cocktail cutter, cut each slice into shapes. Blanch for 3–4 minutes, drain and add to the mushrooms.

4 Scrub the mussels, discarding any that are open or do not close when sharply tapped. Put into a saucepan with ⅔ cup water and the remaining wine. Bring to a boil, cover, and simmer for 3–4 minutes or until they open. Drain, discarding any that are still closed. Reserve 12 mussels for garnish, leaving them on the half shell;

remove the other mussels from the shells and add to the mushroom mixture with the squid or octopus rings and shrimp.

5 Add the sun-dried tomatoes, pasta, and chives to the salad. Toss to mix and turn onto a large platter.

6 Blanch the snow peas for 1 minute and baby corn for 3 minutes, rinse under cold water, and drain. Arrange around the edge of the salad, alternating with the mussels on shells and whole shrimp. Cover with plastic wrap and leave to chill until ready to serve.

Macaroni & Squid Casserole

This pasta dish is easy to make and is a very hearty meal for a large number of guests.

NUTRITIONAL INFORMATION

Calories	237	Sugars	........4g
Protein	........12g	Fat	...........11g
Carbohydrate	...19g	Saturates	.......2g

15 MINS   35 MINS

SERVES 6

INGREDIENTS

2 cups short-cut macaroni, or other
   short pasta shapes

1 tablespoon olive oil

2 tablespoons chopped fresh parsley

salt and pepper

SAUCE

12 ounces cleaned squid,
   cut into 1½ in strips

6 tablespoons olive oil

2 onions, sliced

1 cup fish stock

⅔ cup red wine

12 ounces tomatoes, peeled
   and thinly sliced

2 tablespoons tomato paste

1 teaspoon dried oregano

2 bay leaves

1 Cook the pasta for only 3 minutes in a large pan of boiling salted water, adding the oil. Drain in a colander, return to the pan, cover, and keep warm.

2 To make the sauce, heat the oil in a pan over medium heat and fry the onion until translucent. Add the squid and stock and simmer for 5 minutes. Pour on the wine and add the tomatoes, tomato paste, oregano, and bay leaves. Bring the sauce to a boil, season with salt and pepper to taste, and cook, uncovered, for 5 minutes.

3 Add the pasta, stir well, cover the pan, and continue simmering for 10 minutes, or until the macaroni and squid are almost tender. By this time the sauce should be thick and syrupy. If it is too liquid, uncover the pan and continue cooking for a few minutes. Taste the sauce and adjust the seasoning if necessary.

4 Remove the bay leaves and stir in most of the parsley, reserving a little to garnish. Transfer to a warm serving dish. Sprinkle on the remaining parsley and serve hot. Serve with warm, crusty bread, such as ciabatta.

Vermicelli & Clam Sauce

This recipe is quick to prepare and cook – it's so delicious that it will be devoured even faster!

NUTRITIONAL INFORMATION

Calories	502	Sugars	.........2g
Protein	........27g	Fat	.........17g
Carbohydrate	...58g	Saturates	.......7g

 15 MINS   25 MINS

SERVES 4

I N G R E D I E N T S

14 ounces vermicelli, spaghetti, or other
   long pasta

1 tablespoon olive oil

2 tablespoons butter

2 tablespoons Parmesan shavings, to garnish

sprig of basil, to garnish

S A U C E

1 tablespoon olive oil

2 onions, chopped

2 garlic cloves, chopped

2 x 7-ounce jars clams in brine

½ cup white wine

4 tablespoons chopped fresh parsley

½ teaspoon dried oregano

pinch of freshly grated nutmeg

salt and pepper

1 Cook the pasta in a large pan of boiling salted water, adding the olive oil, for 8–10 minutes or until tender. Drain the pasta in a colander and return to the pan. Add the butter, cover, and shake the pan. Keep warm until required.

2 To make the clam sauce, heat the oil in a pan over medium heat and fry the onion until it is translucent. Stir in the garlic and cook for 1 minute.

3 Strain the liquid from one jar of clams, pour into the pan, and add the wine. Stir well, bring to simmering point and simmer for 3 minutes. Drain the brine from the second jar of clams and discard.

4 Add the shellfish and herbs to the pan, and season with pepper to taste

and the nutmeg. Lower the heat and cook until the sauce is heated through.

5 Transfer the pasta to a warm serving dish and pour on the sauce.

6 Sprinkle with the Parmesan and garnish with the basil sprig. Serve hot.

Pasta & Chili Tomatoes

The pappardelle and vegetables are tossed in a delicious chili and tomato sauce for a quick and economical meal.

NUTRITIONAL INFORMATION

Calories 353	Sugars 7g
Protein 10g	Fat 24g
Carbohydrate ...26g	Saturates 4g

15 MINS   20 MINS

SERVES 4

I N G R E D I E N T S

9½ ounces pappardelle

3 tablespoons peanut oil

2 cloves garlic, crushed

2 shallots, sliced

8 ounces green beans, sliced

3½ ounces cherry tomatoes, halved

1 teaspoon chili flakes

4 tablespoons crunchy
   peanut butter

⅔ cup coconut milk

1 tablespoon tomato paste

sliced green onions, to garnish

1 Cook the pappardelle in a large saucepan of boiling, lightly salted water for 5–6 minutes.

VARIATION

Add slices of chicken or beef to the recipe and stir-fry with the beans and pasta in step 5 for a more substantial main meal.

2 Heat the peanut oil in a large pan or preheated wok.

3 Add the garlic and shallots and stir-fry for 1 minute.

4 Drain the pappardelle thoroughly and set aside.

5 Add the green beans and drained pasta to the wok and stir-fry for 5 minutes.

6 Add the cherry tomatoes to the wok and mix well.

7 Mix together the chili flakes, peanut butter, coconut milk, and tomato paste.

8 Pour the chili mixture over the noodles, toss well to combine, and heat through.

9 Transfer to warm serving dishes and garnish. Serve at once.

Fish & Vegetable Lasagne

Layers of cheese sauce, smoked cod and whole wheat lasagne can be assembled overnight and left ready to cook on the following day.

NUTRITIONAL INFORMATION

Calories 456	Sugars 8g	
Protein 33g	Fat 24g	
Carbohydrate ...24g	Saturates 15g	

  25 MINS   50 MINS

SERVES 6

I N G R E D I E N T S

8 sheets whole wheat lasagne

1 pound 2 ounces smoked cod

2½ cups milk

1 tablespoon lemon juice

8 peppercorns

2 bay leaves

a few parsley stalks

½ cup grated sharp Cheddar cheese

⅓ cup grated Parmesan cheese

salt and pepper

a few whole shrimp, to garnish

S A U C E

¼ cup butter, plus extra for greasing

1 large onion, sliced

1 green bell pepper, cored, deseeded, and
   chopped

1 small zucchini, sliced

½ cup all-purpose flour

⅔ cup white wine

⅔ cup light cream

4½ ounces peeled shrimp

½ cup grated sharp Cheddar cheese

1 Cook the lasagne in a pan of boiling, salted water until almost tender, as described on page 344. Drain and reserve.

2 Place the smoked cod, milk, lemon juice, peppercorns, bay leaves, and parsley stalks in a skillet. Bring to a boil, cover and simmer for 10 minutes.

3 Lift the fish from the pan with a slotted spoon. Remove the skin and any bones. Flake the fish. Strain and reserve the liquid.

4 To make the sauce, melt the butter in a pan and fry the onion, bell pepper, and zucchini for 2–3 minutes. Stir in the flour and cook for 1 minute. Gradually add the fish liquid, then stir in the wine, cream, and shrimp. Simmer for 2 minutes.

Remove from the heat, add the grated cheese, and season.

5 Grease a shallow ovenproof dish. Pour in a quarter of the sauce and spread evenly over the base. Cover the sauce with three sheets of lasagne, then with another quarter of the sauce.

6 Arrange the fish on top, then cover with half of the remaining sauce. Finish with the remaining lasagne, then the rest of the sauce. Sprinkle the Cheddar and Parmesan over the sauce.

7 Bake in a preheated oven, 375°F, for 25 minutes, or until the top is golden brown and bubbling. Garnish and serve.

Macaroni & Tuna Layer

A layer of tuna with garlic, mushrooms, and red bell pepper is sandwiched between two layers of macaroni with a crunchy topping.

NUTRITIONAL INFORMATION

Calories 691   Sugars 10g
Protein . . . . .41g   Fat 33g
Carbohydrate . . .62g   Saturates 15g

20 MINS   50 MINS

SERVES 2

I N G R E D I E N T S

1¼ cups dried macaroni

2 tablespoons oil

1 garlic clove, crushed

¾ cup mushrooms, sliced

½ red bell pepper, thinly sliced

7-ounce can of tuna,
   drained and flaked

½ teaspoon dried oregano

salt and pepper

S A U C E

2 tablespoons butter or margarine

1 tablespoon all-purpose flour

1 cup milk

2 tomatoes, sliced

2 tablespoons dried bread crumbs

¼ cup grated sharp Cheddar or
   Parmesan cheese, grated

1 Cook the macaroni in boiling salted water, with 1 tablespoon of the oil added, for 10–12 minutes or until tender. Drain, rinse, and drain thoroughly.

2 Heat the remaining oil in a saucepan or skillet and fry the garlic, mushrooms, and bell pepper until soft. Add the tuna, oregano, and seasoning, and heat through.

3 Grease an ovenproof dish (about 4-cup capacity), and add half of the cooked macaroni. Cover with the tuna mixture, and then add the remaining macaroni.

4 To make the sauce, melt the butter or margarine in a saucepan, stir in the flour, and cook for 1 minute. Add the milk gradually and bring to a boil. Simmer for 1–2 minutes, stirring continuously, until thickened. Season to taste. Pour the sauce over the macaroni.

5 Lay the sliced tomatoes over the sauce and sprinkle with the bread crumbs and cheese.

6 Place in a preheated oven, at 400°F, for about 25 minutes, or until piping hot and the top is well browned.

VARIATION

Replace the tuna with chopped cooked chicken, beef, pork, or ham or with 3–4 sliced hard-cooked eggs.

Pasta with Nuts & Cheese

Simple and inexpensive, this tasty pasta dish can be prepared fairly quickly.

NUTRITIONAL INFORMATION

Calories 531	Sugars 4g
Protein 20g	Fat 35g
Carbohydrate . . .35g	Saturates 16g

10 MINS   30 MINS

SERVES 4

I N G R E D I E N T S

½ cup pine nuts

3 cups dried pasta shapes

2 zucchini, sliced

1¼ cups broccoli,
    broken into flowerets

1 cup cream cheese

⅔ cup milk

1 tablespoon chopped fresh basil

4½ ounces button mushrooms, sliced

3 ounces blue cheese, crumbled

salt and pepper

sprigs of fresh basil, to garnish

salad greens, to serve

1 Scatter the pine nuts on to a cookie sheet and broil, turning occasionally, until lightly browned all over. Set aside.

2 Cook the pasta in plenty of boiling salted water for 8–10 minutes or until just tender.

3 Meanwhile, cook the zucchini and broccoli in a small amount of boiling, lightly salted water for about 5 minutes or until just tender.

4 Put the cream cheese into a pan and heat gently, stirring constantly. Add the milk and stir to mix. Add the basil and mushrooms and cook gently for 2–3 minutes. Stir in the blue cheese and season to taste.

5 Drain the pasta and the vegetables and mix together. Pour over the cheese and mushroom sauce and add the pine nuts. Toss gently to mix. Garnish with basil sprigs and serve with salad greens.

Basil & Tomato Pasta

Roasting the tomatoes gives a sweeter flavor to this sauce. Buy Italian tomatoes, such as plum, as these have a better flavor and color.

NUTRITIONAL INFORMATION

Calories	177	Sugars	.........4g
Protein	.........5g	Fat	...........4g
Carbohydrate	...31g	Saturates	.......1g

15 MINS   35 MINS

SERVES 4

I N G R E D I E N T S

1 tablespoon olive oil

2 sprigs rosemary

2 cloves garlic

1 pound tomatoes, halved

1 tablespoon sun-dried tomato paste

12 fresh basil leaves, plus extra to garnish

salt and pepper

1½ pounds fresh farfalle or 12 ounces
  dried farfalle

1 Place the oil, rosemary, garlic. and tomatoes, skin side up, in a shallow roasting pan.

2 Drizzle with a little oil and cook under a preheated broiler for 20 minutes or until the tomato skins are slightly charred.

3 Peel the skin from the tomatoes. Roughly chop the tomato flesh and place in a pan.

4 Squeeze the pulp from the garlic cloves and mix with the tomato flesh and sun-dried tomato paste.

5 Roughly tear the fresh basil leaves into smaller pieces and then stir them into the sauce. Season with a little salt and pepper to taste. Set aside.

6 Cook the farfalle in a saucepan of boiling water for 8–10 minutes or until it is cooked through, but still has bite. Drain well.

7 Gently re-heat the tomato and basil sauce, stirring.

8 Transfer the farfalle to serving plates and pour over the basil and tomato sauce. Serve at once.

COOK'S TIP

This sauce tastes just as good when served cold in a pasta salad.

Tagliatelle & Garlic Sauce

This pasta dish can be prepared in a moment—the intense flavors are sure to make this a popular recipe.

NUTRITIONAL INFORMATION

Calories 501   Sugars 3g
Protein . . . . .15g   Fat 31g
Carbohydrate . . .43g   Saturates 11g

15 MINS   20 MINS

SERVES 4

I N G R E D I E N T S

2 tablespoons walnut oil

1 bunch green onions, sliced

2 garlic cloves, sliced thinly

8 ounces mushrooms, sliced

1 pound 2 ounces fresh green and
   white tagliatelle

8 ounces frozen chopped leaf
   spinach, thawed and drained

½ cup cream cheese with
   garlic and herbs

4 tablespoon light cream

½ cup chopped, unsalted
   pistachio nuts

2 tablespoons shredded fresh basil

salt and pepper

sprigs of fresh basil, to garnish

Italian bread, to serve

1 Gently heat the oil in a wok or skillet and fry the green onions and garlic for 1 minute or until just softened. Add the mushrooms, stir well, cover, and cook gently for 5 minutes or until softened.

2 Meanwhile, bring a large saucepan of lightly salted water to a boil and cook the pasta for 3–5 minutes or until just tender. Drain the pasta thoroughly and return to the saucepan.

3 Add the spinach to the mushrooms and heat through for 1–2 minutes. Add the cheese and allow to melt slightly. Stir in the cream and continue to heat without allowing to boil.

4 Pour the mixture over the pasta, season to taste and mix well. Heat gently, stirring, for 2–3 minutes.

5 Pile into a warm serving bowl and sprinkle over the pistachio nuts and shredded basil. Garnish with basil sprigs and serve with Italian bread.

Chili & Bell Pepper Pasta

This roasted bell pepper and chili sauce is sweet and spicy—the perfect combination!

NUTRITIONAL INFORMATION

Calories	423	Sugars	.........5g
Protein	.........9g	Fat	..........27g
Carbohydrate	...38g	Saturates	.......4g

25 MINS   30 MINS

SERVES 4

INGREDIENTS

2 red bell peppers, halved and deseeded

1 small red chili

4 tomatoes, halved

2 garlic cloves

½ cup ground almonds

7 tablespoons olive oil

1½ pounds fresh pasta or 12 ounces dried pasta

fresh oregano leaves, to garnish

1 Place the bell peppers, skin-side up, on a cookie sheet with the chili and tomatoes. Cook under a preheated broiler for 15 minutes or until charred. After 10 minutes turn the tomatoes skin-side up. Place the bell peppers and chilies in a plastic bag and leave to sweat for 10 minutes.

2 Remove the skin from the bell peppers and chilies and slice the flesh into strips, using a sharp knife.

3 Peel the garlic, and peel and deseed the tomatoes.

4 Place the almonds on a cookie sheet and place under the broiler for 2–3 minutes until golden.

5 Using a food processor, blend the bell pepper, chili, garlic, and tomatoes to make a purée. Keep the motor running and slowly add the olive oil to form a thick sauce. Alternatively, mash the mixture

with a fork and gradually beat in the olive oil, drop by drop.

6 Stir the toasted ground almonds into the mixture.

7 Warm the sauce in a saucepan until it is heated through.

8 Cook the pasta in a saucepan of boiling water for 8–10 minutes if using dried, or 3–5 minutes if using fresh. Drain the pasta thoroughly and transfer to a serving dish. Pour over the sauce and toss to mix. Garnish with the fresh oregano leaves.

VARIATION

Add 2 tablespoons of red wine vinegar to the sauce and use as a dressing for a cold pasta salad, if you wish.

Artichoke & Olive Spaghetti

The tasty flavors of artichoke hearts and black olives are a winning combination.

NUTRITIONAL INFORMATION

Calories 393	Sugars 11g	
Protein 14g	Fat 11g	
Carbohydrate ...63g	Saturates 2g	

20 MINS   35 MINS

SERVES 4

I N G R E D I E N T S

2 tablespoons olive oil

1 large red onion, chopped

2 garlic cloves, crushed

1 tablespoon lemon juice

4 baby eggplants, quartered

2½ cups sieved tomatoes

2 teaspoons sugar

2 tablespoons tomato paste

14-ounce can artichoke hearts, drained
    and halved

1 cup pitted black olives

12 ounces whole wheat dried spaghetti

salt and pepper

sprigs of fresh basil,
    to garnish

olive bread, to serve

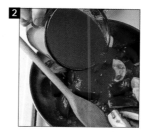

1 Heat 1 tablespoon of the oil in a large skillet and gently fry the onion, garlic, lemon juice, and eggplants for 4–5 minutes or until lightly browned.

2 Pour in the sieved tomatoes, season with salt and pepper to taste, and add the sugar and tomato paste. Bring to a boil, reduce the heat, and simmer for 20 minutes.

3 Gently stir in the artichoke halves and olives and cook for 5 minutes.

4 Meanwhile, bring a large saucepan of lightly salted water to a boil, and cook the spaghetti for 8–10 minutes or until just tender. Drain well, toss in the remaining olive oil, and season with salt and pepper to taste.

5 Transfer the spaghetti to a warm serving bowl and top with the vegetable sauce. Garnish with basil sprigs and serve with olive bread.

Spaghetti with Ricotta Sauce

This makes a quick and easy starter, and is particularly ideal for the summer.

NUTRITIONAL INFORMATION

Calories	 688	Sugars	.... .5g
Protein	.... 17g	Fat	.... .51g
Carbohydrate	...43g	Saturates	...... 16g

15 MINS   20 MINS

SERVES 4

I N G R E D I E N T S

12 ounces spaghetti

3 tablespoons olive oil

3 tablespoons butter, cut into small
   pieces

2 tablespoons chopped parsley

S A U C E

1 cup freshly ground almonds

½ cup ricotta cheese

large pinch of grated nutmeg

large pinch of ground cinnamon

⅔ cup crème fraîche (see page 472)

½ cup hot chicken stock

1 tablespoon pine nuts

pepper

cilantro leaves, to garnish

COOK'S TIP

To toss spaghetti and coat
it with a sauce or dressing, use
the 2 largest forks you can find.
Holding one fork in each hand,
ease the prongs under the spaghetti
from each side and lift them
towards the center. Repeat evenly
until the pasta is well coated.

1 Cook the spaghetti in a large pan of boiling salted water, to which you have added 1 tablespoon of the oil, for 8–10 minutes or until tender. Drain the pasta in a colander, return to the pan, and toss with the butter and parsley. Cover the pan and keep warm.

2 To make the sauce, mix together the ground almonds, ricotta, nutmeg, cinnamon, and crème fraîche to make a thick paste. Gradually pour on the remaining oil, stirring constantly until it is well blended. Gradually pour on the hot stock, stirring all the time, until the sauce is smooth.

3 Transfer the spaghetti to warm serving dishes, pour on the sauce and toss well. Sprinkle each serving with pine nuts and garnish with cilantro leaves. Serve warm.

Tagliatelle with Garlic Butter

Pasta is not difficult to make yourself, just a little time consuming. The resulting pasta only takes a couple of minutes to cook and tastes wonderful.

NUTRITIONAL INFORMATION

Calories	642	Sugars	.........2g
Protein	........16g	Fat	..........29g
Carbohydrate	...84g	Saturates	......13g

45 MINS   5 MINS

SERVES 4

INGREDIENTS

4 cups white flour,
    plus extra for dredging

2 teaspoons salt

4 eggs, beaten

3 tablespoons olive oil

5 tablespoons butter, melted

3 garlic cloves, finely chopped

2 tablespoons chopped, fresh parsley

pepper

1 Sift the flour into a large bowl and stir in the salt.

2 Make a well in the middle of the dry ingredients and add the eggs and 2 tablespoons of oil. Using a wooden spoon, stir in the eggs, gradually drawing in the flour. After a few minutes the dough will be too stiff to use a spoon and you will need to use your fingers.

3 Once all of the flour has been incorporated, turn the dough out on to a floured surface and knead for about 5 minutes, or until smooth and elastic. If you find the dough is too wet, add a little more flour and continue kneading. Cover with plastic wrap and leave to rest for at least 15 minutes.

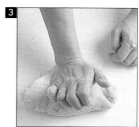

4 The basic dough is now ready; roll out the pasta thinly and create the pasta shapes required. This can be done by hand or using a pasta machine. Results from a machine are usually neater and thinner, but not necessarily better.

5 To make the tagliatelle by hand, fold the thinly rolled pasta sheets into 3 and cut out long, thin strips, about ½ inch wide.

6 To cook, bring a pan of water to a boil, add 1 tablespoon of oil and the pasta. It will take 2–3 minutes to cook, and the texture should have a slight bite to it. Drain.

7 Mix together the butter, garlic, and parsley. Stir into the pasta, season with a little pepper to taste, and serve at once.

COOK'S TIP

Generally allow about 5½ ounces fresh pasta or about 3½ ounces dried pasta per person.

Pasta & Cheese Puddings

These delicious pasta puddings are served with a tasty tomato and bay leaf sauce.

🥘 45 MINS   🕐 50 MINS

SERVES 4

I N G R E D I E N T S

1 tablespoon butter or margarine,
   softened

½ cup dried white
   bread crumbs

6 ounces tricolor spaghetti

1¼ cups Béchamel Sauce
   (see page 28)

1 egg yolk

1 cup grated Swiss cheese

salt and pepper

fresh flat-leaf parsley,
   to garnish

T O M A T O   S A U C E

2 teaspoons olive oil

1 onion, chopped finely

1 bay leaf

⅔ cup dry white wine

⅔ cup sieved tomatoes

1 tablespoon tomato paste

1 Grease four ¾ cup molds or ramekins with the butter or margarine. Evenly coat the insides with half of the bread crumbs.

2 Break the spaghetti into 2-inch lengths. Bring a saucepan of lightly salted water to a boil and cook the spaghetti for 5–6 minutes or until just tender. Drain well and put in a bowl.

3 Mix the Béchamel Sauce, egg yolk, cheese, and seasoning into the cooked pasta and pack into the molds.

4 Sprinkle with the remaining bread crumbs and place the molds on a cookie sheet. Bake in a preheated oven, 425°F, for 20 minutes until golden. Leave to stand for 10 minutes.

5 Meanwhile, make the sauce. Heat the oil in a pan and fry the onion and bay leaf for 2–3 minutes or until just softened.

6 Stir in the wine, sieved tomatoes, tomato paste, and seasoning. Bring to a boil and simmer for 20 minutes or until thickened. Discard the bay leaf.

7 Run a spatula around the inside of the molds. Turn onto serving plates, garnish and serve with the tomato sauce.

Pasta & Bean Casserole

A satisfying winter dish, this is a slow-cooked, one-pot meal. The navy beans need to be soaked overnight, so prepare well in advance.

NUTRITIONAL INFORMATION

Calories 323   Sugars 5g
Protein . . . . .13g   Fat 12g
Carbohydrate . . .41g   Saturates 2g

25 MINS   3¹/₂ HOURS

SERVES 6

I N G R E D I E N T S

1 cup dried navy beans,
   soaked overnight and drained

2 cups penne,
   or other short pasta shapes

6 tablespoons olive oil

3½ cups vegetable stock

2 large onions, sliced

2 cloves garlic, chopped

2 bay leaves

1 teaspoon dried oregano

1 teaspoon dried thyme

5 tablespoons red wine

2 tablespoons tomato paste

2 celery stalks, sliced

1 fennel bulb, sliced

4½ ounces mushrooms, sliced

8 ounces tomatoes, sliced

1 teaspoon brown sugar

4 tablespoons dry white bread crumbs

salt and pepper

TO SERVE

salad greens

crusty bread

1 Put the beans in a large pan, cover them with water, and bring to a boil. Boil the beans rapidly for 20 minutes, then drain them.

2 Cook the pasta for only 3 minutes in a large pan of boiling salted water, adding 1 tablespoon of the oil. Drain in a colander and set aside.

3 Put the beans in a large flameproof casserole, pour on the vegetable stock, and stir in the remaining olive oil, the onions, garlic, bay leaves, herbs, wine, and tomato paste.

4 Bring to a boil, cover the casserole, and cook in a preheated oven, 350°F, for 2 hours.

5 Add the reserved pasta, the celery, fennel, mushrooms, and tomatoes, and season with salt and pepper.

6 Stir in the sugar and sprinkle on the bread crumbs. Cover the casserole and continue cooking for 1 hour. Serve hot, with salad greens and crusty bread.

Spicy Tomato Tagliatelle

A deliciously fresh and slightly spicy tomato sauce which is excellent for lunch or a light supper.

NUTRITIONAL INFORMATION

Calories 306   Sugars 7g
Protein . . . . .8g   Fat 12g
Carbohydrate . . .45g   Saturates 7g

15 MINS   35 MINS

SERVES 4

INGREDIENTS

4 tablespoons butter

1 onion, finely chopped

1 garlic clove, crushed

2 small red chilies,
    deseeded and diced

1 pound fresh tomatoes, peeled,
    deseeded, and diced

¾ cup vegetable stock

2 tablespoons tomato paste

1 teaspoon sugar

salt and pepper

1½ pounds fresh green and white
    tagliatelle, or 12 ounces
    dried tagliatelle

VARIATION

Try topping your pasta dish with 1¾ ounces pancetta or unsmoked bacon, diced and dry-fried for 5 minutes until crispy.

1 Melt the butter in a large saucepan. Add the onion and garlic and cook for 3–4 minutes or until softened.

2 Add the chilies to the pan and continue cooking for about 2 minutes.

3 Add the tomatoes and stock, reduce the heat, and leave to simmer for 10 minutes, stirring.

4 Pour the sauce into a food processor and blend for 1 minute until smooth.

Alternatively, push the sauce through a strainer.

5 Return the sauce to the pan and add the tomato paste sugar, and salt and pepper to taste. Gently reheat over low heat, until piping hot.

6 Cook the tagliatelle in a pan of boiling water for 8–10 minutes or until it is tender, but still has bite. Drain the tagliatelle, transfer to serving plates, and serve with the tomato sauce.

Eggplant Lasagne

This filling eggplant, zucchini, and mozzarella lasagne is an Italian classic.

NUTRITIONAL INFORMATION

Calories	525	Sugars	........14g
Protein	........17g	Fat	..........39g
Carbohydrate	...28g	Saturates	......15g

1¼ HOURS   1 HOUR

SERVES 6

I N G R E D I E N T S

4 ounces eggplants

4 teaspoons salt

8 tablespoon olive oil

2 tablespoons garlic and herb butter or
    margarine

1 pound 2 ounces zucchini, sliced

2 cups grated mozzarella cheese

2½ cups sieved tomatoes

6 sheets pre-cooked
    green lasagne

2½ cups Béchamel Sauce
    (see page 28)

⅔ cup grated Parmesan cheese

1 teaspoon dried oregano

pepper

1 Thinly slice the eggplant. Layer the slices in a bowl, sprinkling with the salt as you go. Set aside for 30 minutes. Rinse well in cold water and pat dry with paper towels.

2 Heat 4 tablespoons of oil in a skillet and fry half of the eggplant slices for 6–7 minutes or until lightly golden all over. Drain on paper towels. Repeat with the remaining eggplant slices and oil.

3 Melt the garlic and herb butter or margarine in the skillet and fry the zucchini for 5–6 minutes until golden. Drain thoroughly on paper towels.

4 Place half of the eggplant and zucchini slices in a large ovenproof dish. Season to taste with pepper and sprinkle over half of the grated mozzarella. Spoon over half of the sieved tomatoes and top with 3 sheets of lasagne.

5 Arrange the remaining eggplant and zucchini slices on top. Season with pepper and top with the remaining mozzarella and sieved tomatoes and another layer of lasagne.

6 Spoon over the Béchamel Sauce and top with Parmesan and oregano. Put on a cookie sheet and bake in a preheated oven, 425°F, for 30–35 minutes or until golden on top.

Pasta with Cheese & Broccoli

Some of the simplest and most satisfying dishes are made with pasta, such as this delicious combination of tagliatelle with two-cheese sauce.

NUTRITIONAL INFORMATION

Calories 624   Sugars 2g
Protein .... 22g   Fat 45g
Carbohydrate ... 34g   Saturates 28g

 5 MINS   15 MINS

SERVES 4

I N G R E D I E N T S

10½ ounces dried tagliatelle tricolore
    (plain, spinach- and tomato-flavored
    noodles)

2½ cups broccoli, broken into
    small flowerets

1½ cups mascarpone cheese

1 cup diced blue cheese

1 tablespoon chopped fresh oregano

2 tablespoons butter

salt and pepper

sprigs of fresh oregano, to garnish

freshly grated Parmesan, to serve

1 Cook the tagliatelle in plenty of boiling salted water for 8–10 minutes or until just tender.

2 Meanwhile, cook the broccoli flowerets in a small amount of lightly salted, boiling water. Avoid overcooking the broccoli, so that it retains much of its color and texture.

3 Heat the mascarpone and blue cheeses together gently in a large saucepan until they are melted. Stir in the oregano and season with salt and pepper to taste.

4 Drain the pasta thoroughly. Return it to the saucepan and add the butter, tossing the tagliatelle to coat it. Drain the broccoli well and add to the pasta with the sauce, tossing gently to mix.

5 Divide the pasta among 4 warmed serving plates. Garnish with sprigs of fresh oregano and serve with freshly grated Parmesan.

Pasta & Vegetable Sauce

A Mediterranean mixture of red bell peppers, garlic, and zucchini cooked in olive oil and tossed with pasta.

NUTRITIONAL INFORMATION

Calories 341   Sugars 8g
Protein . . . . .13g   Fat 20g
Carbohydrate . . .30g   Saturates 8g

 15 MINS   20 MINS

SERVES 4

I N G R E D I E N T S

3 tablespoons olive oil

1 onion, sliced

2 garlic cloves, chopped

3 red bell peppers, deseeded and cut
   into strips

3 zucchini, sliced

14-ounce can diced tomatoes

3 tablespoon sun-dried tomato paste

2 tablespoons chopped fresh basil

8 ounces fresh pasta spirals

1 cup grated Swiss cheese

salt and pepper

fresh basil sprigs,`
   to garnish

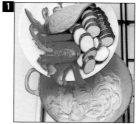

1 Heat the oil in a heavy-based saucepan or flameproof casserole. Add the onion and garlic and cook, stirring occasionally, until softened. Add the bell peppers and zucchini and fry for 5 minutes, stirring occasionally.

2 Add the tomatoes, sun-dried tomato paste, basil, and seasoning, cover, and cook for 5 minutes.

3 Meanwhile, bring a large saucepan of salted water to a boil and add the pasta. Stir and bring back to a boil.

Reduce the heat slightly and cook, uncovered, for 3 minutes, or until just tender. Drain thoroughly and add to the vegetables. Toss gently to mix well.

4 Put the mixture into a shallow flameproof dish and sprinkle over the grated cheese.

5 Cook under a preheated broiler for 5 minutes until the cheese is golden. Garnish with basil sprigs and serve.

COOK'S TIP

Be careful not to overcook fresh pasta—it should be al dente (retaining some bite). It takes only a few minutes to cook as it is still full of moisture.

Tagliatelle with Pumpkin

This unusual pasta dish comes from the Emilia Romagna region of Italy.

NUTRITIONAL INFORMATION

Calories	.454	Sugars	.4g
Protein	.9g	Fat	.33g
Carbohydrate	.33g	Saturates	.12g

15 MINS   35 MINS

SERVES 4

I N G R E D I E N T S

1 pound 2 ounces pumpkin or
 butternut squash

2 tablespoons olive oil

1 onion, chopped finely

2 garlic cloves, crushed

4–6 tablespoon chopped fresh parsley

pinch of ground or freshly grated
nutmeg

1 cup chicken or
 vegetable stock

4½ ounces prosciutto, cut into narrow strips

9 ounces tagliatelle, green or white (fresh
 or dried)

⅔ cup heavy cream

salt and pepper

freshly grated Parmesan, to serve

 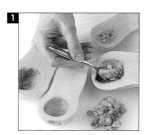 

1 Peel the pumpkin or squash and scoop out the seeds and membrane. Cut the flesh into ½-inch dice.

2 Heat the olive oil in a pan and gently fry the onion and garlic until softened. Add half of the parsley and fry for 1–2 minutes.

3 Add the pumpkin or squash and continue to cook for 2–3 minutes. Season well with salt, pepper, and nutmeg.

4 Add half of the stock, bring to a boil, cover, and simmer for about 10 minutes or until the pumpkin is tender, adding more stock as necessary. Add the prosciutto and continue to cook for 2 minutes, stirring frequently.

5 Meanwhile, cook the tagliatelle in a large saucepan of boiling salted water, allowing 3–4 minutes for fresh pasta or 8–10 minutes for dried. Drain thoroughly and turn into a warm dish.

6 Add the cream to the ham mixture and heat gently. Season and spoon over the pasta. Sprinkle with the remaining parsley and grated Parmesan separately.

Basil & Pine Nut Pesto

Delicious stirred into pasta, soups. and salad dressings, pesto is available in most supermarkets, but making your own gives a concentrated flavor.

NUTRITIONAL INFORMATION

Calories 321   Sugars 1g
Protein . . . . .11g   Fat 17g
Carbohydrate . . .32g   Saturates 4g

 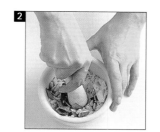 

15 MINS   10 MINS

SERVES 4

I N G R E D I E N T S

about 40 fresh basil leaves,
    washed and dried

3 garlic cloves, crushed

¼ cup pine nuts

⅔ cup finely grated Parmesan cheese

2–3 tablespoons extra virgin olive oil

salt and pepper

1½ pounds fresh pasta or
    12 ounces dried pasta

1 Rinse the basil leaves and pat them dry with paper towels.

2 Put the basil leaves, garlic, pine nuts, and grated Parmesan into a food processor and blend for about 30 seconds or until smooth. Alternatively, pound all of the ingredients by hand, using a mortar and pestle.

3 If you are using a food processor, keep the motor running and slowly add the olive oil. Alternatively, add the oil drop by drop while stirring briskly. Season with salt and pepper to taste.

4 Cook the pasta in a saucepan of boiling water allowing 3–4 minutes for fresh pasta or 8–10 minutes for dried, or until it is cooked through, but still has bite. Drain the pasta thoroughly in a colander.

5 Transfer the pasta to a serving plate and serve with the pesto. Toss to mix well and serve hot.

COOK'S TIP

You can store pesto in the refrigerator for about 4 weeks. Cover the surface of the pesto with olive oil before sealing the container or bottle, to prevent the basil from oxidizing and turning black.

Pasta & Olive Omelet

Use any leftover cooked pasta you may have, such as penne, short-cut macaroni, or shells, to make this fluffy omelet an instant success.

NUTRITIONAL INFORMATION

Calories 521	Sugars 3g
Protein 18g	Fat 34g
Carbohydrate . . .38g	Saturates 6g

20 MINS   20 MINS

SERVES 2

I N G R E D I E N T S

4 tablespoons olive oil

1 small onion, chopped

1 fennel bulb, thinly sliced

½ cup diced and dried raw potato

1 garlic clove, chopped

4 eggs

1 tablespoon chopped parsley

pinch of cayenne pepper

3 ounces short pasta, cooked weight

1 tablespoon stuffed green olives, halved,
   plus extra to garnish

salt and pepper

marjoram sprigs, to garnish

tomato salad, to serve

1 Heat 2 tablespoons of the oil in a heavy skillet over low heat and fry the onion, fennel, and potato for 8-10 minutes, stirring occasionally, until the potato is just tender. Do not allow it to break up. Stir in the garlic and cook for 1 minute. Remove the skillet from the heat, lift out the vegetables with a slotted spoon, and set aside. Rinse and dry the skillet.

2 Break the eggs into a bowl and beat until frothy. Stir in the parsley and season with salt, pepper, and cayenne.

3 Heat 1 tablespoon of the remaining oil in a pan over medium heat. Pour in half of the beaten eggs, then add the cooked vegetables, the pasta, and the olives. Pour on the remaining egg and cook until the sides begin to set.

4 Lift up the edges with a spatula to allow the uncooked egg to spread underneath. Continue cooking the omelet, shaking the pan occasionally, until the underside is golden brown.

5 Slide the omelet out on to a large, flat plate and wipe the pan clean with paper towels. Heat the remaining oil in the pan and invert the omelet. Cook the omelet on the other side until it is also golden brown.

6 Slide the omelet on to a warm serving dish. Garnish with a few olives and sprigs of marjoram, and serve hot, cut into wedges, with a tomato salad, if wished.

Pasta with Green Vegetables

The different shapes and textures of the vegetables make a mouthwatering presentation in this light and summery dish.

NUTRITIONAL INFORMATION

Calories 517	Sugars 5g	
Protein 17g	Fat 32g	
Carbohydrate ...42g	Saturates 18g	

 10 MINS   25 MINS

SERVES 4

I N G R E D I E N T S

2 cups gemelli or other pasta shapes

1 tablespoon olive oil

2 tablespoons chopped fresh parsley

2 tablespoons freshly grated Parmesan cheese

salt and pepper

S A U C E

1 head of green broccoli, cut into flowerets

2 zucchini, sliced

8 ounces asparagus spears, trimmed

4½ ounces snow peas

1 cup frozen peas

2 tablespoons butter

3 tablespoons vegetable stock

5 tablespoons heavy cream

large pinch of freshly grated nutmeg

1 Cook the pasta in a large pan of salted boiling water, adding the olive oil, for 8–10 minutes or until tender. Drain the pasta in a colander, return to the pan, cover, and keep warm.

2 Steam the broccoli, zucchini, asparagus spears, and snow peas over a pan of boiling, salted water until just beginning to soften. Remove from the heat and plunge into cold water to prevent further cooking. Drain thoroughly and set aside.

3 Cook the peas in boiling, salted water for 3 minutes, then drain. Refresh in cold water and drain again.

4 Put the butter and vegetable stock in a pan over medium heat. Add all of the vegetables, except the asparagus spears, and toss carefully with a wooden spoon to heat through, taking care not to break them up. Stir in the cream, allow the sauce to heat through and season with salt, pepper, and nutmeg.

5 Transfer the pasta to a warm serving dish and stir in the chopped parsley. Spoon the sauce over, and sprinkle on the freshly grated Parmesan. Arrange the asparagus spears in a pattern on top. Serve hot.

Italian Tomato Sauce & Pasta

Fresh tomatoes make a delicious Italian-style sauce which goes particularly well with pasta.

NUTRITIONAL INFORMATION

Calories 304	Sugars 8g
Protein 15g	Fat 14g
Carbohydrate ...31g	Saturates 5g

 10 MINS   25 MINS

SERVES 2

INGREDIENTS

1 tablespoon olive oil

1 small onion, chopped finely

1–2 cloves garlic, crushed

12 ounces tomatoes, peeled and chopped

2 teaspoons tomato paste

2 tablespoons water

10½–12 ounces dried pasta shapes

¾ cup derinded and diced lean bacon

½ cup sliced mushrooms

1 tablespoon chopped fresh parsley or

1 teaspoon chopped fresh cilantro

2 tablespoons sour cream (optional)

salt and pepper

COOK'S TIP

Sour cream contains 18–20 % fat, so if you are following a low-fat diet, you can leave it out of this recipe or substitute a low-fat alternative.

 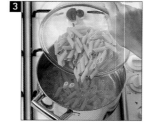 

1 To make the tomato sauce, heat the oil in a saucepan over medium heat and fry the onion and garlic gently, stirring occasionally, until soft.

2 Add the tomatoes, tomato paste, water, and salt and pepper to taste to the mixture in the pan and bring to a boil. Cover and simmer gently for 10 minutes.

3 Meanwhile, cook the pasta in a saucepan of boiling salted water for 8–10 minutes, or until just tender. Drain the pasta thoroughly and transfer to warm individual serving dishes.

4 Heat the bacon gently in a skillet until the fat runs, then add the mushrooms and continue cooking for 3–4 minutes. Drain off any excess oil.

5 Add the bacon and mushrooms to the tomato mixture, together with the parsley or cilantro and the sour cream, if using. Reheat and serve with the pasta.

Mushroom & Pasta Flan

Lightly cooked vermicelli is pressed into a flan ring and baked with a creamy mushroom filling.

10 MINS   1 HR 10 MINS

SERVES 4

INGREDIENTS

8 ounces vermicelli or spaghetti

1 tablespoon olive oil

2 tablespoons butter, plus extra for
    greasing

salt and pepper

tomato and basil salad, to serve

SAUCE

¼ cup butter

1 onion, chopped

5½ ounces mushrooms, trimmed

1 green bell pepper, cored, deseeded, and
    sliced into thin rings

⅔ cup milk

3 eggs, beaten lightly

2 tablespoons heavy cream

1 teaspoon dried oregano

pinch of finely grated nutmeg

1 tablespoon freshly grated Parmesan

1 Cook the pasta in a large pan of salted boiling water, adding the olive oil, for 8–10 minutes or until tender. Drain the pasta in a colander, return to the pan, add the butter, and shake the pan well.

2 Lightly grease an 8-inch loose-based flan pan. Press the cooked pasta onto the base and around the sides of the pan to form a shell.

3 Heat the butter in a skillet over medium heat and fry the onion until it is translucent. Remove with a slotted spoon and spread in the flan base.

4 Add the mushrooms and bell pepper rings to the pan and turn them in the fat until glazed. Fry for 2 minutes on each side, then arrange in the flan base.

5 Beat together the milk, eggs, and cream, stir in the oregano, and season with nutmeg and pepper. Pour the mixture carefully over the vegetables and sprinkle on the cheese.

6 Bake the flan in the preheated oven, 350°F, for 40–45 minutes, or until the filling is set. Slide on to a serving plate and serve warm.

Three-Cheese Macaroni

Based on a traditional family favorite, this pasta bake has plenty of flavor. Serve with a crisp salad for a quick, tasty supper.

NUTRITIONAL INFORMATION

Calories 672	Sugars 10g
Protein 31g	Fat 44g
Carbohydrate ...40g	Saturates 23g

 30 MINS   45 MINS

SERVES 4

I N G R E D I E N T S

2½ cups Béchamel Sauce
  (see page 28)

2 cups macaroni

1 egg, beaten

1 cup grated grated sharp
  Cheddar cheese

1 tablespoon wholegrain mustard

2 tablespoons chopped
  fresh chives

4 tomatoes, sliced

1 cup grated brick cheese

½ cup grated blue cheese

2 tablespoons sunflower seeds

salt and pepper

snipped fresh chives, to garnish

1 Make the Béchamel Sauce, put into a bowl and cover with plastic wrap to prevent a skin forming. Set aside.

2 Bring a saucepan of salted water to a boil and cook the macaroni for 8–10 minutes or until just tender. Drain well and place in an ovenproof dish.

3 Stir the beaten egg, Cheddar, mustard, chives, and seasoning into the Béchamel Sauce and spoon over the macaroni, making sure it is well covered. Top with a layer of sliced tomatoes.

4 Sprinkle over the brick and blue cheeses, and sunflower seeds. Put on a cookie sheet and bake in a preheated oven, 375°F, for 25–30 minutes or until bubbling and golden. Garnish with chives and serve at once.

Vegetable & Pasta Parcels

These small parcels are very easy to make and have the advantage of being filled with your favorite mixture of succulent mushrooms.

NUTRITIONAL INFORMATION

Calories . . . . . . .333 Sugars 1g
Protein . . . . .7g Fat 30g
Carbohydrate . . .10g Saturates 13g

20 MINS 20 MINS

SERVES 4

I N G R E D I E N T S

FILLING

2 tablespoons butter or margarine

2 garlic cloves, crushed

1 small leek, chopped

2 celery stalks, chopped

2⅓ cups mushrooms, chopped

1 egg, beaten

2 tablespoons grated Parmesan cheese

salt and pepper

RAVIOLI

4 sheets phyllo pastry

2 tablespoons margarine

oil, for deep-frying

1 To make the filling, melt the butter or margarine in a skillet and sauté the garlic and leek for 2–3 minutes until softened.

2 Add the celery and mushrooms and cook for a further 4–5 minutes until all of the vegetables are tender.

3 Turn off the heat and stir in the egg and grated Parmesan cheese. Season with salt and pepper to taste.

4 Lay the pastry sheets on a chopping board and cut each into nine squares.

5 Spoon a little of the filling into the center of half of the squares and brush the edges of the pastry with butter or margarine. Lay another square on top and seal the edges to make a parcel.

6 Heat the oil for deep-frying to 350°–375°F or until a cube of bread browns in 30 seconds. Fry the ravioli, in batches, for 2–3 minutes or until golden brown. Remove from the oil with a slotted spoon and pat dry on absorbent paper towels. Transfer the ravioli to a warm serving plate and serve.

Rice & Grains

Rice dishes are particularly popular in the north of Italy as the people in this area are very fond of risottos. Milanese and other risottos are made with short-grain Italian rice,

the best of which is arborio rice. An Italian risotto is far moister than a pilau or other savory rice dish, but it should not be soggy or sticky. Gnocchi are made with maize flour, cornmeal, potatoes, or semolina, often combined with spinach or some sort of cheese. Gnocchi resemble dumplings and are either poached or baked. Polenta is made with cornmeal or polenta flour and can be served either as a soft porridge or a firmer cake, which is then fried until crisp.

Golden Chicken Risotto

Long-grain rice can be used instead of arborio rice, but it won't give you the traditional, creamy texture that is typical of Italian risottos.

NUTRITIONAL INFORMATION

Calories 701	Sugars 7g
Protein 35g	Fat 26g
Carbohydrate . . .88g	Saturates 8g

10 MINS   30 MINS

SERVES 4

INGREDIENTS

2 tablespoons sunflower oil

1 tablespoon butter or margarine

1 medium leek, thinly sliced

1 large yellow bell pepper, diced

3 skinless, boneless chicken breasts, diced

1⅔ cups arborio rice

a few strands of saffron

6¼ cups chicken stock

7-ounce can corn

½ cup toasted unsalted peanuts

⅔ cup grated Parmesan cheese

salt and pepper

1 Heat the sunflower oil and butter or margarine in a large saucepan. Fry the leek and bell pepper for 1 minute, then stir in the chicken and cook, stirring until golden brown.

2 Stir in the arborio rice and cook for 2–3 minutes.

3 Stir in the saffron strands and salt and pepper to taste. Add the chicken stock, a little at a time, cover and cook over low heat, stirring occasionally, for about 20 minutes, or until the rice is tender and most of the liquid has been absorbed. Do not let the risotto dry out—add more stock if necessary.

4 Stir in the corn, peanuts, and Parmesan cheese, then season with salt and pepper to taste. Serve hot.

COOK'S TIP

Risottos can be frozen, before adding the Parmesan cheese, for up to 1 month, but remember to reheat this risotto thoroughly as it contains chicken.

Sun-dried Tomato Risotto

A Milanese risotto can be cooked in a variety of ways—but always with saffron. This version with sun-dried tomatoes has a lovely tangy flavor.

NUTRITIONAL INFORMATION

Calories 558	Sugars 2g	
Protein 16g	Fat 19g	
Carbohydrate ...80g	Saturates 9g	

10 MINS   30 MINS

SERVES 4

INGREDIENTS

1 tablespoon olive oil

2 tablespoons butter

1 large onion, finely chopped

1⅔ cups arborio rice, washed

about 15 strands of saffron

⅔ cup white wine

3¾ cup hot vegetable or
   chicken stock

8 sun-dried tomatoes,
   cut into strips

1 cup frozen peas, thawed

1¾ oz prosciutto, shredded

1 cup grated Parmesan cheese

1 Heat the oil and butter in a large skillet. Add the onion and cook for 4–5 minutes or until softened.

2 Add the rice and saffron to the skillet, stirring well to coat the rice in the oil, and cook for 1 minute.

3 Add the wine and stock gradually to the rice mixture in the pan, a ladleful at a time, stirring and making sure that all the liquid is absorbed before adding the next ladleful of liquid.

4 About halfway through adding the stock, stir in the sun-dried tomatoes.

5 When all of the wine and stock has been absorbed, the rice should be cooked. Test by tasting a grain—if it is still crunchy, add a little more water, and continue cooking. It should take 15–20 minutes to cook.

6 Stir in the peas, prosciutto, and cheese. Cook for 2–3 minutes, stirring, until hot. Serve with extra Parmesan.

COOK'S TIP

The finished risotto should have moist but separate grains. This is achieved by adding the hot stock a little at a time, only adding more when the last addition has been absorbed. Don't leave the risotto to cook by itself: it needs constant checking to see when more liquid is required.

Rice-Filled Eggplants

An eggplant is halved and filled with a risotto mixture, topped with cheese, and baked to make a snack or quick meal for two.

NUTRITIONAL INFORMATION

Calories	435	Sugars	........17g
Protein	........13g	Fat	..........23g
Carbohydrate	...48g	Saturates	.......8g

 20 MINS   1 HOUR

SERVES 2

I N G R E D I E N T S

¼ cup mixed long-grain and
   wild rice

1 eggplant, about 12 ounces

1 tablespoon olive oil

1 small onion, chopped finely

1 garlic clove, crushed

½ small red bell pepper, cored, deseeded,
   and chopped

2 tablespoons water

3 tablespoons raisins

¼ cup cashew nuts, chopped roughly

½ teaspoon dried oregano

½ cup grated sharp Cheddar
   or Parmesan cheese

salt and pepper

fresh oregano or parsley,
   to garnish

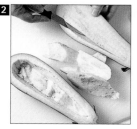  

1 Cook the rice in a pan of boiling salted water for 15 minutes or until tender. Drain, rinse, and drain again.

2 Bring a large pan of water to a boil. Cut the stem off the eggplant and then cut in half lengthwise. Cut out the flesh from the center, leaving a ½-inch shell. Blanch the shells in a boiling water for 3–4 minutes. Drain.

3 Chop the eggplant flesh finely.

4 Heat the oil in a pan and fry the onion and garlic gently until just beginning to soften. Add the bell pepper and eggplant flesh and continue cooking for 2 minutes. Add the water and cook for 2–3 minutes.

5 Stir the raisins, cashew nuts, oregano. and rice into the eggplant mixture and season with salt and pepper to taste.

6 Lay the eggplant shells in an ovenproof dish and spoon in the rice mixture, piling it up well. Cover and place in a preheated oven, at 375°F, for 20 minutes.

7 Remove the lid and sprinkle the cheese over the rice. Place under a preheated moderate broiler for 3–4 minutes or until golden brown. Serve hot garnished with oregano or parsley.

Milanese Risotto

Italian rice is a round, short-grained variety with a nutty flavor, which is essential for a good risotto. Arborio is a good one to use.

NUTRITIONAL INFORMATION

Calories 631   Sugars 1g
Protein . . . . .16g   Fat 29g
Carbohydrate . . .77g   Saturates 17g

🍲 10 MINS   ⏱ 35 MINS

SERVES 4

I N G R E D I E N T S

2 good pinches of saffron threads

1 large onion, chopped finely

1–2 garlic cloves, crushed

6 tablespoons butter

1⅔ cups arborio rice

⅔ cup dry white wine

5 cups boiling stock
   (chicken, beef, or vegetable)

1 cup grated Parmesan

salt and pepper

1 Put the saffron in a small bowl, cover with 3–4 tablespoons of boiling water and leave to soak while cooking the risotto.

2 Fry the onion and garlic in 2 ounces of the butter until soft but not colored. Add the rice and continue to cook for 2–3 minutes or until all of the grains are coated in oil and just beginning to color lightly.

3 Add the wine to the rice and simmer gently, stirring from time to time, until it is all absorbed.

4 Add a boiling stock a little at a time, about ⅔ cup, cooking until the liquid is fully absorbed before adding more, and stirring frequently.

5 When all the stock has been absorbed (this should take about 20 minutes), the rice should be tender but not soft and soggy. Add the saffron liquid, Parmesan, remaining butter, and salt and pepper to taste. Leave to simmer for 2 minutes until piping hot and thoroughly mixed.

6 Cover the pan tightly and leave to stand for 5 minutes off the heat. Give a good stir and serve at once.

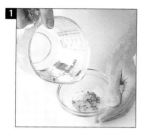

Green Risotto

A simple rice dish cooked with green vegetables and herbs. This recipe has been adapted for the microwave.

NUTRITIONAL INFORMATION

Calories	344	Sugars	.........4g
Protein	........13g	Fat	..........10g
Carbohydrate	...54g	Saturates	.......4g

15 MINS   20 MINS

SERVES 4

I N G R E D I E N T S

1 onion, chopped

2 tablespoons olive oil

1 cup arborio rice

3 cups hot vegetable stock

12 ounces mixed green vegetables, such
   as asparagus, thin green beans,
   snow peas, zucchini, broccoli
   flowerets, frozen peas

2 tablespoons chopped fresh parsley

⅔ cup fresh Parmesan cheese,
   shaved thinly

salt and pepper

1 Place the onion and oil in a large bowl. Cover and cook on HIGH power for 2 minutes.

2 Add the rice and stir until thoroughly coated in the oil. Pour in about ⅓ cup of the hot stock. Cook, uncovered, for 2 minutes, until the liquid has been absorbed. Pour in another ⅓ cup of the stock and cook, uncovered, on HIGH power for 2 minutes. Repeat once more.

3 Chop or slice the vegetables into even-size pieces. Stir into the rice with the remaining stock. Cover and cook on HIGH power for 8 minutes, stirring occasionally, until most of the liquid has been absorbed and the rice is just tender.

4 Stir in the parsley and season generously. Leave to stand, covered, for almost 5 minutes. The rice should be tender and creamy.

5 Scatter the Parmesan cheese over the risotto before serving.

COOK'S TIP

For extra texture, stir in a few toasted pine nuts or coarsely chopped cashew nuts at the end of the cooking time.

Genoese Seafood Risotto

This is cooked in a different way from any of the other risottos. First, you cook the rice, then you prepare a sauce, then you mix the two together.

NUTRITIONAL INFORMATION

Calories 424   Sugars 0g
Protein . . . . .23g   Fat 17g
Carbohydrate . . .46g   Saturates 10g

🧈 10 MINS   🕐 25 MINS

SERVES 4

I N G R E D I E N T S

5 cups hot fish or
  chicken stock

1⅔ cups arborio rice, washed

3 tablespoons butter

2 garlic cloves, chopped

9 ounces mixed seafood, preferably raw,
  such as shrimp, squid, mussels,
  and clams

2 tablespoons chopped oregano, plus extra
  for garnishing

⅔ cups grated Romano or Parmesan
  cheese

1 In a large saucepan, bring the stock to a boil. Add the rice and cook for about 12 minutes, stirring, or until the rice is tender. Drain thoroughly, reserving any excess liquid.

2 Heat the butter in a large skillet and add the garlic, stirring.

3 Add the raw mixed seafood to the skillet and cook for 5 minutes. If you are using cooked seafood, fry for 2–3 minutes.

4 Stir the oregano into the seafood mixture in the skillet.

5 Add the cooked rice to the skillet and cook for 2–3 minutes, stirring, or until hot. Add the reserved stock if the mixture gets too sticky.

6 Add the Romano or Parmesan cheese and mix well.

7 Transfer the risotto to warm serving dishes and serve immediately.

COOK'S TIP

The Genoese are excellent cooks, and they make particularly delicious fish dishes flavored with the local olive oil.

Mushroom & Cheese Risotto

Make this creamy arborio with Italian risotto rice and freshly grated Parmesan cheese for the best results.

NUTRITIONAL INFORMATION

Calories	358	Sugars	........3g
Protein	........11g	Fat	..........14g
Carbohydrate	...50g	Saturates	.......5g

 20 MINS 40 MINS

SERVES 4

INGREDIENTS

2 tablespoons olive or
   vegetable oil

1 cup arborio rice

2 garlic cloves, crushed

1 onion, chopped

2 celery stalks, chopped

1 red or green bell pepper, deseeded
   and chopped

8 ounces mushrooms, sliced

1 tablespoon chopped fresh oregano or
   1 teaspoon dried oregano

4 cups vegetable stock

1 cup sun-dried tomatoes in olive oil,
drained and chopped (optional)

⅔ cup finely grated
   Parmesan cheese

salt and pepper

TO GARNISH

fresh flat-leaf parsley sprigs

fresh bay leaves

1 Heat the oil in a wok or large skillet. Add the rice and cook, stirring, for 5 minutes.

2 Add the garlic, onion, celery, and bell pepper and cook, stirring, for 5 minutes. Add the mushrooms and cook for 3–4 minutes.

3 Stir in the oregano and stock. Heat until just boiling, then reduce the heat, cover, and simmer gently for about 20 minutes or until the rice is tender and creamy.

4 Add the sun-dried tomatoes, if using, and season to taste. Stir in half of the Parmesan cheese. Top with the remaining cheese, garnish with flat-leaf parsley, and bay leaves and serve.

Chicken Risotto Milanese

This famous dish is known throughout the world, and it is perhaps the best known of all Italian risottos, although there are many variations.

NUTRITIONAL INFORMATION

Calories 857	Sugars 1g	
Protein 57g	Fat 38g	
Carbohydrate ...72g	Saturates 21g	

5 MINS   55 MINS

SERVES 4

INGREDIENTS

½ cup butter

2 pounds chicken meat, sliced thinly

1 large onion, chopped

2⅓ cups arborio rice

2½ cups chicken stock

⅔ cup white wine

1 teaspoon crumbled saffron

salt and pepper

⅔ cup grated Parmesan cheese,
   to serve

1 Heat 4 tablespoons of butter in a deep skillet, and fry the chicken and onion until golden brown.

2 Add the rice, stir well, and cook for 15 minutes.

3 Heat the stock until boiling and gradually add to the rice. Add the white wine, saffron, and salt and pepper to taste and mix well. Simmer gently for 20 minutes, stirring occasionally, and adding more stock if the risotto becomes too dry.

4 Let stand for 2–3 minutes. Just before serving, add a little more stock and simmer for 10 minutes. Serve sprinkled with the Parmesan and the remaining butter.

Exotic Mushroom Risotto

This creamy risotto is flavored with a mixture of exotic and cultivated mushrooms and thyme.

NUTRITIONAL INFORMATION

Calories 364   Sugars 1g
Protein ....15g   Fat 16g
Carbohydrate ...44g   Saturates 6g

15 MINS   25 MINS

SERVES 4

I N G R E D I E N T S

2 tablespoons olive oil

1 large onion, finely chopped

1 garlic clove, crushed

7 ounces mixed exotic and cultivated
   mushrooms, such as ceps, oyster, porcini,
   and button, wiped and sliced if large

1½ cups arborio rice, washed

pinch of saffron threads

3 cups hot vegetable stock

⅔ cup white wine

cup grated Parmesan cheese,
   plus extra for serving

2 tablespoons chopped thyme

salt and pepper

1 Heat the oil in a large skillet. Add the onions and garlic and sauté for 3–4 minutes or until just softened.

2 Add the mushrooms to the pan and cook for 3 minutes or until they are just beginning to brown.

3 Add the rice and saffron to the pan and stir to coat the rice in the oil.

4 Mix together the stock and the wine and add to the pan, a ladleful at a time. Stir the rice mixture and allow the liquid to be fully absorbed before adding more liquid, a ladleful at a time.

5 When all of the wine and stock is incorporated, the rice should be cooked. Test by tasting a grain—if it is still crunchy, add a little more water and continue cooking. It should take at least 15 minutes to cook.

6 Stir in the cheese and thyme, and season with pepper to taste.

7 Transfer the risotto to serving dishes and serve sprinkled with extra Parmesan cheese.

COOK'S TIP

Exotic mushrooms each have their own distinctive flavors and make a change from button mushrooms. However, they can be quite expensive, so you can always use a mixture with cremini or button mushrooms instead.

Risotto-stuffed Bell Peppers

Sweet roasted bell peppers are delightful containers for a creamy risotto and especially good topped with mozzarella cheese.

NUTRITIONAL INFORMATION

Calories 613	Sugars 7g
Protein 17g	Fat 32g
Carbohydrate . . .61g	Saturates 15g

🍳 15 MINS   🕐 35 MINS

SERVES 4

I N G R E D I E N T S

4 red or orange bell peppers

1 tablespoon olive oil

1 large onion, finely chopped

1⅔ cups arborio rice, washed

about 15 strands of saffron

⅔ cup white wine

3¾ cups hot vegetable or

    chicken stock

3 tablespoons butter

⅔ cup grated Romano cheese

1¾ ounces Italian sausage, such as

    felino salame or other coarse Italian

    salame, chopped

7 ounces mozzarella cheese, sliced

1 Cut the bell peppers in half, retaining some of the stalk. Remove the seeds.

2 Place the bell peppers, cut side up, under a preheated broiler for 12–15 minutes or until softened and charred.

3 Meanwhile, heat the oil in a large skillet. Add the onion and cook for 3–4 minutes or until softened. Add the rice and saffron, stirring to coat in the oil, and cook for 1 minute.

4 Add the white wine and hot stock gradually, one ladleful at a time, making sure that all of the liquid has been absorbed before adding the next ladleful of liquid. When all of the liquid is absorbed, the rice should be cooked and tender. Test by tasting a grain—if it is still crunchy, add a little more water and continue cooking. It should take at least 15 minutes to cook.

5 Stir in the butter, Romano cheese, and the chopped Italian sausage.

6 Spoon the risotto into the bell peppers. Top with a slice of mozzarella

and broil for 4–5 minutes or until the cheese is bubbling. Serve hot.

VARIATION

Use tomatoes instead of the bell peppers, if you prefer. Halve 4 large tomatoes and scoop out the seeds. Follow steps 3–6, as there is no need to roast them.

Rice & Peas

If you can get fresh peas (and willing helpers to shell them), do use them: you will need 2¼ pounds. Add them to the pan with the stock.

NUTRITIONAL INFORMATION

Calories 409   Sugars 2g
Protein . . . . .15g   Fat 23g
Carbohydrate . . .38g   Saturates 12g

10 MINS   50 MINS

SERVES 4

INGREDIENTS

1 tablespoon olive oil

¼ cup butter

¼ cup chopped pancetta

1 small onion, chopped

6¼ cups hot chicken stock

1 cup arborio rice

3 tablespoons chopped
    fresh parsley

2 cups frozen or canned
    petits pois

⅔ cup grated Parmesan

pepper

1 Heat the oil and half of the butter in a saucepan.

2 Add the pancetta and onion to the pan and fry for 5 minutes.

3 Add the stock and fresh peas, if using, to the pan and bring to a boil.

4 Stir in the rice and season to taste with pepper. Cook until the rice is tender, about 20–30 minutes, stirring occasionally.

5 Add the parsley and frozen or canned petits pois and cook for 8 minutes until the peas are thoroughly heated.

6 Stir in the remaining butter and the Parmesan. Serve immediately, with freshly ground black pepper.

Pesto Rice with Garlic Bread

Try this combination of two types of rice with the richness of pine nuts, basil, and freshly grated Parmesan.

NUTRITIONAL INFORMATION

Calories 918	Sugars 2g
Protein 18g	Fat 64g
Carbohydrate . . .73g	Saturates 19g

🄖 🄖 🄖

🍲 20 MINS 🕐 40 MINS

SERVES 4

INGREDIENTS

1½ cups mixed long-grain and wild rice

fresh basil sprigs, to garnish

tomato and orange salad, to serve

PESTO DRESSING

½ cup fresh basil

1 cup pine nuts

2 garlic cloves, crushed

6 tablespoons olive oil

⅔ cup freshly grated Parmesan

salt and pepper

GARLIC BREAD

2 small whole wheat
    baguettes

6 tablespoons butter or
    margarine, softened

2 garlic cloves, crushed

1 teaspoon dried mixed herbs

1 Place the rice in a saucepan and cover with water. Bring to a boil and cook for 15–20 minutes. Drain well and keep warm.

2 Meanwhile, make the pesto dressing. Remove the basil leaves from the stalks and finely chop the leaves. Reserve ¼ cup of the pine nuts and finely chop the remainder. Mix with the chopped basil and dressing ingredients. Alternatively, put all the ingredients in a food processor or blender and blend for a few seconds until smooth. Set aside.

3 To make the garlic bread, slice the bread at 1-inch intervals, taking care not to slice all the way through. Mix the butter or margarine with the garlic, herbs, and seasoning. Spread thickly between each slice.

4 Wrap the bread in foil and bake in a preheated oven, 400°F, for 10–15 minutes.

5 To serve, toast the reserved pine nuts under a preheated medium broiler for 2–3 minutes until golden. Toss the pesto dressing into the hot rice and pile into a warm serving dish. Sprinkle with toasted pine nuts and garnish with basil sprigs. Serve with the garlic bread and a tomato and orange salad.

Green Easter Pie

This traditional Easter risotto pie is from Piedmont in northern Italy.
Serve it warm or chilled in slices.

NUTRITIONAL INFORMATION

Calories 392	Sugars 3g
Protein 17g	Fat 17g
Carbohydrate ...41g	Saturates 5g

25 MINS   50 MINS

SERVES 4

I N G R E D I E N T S

2 tablespoons olive oil

1 onion, chopped

2 garlic cloves, chopped

1 cup arborio rice

3½ cups hot chicken or vegetable stock

½ cup white wine

⅔ cup grated Parmesan cheese, grated

1 cup frozen peas, thawed

3 ounces arugula

2 tomatoes, diced

4 eggs, beaten

3 tablespoons fresh
marjoram, chopped

1 cup bread crumbs

salt and pepper

1 Lightly grease and then line the base of a 9-inch deep cake pan.

2 Using a sharp knife, roughly chop the arugula.

3 Heat the oil in a large skillet. Add the onion and garlic and cook for 4–5 minutes or until softened.

4 Add the rice to the mixture in the skillet, mix well to combine, then begin adding the stock a ladleful at a time. Wait until all of the stock has been absorbed before adding another ladleful of liquid.

5 Continue to cook the mixture, adding the wine, until the rice is tender. This will take at least 15 minutes.

6 Stir in the Parmesan cheese, peas, arugula, tomatoes, eggs and 2 tablespoons of the marjoram. Season to taste with salt and pepper.

7 Spoon the risotto into the pan and level the surface by pressing down with the back of a wooden spoon.

8 Top with the bread crumbs and the remaining marjoram.

9 Bake in a preheated oven, at 350°F, for 30 minutes or until set. Cut into slices and serve immediately.

Eggplant & Rice Rolls

Slices of eggplant are blanched and stuffed with a savory rice and nut mixture, and baked in a piquant tomato and wine sauce.

NUTRITIONAL INFORMATION

Calories 142	Sugars 3g	
Protein 6g	Fat 9g	
Carbohydrate 9g	Saturates 3g	

30 MINS   1HR 5 MINS

SERVES 8

INGREDIENTS

3 eggplants (total weight about
   1 pound 10 ounces

⅓ cup mixed long-grain
   and wild rice

4 green onions, trimmed and
   thinly sliced

3 tablespoons chopped cashew nuts or
   toasted chopped hazelnuts

2 tablespoons capers

1 garlic clove, crushed

2 tablespoons grated Parmesan cheese

1 egg, beaten

1 tablespoon olive oil

1 tablespoon balsamic vinegar

2 tablespoons tomato paste

⅔ cup water

⅔ cup white wine

salt and pepper

cilantro sprigs, to garnish

1 Using a sharp knife, cut off the stem end of each eggplant, then cut off and discard a strip of skin from alternate sides of each eggplant. Cut each eggplant into thin slices to give a total of 16 slices.

2 Blanch the eggplant slices in boiling water for 5 minutes, then drain on paper towels.

3 Cook the rice in boiling salted water for about 12 minutes or until just tender. Drain and place in a bowl. Add the green onions, nuts, capers, garlic, cheese, egg, and salt and pepper to taste, and mix well.

4 Spread a thin layer of rice mixture over each slice of eggplant and roll up carefully, securing with a toothpick. Place the rolls in a greased ovenproof dish and brush each one with the olive oil.

5 Combine the vinegar, tomato paste, and water, and pour over the eggplant rolls. Cook in a preheated oven, at 350°F, for about 40 minutes or until tender and most of the liquid has been absorbed. Transfer the rolls to a serving dish.

6 Add the wine to the pan juices and heat gently until the sediment loosens and then simmer gently for 2–3 minutes. Adjust the seasoning and strain the sauce over the eggplant rolls. Leave until cold and then chill thoroughly. Garnish with sprigs of cilantro and serve.

Polenta

Polenta is prepared and served in a variety of ways and can be served hot or cold, sweet or savory.

NUTRITIONAL INFORMATION

Calories 661	Sugars 5g
Protein 15g	Fat 34g
Carbohydrate . . . 68g	Saturates 12g

 1¼ HOURS 1 HOUR

SERVES 4

I N G R E D I E N T S

7 cups water

1½ teaspoons salt

2 cups polenta or
    cornmeal flour

2 beaten eggs (optional)

2 cups fresh fine white
    bread crumbs (optional)

vegetable oil, for frying and oiling

2 quantities Basic Tomato Sauce (see
    page 28)

M U S H R O O M   S A U C E

3 tablespoons olive oil

8 ounces mushrooms, sliced

2 garlic cloves, crushed

⅔ cup dry white wine

4 tablespoons heavy cream

2 tablespoons chopped fresh mixed herbs

salt and pepper

1 Bring the water and salt to a boil in a large pan and gradually sprinkle in the polenta or cornmeal flour, stirring all the time to prevent lumps forming. Simmer the mixture very gently, stirring frequently, until the polenta becomes very thick and starts to draw away from the sides of the pan, about 30–35 minutes. It is likely to splatter, in which case partially cover the pan with a lid.

2 Thoroughly oil a shallow pan, about 11 x 7 inches, and spoon in the polenta. Spread out evenly, using a wet wooden spoon or spatula. Leave to cool, then leave to stand for a few hours at room temperature, if possible.

3 Cut the polenta into 30–36 squares. Heat the oil in a skillet and fry the pieces until golden brown all over, turning several times—about 5 minutes.

Alternatively, dip each piece of polenta in beaten egg and coat in bread crumbs before frying in the hot oil.

4 To make the mushroom sauce, heat the oil in a pan and fry the mushrooms with the crushed garlic for 3–4 minutes. Add the wine, season well, and simmer for 5 minutes. Add the cream and chopped herbs and simmer for 1–2 minutes.

5 Serve the polenta with either the tomato sauce or mushroom sauce.

Smoked Cod Polenta

Using polenta as a crust for a gratin dish gives a lovely crispy outer texture and a smooth inside. It works well with smoked fish and chicken.

NUTRITIONAL INFORMATION

Calories 616	Sugars 3g	
Protein 41g	Fat 24g	
Carbohydrate . . .58g	Saturates 12g	

30 MINS   1¼ HOURS

SERVES 4

INGREDIENTS

2⅓ cups instant polenta

6½ cups water

7 ounces chopped frozen
   spinach, thawed

3 tablespoons butter

⅔ cup grated Romano cheese, grated

¾ cup milk

1 pound smoked cod fillet,
   skinned and boned

4 eggs, beaten

salt and pepper

1 Cook the polenta, using 6½ cups of water to 2⅓ cups polenta, stirring, for 30–35 minutes.

2 Stir the spinach, butter, and half of the Romano cheese into the polenta. Season to taste with salt and pepper.

3 Divide the polenta among 4 individual ovenproof dishes, spreading the polenta evenly across the bottom and up the sides of the dishes.

4 In a skillet, bring the milk to a boil. Add the fish and cook for 8–10 minutes, turning once, or until tender. Remove the fish with a perforated spoon.

5 Remove the pan from the heat. Pour the eggs into the milk in the pan and mix together.

6 Using a fork, flake the fish into smaller pieces and place it in the center of the dishes.

7 Pour the milk and egg mixture over the fish.

8 Sprinkle with the remaining cheese and bake in a preheated oven, at 375°F, for 25–30 minutes or until set and golden. Serve hot.

VARIATION

Try using 12 ounces cooked chicken breast with 2 tablespoons of chopped tarragon, instead of the smoked cod, if you prefer.

Polenta with Rabbit Stew

Polenta can be served fresh, as in this dish, or it can be cooled, then sliced and broiled.

20 MINS 1³/₄ MINUTES

SERVES 4

I N G R E D I E N T S

2 cups polenta or cornmeal

1 tablespoon coarse sea salt

5 cups water

4 tablespoons olive oil

4½ pounds rabbit pieces

3 garlic cloves, peeled

3 shallots, sliced

⅔ cup red wine

1 carrot, sliced

1 celery stalk, sliced

2 bay leaves

1 sprig rosemary

3 tomatoes, peeled and diced

¾ cups pitted black olives

salt and pepper

1 Butter a large ovenproof dish. Mix the polenta, salt, and water in a large pan, whisking well to prevent lumps forming. Bring to a boil and boil for 10 minutes, stirring vigorously. Turn into the buttered dish and bake in a preheated oven, 375°F, for 40 minutes.

2 Meanwhile, heat the oil in a large saucepan and add the rabbit pieces, garlic, and shallots. Fry for 10 minutes until browned.

3 Stir in the wine and cook for a further 5 minutes.

4 Add the carrot, celery, bay leaves, rosemary, tomatoes, olives, and 1¼ cups water. Cover the pan and simmer for about 45 minutes or until the rabbit is tender. Season well with salt and pepper to taste.

5 To serve, spoon or cut a portion of polenta and place on each serving plate. Top with a ladleful of rabbit stew. Serve at once.

Chili Polenta Chips

Polenta is used in Italy in the same way as potatoes and rice. It has little flavor, but combined with butter, garlic, and herbs, it is transformed.

NUTRITIONAL INFORMATION

Calories 365	Sugars 1g	
Protein 8g	Fat 12g	
Carbohydrate . . .54g	Saturates 5g	

5 MINS   20 MINS

SERVES 4

INGREDIENTS

2⅓ cups instant polenta

2 teaspoon chili powder

1 tablespoon olive oil

⅔ cup sour cream

1 tablespoon chopped parsley

salt and pepper

1 Place 6¼ cups of water in a saucepan and bring to a boil. Add 2 teaspoons of salt and then add the polenta in a steady stream, stirring constantly.

2 Reduce the heat slightly and continue stirring for about 5 minutes. It is essential to stir the polenta, otherwise it will stick and burn. The polenta should have a thick consistency at this point and should be stiff enough to hold the spoon upright in the pan.

3 Add the chili powder to the polenta mixture and stir well. Season to taste with a little salt and pepper.

4 Spread the polenta out on a board or cookie sheet to about 1½ inches thick. Leave to cool and set.

5 Cut the cooled polenta mixture into thin wedges.

6 Heat 1 tablespoon of oil in a pan. Add the polenta wedges and fry for 3–4 minutes on each side or until golden and crispy. Alternatively, brush with melted butter and broil for 6–7 minutes until golden. Drain the cooked polenta on paper towels.

7 Mix the sour cream with parsley and place in a bowl.

8 Serve the polenta with the sour cream and parsley dip.

COOK'S TIP

Easy-cook instant polenta is widely available in supermarkets and is quick to make. It will keep for up to 1 week in the refrigerator. The polenta can also be baked in a preheated oven, at 400°F, for 20 minutes.

Polenta Kabobs

Here, skewers of thyme-flavored polenta, wrapped in prosciutto, are broiled or barbecued.

NUTRITIONAL INFORMATION

Calories	.212	Sugars	.0g
Protein	.8g	Fat	.6g
Carbohydrate	.32g	Saturates	.1g

20 MINS   45 MINS

SERVES 4

I N G R E D I E N T S

1 cup instant polenta

3¼ cups water

2 tablespoons fresh thyme, stalks removed

8 slices prosciutto
   (about 2¾ ounces)

1 tablespoon olive oil

salt and pepper

fresh salad greens, to serve

1 Cook the polenta, using 3¼ cups of water to a generous cup polenta, stirring occasionally, for 30–35 minutes. Alternatively, follow the instructions on the packet.

2 Add the fresh thyme to the polenta mixture and season to taste with salt and pepper.

COOK'S TIP

Try flavoring the polenta with chopped oregano, basil, or marjoram instead of the thyme, if you prefer. You should use 3 tablespoons of chopped herbs to every 2½ cups instant polenta.

3 Spread out the polenta, about 1 inch thick, on a board. Set aside to cool.

4 Using a sharp knife, cut the cooled polenta into 1-inch cubes.

5 Cut the prosciutto slices into 2 pieces lengthwise. Wrap the prosciutto around the polenta cubes.

6 Thread the prosciutto-wrapped polenta cubes onto skewers.

7 Brush the kabobs with a little oil and cook under a preheated broiler, turning frequently, for 7–8 minutes. Alternatively, barbecue the kabobs until golden. Transfer to serving plates and serve with a salad.

Gnocchi with Herb Sauce

These little potato dumplings are a traditional Italian appetizer but, served with a salad and bread, they make a substantial main course.

NUTRITIONAL INFORMATION

Calories 619   Sugars 3g
Protein . . . . .11g   Fat 30g
Carbohydrate . . .81g   Saturates 9g

30 MINS   30 MINS

SERVES 6

INGREDIENTS

2¼ pounds old potatoes, cut into
  ½-inch pieces

¼ cup butter or margarine

1 egg, beaten

2½ cups all-purpose flour

salt

SAUCE

½ cup olive oil

2 garlic cloves, very finely chopped

1 tablespoon chopped fresh oregano

1 tablespoon chopped fresh basil

salt and pepper

TO SERVE

freshly grated Parmesan
  (optional)

tossed salad

warm ciabatta or other Italian bread

1 Cook the potatoes in a saucepan of boiling salted water for about 10 minutes or until tender. Drain well.

2 Press the hot potatoes through a strainer into a large bowl. Add 1 teaspoon of salt, the butter or margarine, egg, and 1¼ cups of the flour. Mix well to bind together.

3 Turn on to a lightly floured surface and knead, gradually adding the remaining flour, until a smooth, soft, slightly sticky dough is formed.

4 Dust your hands with flour and roll the dough into ¾-inch thick rolls. Cut the rolls into ½-inch pieces. Press the top of each piece with the lightly floured prongs of a fork and spread out on a floured dish cloth.

5 Bring a large saucepan of salted water to a simmer. Add the gnocchi and cook in batches for 2–3 minutes or until they rise to the surface.

6 Remove the gnocchi with a perforated spoon and put in a warmed, greased serving dish. Cover and keep warm.

7 To make the sauce, put the oil, garlic and seasoning in a pan and cook, stirring, for 3–4 minutes until the garlic is golden. Remove from the heat and stir in the herbs. Pour over the gnocchi and serve, sprinkled with Parmesan, and accompanied by salad and warm ciabatta.

Spinach Gnocchi

These gnocchi or small dumplings are made with potato and flavored with spinach and nutmeg and served in a tomato and basil sauce.

NUTRITIONAL INFORMATION

Calories 337	Sugars 4g
Protein 9g	Fat 10g
Carbohydrate . . .52g	Saturates 4g

  25 MINS   1 HOUR

SERVES 4

I N G R E D I E N T S

1 pound baking potatoes

2¾ ounces spinach

1 teaspoon water

2 tablespoons butter or margarine

1 small egg, beaten

¾ cup all-purpose flour

fresh basil sprigs, to garnish

TOMATO SAUCE

1 tablespoon olive oil

1 shallot, chopped

1 tablespoon tomato paste

8-ounce can diced tomatoes

2 tablespoons chopped basil

6 tablespoons red wine

1 teaspoon sugar

salt and pepper

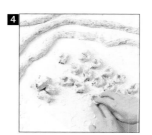

1 Cook the potatoes in their skins in a pan of boiling salted water for 20 minutes. Drain well and press through a strainer into a bowl.

2 Cook the spinach in 1 teaspoon of water for 5 minutes or until wilted. Drain and pat dry with paper towels. Chop and stir into the potatoes.

3 Add the butter or margarine, egg, and half of the flour to the spinach mixture, mixing well. Turn out onto a floured surface, gradually kneading in the remaining flour to form a soft dough.

4 With floured hands, roll the dough into thin ropes and cut off ¾-inch pieces. Press the center of each dumpling with your finger, drawing it toward you to curl the sides of the gnocchi. Cover the gnocchi and leave to chill.

5 Heat the oil for the sauce in a pan and sauté the chopped shallots for 5 minutes. Add the tomato paste, tomatoes, basil, red wine, and sugar and season well. Bring to a boil and then simmer for 20 minutes.

6 Bring a pan of salted water to a boil and cook the gnocchi for 2–3 minutes or until they rise to the top of the pan. Drain well and transfer to serving dishes. Spoon the tomato sauce over the gnocchi. Garnish and serve.

Gnocchi Romana

This is a traditional Italian recipe but, for a less rich version, simply omit the eggs.

NUTRITIONAL INFORMATION

Calories 709   Sugars 9g
Protein . . . . .32g   Fat 41g
Carbohydrate . . .58g   Saturates 25g

  1¼ HOURS   45 MINS

SERVES 4

INGREDIENTS

3 cups milk

pinch of freshly grated
  nutmeg

6 tablespoons butter, plus extra
  for greasing

1¼ cups semolina

1½ cups grated Parmesan cheese

2 eggs, beaten

½ cup grated Swiss cheese

salt and pepper

fresh basil sprigs,
  to garnish

1 Pour the milk into a pan and bring to a boil. Remove the pan from the heat and stir in the nutmeg, 2 tablespoons of butter and salt and pepper.

2 Gradually stir the semolina into the milk, whisking to prevent lumps forming, and return the pan to low heat. Simmer, stirring constantly, for about 10 minutes, or until very thick.

3 Beat ⅔ cup of Parmesan cheese into the semolina mixture, then beat in the eggs. Continue beating the mixture until smooth. Set the mixture aside for a few minutes to cool slightly.

4 Spread out the cooled semolina mixture in an even layer on a sheet of baking parchment or in a large, oiled baking pan, smoothing the surface with a damp spatula—it should be ½ inch thick. Set aside to cool completely, then chill in the refrigerator for 1 hour.

5 Once chilled, cut out rounds of gnocchi, measuring about 1½ inches in diameter, using a plain, greased cookie cutter.

6 Grease a shallow ovenproof dish or 4 individual dishes. Lay the gnocchi trimmings in the base of the dish or dishes and cover with overlapping rounds of gnocchi.

7 Melt the remaining butter and drizzle over the gnocchi. Sprinkle over the remaining Parmesan cheese, then sprinkle over the Swiss cheese.

8 Bake in a preheated oven, at 400°F, for 25-30 minutes, until the top is crisp and golden brown. Serve hot, garnished with the basil.

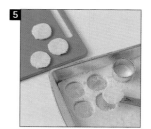

Spinach & Ricotta Gnocchi

Try not to handle the mixture too much when making gnocchi, as this will make the dough a little heavy.

NUTRITIONAL INFORMATION

Calories	712	Sugars	. . . . .15g
Protein	. . . . .29g	Fat	. . . . .59g
Carbohydrate	. . .16g	Saturates	. . . . . .33g

  20 MINS   15 MINS

SERVES 4

I N G R E D I E N T S

2¼ pounds spinach

1½ cups ricotta cheese

1½ cups grated Romano cheese

3 eggs, beaten

¼ teaspoon freshly grated nutmeg

all-purpose flour, to mix

½ cup butter

¼ cup pine nuts

⅓ cup raisins

salt and pepper

1 Wash and drain the spinach well and cook in a covered saucepan without any extra liquid until softened, about 8 minutes. Place the spinach in a colander and press well to remove as much juice as possible. Either rub the spinach through a strainer or purée in a blender.

2 Combine the spinach purée with the ricotta, half of the Romano, the eggs, nutmeg, and seasoning to taste, mixing lightly but thoroughly. Work in enough flour, lightly and quickly, to make the mixture easy to handle.

3 Shape the dough quickly into small lozenge shapes, and dust lightly with a little flour.

4 Add a dash of oil to a large saucepan of salted water and bring to a boil. Add the gnocchi carefully and boil for about 2 minutes or until they float to the surface. Using a perforated spoon, transfer the gnocchi to a buttered ovenproof dish. Keep warm.

5 Melt the butter in a skillet. Add the pine nuts and raisins and fry until the nuts start to brown slightly, but do not allow the butter to burn. Pour the mixture over the gnocchi and serve sprinkled with the remaining grated Romano.

Gnocchi & Tomato Sauce

Freshly made potato gnocchi are delicious, especially when they are topped with a fragrant tomato sauce.

NUTRITIONAL INFORMATION

Calories 216   Sugars 5g
Protein . . . . .5g   Fat 6g
Carbohydrate . . .39g   Saturates 1g

30 MINS   45 MINS

SERVES 4

I N G R E D I E N T S

12 ounces russet potatoes, halved

⅔ cup self-rising flour, plus extra for
   rolling out

2 teaspoons dried oregano

2 tablespoons oil

1 large onion, chopped

2 garlic cloves, chopped

14-ounce can diced tomatoes

½ vegetable stock cube dissolved in
   ⅓ cup boiling water

2 tablespoons basil, shredded, plus whole
   leaves to garnish

salt and pepper

Parmesan cheese, grated, to serve

1 Bring a large saucepan of water to a boil. Add the potatoes and cook for 12–15 minutes or until tender. Drain and leave to cool.

2 Peel and then mash the potatoes with the salt and pepper, sifted flour, and oregano. Mix together with your hands to form a dough.

3 Heat the oil in a pan. Add the onions and garlic and cook for 3–4 minutes.

Add the tomatoes and stock and cook, uncovered, for 10 minutes. Season with salt and pepper to taste.

4 Roll the potato dough into a sausage about 1 inch in diameter. Cut the sausage into 1-inch lengths. Flour your hands, then press a fork into each piece to create a series of ridges on one side and the indent of your index finger on the other.

5 Bring a large saucepan of water to a boil and cook the gnocchi, in batches, for 2–3 minutes. They should rise to the surface when cooked. Drain well and keep warm.

6 Stir the basil into the tomato sauce and pour over the gnocchi. Garnish with basil leaves and season with pepper to taste. Sprinkle with Parmesan and serve at once.

VARIATION

Try serving the gnocchi with Pesto Sauce (see page 377) for a change.

Gnocchi Piemontese

Gnocchi, a specialty from northern Italy, are small dumplings that are either poached or baked. Prepare the Espagnole Sauce well in advance.

NUTRITIONAL INFORMATION

Calories ....643 Sugars 4g
Protein ....25g Fat 44g
Carbohydrate ...34g Saturates 21g

4³/₄ HOURS   15 MINS

SERVES 4

I N G R E D I E N T S

1 pound warm mashed potato

²/₃ cup self-rising flour

1 egg

2 egg yolks

1 tablespoon olive oil

²/₃ cup Espagnole Sauce
  (see page 29)

4 tablespoons butter

2 cups freshly grated Parmesan cheese

salt and pepper

freshly chopped herbs,
  to garnish

1 In a large bowl, mix together the mashed potato and flour. Add the egg and egg yolks, season with salt and pepper, and mix together to form a dough.

VARIATION

Serve with a tomato sauce. Mix 2 cups chopped sun-dried tomatoes, 1 sliced celery stalk, 1 crushed garlic clove and 6 tablespoons red wine in a pan. Cook over low heat for 15–20 minutes. Stir in 8 peeled, chopped plum tomatoes, season and simmer for 10 minutes.

2 Break off pieces of the dough and roll between the palms of your hands to form small balls the size of a walnut. Flatten the balls with a fork into the shape of small cylinders.

3 Bring a large pan of lightly salted water to a boil. Add the gnocchi and olive oil and poach for 10 minutes.

4 Mix together the Espagnole Sauce and the butter in a large saucepan over gentle heat. Gradually blend in the grated Parmesan cheese.

5 Remove the gnocchi from the pan with a slotted spoon. Toss the gnocchi in the sauce, transfer to 4 serving plates, garnish, and serve immediately.

Potato & Spinach Gnocchi

These small potato dumplings are flavored with spinach, cooked in boiling water, and served with a simple tomato sauce.

NUTRITIONAL INFORMATION

Calories 315   Sugars 7g
Protein . . . . .8g   Fat 8g
Carbohydrate . . .56g   Saturates 1g

20 MINS   30 MINS

SERVES 4

I N G R E D I E N T S

10½ ounces russet potatoes, diced

6 ounces spinach

1 egg yolk

1 teaspoon olive oil

1 cup all-purpose flour

salt and pepper

spinach leaves, to garnish

S A U C E

1 tablespoon olive oil

2 shallots, chopped

1 garlic clove, crushed

1¼ cups sieved tomatoes

2 teaspoon soft light
  brown sugar

1 Cook the diced potatoes in a saucepan of boiling water for 10 minutes or until cooked through. Drain and mash the potatoes.

2 Meanwhile, in a separate pan, blanch the spinach in a little boiling water for 1-2 minutes. Drain the spinach and shred the leaves.

3 Transfer the mashed potato to a lightly floured chopping board and make a well in the center. Add the egg yolk, olive oil, spinach, and a little of the flour and quickly mix the ingredients into the potato, adding more flour as you go, until you have a firm dough. Divide the mixture into very small dumplings.

4 Cook the gnocchi, in batches, in a saucepan of boiling salted water for about 5 minutes or until they rise to the surface.

5 Meanwhile, make the sauce. Put the oil, shallots, garlic, sieved tomatoes, and sugar into a saucepan and cook over low heat for 10-15 minutes or until the sauce has thickened.

6 Drain the gnocchi using a perforated spoon and transfer to warm serving dishes. Spoon the sauce over the gnocchi and garnish with the fresh spinach leaves.

VARIATION

Add chopped fresh herbs and cheese to the gnocchi dough instead of the spinach, if you prefer.

Baked Semolina Gnocchi

Semolina has a similar texture to polenta, but is slightly grainier. These gnocchi, which are flavored with cheese and thyme, are easy to make.

NUTRITIONAL INFORMATION

Calories 259	Sugars 0g	
Protein 9g	Fat 16g	
Carbohydrate ...20g	Saturates 10g	

 15 MINS   30 MINS

SERVES 4

INGREDIENTS

scant 1 cup vegetable stock

½ cup semolina

1 tablespoon thyme, stalks removed

1 egg, beaten

⅔ cup grated Parmesan cheese

4 tablespoons butter

2 garlic cloves, crushed

salt and pepper

1 Place the stock in a large saucepan and bring to a boil. Add the semolina in a steady trickle, stirring continuously. Keep stirring for 3–4 minutes until the mixture is thick enough to hold a spoon upright. Set aside and leave to cool slightly.

VARIATION

Try adding 1½ teaspoons of sun-dried tomato paste or 1¾ ounces finely chopped mushrooms, fried in butter, to the semolina mixture in step 2. Follow the same cooking method.

2 Add the thyme, egg, and half of the cheese to the semolina mixture, and season to taste with salt and pepper.

3 Spread the semolina mixture on to a board to about ½ inch thick. Set aside to cool and set.

4 When the semolina is cold, cut it into 1-inch squares, reserving any offcuts.

5 Grease an ovenproof dish, placing the reserved offcuts in the bottom. Arrange the semolina squares on top and sprinkle with the remaining cheese.

6 Melt the butter in a pan, add the garlic and season with pepper to taste. Pour the butter mixture over the gnocchi. Bake in a preheated oven, at 425°F, for 15–20 minutes until puffed up and golden. Serve hot.

Potato Noodles

Potatoes are used to make a "pasta" dough which is cut into thin noodles and boiled. They are served with a bacon and mushroom sauce.

NUTRITIONAL INFORMATION

Calories	.810	Sugars	.5g
Protein	.21g	Fat	.47g
Carbohydrate	.81g	Saturates	.26g

 30 MINS   25 MINS

SERVES 4

I N G R E D I E N T S

1 pound russet potatoes, diced

2 cups all-purpose flour

1 egg, beaten

1 tablespoon milk

salt and pepper

parsley sprig, to garnish

S A U C E

1 tablespoon vegetable oil

1 onion, chopped

1 garlic clove, crushed

4½ ounces mushrooms, sliced

3 smoked bacon slices, chopped

⅔ cup Parmesan cheese, grated

1¼ cups heavy cream

2 tablespoons chopped
   fresh parsley

1 Cook the diced potatoes in a saucepan of boiling water for 10 minutes or until cooked through. Drain well. Mash the potatoes until smooth, then beat in the flour, egg, and milk. Season with salt and pepper to taste and bring together to form a stiff paste.

2 On a lightly floured surface, roll out the paste to form a thin sausage shape. Cut the sausage into 1-inch lengths. Bring a large pan of salted water to a boil, drop in the dough pieces and cook for 3-4 minutes. They will rise to the surface when cooked.

3 To make the sauce, heat the oil in a pan and sauté the onion and garlic for 2 minutes. Add the mushrooms and bacon and cook for 5 minutes. Stir in the cheese, cream, and parsley, and season.

4 Drain the noodles and transfer to a warm pasta bowl. Spoon the sauce over the top and toss to mix. Garnish with a parsley sprig and serve.

COOK'S TIP

Make the dough in advance, then wrap and store the noodles in the refrigerator for up to 24 hours.

Pizzas & Breads

There is little to beat the irresistible aroma and taste of a freshly-made pizza cooked in a wood-fired oven. The recipes for the homemade dough base and freshly made

tomato sauce in this chapter will give you the closest thing possible to an authentic Italian pizza. You can add any type of topping, from salamis and cooked meats, to vegetables and

fragrant herbs—the choice is yours! The Italians make delicious bread, combining all of the flavors of the Mediterranean. You can use the breads in this chapter to mop up the juices from a range of Italian dishes, or you can eat them on their own as a tasty snack.

Bread Dough Base

Traditionally, pizza bases are made from bread dough; this recipe will give you a base similar to an Italian pizza.

NUTRITIONAL INFORMATION

Calories 182   Sugars 2g
Protein ....5g   Fat 3g
Carbohydrate ...36g   Saturates 0.5g

1¹/₂ HOURS   0 MINS

SERVES 4

INGREDIENTS

½ oz fresh yeast or 1 teaspoon active
  dry yeast

6 tablespoons tepid water

½ teaspoon sugar

1 tablespoon olive oil

1½ cups all-purpose flour

1 teaspoon salt

1 Combine the fresh yeast with the water and sugar in a bowl. If using dried yeast, sprinkle it over the surface of the water and whisk in until dissolved.

2 Leave the mixture to rest in a warm place for 10–15 minutes until frothy on the surface. Stir in the olive oil.

3 Sift the flour and salt into a large bowl. If using active dry yeast, stir it in at this point. Make a well in the center and pour in the yeast liquid, or water and oil (without the sugar for active dry yeast).

4 Using either floured hands or a wooden spoon, mix together to form a dough. Turn out onto a floured work surface and knead for about 5 minutes or until smooth and elastic.

5 Place the dough in a large greased plastic bag and leave in a warm place for about 1 hour or until doubled in size. Airing cupboards are often the best places for this process, as the temperature remains constant.

6 Turn out onto a lightly floured work surface and punch down by punching the dough. This releases any air bubbles which would make the pizza uneven. Knead 4 or 5 times. The dough is now ready to use.

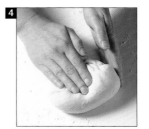

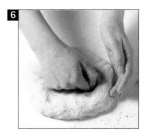

Biscuit Base

This is a quicker alternative to the bread dough base. If you do not have time to wait for bread dough to rise, a biscuit base is ideal.

NUTRITIONAL INFORMATION

Calories	215	Sugars	........3g
Protein	.........5g	Fat	..........7g
Carbohydrate	...35g	Saturates	.......4g

20 MINS   0 MINS

SERVES 4

I N G R E D I E N T S

1½ cups self-rising flour

½ teaspoon salt

2 tablespoons butter

½ cup milk

1 Sift the flour and salt into a large mixing bowl.

2 Rub in the butter with your fingertips until it resembles fine bread crumbs.

3 Make a well in the center of the flour and butter mixture and pour in nearly all of the milk at once. Mix in quickly with a knife. Add the remaining milk only if necessary to mix to a soft dough.

4 Turn the dough out onto a floured work surface and knead by turning and pressing with the heel of your hand 3 or 4 times.

5 Either roll out or press the dough into a 10-inch round on a lightly greased cookie sheet or pizza pan. Push up the edge slightly all round to form a ridge and use immediately.

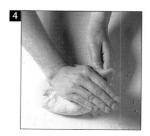

Potato Base

This is an unusual pizza base made from mashed potatoes and flour and is a great way to use up any leftover boiled potatoes.

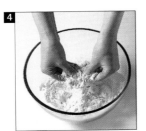

NUTRITIONAL INFORMATION

Calories	170	Sugars	1g
Protein	4g	Fat	3g
Carbohydrate	34g	Saturates	1g

2¼ HOURS   0 MINS

SERVES 4

INGREDIENTS

8 ounces boiled potatoes

¼ cup butter or margarine

1 cup self-rising flour

½ teaspoon salt

1 If the potatoes are hot, mash them, then stir in the butter until it has melted and is distributed evenly throughout the potatoes. Leave to cool.

2 Sift the flour and salt together and stir into the mashed potato to form a soft dough.

3 If the potatoes are cold, mash them without adding the butter. Sift the flour and salt into a bowl.

4 Rub in the butter with your fingertips until the mixture resembles fine bread crumbs, then stir the flour and butter mixture into the mashed potatoes to form a soft dough.

5 Either roll out or press the dough into a 10-inch round on a lightly greased cookie sheet or pizza pan, pushing up the edge slightly all round to form a ridge before adding the topping of your choice. This potato base is rather tricky to lift before it is cooked, so you will find it much easier to handle if you roll it out directly onto the cookie sheet.

6 If the base is not required for cooking immediately, cover it with plastic wrap and chill it for up to 2 hours.

Tomato Sauce

This is a basic topping sauce for pizzas. Using canned diced tomatoes for this dish saves time.

NUTRITIONAL INFORMATION

Calories 41   Sugars 3g
Protein . . . . .1g   Fat 3g
Carbohydrate . . . .3g   Saturates 0.4g

5 MINS   25 MINS

SERVES 4

INGREDIENTS

1 small onion, chopped

1 garlic clove, crushed

1 tablespoon olive oil

7-ounce can diced tomatoes

2 teaspoons tomato paste

½ teaspoon sugar

½ teaspoon dried oregano

1 bay leaf

salt and pepper

1 Fry the onion and garlic gently in the oil for 5 minutes or until softened but not browned.

2 Add the tomatoes, tomato paste, sugar, oregano, bay leaf, and salt and pepper to taste. Stir well.

3 Bring the sauce to the boil, cover, and leave to simmer gently for 20 minutes, stirring occasionally, until you have a thickish sauce.

4 Remove the bay leaf and season to taste. Leave to cool completely before using. This sauce keeps well in a screw-top jar in the refrigerator for up to 1 week.

Special Tomato Sauce

This sauce is made with fresh tomatoes. Use the plum variety whenever available and always choose the reddest ones for the best flavor.

NUTRITIONAL INFORMATION

Calories . . . . .81 Sugars 6g
Protein . . . . .1g Fat 6g
Carbohydrate . . . .6g Saturates 1g

10 MINS   35 MINS

SERVES 4

INGREDIENTS

1 small onion, chopped

1 small red bell pepper, chopped

1 garlic clove, crushed

2 tablespoons olive oil

8 ounces tomatoes

1 tablespoon tomato paste

1 teaspoon soft brown sugar

2 teaspoons chopped fresh basil

½ teaspoon dried oregano

1 bay leaf

salt and pepper

1 Fry the onion, bell pepper, and garlic gently in the oil for 5 minutes until softened but not browned.

2 Cut a cross in the base of each tomato and place them in a bowl. Pour on boiling water and leave for about 45 seconds. Drain, and then plunge in cold water. The skins will slide off easily.

3 Chop the tomatoes, discarding any hard cores.

4 Add the tomatoes to the onion mixture with the tomato paste, sugar, herbs, and seasoning. Stir well. Bring to the boil, cover, and leave to simmer gently for about 30 minutes, stirring occasionally, or until you have a thickish sauce.

5 Remove the bay leaf and adjust the seasoning to taste. Leave to cool completely before using.

6 This sauce will keep well in a screw-top jar in the refrigerator for up to 1 week.

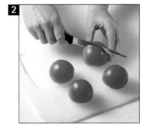

Pizza Margherita

Pizza means "pie" in Italian. The fresh bread dough is not difficult to make but it does take a little time.

NUTRITIONAL INFORMATION

Calories 456	Sugars 7g
Protein 16g	Fat 13g
Carbohydrate ...74g	Saturates 5g

 1 HOUR   45 MINS

SERVES 4

I N G R E D I E N T S

BASIC PIZZA DOUGH

¼ ounce active dry yeast

1 teaspoon sugar

1 cup hand-hot water

3 cups flour

1 teaspoon salt

1 tablespoon olive oil

TOPPING

14-ounce can tomatoes, chopped

2 garlic cloves, crushed

2 teaspoons dried basil

1 tablespoon olive oil

2 tablespoons tomato paste

3½ ounces mozzarella cheese, chopped

2 tablespoons grated Parmesan cheese

salt and pepper

1 Place the yeast and sugar in a measuring cup and mix with 4 tablespoons of the water. Leave the yeast mixture in a warm place for 15 minutes or until frothy.

2 Mix the flour with the salt and make a well in the center. Add the oil, the yeast mixture, and the remaining water. Using a wooden spoon, mix to form a smooth dough.

3 Turn the dough out onto a floured surface and knead for 4–5 minutes or until smooth.

4 Return the dough to the bowl, cover with an oiled sheet of plastic wrap, and leave to rise for 30 minutes or until doubled in size.

5 Knead the dough for 2 minutes. Stretch the dough with your hands, then place it on an oiled cookie sheet, pushing out the edges until even. The dough should be no more than ¼ inch thick because it will rise during cooking.

6 To make the topping, place the tomatoes, garlic, dried basil, olive oil, and salt and pepper to taste in a large skillet and leave to simmer for 20 minutes or until the sauce has thickened. Stir in the tomato paste and leave to cool slightly.

7 Spread the topping evenly over the pizza base. Top with the mozzarella and Parmesan cheeses and bake in a preheated oven, at 400°F, for 20–25 minutes. Serve hot.

Tomato Sauce & Bell Peppers

This pizza is made with a pastry base flavored with cheese and topped with a delicious tomato sauce and roasted bell peppers.

NUTRITIONAL INFORMATION

Calories 611   Sugars 8g
Protein . . . . .14g   Fat 38g
Carbohydrate . . .56g   Saturates 21g

🐚 🐚 🐚

1½ HOURS   55 MINS

SERVES 4

INGREDIENTS

2 cups all-purpose flour

9 tablespoons butter, diced

½ teaspoon salt

2 tablespoons dried Parmesan cheese

1 egg, beaten

2 tablespoons cold water

2 tablespoons olive oil

1 large onion, finely chopped

1 garlic clove, chopped

14-ounce can diced tomatoes

4 tablespoons tomato paste

1 red bell pepper, halved

5 sprigs of thyme, stalks removed

6 black olives, pitted and halved

⅓ cup grated Parmesan cheese

1 Sift the flour and rub in the butter to make bread crumbs. Stir in the salt and dried Parmesan. Add the egg and 1 tablespoon of the water and mix with a round-bladed knife. Add more water if necessary to make a soft dough. Cover the dough with plastic wrap and chill for 30 minutes.

2 Meanwhile, heat the oil in a skillet and cook the onions and garlic for about 5 minutes or until golden. Add the tomatoes and cook for 8–10 minutes. Stir in the tomato paste.

3 Place the bell peppers, skin-side up, on a cookie sheet and cook under a preheated broiler for 15 minutes until charred. Place in a plastic bag and leave to sweat for 10 minutes. Peel off the skin and slice the flesh into thin strips.

4 Roll out the dough to fit a 9-inch loose-based fluted flan pan. Line with foil and bake in a preheated oven, at 400°F, for 10 minutes or until just set. Remove the foil and bake for a further 5 minutes until lightly golden. Leave to cool slightly.

5 Spoon the tomato sauce over the pastry base and top with the bell peppers, thyme, olives, and fresh Parmesan. Return to the oven for 15 minutes or until the pastry is crisp. Serve warm or cold.

Vegetable & Goat Cheese

Wonderfully colorful vegetables are roasted in olive oil with thyme and garlic. The goat cheese adds a nutty, piquant flavor.

NUTRITIONAL INFORMATION

Calories 387   Sugars 9g
Protein ....10g   Fat 21g
Carbohydrate ...42g   Saturates 5g

  2½ HOURS   40 MINS

SERVES 4

INGREDIENTS

2 small zucchini,
  halved lengthwise

2 small eggplants,
  quartered lengthwise

½ red bell pepper, cut into 4 strips

½ yellow bell pepper, cut into 4 strips

1 small red onion, cut into wedges

2 garlic cloves, unpeeled

4 tablespoons olive oil

1 tablespoon red wine vinegar

1 tablespoon chopped fresh thyme

Bread Dough Base (see page 416)

Tomato Sauce (see page 419)

3 ounces goat cheese

salt and pepper

fresh basil leaves, to garnish

1 Place all of the prepared vegetables in a large roasting pan. Mix together the olive oil, vinegar, thyme, and plenty of seasoning and pour over, coating well.

2 Roast the vegetables in a preheated oven, at 400°F, for 15–20 minutes or until the skins have started to blacken in places, turning halfway through. Leave to rest for 5 minutes after roasting.

3 Carefully peel off the skins from the roast bell peppers and the garlic cloves. Slice the garlic.

4 Roll out or press the dough, using a rolling pin or your hands, into a 10-inch round on a lightly floured counter . Place on a large greased cookie sheet or pizza pan and raise the edge a little. Cover and leave for 10 minutes to rise slightly in a warm place. Spread with the tomato sauce almost to the edge.

5 Arrange the roasted vegetables on top and dot with the cheese. Drizzle the oil and juices from the roasting pan over the pizza and season.

6 Bake in a preheated oven, at 400°F, for 18–20 minutes, or until the edge is crisp and golden. Serve immediately, garnished with basil leaves.

Vegetable Calzone

These pizza base parcels are great for making in advance and freezing—they can be thawed when required for a quick snack.

NUTRITIONAL INFORMATION

Calories 499   Sugars 7g
Protein . . . . .16g   Fat 9g
Carbohydrate . . .95g   Saturates 2g

  1½ HOURS   40 MINS

SERVES 4

I N G R E D I E N T S

D O U G H

4 cups white flour

2 teaspoon active dry yeast

1 teaspoon sugar

⅔ cup vegetable stock

⅔ cup sieved tomatoes

beaten egg

F I L L I N G

1 tablespoon vegetable oil

1 onion, chopped

1 garlic clove, crushed

2 tablespoons chopped sun-
  dried tomatoes

3½ ounces spinach, chopped

3 tablespoons canned and drained corn

¼ cup green beans, cut into 3

1 tablespoon tomato paste

1 tablespoon chopped oregano

1¾ ounces mozzarella
  cheese, sliced

salt and pepper

1 Sift the flour into a bowl. Add the yeast and sugar and beat in the stock and sieved tomatoes to make a smooth dough.

2 Knead the dough on a lightly floured surface for 10 minutes, then place in a clean, lightly oiled bowl, and leave to rise in a warm place for 1 hour.

3 Heat the oil in a skillet and sauté the onion for 2–3 minutes.

4 Stir in the garlic, tomatoes, spinach, corn, and beans and cook for 3–4 minutes. Add the tomato paste and oregano and season with salt and pepper to taste.

5 Divide the risen dough into 4 equal portions and roll each on a floured surface to form a 7-inch round.

6 Spoon a quarter of the filling onto one half of each round and top with cheese. Fold the dough over to encase the filling, sealing the edge with a fork. Glaze with beaten egg. Put the calzone on a lightly greased cookie sheet and cook in a preheated oven, at 425°F, for 25–30 minutes until risen and golden. Serve warm.

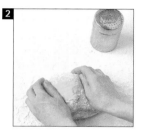

Mushroom Pizza

Juicy mushrooms and stringy mozzarella top this tomato-based pizza. Use exotic mushrooms or a combination of exotic and cultivated.

NUTRITIONAL INFORMATION

Calories	302	Sugars	.........7g
Protein	........10g	Fat	..........12g
Carbohydrate	...41g	Saturates	.......4g

🍲 1¼ HOURS   🕐 45 MINS

SERVES 4

I N G R E D I E N T S

1 portion Basic Pizza Dough (see page 421)

T O P P I N G

14-ounce can diced tomatoes

2 garlic cloves, crushed

1 teaspoon dried basil

1 tablespoon olive oil

2 tablespoons tomato paste

7 ounces mushrooms

1¼ cups grated mozzarella cheese

salt and pepper

basil leaves, to garnish

1 Place the yeast and sugar in a measuring cup and mix with 4 tablespoons of the water. Leave the yeast mixture in a warm place for 15 minutes or until frothy.

2 Mix the flour with the salt and make a well in the center. Add the oil, the yeast mixture, and the remaining water. Using a wooden spoon, mix to form a smooth dough.

3 Turn the dough out onto a floured surface and knead for 4–5 minutes or until smooth. Return the dough to the bowl, cover with an oiled sheet of plastic wrap and leave to rise for 30 minutes or until doubled in size.

4 Remove the dough from the bowl. Knead the dough for 2 minutes. Using a rolling pin, roll out the dough to form an oval or a circular shape, then place it on an oiled cookie sheet, pushing out the edges until even. The dough should be no more than ¼ inch thick because it will rise during cooking.

5 Using a sharp knife, chop the mushrooms into slices.

6 To make the topping, place the tomatoes, garlic, dried basil, olive oil, and salt and pepper in a large pan and simmer for 20 minutes or until the sauce has thickened. Stir in the tomato paste and leave to cool slightly.

7 Spread the sauce over the base of the pizza, top with the mushrooms, and scatter over the mozzarella. Bake in a preheated oven, at 400°F, for 25 minutes. Garnish with basil leaves.

Giardiniera Pizza

As the name implies, this colorful pizza should be topped with fresh vegetables from the garden, especially in the summer months.

NUTRITIONAL INFORMATION

Calories 362	Sugars 10g	
Protein 13g	Fat 15g	
Carbohydrate ...48g	Saturates 5g	

3¹/₂ HOURS   20 MINS

SERVES 4

INGREDIENTS

6 spinach leaves

Potato Base (see page 418)

Special Tomato Sauce
   (see page 420)

1 tomato, sliced

1 celery stalk, sliced thinly

½ green bell pepper, sliced thinly

1 baby zucchini, sliced

1 ounce asparagus tips

1 ounce corn, thawed if frozen

¼ cup peas, thawed if frozen

4 green onions, trimmed and chopped

1 tablespoon chopped fresh mixed herbs

½ cup grated mozzarella cheese

2 tablespoons freshly grated Parmesan

1 artichoke heart

olive oil, for drizzling

salt and pepper

1 Remove any tough stalks from the spinach and wash the leaves in cold water. Pat dry with paper towels.

2 Roll out or press the potato base, using a rolling pin or your hands, into a large 10-inch round on a lightly floured work surface. Place the round on a large greased cookie sheet or pizza pan and push up the edge a little. Spread with the tomato sauce.

3 Arrange the spinach leaves on the sauce, followed by the tomato slices. Top with the remaining vegetables and the herbs.

4 Mix together the cheeses and sprinkle over. Place the artichoke heart in the center. Drizzle the pizza with a little olive oil and season.

5 Bake in a preheated oven, at 400°F, for 18–20 minutes, or until the edges are crisp and golden brown. Serve immediately.

Tomato & Ricotta Pizza

This is a traditional dish from the Calabrian Mountains in southern Italy, where it is made with naturally sun-dried tomatoes and ricotta cheese.

NUTRITIONAL INFORMATION

Calories 274	Sugars 4g
Protein 8g	Fat 11g
Carbohydrate ...38g	Saturates 4g

🍲 1¼ HOURS 🕐 30 MINS

SERVES 4

I N G R E D I E N T S

1 portion Basic Pizza Dough (see page 421)

T O P P I N G

4 tablespoons sun-dried tomato paste

¾ cup ricotta cheese

10 sun-dried tomatoes

1 tablespoon fresh thyme

salt and pepper

1 Place the yeast and sugar in a measuring cup and mix with 4 tablespoons of the water. Leave the yeast mixture in a warm place for 15 minutes or until frothy.

2 Mix the flour with the salt and make a well in the center. Add the oil, the yeast mixture, and the remaining water. Using a wooden spoon, mix to form a dough.

3 Turn the dough out onto a floured surface and knead for 4–5 minutes or until smooth.

4 Return the dough to the bowl, cover with an oiled sheet of plastic wrap, and leave to rise for 30 minutes or until doubled in size.

5 Remove the dough from the bowl. Knead the dough for 2 minutes.

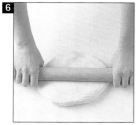  

6 Using a rolling pin, roll out the dough to form a round, then place it on an oiled cookie sheet, pushing out the edges until even. The dough should be no more than ¼ inch thick because it will rise during cooking.

7 Spread the sun-dried tomato paste over the dough, then add spoonfuls of ricotta cheese.

8 Cut the sun-dried tomatoes into strips and arrange these on top of the pizza.

9 Sprinkle the thyme, and salt and pepper to taste over the top of the pizza. Bake in a preheated oven, at 400°F, for 30 minutes or until the crust is golden. Serve hot.

Florentine Pizza

A pizza adaptation of Eggs Florentine—sliced hard-cooked eggs on freshly cooked spinach, with a crunchy almond topping.

NUTRITIONAL INFORMATION

Calories	462	Sugars	.........6g
Protein	........18g	Fat	.........26g
Carbohydrate	...41g	Saturates	.......8g

3 HOURS   20 MINS

SERVES 4

INGREDIENTS

2 tablespoons grated Parmesan cheese

Potato Base (see page 418)

Tomato Sauce (see page 419)

6 ounces spinach

1 small red onion, sliced thinly

2 tablespoons olive oil

¼ teaspoon freshly grated nutmeg

2 hard-cooked eggs

¼ cup fresh white bread crumbs

½ cup grated Jarlsberg, Cheddar, or
    Swiss cheese

2 tablespoons slivered almonds

olive oil, for drizzling

salt and pepper

1 Mix the Parmesan with the potato base. Roll out or press the dough, using a rolling pin or your hands, into a 10-inch round on a lightly floured counter. Place on a large greased cookie sheet or pizza pan and push up the edge slightly. Spread the tomato sauce almost to the edge.

2 Remove the stalks from the spinach and wash the leaves thoroughly in plenty of cold water. Drain well and pat off the excess water with paper towels.

3 Fry the onion gently in the oil for 5 minutes or until softened. Add the spinach and continue to fry until just wilted. Drain off any excess liquid. Arrange on the pizza and sprinkle over the nutmeg.

4 Remove the shells from the eggs and slice. Arrange the slices of egg on top of the spinach.

5 Mix together the bread crumbs, cheese, and almonds, and sprinkle over. Drizzle with a little olive oil and season with salt and pepper to taste.

6 Bake in a preheated oven, at 400°F, for 18–20 minutes, or until the edge is crisp and golden. Serve immediately.

Potato & Tomato Calzone

These pizza dough Italian pasties are best served hot with a salad as a delicious lunch or supper dish.

NUTRITIONAL INFORMATION

Calories ....508 Sugars 8g
Protein ....14g Fat 7g
Carbohydrate ..104g Saturates 2g

🍐 🍐 🍐

🥔 1½ HOURS   🕐 35 MINS

SERVES 4

INGREDIENTS

DOUGH

4 cups white bread flour

1 teaspoon active dry yeast

1¼ cups vegetable stock

1 tablespoon liquid honey

1 teaspoon caraway seeds

milk, for glazing

FILLING

8 ounces potatoes, diced

1 tablespoon vegetable oil

1 onion, halved and sliced

2 garlic cloves, crushed

¾ cup sun-dried tomatoes

2 tablespoons chopped fresh basil

2 tablespoons tomato paste

2 celery stalks, sliced

½ cup grated mozzarella cheese

1 To make the dough, sift the flour into a large bowl and stir in the yeast. Make a well in the center of the mixture.

2 Stir in the vegetable stock, honey, and caraway seeds and bring the mixture together to form a dough.

3 Turn the dough out onto a lightly floured surface and knead for 8 minutes until smooth. Place the dough in a lightly oiled mixing bowl, cover, and leave to rise in a warm place for 1 hour or until it has doubled in size.

4 Meanwhile, make the filling. Heat the oil in a skillet and add all of the remaining ingredients except for the cheese. Cook for 5 minutes, stirring.

5 Divide the risen dough into 4 pieces. On a lightly floured surface, roll them out to form four 7-inch rounds. Spoon equal amounts of the filling onto one half of each round.

6 Sprinkle the cheese over the filling. Brush the edge of the dough with milk, and fold the dough over to form 4 semi-circles, pressing to seal the edges.

7 Place on a nonstick cookie sheet and brush with milk. Cook in a preheated oven, at 425°F, for 30 minutes until golden and risen. Serve hot.

Bell Peppers & Red Onion Pizza

The vibrant colors of the bell peppers and onion make this a delightful pizza. Served cut into fingers, it is ideal for a party or buffet.

NUTRITIONAL INFORMATION

Calories 380	Sugars 19g
Protein 7g	Fat 17g
Carbohydrate ...53g	Saturates 2g

2½ HOURS   25 MINS

SERVES 8

I N G R E D I E N T S

Bread Dough Base (see page 416)

2 tablespoons olive oil

½ each red, green, and yellow bell pepper,
   sliced thinly

1 small red onion, sliced thinly

1 garlic clove, crushed

Tomato Sauce (see page 419)

3 tablespoons raisins

¼ cup pine nuts

1 tablespoon chopped fresh thyme

olive oil, for drizzling

salt and pepper

1 Roll out or press the dough, using a rolling pin or your hands, on a lightly floured counter to fit a 12 x 7 inch greased jelly roll pan. Place in the pan and push up the edges slightly.

2 Cover and leave the dough to rise slightly in a warm place for about 10 minutes.

3 Heat the oil in a large skillet. Add the bell peppers, onion, and garlic, and fry gently for 5 minutes until they have softened but not browned. Leave to cool.

4 Spread the tomato sauce over the base of the pizza almost to the edge.

5 Sprinkle over the raisins and top with the cooled bell pepper mixture. Add the pine nuts and thyme. Drizzle with a little olive oil and season well.

6 Bake in a preheated oven, at 400°F, for 18–20 minutes, or until the edges are crisp and golden. Cut into fingers and serve immediately.

Gorgonzola & Pumpkin Pizza

A combination of blue Gorgonzola cheese and pears combine to give a colorful pizza. The whole wheat base adds a nutty flavor and texture.

NUTRITIONAL INFORMATION

Calories	470	Sugars	5g
Protein	17g	Fat	15g
Carbohydrate	72g	Saturates	6g

1¼ HOURS   35 MINS

SERVES 4

I N G R E D I E N T S

PIZZA DOUGH

¼ ounce active dry yeast

1 teaspoon sugar

1 cup hand-hot water

1½ cups whole wheat flour

1½ cups white flour

1 teaspoon salt

1 tablespoon olive oil

TOPPING

14 ounces pumpkin or squash,
   peeled and cubed

1 tablespoon olive oil

1 pear, cored, peeled, and sliced

3½ ounces Gorgonzola cheese

1 sprig fresh rosemary, to garnish

1 Place the yeast and sugar in a measuring cup and mix with 4 tablespoons of the water. Leave the yeast mixture in a warm place for 15 minutes or until frothy.

2 Mix both of the flours with the salt and make a well in the center. Add the oil, the yeast mixture, and the remaining water. Using a wooden spoon, mix to form a dough.

3 Turn the dough out onto a floured surface and knead for 4–5 minutes or until smooth.

4 Return the dough to the bowl, cover with an oiled sheet of plastic wrap, and leave to rise for 30 minutes or until doubled in size.

5 Remove the dough from the bowl. Knead the dough for 2 minutes. Using a rolling pin, roll out the dough to form a long oval shape, then place it on an oiled cookie sheet, pushing out the edges until even. The dough should be no more than ¼ inch thick because it will rise during cooking.

6 To make the topping, place the pumpkin in a shallow roasting pan. Drizzle with the olive oil and cook under a preheated broiler for 20 minutes or until soft and lightly golden.

7 Top the dough with the pear and the pumpkin, brushing with the oil from the pan. Sprinkle over the Gorgonzola. Bake in a preheated oven, at 400°F, for 15 minutes or until the base is golden. Garnish with rosemary.

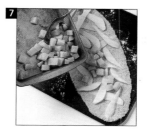

Ratatouille & Lentil Pizza

Ratatouille and lentils on a whole wheat base are topped with cheese and sunflower seeds. The lentils need soaking so prepare in advance.

NUTRITIONAL INFORMATION

Calories	377	Sugars	.........6g
Protein	........11g	Fat	..........19g
Carbohydrate	...44g	Saturates	.......5g

2¹/₂ HOURS   55 MINS

SERVES 4

I N G R E D I E N T S

¼ cups green lentils

½ small eggplant, diced

1 small onion, sliced

1 garlic clove, crushed

3 tablespoons olive oil

½ zucchini, sliced

½ red bell pepper, sliced

½ green bell pepper, sliced

7-ounce can chopped tomatoes

1 tablespoon chopped fresh oregano

Bread Dough Base (see page 416), made
    with whole wheat flour

2 ounces Cheddar, sliced thinly

1 tablespoon sunflower seeds

olive oil, for drizzling

salt and pepper

1 Soak the lentils in hot water for 30 minutes. Drain and rinse; then cover with fresh water, and simmer over low heat for 10 minutes.

2 Place the eggplant in a colander, sprinkle with a little salt, and leave the bitter juices to drain for about 20 minutes. Rinse well and pat dry with paper towels.

3 Fry the onion and garlic gently in the oil for 3 minutes. Add the zucchini, bell peppers, and eggplant. Cover and leave to cook over low heat for about 5 minutes.

4 Add the tomatoes, drained lentils, oregano, 2 tablespoons of water, and seasoning. Cover and simmer for 15 minutes, stirring occasionally, adding more water if necessary.

5 Roll out or press the dough, using a rolling pin or your hands, into a 10-inch round on a lightly floured counter. Place on a large greased cookie sheet or pizza pan and push up the edge slightly. Cover and leave the dough to rise slightly for 10 minutes in a warm place.

6 Spread the ratatouille over the dough base almost to the edge. Arrange the cheese slices on top and sprinkle over the sunflower seeds. Drizzle with a little olive oil and season with a little salt and pepper to taste.

7 Bake in a preheated oven, at 400°F, for 18–20 minutes, or until the edge is crisp and golden brown. Serve immediately.

Cheese & Artichoke Pizza

Sliced artichokes combined with sharp Cheddar, Parmesan, and blue cheese give a really delicious topping to this pizza.

NUTRITIONAL INFORMATION

Calories 424	Sugars 9g
Protein 16g	Fat 20g
Carbohydrate ...47g	Saturates 8g

 1³/₄ HOURS   20 MINS

SERVES 4

I N G R E D I E N T S

Bread Dough Base (see page 416)

Special Tomato Sauce (see page 420)

2 ounces blue cheese, sliced

4½ ounces marinated artichoke hearts in oil, sliced

½ small red onion, chopped

½ cup grated Cheddar cheese

2 tablespoons grated Parmesan cheese

1 tablespoon chopped fresh thyme

oil from artichokes for drizzling

salt and pepper

T O   S E R V E

salad greens

cherry tomatoes, halved

1 Roll out or press the dough, using a rolling pin or your hands, to form a 10-inch round on a lightly floured counter.

2 Place the pizza base on a large greased cookie sheet or pizza pan and push up the edge slightly. Cover and leave to rise for 10 minutes in a warm place.

3 Spread the tomato sauce almost to the edge of the base. Arrange the blue cheese on top of the tomato sauce, followed by the artichoke hearts and red onion.

4 Mix the Cheddar and Parmesan cheeses together with the thyme and sprinkle the mixture over the pizza. Drizzle a little of the oil from the jar of artichokes over the pizza and season to taste.

5 Bake in a preheated oven, at 400°F, for 18–20 minutes, or until the edge is crisp and golden and the cheese is bubbling.

6 Mix the fresh salad greens and cherry tomato halves together and serve with the pizza, cut into slices.

Cheese & Garlic Mushroom

This pizza dough is flavored with garlic and herbs and topped with mixed mushrooms and melting cheese for a really delicious pizza.

NUTRITIONAL INFORMATION

Calories	.541	Sugars	.5g
Protein	.16g	Fat	.15g
Carbohydrate	.91g	Saturates	.6g

45 MINS   30 MINS

SERVES 4

I N G R E D I E N T S

DOUGH

4 cups white flour

2 teaspoons active dry yeast

2 garlic cloves, crushed

2 tablespoons chopped thyme

2 tablespoons olive oil

1¼ cups tepid water

TOPPING

2 tablespoons butter or margarine

12 ounces mixed mushrooms, sliced

2 garlic cloves, crushed

2 tablespoons chopped parsley

2 tablespoons tomato paste

6 tablespoons sieved tomatoes

¾ cup grated mozzarella cheese

salt and pepper

chopped parsley, to garnish

1 Put the flour, yeast, garlic, and thyme in a bowl. Make a well in the center and gradually stir in the oil and water. Bring together to form a soft dough.

2 Turn the dough onto a floured surface and knead for 5 minutes or until smooth. Roll into a 14-inch round and place on a greased cookie sheet. Leave in a warm place for 20 minutes or until the dough puffs up.

3 Meanwhile, make the topping. Melt the margarine or butter in a skillet and sauté the mushrooms, garlic, and parsley for 5 minutes.

4 Mix the tomato paste and sieved tomatoes and spoon onto the pizza base, leaving a ½-inch edge of dough. Spoon the mushroom mixture on top. Season well and sprinkle the cheese on top.

5 Cook the pizza in a preheated oven, at 375°F, for 20–25 minutes or until the base is crisp and the cheese has melted. Garnish with chopped parsley and serve at once.

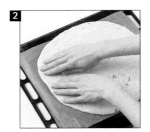

Tofu, Corn, & Peas

Chunks of tofu marinated in ginger and soy sauce impart something of an eastern flavor to this pizza.

NUTRITIONAL INFORMATION

Calories 596	Sugars 17g
Protein 33g	Fat 23g
Carbohydrate . . .66g	Saturates 9g

 1 HOUR   35 MINS

SERVES 4

INGREDIENTS

4 cups milk

1 teaspoon salt

1⅓ cups semolina

1 tablespoon soy sauce

1 tablespoon dry sherry

½ teaspoon grated fresh ginger root

9 ounces tofu, cut into chunks

2 eggs

⅔ cup grated Parmesan cheese

Tomato Sauce (see page 419)

1 ounce baby corn, cut into 4

1 ounce snow peas, trimmed
 and cut into 4

4 green onions, trimmed and cut into
 1-inch strips

2 ounces mozzarella, sliced thinly

2 teaspoons sesame oil

salt and pepper

1 Bring the milk to the boil with the salt. Sprinkle the semolina over the surface, stirring all the time. Cook for 10 minutes over low heat, stirring occasionally, taking care not to let it burn. Remove from the heat and leave to cool until tepid.

2 Mix the soy sauce, sherry, and ginger together in a bowl, add the tofu, and stir gently to coat. Leave to marinate in a cool place for 20 minutes.

3 Beat the eggs with a little pepper. Add to the semolina with the Parmesan and mix well. Place on a large greased cookie sheet or pizza pan and pat into a 10-inch round, using the back of a metal spoon. Spread the tomato sauce almost to the edge.

4 Blanch the corn and snow peas in a saucepan of boiling water for 1 minute, drain, and place on the pizza with the drained tofu. Top with the green onions and slices of cheese. Drizzle over the sesame oil and season with salt and pepper.

5 Bake in a preheated oven, at 400°F, for 18–20 minutes, or until the edge is crisp and golden. Serve immediately.

Exotic Mushroom & Walnut

Exotic mushrooms make a delicious pizza topping when mixed with walnuts and Roquefort cheese.

NUTRITIONAL INFORMATION

Calories	499	Sugars	.........9g
Protein	........13g	Fat	.........32g
Carbohydrate	...42g	Saturates	......11g

 1¼ HOURS   25 MINS

SERVES 4

I N G R E D I E N T S

Biscuit Base (see page 417)

Special Tomato Sauce (see page 420)

½ cup cream cheese

1 tablespoon chopped fresh mixed herbs, such as parsley, oregano, and basil

8 ounces exotic mushrooms, such as oyster, shiitake, or porcini, or 4 ounces each exotic and button mushrooms

2 tablespoons olive oil

¼ teaspoon fennel seeds

¼ cup walnuts, chopped roughly

1½ ounces blue cheese

olive oil, for drizzling

salt and pepper

sprig of flat-leaf parsley, to garnish

1 Roll out or press the biscuit base, using a rolling pin or your hands, into a 10-inch round on a lightly floured work surface. Place on a large greased cookie sheet or pizza pan and push up the edge a little with your fingers to form a rim.

2 Carefully spread the tomato sauce almost to the edge of the pizza base. Dot with the cream cheese and chopped fresh herbs.

3 Wipe and slice the mushrooms. Heat the oil in a large skillet or wok and stir-fry the mushrooms and fennel seeds for 2–3 minutes. Spread over the pizza with the walnuts.

4 Crumble the cheese over the pizza, drizzle with a little olive oil, and season with salt and pepper to taste.

5 Bake in a preheated oven, at 400°F, for 18–20 minutes, or until the edge is crisp and golden. Serve immediately, garnished with a sprig of flat-leaf parsley.

Tomato & Olive Pizzas

Halved ciabatta bread or baguettes are a ready-made pizza base. The colors of the tomatoes and cheese contrast beautifully on top.

NUTRITIONAL INFORMATION

Calories 181	Sugars 4g	
Protein 7g	Fat 10g	
Carbohydrate ...18g	Saturates 4g	

45 MINS   25 MINS

SERVES 4

INGREDIENTS

2 loaves of ciabatta or 2 baguettes

Tomato Sauce (see page 419)

4 plum tomatoes, sliced thinly lengthwise

5½ ounces mozzarella, sliced thinly

10 black olives, cut into rings

8 fresh basil leaves, shredded

olive oil, for drizzling

salt and pepper

1 Cut the bread in half lengthwise and toast the cut side of the bread lightly. Carefully spread the toasted bread with the tomato sauce.

2 Arrange the tomato and mozzarella slices alternately along the length.

3 Top with the olive rings and half of the basil. Drizzle over a little olive oil and season with salt and pepper.

4 Either place under a preheated medium broiler and cook until the cheese is melted and bubbling or bake in a preheated oven, 400°F, for 15–20 minutes.

5 Sprinkle over the remaining basil and serve immediately.

Marinara Pizza

This pizza is topped with a cocktail of mixed seafood, such as shrimp, mussels, clams, and squid rings.

NUTRITIONAL INFORMATION

Calories	359	Sugars	.........9g
Protein	........19g	Fat	..........14g
Carbohydrate	...42g	Saturates	.......4g

 3¼ HOURS 20 MINS

SERVES 4

INGREDIENTS

Potato Base (see page 418)

Special Tomato Sauce (see page 420)

7 ounces frozen seafood cocktail, thawed

1 tablespoon capers

1 small yellow bell pepper, chopped

1 tablespoon chopped fresh marjoram

½ teaspoon dried oregano

½ cup grated mozzarella cheese

3 tablespoons grated Parmesan cheese

12 black olives

olive oil, for drizzling

salt and pepper

sprig of fresh marjoram or oregano, to garnish

1 Roll out or press out the potato dough, using a rolling pin or your hands, into a 10-inch round on a lightly floured work surface.

2 Place the dough on a large greased cookie sheet or pizza pan and push up the edge a little with your fingers to form a rim.

3 Spread the tomato sauce evenly over the base almost to the edge.

4 Arrange the seafood cocktail, capers, and yellow bell pepper on top of the tomato sauce.

5 Sprinkle over the herbs and cheeses. Arrange the olives on top. Drizzle over a little olive oil and season with salt and pepper to taste.

6 Bake in a preheated oven, at 400°F, for 18–20 minutes or until the edge of the pizza is crisp and golden brown.

7 Transfer to a warm serving plate, garnish with a sprig of marjoram or oregano, and serve immediately.

Onion & Anchovy Pizza

This tasty onion pizza is topped with a lattice pattern of anchovies and black olives. Cut the pizza into squares to serve.

NUTRITIONAL INFORMATION

Calories 373   Sugars 5g
Protein ....12g   Fat 20g
Carbohydrate ...39g   Saturates 4g

1³/₄ HOURS   30 MINS

MAKES 6

INGREDIENTS

4 tablespoons olive oil

3 onions, sliced thinly

1 garlic clove, crushed

1 teaspoon soft brown sugar

½ teaspoon crushed fresh rosemary

7-ounces can diced tomatoes

Bread Dough Base (see page 416)

2 tablespoons freshly grated Parmesan

1³/₄-ounce can anchovies

12–14 black olives

salt and pepper

1 Heat 3 tablespoons of the oil in a large saucepan and add the onions, garlic, sugar, and rosemary. Cover and fry gently, stirring occasionally, for 10 minutes or until the onions are soft but not brown.

2 Add the tomatoes to the pan, stir, and season with salt and pepper to taste. Leave to cool slightly.

3 Roll out or press the dough, using a rolling pin or your hands, on a lightly floured work surface to fit a 12 x 7 inch greased jelly roll pan. Place in the pan and push up the edges slightly to form a rim.

4 Brush the remaining oil over the dough and sprinkle with the cheese. Cover and leave to rise slightly in a warm place for about 10 minutes.

5 Spread the onion and tomato topping over the base. Drain the anchovies, reserving the oil. Split each anchovy in half lengthwise and arrange on the pizza in a lattice pattern. Place olives in between the anchovies and drizzle over a little of the reserved oil. Season to taste.

6 Bake in a preheated oven, at 400°F, for 18–20 minutes, or until the edges are crisp and golden. Cut the pizza into 6 squares and serve immediately.

Salmon Pizza

You can use either red or pink salmon for this tasty pizza. Red salmon will give a better color and flavor but it can be expensive.

NUTRITIONAL INFORMATION

Calories 321	Sugars 6g	
Protein 12g	Fat 14g	
Carbohydrate . . .39g	Saturates 6g	

   1¼ HOURS   20 MINS

SERVES 4

I N G R E D I E N T S

1 quantity Biscuit Base (see
page 417)

1 quantity Tomato Sauce (see page 419)

1 zucchini, grated

1 tomato, sliced thinly

3½-ounce can red or pink salmon

2 ounces mushrooms,
wiped and sliced

1 tablespoon chopped fresh dill

½ teaspoon dried oregano

½ cup grated mozzarella cheese

olive oil, for drizzling

salt and pepper

sprig of fresh dill, to garnish

1 Roll out or press the dough, using a rolling pin or your hands, into a 10-inch round on a lightly floured counter. Place on a large greased cookie sheet or pizza pan and gently push up the edge a little with your fingers to form a rim.

2 Spread the tomato sauce over the pizza base, almost to the edge.

3 Top the tomato sauce with the grated zucchini, then lay the tomato slices on top.

4 Drain the can of salmon. Remove any bones and skin and flake the fish. Arrange on the pizza with the mushrooms. Sprinkle over the herbs and cheese. Drizzle with a little olive oil and season with salt and pepper.

5 Bake in a preheated oven, at 400°F, for 18–20 minutes or until the edge is golden and crisp.

6 Transfer to a warm serving plate and serve immediately, garnished with a sprig of dill.

COOK'S TIP

If salmon is too pricey, use either canned tuna or sardines to make a delicious everyday fish pizza. Choose canned fish in brine for a healthier topping. If fresh dill is unavailable, you can use parsley instead.

Pissaladière

This is a variation of the classic Italian pizza but is made with ready-made puff pastry. It is perfect for outdoor eating.

NUTRITIONAL INFORMATION

Calories ....612 Sugars 13g
Protein ....12g Fat 43g
Carbohydrate ...47g Saturates 11g

20 MINS 55 MINS

SERVES 8

I N G R E D I E N T S

4 tablespoons olive oil

1 pound 9 ounces red onions, sliced thinly

2 garlic cloves, crushed

2 teaspoons sugar

2 tablespoons red wine vinegar

12 ounces fresh ready-made
   puff pastry

salt and pepper

T O P P I N G

2 x 1¾-ounce cans anchovy fillets

12 green pitted olives

1 teaspoon dried marjoram

1 Lightly grease a jelly roll pan. Heat the olive oil in a large saucepan. Add the red onions and garlic and cook over low heat for about 30 minutes, stirring occasionally.

2 Add the sugar and red wine vinegar to the pan and season with plenty of salt and pepper.

3 On a lightly floured surface, roll out the pastry to a rectangle, about 13 x 9 inches. Place the pastry rectangle onto the prepared pan, pushing the pastry into the corners of the pan.

4 Spread the onion mixture over the pastry.

5 Arrange the anchovy fillets and green olives on top, then sprinkle with the marjoram.

6 Bake in a preheated oven, at 425°F, for 20-25 minutes or until the pissaladière is lightly golden. Serve the pissaladière piping hot, straight from the oven.

VARIATION

Cut the pissaladière into squares or triangles for easy finger food at a party or barbecue.

Mini Pizzas

Pizette, as they are known in Italy, are tiny pizzas. This quantity will make 8 individual pizzas, or 16 cocktail pizzas to go with drinks.

NUTRITIONAL INFORMATION

Calories	139	Sugars	.........1g
Protein	.........4g	Fat	...........6g
Carbohydrate	...18g	Saturates	.......1g

1¼ HOURS   15 MINS

SERVES 8

INGREDIENTS

1 portion Basic Pizza Dough (see page 421)

TOPPING

2 zucchini

½ cup sieved tomatoes

½ cup diced pancetta

½ cup ounces black olives, pitted and chopped

1 tablespoon mixed dried herbs

2 tablespoons olive oil

1 Place the yeast and sugar in a measuring cup and mix with 4 tablespoons of the water. Leave the yeast mixture in a warm place for 15 minutes or until frothy.

2 Mix the flour with the salt and make a well in the center. Add the oil, the yeast mixture, and the remaining water. Using a wooden spoon, mix to form a smooth dough.

3 Turn the dough out onto a floured surface and knead for 4–5 minutes or until smooth. Return the dough to the bowl, cover with an oiled sheet of plastic wrap and leave to rise for 30 minutes or until the dough has doubled in size.

4 Knead the dough for 2 minutes and divide it into 8 balls.

5 Roll out each portion thinly to form rounds or squares, then place them on an oiled cookie sheet, pushing out the edges until even. The dough should be no more than ¼ inch thick because it will rise during cooking.

6 To make the topping, grate the zucchini finely. Cover with paper towels and leave to stand for 10 minutes to absorb some of the juices.

7 Spread 2–3 teaspoons of the sieved tomatoes over the pizza bases and top each with the grated zucchini, pancetta, and olives. Season with pepper to taste, a sprinkling of mixed dried herbs and drizzle with olive oil.

8 Bake in a preheated oven at 400°F for 15 minutes or until crispy. Season with salt and pepper to taste and serve hot.

Four Seasons Pizza

This is a traditional pizza on which the toppings are divided into four sections, each of which is supposed to depict a season of the year.

NUTRITIONAL INFORMATION

Calories 313   Sugars 8g
Protein . . . . .8g   Fat 13g
Carbohydrate . . .44g   Saturates 3g

 2³/₄ HOURS   20 MINS

SERVES 4

I N G R E D I E N T S

Bread Dough Base (see page 416)

Special Tomato Sauce (see page 420)

1 ounce chorizo sausage, sliced thinly

1 ounce mushrooms, wiped and
sliced thinly

1½ ounces artichoke hearts, sliced thinly

1 ounce mozzarella, sliced thinly

3 anchovies, halved lengthwise

2 teaspoons capers

4 pitted black olives, sliced

4 fresh basil leaves, shredded

olive oil, for drizzling

salt and pepper

1 Roll out or press the dough, using a rolling pin or your hands, into a 10-inch round on a lightly floured surface. Place on a large greased cookie sheet or pizza pan and push up the edge a little.

2 Cover and leave to rise slightly for 10 minutes in a warm place. Spread the tomato sauce over the pizza base, almost to the edge.

3 Put the sliced chorizo onto one quarter of the pizza, the sliced mushrooms on a second quarter, the artichoke hearts on a third quarter, and the mozzarella and anchovies on the fourth quarter.

4 Dot with the capers, olives, and basil leaves. Drizzle with a little olive oil and season. Do not put any salt on the anchovy section as the fish are very salty.

5 Bake in a preheated oven, at 400°F, for 18–20 minutes, or until the crust is golden and crisp. Serve immediately.

Eggplant & Lamb Pizza

An unusual fragrant, spiced pizza topped with ground lamb and eggplant on a bread base.

NUTRITIONAL INFORMATION

Calories	430	Sugars	........10g
Protein	........18g	Fat	..........22g
Carbohydrate	...44g	Saturates	.......7g

3 HOURS   30 MINS

SERVES 4

I N G R E D I E N T S

1 small eggplant, diced

Bread Dough Base (see page 416)

1 small onion, sliced thinly

1 garlic clove, crushed

1 teaspoon cumin seeds

1 tablespoon olive oil

6 ounces ground lamb

1 ounce canned pimento, thinly sliced

2 tablespoons chopped fresh cilantro

Special Tomato Sauce (see page 420)

3 ounces mozzarella, sliced thinly

olive oil, for drizzling

salt and pepper

1 Place the diced eggplant in a colander, sprinkle with the salt, and let the bitter juices drain for about 20 minutes. Rinse thoroughly, then pat dry with paper towels.

2 Roll out or press the dough, using a rolling pin or your hands, into a 10-inch round on a lightly floured counter. Place on a large greased cookie sheet or pizza pan and gently push up the edge to form a rim.

3 Cover and leave to rise slightly for 10 minutes in a warm place.

4 Fry the onion, garlic, and cumin seeds gently in the oil for 3 minutes. Increase the heat slightly and add the lamb, eggplant, and pimento. Fry for 5 minutes, stirring occasionally. Add the cilantro and season with salt and pepper to taste.

5 Spread the tomato sauce over the dough base, almost to the edge. Top with the lamb mixture.

6 Arrange the mozzarella slices on top. Drizzle over a little olive oil and season with salt and pepper.

7 Bake in a preheated oven, at 400°F, for 18–20 minutes, or until the crust is crisp and golden. Serve immediately.

Onion, Ham, & Cheese Pizza

This pizza was a favorite of the Romans. It is slightly unusual because the topping is made without a tomato sauce base.

NUTRITIONAL INFORMATION

Calories	333	Sugars	.........8g
Protein	........12g	Fat	..........14g
Carbohydrate	...43g	Saturates	.......4g

 1 HOUR   40 MINS

SERVES 4

I N G R E D I E N T S

1 portion of Basic Pizza Dough (see page 421)

T O P P I N G

2 tablespoons olive oil

9 ounces onions, sliced into rings

2 garlic cloves, crushed

1 red bell pepper, diced

3½ ounces raw prosciutto, cut into strips

3½ ounces mozzarella cheese, sliced

2 tablespoons rosemary, stalks removed and roughly chopped

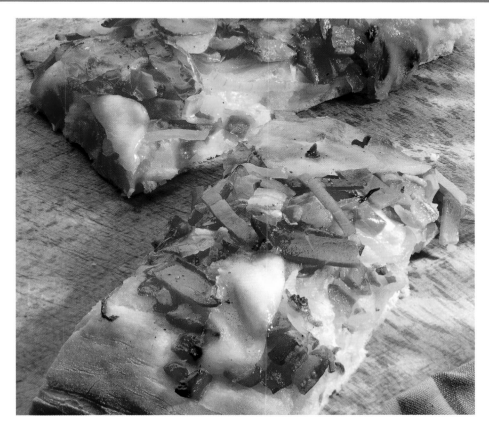

1 Place the yeast and sugar in a measuring cup and mix with 4 tablespoons of the water. Leave the mixture in a warm place for 15 minutes or until frothy.

2 Mix the flour with the salt and make a well in the center. Add the oil, the yeast mixture, and the remaining water. Using a wooden spoon, mix to form a smooth dough.

3 Turn the dough out onto a floured surface and knead for 4–5 minutes or until smooth. Return the dough to the bowl, cover with an oiled sheet of plastic wrap, and leave to rise for 30 minutes or until doubled in size.

4 Remove the dough from the bowl. Knead the dough for 2 minutes. Using a rolling pin, roll out the dough to form a square shape, then place it on an oiled cookie sheet, pushing out the edges until even. The dough should be no more than ¼ inch thick because it will rise during cooking.

5 To make the topping, heat the oil in a pan. Add the onions and garlic and cook for 3 minutes. Add the bell pepper and fry for 2 minutes.

6 Cover the pan and cook the vegetables over low heat for 10 minutes, stirring occasionally, until the onions are slightly caramelized. Leave to cool slightly.

7 Spread the topping evenly over the pizza base. Arrange the prosciutto, mozzarella, and rosemary over the top.

8 Bake in a preheated oven, at 400°F, for 20–25 minutes. Serve hot.

Tomato & Chorizo Pizza

Spicy chorizo sausage blends beautifully with juicy tomatoes and mild, melting mozzarella cheese. This pizza makes a delicious light lunch.

NUTRITIONAL INFORMATION

Calories	574	Sugars	.........8g
Protein	........17g	Fat	..........38g
Carbohydrate	...43g	Saturates	.......8g

 15 MINS 15 MINS

SERVES 2

I N G R E D I E N T S

9-inch ready-made pizza base

1 tablespoon black olive paste

1 tablespoon olive oil

1 onion, sliced

1 garlic clove, crushed

4 tomatoes, sliced

3 ounces chorizo sausages, sliced

1 teaspoon fresh oregano

4½ ounces mozzarella cheese, sliced

6 black olives, pitted and halved

pepper

1 Put the pizza base on a cookie sheet and spread the black olive paste to within ½ inch of the edge.

2 Heat the oil in a skillet and cook the onion for 2 minutes. Add the garlic and cook for 1 minute.

COOK'S TIP

There are several varieties of pizza base available. Those with added olive oil are preferable because the dough is much lighter and tastier.

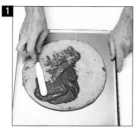

3 Spread the onion mixture over the pizza base and arrange the tomato and chorizo slices on top. Sprinkle with the oregano, season with pepper to taste, and arrange the mozzarella cheese and olives on top.

4 Bake in a preheated oven, at 450°F, for 10 minutes until the cheese is melted and golden. Serve immediately.

Smoky Bacon & Pepperoni Pizza

This more traditional kind of pizza is topped with pepperoni, smoked bacon, and bell peppers covered in a smoked cheese.

NUTRITIONAL INFORMATION

Calories .... .450	Sugars 6g	
Protein 19g	Fat .... .24g	
Carbohydrate ...41g	Saturates 6g	

  1½ HOURS 20 MINS

SERVES 4

INGREDIENTS

Bread Dough Base (see page 416)

1 tablespoon olive oil

1 tablespoon freshly grated Parmesan

Tomato Sauce (see page 419)

4½ ounces lightly smoked bacon, diced

½ green bell pepper, sliced thinly

½ yellow bell pepper, sliced thinly

2 ounces pepperoni-style sliced spicy
    sausage

½ cup grated smoked Bavarian cheese

½ teaspoon dried oregano

olive oil, for drizzling

salt and pepper

1 Roll out or press the dough, using a rolling pin or your hands, into a 10-inch round on a lightly floured work surface.

2 Place the dough base on a large greased cookie sheet or pizza pan and push up the edge a little with your fingers, to form a rim.

3 Brush the base with the olive oil and sprinkle with the Parmesan. Cover and leave to rise slightly in a warm place for about 10 minutes.

4 Spread the tomato sauce over the base almost to the edge. Top with the bacon and bell peppers. Arrange the pepperoni on top and sprinkle with the smoked cheese.

5 Sprinkle over the oregano and drizzle with a little olive oil. Season well.

6 Bake in a preheated oven, at 400°F, for 18–20 minutes, or until the crust is golden and crisp around the edge. Cut the pizza into wedges and serve immediately.

Corned Beef Hash Pizza

A combination of corned beef and baked eggs on a sour cream and potato base makes a really unusual pizza.

NUTRITIONAL INFORMATION

Calories 563	Sugars 16g
Protein 36g	Fat 28g
Carbohydrate ...45g	Saturates 12g

 1¼ HOURS   35 MINS

SERVES 4

INGREDIENTS

1 pound 2 ounces potatoes

3 tablespoons sour cream

11½-ounce can corned beef

1 small onion, chopped finely

1 green bell pepper, chopped

3 tablespoons tomato and chili relish

Special Tomato Sauce (see page 420)

4 eggs

¼ cup grated mozzarella cheese

¼ cup grated Cheddar cheese

paprika

salt and pepper

chopped fresh parsley, to garnish

1 Peel the potatoes and cut into even-size chunks. Parboil them in a pan of boiling salted water for 5 minutes. Drain, rinse in cold water and cool.

COOK'S TIP

For extra color, mix a grated carrot with the potato base. This will look and taste good, and will help to persuade children to eat their vegetables, if they are fussy eaters. Use the tomato and chili relish sparingly if you are serving this to children.

2 Grate the potatoes and mix with the sour cream and seasoning to taste in a bowl. Place on a large greased cookie sheet or pizza pan and pat out into a 10-in round, pushing up the edge slightly to form a rim.

3 Mash the corned beef roughly with a fork and stir in the onion, green bell pepper, and relish. Season well.

4 Spread the tomato sauce over the potato base almost to the edge. Top with the corned beef mixture. Using a spoon, make 4 wells in the corned beef. Break an egg into each.

5 Mix the cheeses together and sprinkle over the pizza with a little paprika. Season with salt and pepper.

6 Bake in a preheated oven, at 400°F, for 20–25 minutes until the eggs have cooked but still have slightly runny yolks.

7 Serve immediately, garnished with chopped parsley.

Italian Calzone

A calzone is like a pizza in reverse—it resembles a large turnover with the dough on the outside and the filling on the inside.

NUTRITIONAL INFORMATION

Calories 405   Sugars 7g
Protein ....19g   Fat 17g
Carbohydrate ...48g   Saturates 5g

1¼ HOURS   20 MINS

SERVES 4

INGREDIENTS

Bread Dough Base (see page 416)

1 egg, beaten

1 tablespoon tomato paste

1 ounce Italian salami, chopped

1 ounce mortadella ham, chopped

1 tomato, peeled and chopped

1 ounce ricotta cheese

2 green onions, trimmed and
    chopped

¼ teaspoon dried oregano

salt and pepper

1 Roll out the dough to form a 9-inch round on a lightly floured work surface.

2 Brush the edge of the dough with a little beaten egg.

3 Spread the tomato paste over half of the round nearest to you.

4 Scatter the salami, mortadella, and chopped tomato on top.

5 Dot with the ricotta and sprinkle over the green onions and oregano. Season with salt and pepper to taste.

6 Fold over the other half of the dough to form a half moon shape. Press the edges together well to prevent the filling from coming out.

7 Place the calzone on a cookie sheet and brush with beaten egg to glaze. Make a hole in the top in order to allow any steam from the vegetables to escape during the cooking time.

8 Bake in a preheated oven, at 400°F, for 20 minutes, or until golden. Serve immediately.

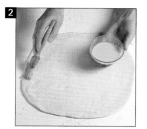

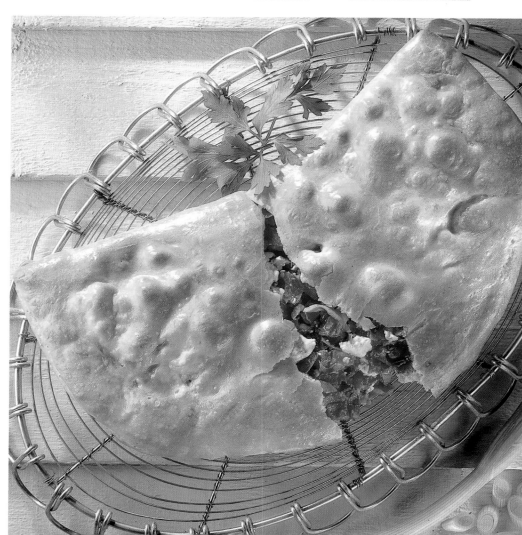

Potato & Pepperoni Pizza

Potatoes make a great pizza base and this recipe is well worth making, rather than using a ready-made base, both for texture and flavor.

NUTRITIONAL INFORMATION

Calories	234	Sugars	.........5g
Protein	.........4g	Fat	..........12g
Carbohydrate	...30g	Saturates	.......1g

20 MINS   45 MINS

SERVES 4

INGREDIENTS

2 pound russet potatoes, diced

1 tablespoon butter

2 garlic cloves, crushed

2 tablespoons mixed chopped fresh herbs

1 egg, beaten

⅓ cup sieved tomatoes

2 tablespoons tomato paste

1¾ ounces pepperoni slices

1 green bell pepper, cut into strips

1 yellow bell pepper, cut into strips

2 large mushrooms, sliced

¼ cup pitted black olives, quartered

4½ ounces mozzarella cheese, sliced

COOK'S TIP

This pizza base is softer in texture than a normal bread dough and is ideal served from the pan. Top with any of your favorite pizza ingredients that you have available.

1 Grease and flour a 9-inch pizza pan.

2 Cook the diced potatoes in a saucepan of boiling water for 10 minutes or until cooked through. Drain and mash until smooth. Transfer the mashed potato to a mixing bowl and stir in the butter, garlic, herbs and egg.

3 Spread the mixture into the prepared pizza pan. Cook in a preheated oven, at 425°F, for 7-10 minutes or until the pizza base begins to set.

4 Mix the sieved tomatoes and tomato paste together and spoon it over the pizza base, to within ½ inch of the edge of the base.

5 Arrange the pepperoni, bell peppers, mushrooms, and olives on top of the sieved tomatoes.

6 Scatter the mozzarella cheese on top of the pizza. Return to the oven for 20 minutes or until the base is cooked through and the cheese has melted on top. Serve hot.

Hot Chili Beef Pizza

This deep-pan pizza is topped with ground beef, red kidney beans, and jalapeño chilies, which are small, green and very hot.

NUTRITIONAL INFORMATION

Calories 550	Sugars 5g
Protein 24g	Fat 26g
Carbohydrate ...60g	Saturates 9g

  1½ HOURS   30 MINS

SERVES

INGREDIENTS

¾ ounces fresh yeast or 1½ teaspoon active dry yeast

½ cup tepid water

1 teaspoon sugar

3 tablespoons olive oil

2 cups all-purpose flour

1 teaspoon salt

TOPPING

1 small onion, sliced thinly

1 garlic clove, crushed

½ yellow bell pepper, chopped

1 tablespoon olive oil

6 ounces lean ground beef

¼ teaspoon chili powder

¼ teaspoon ground cumin

7-ounce can red kidney beans, drained

Tomato Sauce (see page 419)

3 jalapeño chilies, sliced

2 ounces mozzarella, sliced thinly

½ cup grated sharp Cheddar or Monterey Jack cheese

olive oil, for drizzling

salt and pepper

chopped parsley, to garnish

1 For the deep-pan dough base, use the same method as the Bread Dough Base recipe.

2 Roll out or press the dough, using a rolling pin or your hands, into a 9-inch round on a lightly floured counter. Place on a large greased cookie sheet or pizza pan and push up the edge to form a small rim. Cover and leave to rise slightly for about 10 minutes.

3 Fry the onion, garlic, and bell pepper gently in the oil for 5 minutes until soft but not browned. Increase the heat slightly and add the beef, chili, and cumin. Fry for 5 minutes, stirring occasionally. Remove from the heat and stir in the kidney beans. Season well.

4 Spread the tomato sauce over the dough, almost to the edge. Top with the meat mixture.

5 Top with the sliced chilies and mozzarella and sprinkle over the grated cheese. Drizzle with a little olive oil and season with salt and pepper to taste.

6 Bake in a preheated oven, at 400°F, for 18–20 minutes, or until the crust is golden. Serve immediately sprinkled with chopped parsley.

Folded-over Pizza

This recipe makes 4 large *calzones* (as these pizzas are known) or 8 small *calzones*.

NUTRITIONAL INFORMATION

Calories 402	Sugars 3g
Protein 16g	Fat 22g
Carbohydrate ...37g	Saturates 5g

  1¼ HOURS   15 MINS

SERVES 4

I N G R E D I E N T S

1 portion of Basic Pizza Dough (see
   page 421)

freshly grated Parmesan cheese, to serve

T O P P I N G

2¾ ounces mortadella or other Italian pork
   sausage, chopped

1¾ ounces Italian sausage, chopped

1¾ ounces Parmesan cheese, sliced

3½ ounces mozzarella, cut into chunks

2 tomatoes, diced

4 tablespoons fresh oregano

salt and pepper

1 Place the yeast and sugar in a measuring cup and mix with 4 tablespoons of the water. Leave the yeast mixture in a warm place for 15 minutes or until frothy.

2 Mix the flour with the salt and make a well in the center. Add the oil, yeast mixture, and remaining water. Using a wooden spoon, mix to form a dough.

3 Turn the dough out onto a floured surface and knead for 4–5 minutes or until smooth. Return the dough to the bowl, cover with an oiled sheet of plastic wrap, and leave to rise for 30 minutes or until doubled in size.

4 Knead the dough for 2 minutes and divide it into 4 pieces. Roll out each portion thinly to form rounds. Place them on an oiled cookie sheet. The dough should be no more than about ¼ inch thick because it will rise during the cooking time.

5 To make the topping, place both Italian sausages, the Parmesan, and the mozzarella on one side of each round. Top with the tomatoes and oregano. Season to taste with salt and pepper.

6 Brush around the edges of the dough with a little water then fold over the round to form a turnover shape. Squeeze the edges together to seal so that none of the filling leaks out during cooking.

7 Bake in a preheated oven, at 400°F, for 10–15 minutes or until golden. If you are making the smaller pizzas, reduce the cooking time to 8–10 minutes. Garnish with freshly grated Parmesan cheese and serve with salad greens, if desired.

English Muffin Pizzas

Toasted English muffins are topped with pineapple and prosciutto. Plain, whole wheat, or cheese muffins will all make great pizza bases.

NUTRITIONAL INFORMATION

Calories	259	Sugars	.........7g
Protein	.........9g	Fat	..........15g
Carbohydrate	...24g	Saturates	.......3g

 45 MINS   5 MINS

SERVES 4

INGREDIENTS

4 English muffins

1 quantity Tomato Sauce (see page 419)

2 sun-dried tomatoes in oil, chopped

2 ounces prosciutto

2 rings canned pineapple, chopped

½ green bell pepper, chopped

4½ ounces mozzarella cheese, sliced thinly

olive oil, for drizzling

salt and pepper

fresh basil leaves, to garnish

1 Cut the muffins in half and toast the cut side lightly.

2 Spread the tomato sauce evenly over the muffins.

3 Sprinkle the sun-dried tomatoes on top of the tomato sauce.

4 Cut the prosciutto into thin strips and place on the muffins with the pineapple and green bell pepper.

5 Carefully arrange the mozzarella slices on top.

6 Drizzle a little olive oil over each pizza, and season.

7 Place under a preheated medium broiler and cook until the cheese melts and bubbles.

8 Serve immediately garnished with small basil leaves.

COOK'S TIP

You don't have to use plain English muffins for your base; whole wheat or cheese muffins will also make ideal pizza bases. Muffins freeze well, so always keep some in the freezer for an instant pizza.

Calabrian Pizza

Traditionally, this pizza has a double layer of dough to make it robust and filling. Alternatively, it can be made as a single pizza (as shown here).

NUTRITIONAL INFORMATION

Calories 574	Sugars 6g
Protein 20g	Fat 30g
Carbohydrate ...60g	Saturates 7g

2½ HOURS   55 MINS

SERVES 6

INGREDIENTS

3½ cups all-purpose flour

½ teaspoon salt

1 envelope active dry yeast

2 tablespoons olive oil

1 cup warm water

FILLING

2 tablespoons olive oil

2 garlic cloves, crushed

1 red bell pepper, cored, deseeded, and sliced

1 yellow bell pepper, cored, deseeded, and sliced

½ cup ricotta cheese

6 ounces sun-dried tomatoes in oil, drained

3 hard-cooked eggs, sliced thinly

1 tablespoon chopped fresh mixed herbs

4½ ounces salami, cut into strips

1–1½ cups grated mozzarella

milk, to glaze

salt and pepper

1 Sift the flour and salt into a bowl and mix in the active dry yeast.

2 Add the olive oil and enough warm water to mix to a smooth, pliable dough. Knead for 10–15 minutes by hand, or process for 5 minutes in a mixer.

3 Shape the dough into a ball, place in a lightly oiled plastic bag, and put in a warm place for 1–1½ hours or until doubled in size.

4 To make the filling, heat the oil in a skillet and fry the garlic and bell peppers slowly in the oil until softened.

5 Knock back the dough and roll out half to fit the base of a 12 x 10 inch oiled roasting pan.

6 Season the dough and spread with the ricotta, then cover with sun-dried tomatoes, hard-cooked eggs, herbs, and the bell pepper mixture. Arrange the salami strips on top and sprinkle with the grated cheese.

7 Roll out the remaining dough and place over the filling, sealing the edges well, or use to make a second pizza. Leave to rise for 1 hour in a warm place. An uncovered pizza will only take about 30–40 minutes to rise.

8 Prick the double pizza with a fork about 20 times, brush the top with milk, and cook in a preheated oven, at 350°F, for about 50 minutes or until lightly browned. The uncovered pizza will take only 35–40 minutes. Serve hot.

Funny Faces Pizza

These individual pizzas have faces made from sliced vegetables and pasta. Children love pizzas and will enjoy making their own funny faces.

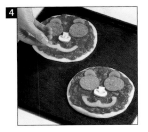

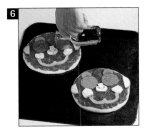

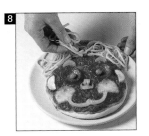

NUTRITIONAL INFORMATION

Calories 343	Sugars 5g	
Protein 10g	Fat 15g	
Carbohydrate ...45g	Saturates 2g	

2¼ HOURS   30 MINS

SERVES 4

INGREDIENTS

Bread Dough Base (see page 416)

1 ounce spaghetti or egg noodles

Tomato Sauce (see page 419)

8 slices pepperoni-style sausage

8 thin slices celery

4 slices mushrooms

4 slices yellow bell pepper

4 slices mozzarella

4 slices zucchini

olive oil, for drizzling

8 peas

1 Divide the dough into 4 pieces. Roll each piece out into a 5-inch diameter round and place on greased cookie sheets. Cover and leave to rise slightly in a warm place for about 10 minutes.

2 Cook the spaghetti or egg noodles in a pan of boiling water according to the packet instructions.

3 Divide the tomato sauce evenly between each pizza base and spread out almost to the edge.

4 To make the faces, use pepperoni slices for the main part of the eyes, celery for the eyebrows, mushrooms for the noses, and bell pepper slices for the mouths.

5 Cut the mozzarella and zucchini slices in half. Use the mozzarella cheese for the cheeks and the zucchini for the ears.

6 Drizzle a little olive oil over each pizza and bake in a preheated oven, at 400°F, for 12–15 minutes or until the edges are crisp and golden.

7 Transfer the pizzas to serving plates and place the peas in the center of the eyes.

8 Drain the spaghetti and arrange around the tops of the pizzas for hair. Serve immediately.

Avocado & Ham Pizza

A smoked ham and avocado salad is served on a pizza with a base enriched with chopped sun-dried tomatoes and black olives.

NUTRITIONAL INFORMATION

Calories	397	Sugars	.........9g
Protein	........10g	Fat	..........22g
Carbohydrate	...43g	Saturates	.......5g

2³/₄ HOURS   20 MINS

SERVES 4

I N G R E D I E N T S

Bread Dough Base (see page 416)

4 sun-dried tomatoes, chopped

¼ cup black olives, chopped

Special Tomato Sauce (see page 420)

4 small endive leaves, shredded

4 small radicchio leaves, shredded

1 avocado, peeled, pitted, and sliced

2 ounces wafer-thin smoked ham

2 ounces blue cheese, cut into small pieces

olive oil, for drizzling

salt and pepper

chopped fresh chervil, to garnish

1 Make the dough according to the instructions on page 416. Knead the dough gently with the sun-dried tomatoes and olives until well mixed.

2 Roll out or press the dough, using a rolling pin or your hands, into a 10-inch round on a lightly floured counter. Place on a greased cookie sheet or pizza pan and push up the edge a little to form a rim.

3 Cover the dough and leave to rise slightly in a warm place for 10 minutes. Spread the tomato sauce almost to the edge of the pizza base.

4 Top the pizza with shredded lettuce leaves and avocado slices. Scrunch up the ham and add together with the blue cheese.

5 Drizzle with a little olive oil and season with salt and pepper to taste.

6 Bake in a preheated oven, at 400°F, for 18–20 minutes, or until the edge is crisp and a golden brown color.

7 Sprinkle with chervil to garnish and serve immediately.

Creamy Ham & Cheese Pizza

This traditional pizza uses a pastry case and Béchamel Sauce to make a type of savory flan. Grating the pastry gives it a lovely nutty texture.

NUTRITIONAL INFORMATION

Calories	628	Sugars	........5g
Protein	........19g	Fat	.........47g
Carbohydrate	...35g	Saturates	......16g

20 MINS   40 MINS

SERVES 4

I N G R E D I E N T S

9 ounces flaky pastry, well chilled

3 tablespoons butter

1 red onion, chopped

1 garlic clove, chopped

⅓ cup flour

1¼ cups milk

⅔ cup grated Parmesan cheese, plus
extra for sprinkling

2 eggs, hard-cooked, cut
into quarters

3½ ounces Italian pork sausage, such as
feline salame, cut into strips

salt and pepper

sprigs of fresh thyme, to garnish

1 Fold the pastry in half and grate it into 4 individual flan pans, measuring 4 inches across. Using a floured fork, press the pastry flakes down so they are even, there are no holes and the pastry comes up the sides of the pan.

2 Line with foil and bake blind in a preheated oven, at 425°F, for 10 minutes. Reduce the heat to 400°F, remove the foil and cook for 15 minutes or until golden and set.

3 Heat the butter in a pan. Add the onion and garlic and cook for 5–6 minutes or until softened.

4 Add the flour, stirring well to coat the onions. Gradually stir in the milk to make a thick sauce.

5 Season the sauce with salt and pepper to taste and then stir in the Parmesan cheese. Do not reheat once the cheese has been added or the sauce will become too stringy.

6 Spread the sauce over the pastry cases. Decorate with the egg and strips of sausage.

7 Sprinkle with a little extra Parmesan cheese, return to the oven, and bake for 5 minutes, just to heat through.

8 Serve immediately, garnished with sprigs of fresh thyme.

COOK'S TIP

This pizza is just as good cold, but do not prepare it too far in advance as the pastry will turn soggy.

Spicy Meatball Pizza

Small ground beef meatballs, spiced with chilies and cumin seeds, are baked on a biscuit base.

NUTRITIONAL INFORMATION

Calories 568   Sugars 5g
Protein . . . . .24g   Fat 37g
Carbohydrate . . .38g   Saturates 15g

2¼ HOURS   25 MINS

SERVES 4

I N G R E D I E N T S

8 ounces ground lean beef

3 jalapeño chilies in brine, chopped

1 teaspoon cumin seeds

1 tablespoon chopped fresh parsley

1 tablespoon beaten egg

3 tablespoons olive oil

Biscuit Base (see page 417)

Tomato Sauce (see page 419)

1 ounces canned pimento, sliced

2 slices bacon, cut into strips

½ cup grated sharp Cheddar

olive oil, for drizzling

salt and pepper

chopped fresh parsley, to garnish

1 Mix the beef, chilies, cumin seeds, parsley, and egg together in a bowl and season. Form into 12 small meatballs. Cover and chill for 1 hour.

2 Heat the oil in a large skillet. Add the meatballs and brown all over. Remove with a perforated spoon or fish slice and drain on paper towels.

3 Roll out or press the dough into a 10-inch round on a lightly floured work surface. Place on a greased cookie sheet or pizza pan and push up the edge slightly to form a rim. Spread with the tomato sauce, almost to the edge.

4 Arrange the meatballs on the pizza with the pimento and bacon. Sprinkle over the cheese and drizzle with a little olive oil. Season with salt and pepper.

5 Bake in a preheated oven, at 400°F, for 18–20 minutes, or until the edge is crisp and a golden brown color.

6 Serve immediately, garnished with chopped parsley.

Mini Pita Bread Pizzas

Smoked salmon and asparagus make extra special party pizza canapés.
Mini pita breads make great bases and are really quick to cook.

NUTRITIONAL INFORMATION

Calories	...518	Sugars	...10g
Protein	...21g	Fat	...12g
Carbohydrate	...87g	Saturates	...4g

55 MINS   15 MINS

SERVES 4

INGREDIENTS

8 thin asparagus spears

16 mini pita breads

1 quantity Special Tomato Sauce (see
   page 420)

¼ cup grated mild Cheddar cheese

2 tablespoons ricotta cheese

2 ounces smoked salmon

olive oil, for drizzling

pepper

1 Cut the asparagus spears into 1-inch lengths; then cut each piece in half lengthwise.

2 Blanch the asparagus in a saucepan of boiling water for 1 minute. Drain the asparagus, plunge into cold water, and drain again.

3 Place the pita breads onto 2 cookie sheets. Spread about 1 teaspoon of tomato sauce on each pita bread.

4 Mix the cheeses together and divide between the 16 pita breads.

5 Cut the smoked salmon into 16 long thin strips. Arrange one strip on each pita bread with the asparagus spears.

6 Drizzle over a little olive oil and season with pepper to taste.

7 Bake in a preheated oven, at 400°F, for 8–10 minutes. Serve immediately.

COOK'S TIP

Smoked salmon is expensive, so for a cheaper version, use smoked trout. It is often half the price of smoked salmon, and tastes just as good. Try experimenting with other smoked fish, such as smoked mackerel, with its strong, distinctive flavor, for a bit of variety.

Chicken & Peanut Pizza

This pizza is topped with chicken which has been marinated in a delicious peanut sauce.

NUTRITIONAL INFORMATION

Calories 418	Sugars 7g
Protein 22g	Fat 19g
Carbohydrate . . .43g	Saturates 5g

  2³/₄ HOURS   20 MINS

SERVES 4

I N G R E D I E N T S

2 tablespoons crunchy peanut butter

1 tablespoon lime juice

1 tablespoon soy sauce

3 tablespoons milk

1 red chili, deseeded
    and chopped

1 garlic clove, crushed

6 ounces cooked chicken, diced

1 quantity Bread Dough Base (see
    page 416)

1 quantity Special Tomato Sauce (see
    page 420)

4 green onions, trimmed and chopped

½ cup grated mozzarella cheese

olive oil, for drizzling

salt and pepper

1 Mix together the peanut butter, lime juice, soy sauce, milk, chili, and garlic in a bowl to form a sauce. Season well.

2 Add the chicken to the peanut sauce and stir until well coated. Cover and leave to marinate in a cool place for about 20 minutes.

3 Roll out or press the dough, using a rolling pin or your hands, into a 10-inch round on a lightly floured counter. Place on a large greased cookie sheet or pizza pan and push up the edge a little. Cover and leave to rise slightly for 10 minutes in a warm place.

4 When the dough has risen, spread the tomato sauce over the base, almost to the edge.

5 Top with the green onions and chicken pieces, spooning over the peanut sauce.

6 Sprinkle over the cheese. Drizzle with a little olive oil and season well. Bake in a preheated oven, at 400°F, for 18–20 minutes, or until the crust is golden. Serve at once.

Cheese & Potato Braid

This bread has a delicious cheese, garlic, and rosemary flavor, and is best eaten straight from the oven. This recipe makes a 1-pound loaf.

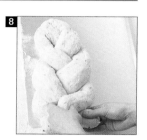

NUTRITIONAL INFORMATION

Calories 724	Sugars 4g	
Protein 22g	Fat 10g	
Carbohydrate ..147g	Saturates 4g	

 2½ HOURS 40 MINS

SERVES 4

INGREDIENTS

6 ounces russet potatoes, diced

2 x ¼ ounce envelopes active dry yeast

6 cups white bread flour

1 tablespoon salt

2 cups vegetable stock

2 garlic cloves, crushed

2 tablespoons chopped fresh rosemary

1 cup grated Swiss cheese

1 tablespoon vegetable oil

1 Lightly grease and flour a cookie sheet.

2 Cook the potatoes in a saucepan of boiling water for 10 minutes or until soft. Drain and mash the potatoes.

3 Transfer the mashed potatoes to a large mixing bowl.

4 Stir the yeast, flour, salt and stock into the mashed potatoes and mix to form a smooth dough.

5 Add the garlic, rosemary and ¾ cup of the cheese and knead the dough for 5 minutes. Make a hollow in the dough, pour in the oil, and knead the dough.

6 Cover the dough and leave it to rise in a warm place for 1½ hours or until doubled in size.

7 Knead the dough again and divide it into 3 equal portions. Roll each portion into a 14-inch sausage shape.

8 Pressing one end of each of the sausage shapes together, braid the dough and fold the remaining ends underneath. Place the braid on the cookie sheet, cover and leave to rise for 30 minutes.

9 Sprinkle the remaining cheese over the top of the braid and bake in a preheated oven, at 375°F, for 40 minutes or until the base of the loaf sounds hollow when tapped. Serve warm.

VARIATION

Instead of making a braid, use the mixture to make a batch of cheesey rolls which would be ideal to serve with hot soup.

Roman Focaccia

Roman focaccia makes a delicious snack on its own or serve it with cured meats and salad for a quick supper.

NUTRITIONAL INFORMATION

Calories 119	Sugars 2g	
Protein 3g	Fat 2g	
Carbohydrate . . .24g	Saturates 0.3g	

1 HOUR   45 MINS

Makes 16 squares

I N G R E D I E N T S

¼ ounce dried yeast

1 teaspoon sugar

1¼ cups hot water

4 cups white flour

2 teaspoons salt

3 tablespoons rosemary, chopped

2 tablespoons olive oil

1 pound mixed red and white onions,

sliced into rings

4 garlic cloves, sliced

1 Place the yeast and the sugar in a small bowl and mix with 8 tablespoons of the water. Leave to ferment in a warm place for 15 minutes.

2 Mix the flour with the salt in a large bowl. Add the yeast mixture, half of the rosemary, and the remaining water and mix to form a smooth dough. Knead the dough for 4 minutes.

3 Cover the dough with oiled plastic wrap and leave to rise for 30 minutes or until doubled in size.

4 Meanwhile, heat the oil in a large pan. Add the onions and garlic and fry for 5 minutes or until softened. Cover the pan and continue to cook for 7–8 minutes or until the onions are lightly caramelized.

5 Remove the dough from the bowl and knead it again for 1–2 minutes.

6 Roll the dough out to form a square shape. The dough should be no more than ¼ inch thick because it will rise during cooking. Place the dough onto a large cookie sheet, pushing out the edges until even.

7 Spread the onions over the dough, and sprinkle with the remaining rosemary.

8 Bake in a preheated oven, at 400°F, for 25–30 minutes or until a golden brown color. Cut the focaccia into 16 squares and serve immediately.

Mini Focaccia

This is a delicious Italian bread made with olive oil. The topping of red onions and thyme is particularly flavorful.

NUTRITIONAL INFORMATION

Calories 439	Sugars 3g	
Protein 9g	Fat 15g	
Carbohydrate 71g	Saturates 2g	

🍲 2¼ HOURS 🕐 25 MINS

SERVES 4

INGREDIENTS

3 cups white flour

½ teaspoon salt

1 envelope active dry yeast

2 tablespoons olive oil

generous 1 cup tepid water

1 cup green or black olives, halved

TOPPING

2 red onions, sliced

2 tablespoons olive oil

1 teaspoon sea salt

1 tablespoon thyme leaves

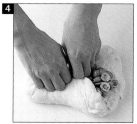  

1 Lightly oil several cookie sheets. Sift the flour and salt into a large mixing bowl, then stir in the yeast. Pour in the olive oil and tepid water and mix everything together to form a dough.

2 Turn the dough out onto a lightly floured surface and knead it for about 5 minutes (alternatively, use an electric mixer with a dough hook and knead for 7–8 minutes).

3 Place the dough in a greased bowl, cover, and leave in a warm place for about 1–1½ hours or until it has doubled in size. Punch down the dough by kneading it again for 1-2 minutes.

4 Knead half of the olives into the dough. Divide the dough into quarters and then shape the quarters into rounds. Place them on the cookie sheets and push your fingers into the dough to achieve a dimpled effect.

5 To make the topping, sprinkle the red onions and remaining olives over the rounds. Drizzle the oil over the top and sprinkle with the sea salt and thyme leaves. Cover and leave to rise for 30 minutes.

6 Bake in a preheated oven, at 375°F, for 20-25 minutes or until the focaccia are golden.

7 Transfer to a wire rack and leave to cool before serving.

VARIATION

Use this quantity of dough to make 1 large focaccia, if you prefer.

Italian Bruschetta

It is important to use a good quality olive oil for this recipe. Serve the bruschetta with kabobs or fish for a really summery taste.

NUTRITIONAL INFORMATION	
Calories 415	Sugars 2g
Protein 8g	Fat 24g
Carbohydrate . . .45g	Saturates 4g

 10 MINS   10 MINS

Makes 1 loaf

I N G R E D I E N T S

1 ciabatta loaf or baguette

1 plump clove garlic

extra virgin olive oil

fresh Parmesan cheese, grated (optional)

1 Slice the bread in half crosswise and again lengthwise to give 4 portions.

2 Do not peel the garlic clove, but cut it in half.

3 Barbecue the bread over hot coals for 2–3 minutes on both sides or until golden brown.

4 Rub the garlic, cut side down, all over the toasted surface of the bread.

COOK'S TIP

As ready-grated Parmesan quickly loses its pungency and bite, it is better to buy small quantities of the cheese in one piece and grate it yourself as needed. Tightly wrapped in plastic wrap or foil, it will keep in the refrigerator for several months.

 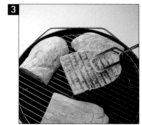 

5 Drizzle the olive oil over the bread and serve hot as an accompaniment.

6 If using Parmesan cheese, sprinkle the cheese over the bread.

7 Return the bread to the barbecue , cut side up, for 1–2 minutes or until the cheese just begins to melt. Serve hot.

Roasted Bell Pepper Bread

Bell peppers become sweet and mild when they are roasted and make this bread delicious.

NUTRITIONAL INFORMATION

Calories 426	Sugars 4g	
Protein 12g	Fat 4g	
Carbohydrate ...90g	Saturates 1g	

 1¾ HOURS   1 HR 5 MINS

SERVES 4

INGREDIENTS

1 red bell pepper, halved and deseeded

1 yellow bell pepper, halved and deseeded

2 sprigs of rosemary

1 tablespoon olive oil

¼ ounce active dry yeast

1 teaspoon sugar

1¼ cups hand-hot water

4 cups white flour

1 teaspoon salt

1 Grease a 9-inch deep round cake pan.

2 Place the bell peppers and rosemary in a shallow roasting pan. Pour over the oil and roast in a preheated oven, at 400°F, for 20 minutes or until slightly charred. Remove the skin from the bell peppers and cut the flesh into slices.

3 Place the yeast and sugar in a small bowl and mix with 8 tablespoons of hand-hot water. Leave to ferment in a warm place for 15 minutes.

4 Mix the flour and salt together in a large bowl. Stir in the yeast mixture and the remaining water and mix to form a smooth dough.

5 Knead the dough for about 5 minutes until smooth. Cover with oiled plastic wrap and leave to rise for about 30 minutes or until doubled in size.

6 Cut the dough into 3 equal portions. Roll the portions into rounds slightly larger than the cake pan.

7 Place 1 round in the base of the pan so that it reaches up the sides of the pan by about ¾ inch. Top with half of the bell pepper mixture.

8 Place the second round of dough on top, followed by the remaining bell pepper mixture. Place the last round of dough on top, pushing the edges of the dough down the sides of the pan.

9 Cover the dough with oiled plastic wrap and leave to rise for 30–40 minutes. Return to the oven and bake for 45 minutes until golden or the base sounds hollow when lightly tapped. Serve warm.

Olive Oil Bread with Cheese

This flat cheese bread is sometimes called *focaccia*. It is delicious served with *antipasto* or simply on its own. This recipe makes one loaf.

NUTRITIONAL INFORMATION

Calories 586   Sugars 3g
Protein . . . . .22g   Fat 26g
Carbohydrate . . .69g   Saturates 12g

1 HOUR   30 MINS

SERVES 4

I N G R E D I E N T S

½ ounces active dry yeast

1 teaspoon sugar

1 cup hot water

3 cups flour

1 teaspoon salt

3 tablespoons olive oil

7 ounces Romano cheese, cubed

½ tablespoons fennel seeds, lightly crushed

1 Mix the yeast with the sugar and 8 tablespoons of the water. Leave to ferment in a warm place for about 15 minutes.

2 Mix the flour with the salt. Add 1 tablespoon of the oil, the yeast mixture, and the remaining water to form a smooth dough. Knead the dough for 4 minutes.

COOK'S TIP

Romano is a hard, quite salty cheese, which is sold in most large supermarkets and Italian delicatessens. If you cannot obtain Romano, use strong Cheddar or Parmesan cheese instead.

3 Divide the dough into 2 equal portions. Roll out each portion to a form a round ¼ inch thick. Place 1 round on a cookie sheet.

4 Scatter the cheese and half of the fennel seeds evenly over the round.

5 Place the second round on top and squeeze the edges together to seal so that the filling does not leak during the cooking time.

6 Using a sharp knife, make a few slashes in the top of the dough and brush with the remaining olive oil.

7 Sprinkle with the remaining fennel seeds and leave the dough to rise for 20–30 minutes.

8 Bake in a preheated oven, at 400°F, for 30 minutes or until golden brown. Serve immediately.

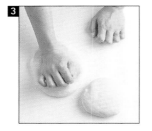

Sun-dried Tomato Loaf

This delicious tomato bread is great with cheese or soup or to make an unusual sandwich. This recipe makes one loaf.

NUTRITIONAL INFORMATION

Calories 403   Sugars 5g
Protein ....12g   Fat 2g
Carbohydrate ...91g   Saturates 0.3g

 1¼ HOURS   35 MINS

SERVES 4

I N G R E D I E N T S

¼ ounce active dry yeast

1 teaspoon sugar

1¼ cups hot water

1 teaspoon salt

2 teaspoons dried basil

4 cups white flour

2 tablespoons sun-dried tomato paste or tomato paste

12 sun-dried tomatoes, cut into strips

 1 Place the yeast and sugar in a bowl and mix with 8 tablespoons of the water. Leave to ferment in a warm place for 15 minutes.

2 Place the flour in a bowl and stir in the salt. Make a well in the dry ingredients and add the basil, the yeast mixture, tomato paste, and half of the remaining water. Using a wooden spoon, draw the flour into the liquid and mix to form a dough, adding the rest of the water gradually.

3 Turn out the dough onto a floured surface and knead for 5 minutes or until smooth. Cover with oiled plastic wrap and leave in a warm place to rise for about 30 minutes or until doubled in size.

4 Lightly grease a 2-pound loaf pan.

5 Remove the dough from the bowl and knead in the sun-dried tomatoes. Knead again for 2–3 minutes.

6 Place the dough in the pan and leave to rise for 30–40 minutes or until it has doubled in size again. Bake in a preheated oven, at 375°F, for 30–35 minutes or until golden and the base sounds hollow when tapped.

COOK'S TIP

You could make mini sun-dried tomato loaves for children. Divide the dough into 8 equal portions, leave to rise, and bake in mini-loaf pans for 20 minutes. Alternatively, make 12 small rounds, leave to rise and bake as rolls for 12–15 minutes.

Sun-dried Tomato Rolls

These white rolls have the addition of finely chopped sun-dried tomatoes.
The tomatoes are sold in jars and are available at most supermarkets.

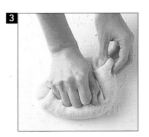

NUTRITIONAL INFORMATION

Calories 214	Sugars 1g
Protein 5g	Fat 12g
Carbohydrate . . .22g	Saturates 7g

2¼ HOURS   15 MINS

SERVES 8

I N G R E D I E N T S

2 cups white bread flour

½ teaspoon salt

1 envelope active dry yeast

7 tablespoons butter, melted and
   cooled slightly

3 tablespoons milk, warmed

2 eggs, beaten

¾ cup sun-dried tomatoes, well
   drained and chopped finely

milk, for brushing

1 Lightly grease a cookie sheet.

2 Sift the flour and salt into a large mixing bowl. Stir in the yeast, then pour in the butter, milk, and eggs. Mix together to form a dough.

VARIATION

Add some finely chopped anchovies or olives to the dough in step 5 for extra flavor.

3 Turn the dough onto a lightly floured surface and knead for about 5 minutes (alternatively, use an electric mixer with a dough hook).

4 Place the dough in a greased bowl, cover, and leave to rise in a warm place for 1-1½ hours or until the dough has doubled in size. Punch down the dough for 2–3 minutes.

5 Knead the sun-dried tomatoes into the dough, sprinkling the counter with extra flour as the tomatoes are quite oily.

6 Divide the dough into 8 balls and place them on the cookie sheet. Cover and leave to rise for about 30 minutes or until the rolls have doubled in size.

7 Brush the rolls with milk and bake in a preheated oven, at 450°F, for 10-15 minutes or until the rolls are golden brown.

8 Transfer the rolls to a wire rack and leave to cool slightly before serving.

Garlic Bread

A perennial favorite, garlic bread is perfect with a range of barbecue meals and excellent with soups.

NUTRITIONAL INFORMATION

Calories	261	Sugars	.........1g
Protein	.........3g	Fat	..........22g
Carbohydrate	...15g	Saturates	......14g

10 MINS   15 MINS

SERVES 6

I N G R E D I E N T S

11 tablespoons butter, softened

3 cloves garlic, crushed

2 tablespoons chopped, fresh parsley

pepper

1 large or 2 small baguettes

1   Mix together the butter, garlic, and parsley in a bowl until well combined. Season with pepper to taste and mix well.

2   Cut the small baguettes into thick slices.

3   Spread the flavored butter over one side of each slice and reassemble the loaf on a large sheet of thick kitchen foil.

4   Wrap the bread well and barbecue over hot coals for 10–15 minutes until the butter melts and the bread is piping hot.

5   Serve as an accompaniment to a wide range of dishes.

Desserts

The Italians love their desserts, but when there is an important gathering or celebration, then an extra special effort is made and a wide range of exquisite delicacies appear. The Sicilians are said to have the sweetest tooth of all, and many Italian desserts are thought to have originated there. Indeed, you have to go a very long way to

beat a Sicilian ice cream—they truly are the best in the world! Fresh fruit also features in many Italian desserts—oranges are often peeled and served whole, marinated in a fragrant syrup and liqueur. Chocolate, too, is very popular in Italy—try the different varieties of the classic Tiramisu that are included in this chapter. Whatever your dessert preference, there is sure to be at least one Italian dessert to tempt and satisfy you—you'll never be disappointed!

Tuscan Pudding

These baked mini-ricotta puddings are delicious served warm or chilled and will keep in the refrigerator for 3–4 days.

NUTRITIONAL INFORMATION

Calories 293   Sugars 28g
Protein . . . . .9g   Fat 17g
Carbohydrate . . .28g   Saturates 9g

 20 MINS   15 MINS

SERVES 4

I N G R E D I E N T S

1 tablespoon butter

½ cup mixed dried fruit

1 cup ricotta cheese

3 egg yolks

¼ cup sugar

1 teaspoon cinnamon

finely grated rind of 1 orange,
    plus extra to decorate

crème fraîche (see Cook's Tip), to serve

1 Lightly grease 4 mini pudding bowls or ramekin dishes with the butter.

2 Put the dried fruit in a bowl and cover with warm water. Leave to soak for 10 minutes.

COOK'S TIP

Crème fraîche has a slightly sour, nutty taste and is very thick. It is suitable for cooking, but has the same fat content as heavy cream. It can be made by stirring cultured buttermilk into heavy cream and refrigerating overnight.

3 Beat the ricotta cheese with the egg yolks in a bowl. Stir in the superfine sugar, cinnamon, and orange rind and mix to combine.

4 Drain the dried fruit in a strainer set over a bowl. Mix the drained fruit with the ricotta cheese mixture.

5 Spoon the mixture into the bowls or ramekin dishes.

6 Bake in a preheated oven, at 350°F, for 15 minutes. The tops should be firm to the touch but not brown.

7 Decorate the puddings with grated orange rind. Serve warm or chilled decorated with crème fraîche if liked.

Tiramisu Layers

This is a modern version of the well-known and very traditional chocolate dessert from Italy.

NUTRITIONAL INFORMATION

Calories	798	Sugars	........60g
Protein	........12g	Fat	.........50g
Carbohydrate	...76g	Saturates	......25g

 1¼ HOURS   5 MINS

SERVES 6

I N G R E D I E N T S

10½ ounces dark chocolate

1¾ cups mascarpone cheese

⅔ cup heavy cream, whipped until
   it just holds its shape

1¾ cups black coffee with
   ¼ cup sugar, cooled

6 tablespoons dark rum or brandy

36 ladyfingers,
   about 14 ounces

unsweetened cocoa, to dust

1 Melt the chocolate in a bowl set over a saucepan of simmering water, stirring occasionally. Leave the chocolate to cool slightly, then stir it into the mascarpone and cream.

2 Mix the coffee and rum together in a bowl. Dip the ladyfingers into the mixture briefly so that they absorb the coffee and rum liquid, but they do not become soggy.

3 Place 3 ladyfingers on to 3 serving plates.

4 Spoon a layer of the mascarpone and chocolate mixture over the ladyfingers.

5 Place 3 more ladyfingers on top of the mascarpone layer. Spread another layer of mascarpone and chocolate mixture, and place 3 more ladyfingers on top.

6 Leave the tiramisu to chill in the refrigerator for at least 1 hour. Dust all over with a little unsweetened cocoa just before serving.

VARIATION

Try adding ½ cup toasted, chopped hazelnuts to the chocolate cream mixture in step 1, if you prefer.

Orange & Almond Cake

This light and tangy citrus cake from Sicily is better eaten as a dessert than as a cake. It is especially good served after a large meal.

NUTRITIONAL INFORMATION

Calories ....399 Sugars 20g
Protein ....8g Fat 31g
Carbohydrate ...23g Saturates 13g

30 MINS   40 MINS

SERVES 8

INGREDIENTS

4 eggs, separated

¾ cup sugar, plus

2 teaspoons for the cream

finely grated rind and juice of 2 oranges

finely grated rind and juice of 1 lemon

1 cup ground almonds

¼ cup self-rising flour

¾ cup light cream

1 teaspoon cinnamon

¼ cup slivered almonds, toasted

icing sugar, to dust

1 Grease and line the base of a 7-inch round deep cake pan.

2 Blend the egg yolks with the sugar until the mixture is thick and creamy. Whisk half of the orange rind and all of the lemon rind into the egg yolks.

VARIATION

You could serve this cake with a syrup. Boil the juice and finely grated rind of 2 oranges, ⅓ cup superfine sugar and 2 tablespoons of water for 5–6 minutes until slightly thickened. Stir in 1 tablespoon of orange liqueur just before serving.

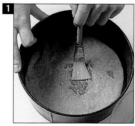

3 Mix the juice from both oranges and the lemon with the ground almonds and stir into the egg yolks. The mixture will become quite runny at this point. Fold in the flour.

4 Whisk the egg whites until stiff and gently fold into the egg yolk mixture.

5 Pour the mixture into the pan and bake in a preheated oven, at 350°F, for 35–40 minutes, or until golden and

springy to the touch. Leave to cool in the pan for 10 minutes and then turn out. It is likely to sink slightly at this stage.

6 Whip the cream to form soft peaks. Stir in the remaining orange rind, cinnamon, and sugar.

7 Once the cake is cold, cover with the almonds, dust with icing sugar, and serve with the cream.

Panforte di Siena

This famous Tuscan honey and nut cake is a Christmas specialty. In Italy it is sold in pretty boxes, and served in very thin slices.

NUTRITIONAL INFORMATION

Calories	257	Sugars	........29g
Protein	.........5g	Fat	..........13g
Carbohydrate	...33g	Saturates	.......1g

 10 MINS 1¼ HOURS

SERVES 12

INGREDIENTS

1 cup split whole almonds

1 cup hazelnuts

½ cup cut mixed peel

⅓ cup dried apricots

2 ounces glacé or crystallized pineapple

grated rind of 1 large orange

½ cup all-purpose flour

2 tablespoons unsweetened cocoa

2 teaspoons ground cinnamon

½ cup sugar

½ cup honey

icing sugar, for dredging

1 Toast the almonds under the broiler until lightly browned and place in a bowl.

2 Toast the hazelnuts until the skins split. Place on a dry dish cloth and rub off the skins. Roughly chop the hazelnuts and add to the almonds with the mixed peel.

3 Chop the apricots and pineapple fairly finely, add to the nuts with the orange rind and mix well.

4 Sift the flour with the cocoa and cinnamon, add to the nut mixture; mix.

5 Line a round 8-inch cake pan or deep loose-based flan pan with baking parchment.

6 Put the sugar and honey into a saucepan and heat until the sugar dissolves, then boil gently for about 5 minutes or until the mixture thickens and begins to turn a deeper shade of brown. Quickly add to the nut mixture and mix evenly. Turn into the prepared pan and level the top using the back of a damp spoon.

7 Cook in a preheated oven, at 300°F, for 1 hour. Remove from the oven and leave in the pan until cold. Take out of the pan and carefully peel off the paper. Before serving, dredge the cake heavily with sifted icing sugar. Serve in very thin slices.

Pear Cake

This is a really moist cake, deliciously flavored with chopped pears and cinnamon.

NUTRITIONAL INFORMATION

Calories 119	Sugars 16g
Protein 2g	Fat 0.3g
Carbohydrate . . .29g	Saturates 0g

🥧 25 MINS 🕐 1½ HOURS

SERVES 12

INGREDIENTS

4 pears, peeled and cored

margarine, for greasing

2 tablespoons water

1½ cups all-purpose flour

2 teaspoons baking powder

½ cup soft light brown sugar

4 tablespoons milk

2 tablespoons liquid honey and extra to pour

2 teaspoons ground cinnamon

2 egg whites

1 Grease and line the base of an 8-inch cake pan.

2 Put 1 pear in a food processor with the water and blend until almost smooth. Transfer to a mixing bowl.

3 Sift in the all-purpose flour and baking powder. Beat in the sugar, milk, honey, and cinnamon and mix well.

4 Chop all but one of the remaining pears and add to the mixture.

5 Whisk the egg whites until peaking and gently fold into the mixture until fully blended.

6 Slice the remaining pear and arrange in a fan pattern on the base of the pan.

7 Spoon the cake mixture into the pan and cook in a preheated oven, at 300°F, for 1¼–1½ hours or until cooked through.

8 Remove the cake from the oven and leave to cool in the pan for 10 minutes.

9 Turn the cake out on to a wire cooling rack and drizzle with honey. Leave to cool completely, then cut into slices to serve.

COOK'S TIP

To test if the cake is cooked through, insert a toothpick into the center—if it comes out clean the cake is cooked. If not, return the cake to the oven and test at frequent intervals.

Pear & Ginger Cake

This deliciously buttery pear and ginger cake is ideal for coffee time or you can serve it with cream for a delicious dessert.

NUTRITIONAL INFORMATION

Calories . . . . .531 Sugars 41g
Protein . . . . .6g Fat 30g
Carbohydrate . . .62g Saturates 19g

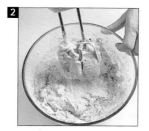

 15 MINS   40 MINS

SERVES 6

I N G R E D I E N T S

14 tablespoons butter, softened

1 cup sugar

1½ cups self-rising flour, sifted

1 tablespoon ginger

3 eggs, beaten

1 pound pears, peeled, cored and
    thinly sliced

1 tablespoon soft brown sugar

1 Lightly grease and line the base of a deep 8-inch cake pan.

2 Using a whisk, combine ¾ cup of the butter with the sugar, flour, ginger, and eggs and mix to form a smooth consistency.

3 Spoon the cake mixture into the prepared pan, leveling out the surface.

4 Arrange the pear slices over the cake mixture. Sprinkle with the brown sugar and dot with the remaining butter.

5 Bake in a preheated oven, at 350°F, for 35–40 minutes or until the cake is golden and feels springy to the touch.

6 Serve the pear and ginger cake warm, with ice cream or cream, if you wish.

COOK'S TIP

Soft brown sugar is sometimes known as Barbados sugar. It is a darker form of light brown soft sugar.

Italian Bread Pudding

This deliciously rich pudding is cooked with cream and apples and is delicately flavored with orange.

45 MINS   25 MINS

SERVES 4

I N G R E D I E N T S

1 tablespoon butter

2 small apples, peeled, cored and
sliced into rings

⅓ cup sugar

2 tablespoons white wine

3½ ounces bread, sliced with crusts
    removed (slightly stale French baguette
    is ideal)

1¼ cups light cream

2 eggs, beaten

pared rind of 1 orange, cut into matchsticks

1 Lightly grease a 5-cup deep ovenproof dish with the butter.

2 Arrange the apple rings in the base of the dish. Sprinkle half of the sugar over the apples.

3 Pour the wine over the apples. Add the bread slices, pushing them down with your hands to flatten them slightly.

4 Mix the cream with the eggs, the remaining sugar and the orange rind and pour the mixture over the bread. Leave to soak for 30 minutes.

5 Bake the pudding in a preheated oven, at 350°F, for 25 minutes until golden and set. Serve warm.

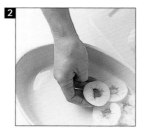

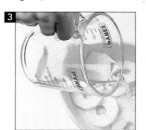

VARIATION

For a variation, try adding dried fruit, such as apricots, cherries, or dates, to the pudding, if you prefer.

Baked Sweet Ravioli

These scrumptious little parcels are the perfect dessert for anyone with a really sweet tooth.

NUTRITIONAL INFORMATION

Calories 765	Sugars 56g	
Protein 16g	Fat 30g	
Carbohydrate . . .114g	Saturates 15g	

1½ HOURS   20 MINS

SERVES 4

INGREDIENTS

PASTA

3¾ cups all-purpose flour

10 tablespoons butter, plus extra
for greasing

¾ cup sugar

4 eggs

1 ounce yeast

1 cup warm milk

FILLING

⅔ cup chestnut purée

½ cup unsweetened cocoa

¼ cup sugar

½ cup chopped almonds

1 cup crushed amaretti cookies

⅔ cup orange marmalade

1 To make the sweet pasta dough, sift the flour into a mixing bowl, then mix in the butter, sugar, and 3 eggs.

2 Mix together the yeast and warm milk in a small bowl and when thoroughly combined, mix into the dough.

3 Knead the dough for 20 minutes, cover with a clean cloth, and set aside in a warm place for 1 hour to rise.

4 Mix together the chestnut purée, unsweetened cocoa, sugar, almonds, crushed amaretti cookies, and orange marmalade in a separate bowl.

5 Grease a cookie sheet with butter.

6 Lightly flour the counter. Roll out the pasta dough into a thin sheet and cut into 2-inch rounds with a plain cookie cutter.

7 Put a spoonful of filling onto each round and then fold in half, pressing the edges to seal. Arrange on the prepared cookie sheet, spacing the ravioli out well.

8 Beat the remaining egg and brush all over the ravioli to glaze. Bake in a preheated oven, at 350°F, for 20 minutes. Serve hot.

Mascarpone Cheesecake

The mascarpone gives this baked cheesecake a wonderfully tangy flavor. Ricotta cheese could be used as an alternative.

NUTRITIONAL INFORMATION

Calories . . . . . . .327 Sugars 25g
Protein . . . . .9g Fat 18g
Carbohydrate . . .33g Saturates 11g

15 MINS   50 MINS

SERVES 8

INGREDIENTS

1½ tablespoons butter

5½ ounces ginger snaps, crushed

2 tablespoons chopped candied ginger

1 pound 2 ounces mascarpone cheese

finely grated rind and juice of 2 lemons

½ cup sugar

2 large eggs, separated

fruit coulis (see Cook's Tip),
   to serve

1 Grease and line the base of a 10-inch spring-form cake pan or loose-bottomed pan.

2 Melt the butter in a pan and stir in the crushed cookies and chopped ginger. Use the mixture to line the pan, pressing the mixture about ¼ inch up the sides.

COOK'S TIP

Fruit coulis can be made by cooking 14 ounces fruit, such as blueberries, for 5 minutes with 2 tablespoons of water. Strain the mixture, then stir in 1 tablespoon (or more to taste) of sifted icing sugar. Leave to cool before serving.

3 Beat together the cheese, lemon rind and juice, sugar, and egg yolks until quite smooth.

4 Whisk the egg whites until they are stiff and fold into the cheese and lemon mixture.

5 Pour the mixture into the pan and bake in a preheated oven, at 350°F, for 35–45 minutes until just set. Don't worry if it cracks or sinks—this is quite normal.

6 Leave the cheesecake in the pan to cool. Serve with fruit coulis (see Cook's Tip).

Zabaglione

This well-known dish is really a light but rich egg mousse flavored with Marsala.

NUTRITIONAL INFORMATION

Calories 158	Sugars 29g	
Protein 1g	Fat 1g	
Carbohydrate ...29g	Saturates 0.2g	

5 MINS   15 MINS

SERVES 4

I N G R E D I E N T S

5 egg yolks

½ cup sugar

⅔ cup Marsala or
  sweet sherry

amaretti cookies, to serve
  (optional)

1 Place the egg yolks in a large mixing bowl.

2 Add the sugar to the egg yolks and whisk until the mixture is thick and very pale and has doubled in volume.

3 Place the bowl containing the egg yolk and sugar mixture over a saucepan of gently simmering water.

4 Add the Marsala or sherry to the egg yolk and sugar mixture and continue whisking until the foam mixture becomes warm. This process may take as long as 10 minutes.

5 Pour the mixture, which should be frothy and light, into 4 wine glasses.

6 Serve the zabaglione warm with fresh fruit or amaretti cookies, if you wish.

Chocolate Zabaglione

As this recipe only uses a little chocolate, choose one with a minimum of 70 percent cocoa solids for a good flavor.

NUTRITIONAL INFORMATION

Calories	224	Sugars	.......23g
Protein	.........4g	Fat	..........10g
Carbohydrate	...23g	Saturates	.......4g

🧈 10 MINS   🕐 5 MINS

SERVES 4

I N G R E D I E N T S

4 egg yolks

4 tablespoons sugar

1¾ ounces dark chocolate

1 cup Marsala wine

unsweetened cocoa, to dust

1 In a large glass mixing bowl, whisk together the egg yolks and sugar until you have a very pale mixture, using electric beaters.

2 Grate the chocolate finely and fold into the egg mixture.

3 Fold the Marsala wine into the chocolate mixture.

4 Place the mixing bowl over a saucepan of gently simmering water

and set the beaters on the lowest speed or switch to a balloon whisk. Cook gently, whisking continuously until the mixture thickens; take care not to overcook or the mixture will curdle.

5 Spoon the hot mixture into warmed individual glass dishes or coffee cups (as here) and dust with unsweetened cocoa. Serve the zabaglione as soon as possible so that it is warm, light and fluffy.

COOK'S TIP

Make the dessert just before serving as it will separate if left to stand. If it begins to curdle, remove it from the heat immediately and place it in a bowl of cold water to stop the cooking. Whisk furiously until the mixture comes together.

Chocolate Chip Ice Cream

This marvellous frozen dessert offers the best of both worlds, delicious chocolate chip cookies and a rich dairy-flavored ice.

NUTRITIONAL INFORMATION

Calories 238	Sugars 23g
Protein 9g	Fat 10g
Carbohydrate ...30g	Saturates 4g

6 HOURS   5 MINS

SERVES 6

I N G R E D I E N T S

1¼ cups milk

1 vanilla bean

2 eggs

2 egg yolks

¼ cup sugar

1¼ cups plain yogurt

4½ ounces chocolate chip cookies, broken into small pieces

1 Pour the milk into a small pan, add the vanilla bean and bring to the boil over a low heat. Remove from the heat, cover the pan and set aside to cool.

2 Beat the eggs and egg yolks in a double boiler or in a bowl set over a pan of simmering water. Add the sugar and continue beating until the mixture is pale and creamy.

3 Reheat the milk to simmering point and strain it over the egg mixture. Stir continuously until the custard is thick enough to coat the back of a spoon. Remove the custard from the heat and stand the pan or bowl in cold water to prevent any further cooking. Wash and dry the vanilla bean for future use.

4 Stir the yogurt into the cooled custard and beat until it is well blended. When the mixture is thoroughly cold, stir in the broken cookies.

5 Transfer the mixture to a chilled metal cake pan or plastic container, cover and freeze for 4 hours. Remove from the freezer every hour, transfer to a chilled bowl and beat vigorously to prevent ice crystals from forming then return to the freezer. Alternatively, freeze the mixture in an ice-cream maker, following the manufacturer's instructions.

6 To serve the ice-cream, transfer it to the main part of the refrigerator for 1 hour. Serve in scoops.

Honey & Pistachio Nests

Pistachio nuts and honey are combined with crisp cooked angel hair pasta in this unusual dessert.

NUTRITIONAL INFORMATION

Calories 802	Sugars 53g	
Protein 13g	Fat 48g	
Carbohydrate . . .85g	Saturates 16g	

 10 MINS   1 HOUR

SERVES 4

I N G R E D I E N T S

8 ounces angel-hair pasta

8 tablespoons butter

1½ cups shelled pistachio nuts, chopped

½ cup sugar

⅓ cup liquid honey

⅔ cup water

2 teaspoons lemon juice

salt

strained yogurt, to serve

1 Bring a large saucepan of lightly salted water to a boil. Add the angel-hair pasta and cook for 8–10 minutes or until tender, but still firm to the bite. Drain the pasta and return to the pan. Add the butter and toss to coat the pasta thoroughly. Set aside to cool.

2 Arrange 4 small flan or poaching rings on a cookie sheet. Divide the angel-hair pasta into 8 equal quantities and spoon 4 of them into the rings. Press down lightly. Top the pasta with half of the nuts, then add the remaining pasta.

3 Bake in a preheated oven, at 350°F, for 45 minutes, or until golden brown.

4 Meanwhile, put the sugar, honey, and water in a saucepan and bring to a boil over low heat, stirring constantly until the sugar has dissolved completely. Simmer for 10 minutes, add the lemon juice and simmer for 5 minutes.

5 Using a spatula, carefully transfer the angel hair nests to a serving dish. Pour over the honey syrup, sprinkle over the remaining nuts and set aside to cool completely before serving. Serve the yogurt separately.

COOK'S TIP

Angel-hair pasta is also known as *capelli d'Angelo*. Long and very fine, it is usually sold in small bunches that already resemble nests.

Pear Tart

Pears are a very popular fruit in Italy. In this recipe from Trentino they are flavored with almonds, cinnamon, raisins, and apricot preserves.

NUTRITIONAL INFORMATION

Calories 629   Sugars 70g
Protein . . . . .7g   Fat 21g
Carbohydrate . .109g   Saturates 13g

1¹/₂ HOURS   50 MINS

SERVES 6

INGREDIENTS

2¼ cups all-purpose flour

pinch of salt

½ cup icing sugar

½ cup butter, diced

1 egg

1 egg yolk

few drops of vanilla extract

2–3 teaspoons water

sifted sugar, for sprinkling

FILLING

4 tablespoons apricot
   preserves

2 ounces amaretti or ratafia
   cookies, crumbled

1¾–2 pound 4 ounces pears, peeled
   and cored

1 teaspoon ground cinnamon

½ cup raisins

⅓ cup soft brown or raw
   crystal sugar

1 Sift the flour and salt onto a flat surface, make a well in the center and add the sugar, butter, egg, egg yolk, vanilla extract, and most of the water.

2 Using your fingers, gradually work the flour into the other ingredients to give a smooth dough, adding more water if necessary. Wrap in plastic wrap and chill for 1 hour or until firm. Alternatively, put all the ingredients into a food processor and work until smooth.

3 Roll out three-quarters of the dough and use to line a shallow 10-inch cake pan or deep flan pan. Spread the preserves over the base and sprinkle with the crushed cookies.

4 Slice the pears very thinly. Arrange over the cookies in the pastry case. Sprinkle with cinnamon, then with raisins, and finally with brown sugar.

5 Roll out a thin sausage shape using one-third of the remaining dough, and place around the edge of the pie. Roll the remainder into thin sausages and arrange in a lattice over the pie, 4 or 5 strips in each direction, attaching them to the strip around the edge.

6 Cook in a preheated oven, at 400°F, for 50 minutes until golden and cooked through. Leave to cool, then serve warm or chilled, sprinkled with sifted icing sugar.

Quick Tiramisu

This quick version of one of the most popular Italian desserts is ready in minutes.

NUTRITIONAL INFORMATION

Calories 387   Sugars 17g
Protein ....9g   Fat 28g
Carbohydrate ...22g   Saturates 15g

15 MINS   0 MINS

SERVES 4

INGREDIENTS

1 cup mascarpone cheese

1 egg, separated

2 tablespoons plain yogurt

2 tablespoons sugar

2 tablespoons dark rum

2 tablespoons strong black coffee

8 ladyfingers

2 tablespoons grated
   dark chocolate

1 Put the cheese in a large bowl, add the egg yolk and yogurt and beat until smooth.

2 Whisk the egg white until stiff but not dry, then whisk in the sugar, and carefully fold into the cheese mixture.

COOK'S TIP

Mascarpone is an Italian soft cream cheese made from cow's milk. It has a rich, silky smooth texture and a deliciously creamy flavor. It can be eaten as it is with fresh fruits or flavored with coffee or chocolate.

3 Spoon half of the mixture into 4 sundae glasses.

4 Mix together the rum and coffee in a shallow dish. Dip the ladyfingers into the rum mixture, break them in half, or into smaller pieces if necessary, and divide among the glasses.

5 Stir any remaining coffee mixture into the remaining cheese and spoon over the top

6 Sprinkle with grated chocolate. Serve immediately or chill until required.

Raspberry Fusilli

This is the ultimate in self-indulgence—a truly delicious dessert that tastes every bit as good as it looks.

NUTRITIONAL INFORMATION

Calories ....235 Sugars 20g
Protein ....7g Fat 7g
Carbohydrate ...36g Saturates 1g

5 MINS   20 MINS

SERVES 4

INGREDIENTS

1½ cups fusilli

4 cups raspberries

2 tablespoons sugar

1 tablespoon lemon juice

4 tablespoons slivered almonds

3 tablespoons raspberry liqueur

1 Bring a large saucepan of lightly salted water to a boil. Add the fusilli and cook for 8–10 minutes until tender, but still firm to the bite. Drain the fusilli thoroughly, return to the pan and set aside to cool.

2 Using a spoon, firmly press 1⅓ cups of the raspberries through a strainer set over a large mixing bowl to form a smooth purée.

3 Put the raspberry purée and sugar in a small saucepan and simmer over low heat, stirring occasionally, for 5 minutes.

4 Stir in the lemon juice and set the sauce aside until required.

5 Add the remaining raspberries to the fusilli in the pan and mix together well. Transfer the raspberry and fusilli mixture to a serving dish.

6 Spread the almonds out on a cookie sheet and toast under the broiler until golden brown. Remove and set aside to cool slightly.

7 Stir the raspberry liqueur into the reserved raspberry sauce and mix together well until very smooth. Pour the raspberry sauce over the fusilli, sprinkle over the toasted almonds, and serve.

VARIATION

You could use any sweet, ripe berry for making this dessert. Strawberries and blackberries are especially suitable, combined with the correspondingly flavored liqueur. Alternatively, you could use a different berry mixed with the fusilli, but still pour over raspberry sauce.

Rich Chocolate Loaf

Another rich chocolate dessert, this loaf is very simple to make and can be served as a treat with coffee as well.

NUTRITIONAL INFORMATION

Calories	180	Sugars	........16g
Protein	.........3g	Fat	...........11g
Carbohydrate	...18g	Saturates	.......5g

 1¼ HOURS   5 MINS

MAKES 16 SLICES

I N G R E D I E N T S

5½ ounces dark chocolate

6 tablespoons butter

7¼-ounce can of condensed milk

2 teaspoons cinnamon

¾ cup almonds

1 cup broken amaretti cookies

1¾ ounces dried apricots, soaked and
   patted dry, roughly chopped

1 Line a 1½-pound loaf pan with a sheet of foil.

2 Using a sharp knife, roughly chop the almonds.

3 Place the chocolate, butter, milk, and cinnamon in a heavy-based saucepan.

COOK'S TIP

To melt chocolate, first break it into manageable pieces. The smaller the pieces, the quicker it will melt.

4 Heat the chocolate mixture over low heat for 3–4 minutes, stirring with a wooden spoon, or until the chocolate has melted. Beat the mixture well.

5 Stir the almonds, cookies and apricots into the chocolate mixture, stirring with a wooden spoon, until well mixed.

6 Pour the mixture into the prepared pan and leave to chill in the refrigerator for about 1 hour or until set.

7 Cut the rich chocolate loaf into slices to serve.

Caramelized Oranges

The secret of these oranges is to allow them to marinate in the syrup for at least 24 hours, so the flavors amalgamate.

NUTRITIONAL INFORMATION

Calories .... 235 Sugars .... .59g
Protein .... .2g Fat 0.2g
Carbohydrate ...59g Saturates 0g

3¼ HOURS   20 MINS

SERVES 6

INGREDIENTS

6 large oranges

1 cup sugar

1 cup water

6 whole cloves (optional)

2–4 tablespoons orange-flavored liqueur
   or brandy

1 Using a citrus zester or potato peeler, pare the rind from 2 of the oranges in narrow strips without any white pith attached. If using a potato peeler, cut the peel into very thin julienne strips.

2 Put the strips into a small saucepan and barely cover with water. Bring to a boil and simmer for 5 minutes. Drain the strips and reserve the water.

3 Cut away all the white pith and peel from the remaining oranges using a very sharp knife. Then cut horizontally into 4 slices. Reassemble the oranges and hold in place with wooden toothpicks. Stand in a heatproof dish.

4 Put the sugar and water into a heavy-based saucepan with the cloves, if using. Bring to a boil and simmer gently until the sugar has dissolved, then boil hard without stirring until the syrup thickens and begins to color. Continue to cook until a light golden brown, then quickly remove from the heat and carefully pour in the reserved orange rind liquid.

5 Place over a gentle heat until the caramel has fully dissolved again, then remove from the heat and add the liqueur or brandy. Pour over the oranges.

6 Sprinkle the orange strips over the oranges, cover with plastic wrap and leave until cold. Chill for at least 3 hours and preferably for 24–48 hours before serving. If time allows, spoon the syrup over the oranges several times while they are marinating. Discard the toothpicks before serving.

Cream Custards

Individual pan-cooked cream custards are flavored with nutmeg and topped with caramelized orange strips.

NUTRITIONAL INFORMATION

Calories	406	Sugars	.......38g
Protein	.........8g	Fat	..........26g
Carbohydrate	...38g	Saturates	......15g

2¼ HOURS   25 MINS

SERVES 4

INGREDIENTS

2 cups light cream

½ cup sugar

1 orange

2 teaspoons grated nutmeg

3 large eggs, beaten

1 tablespoon honey

1 teaspoon cinnamon

1 Place the cream and sugar in a large nonstick saucepan and heat gently, stirring, until the sugar caramelizes.

2 Finely grate half of the orange rind and add it to the pan along with the nutmeg.

3 Add the eggs to the mixture in the pan and cook over low heat for 10–15 minutes, stirring constantly. The custard will eventually thicken.

COOK'S TIP

The cream custards will keep for 1–2 days in the refrigerator. Decorate with the caramelized orange rind just before serving.

4 Strain the custard through a fine strainer into 4 shallow serving dishes. Leave to chill in the refrigerator for 2 hours.

5 Meanwhile, pare the remaining orange rind and cut it into matchsticks.

6 Place the honey and cinnamon in a pan with 2 tablespoons of water and heat gently. Add the orange rind to the pan and cook for 2–3 minutes, stirring, until the mixture has caramelized.

7 Pour the mixture into a bowl and separate out the orange strips. Leave to cool until set.

8 Once the custards have set, decorate them with the caramelized orange rind and serve.

Peaches in White Wine

A very simple but incredibly pleasing dessert, which is especially good for a dinner party on a hot summer day.

NUTRITIONAL INFORMATION

Calories 89   Sugars 14g
Protein ....1g   Fat 0g
Carbohydrate ...14g   Saturates 0g

 1¼ HOURS   0 MINS

SERVES 4

INGREDIENTS

4 large ripe peaches

2 tablespoons icing sugar, sifted

1 orange

1 cup medium or sweet
  white wine, chilled

1 Using a sharp knife, halve the peaches, remove the pits, and discard them. Peel the peaches, if you prefer. Slice the peaches into thin wedges.

2 Place the peach wedges in a serving bowl and sprinkle over the sugar.

3 Using a sharp knife, pare the rind from the orange. Cut the orange rind into matchsticks, place them in a bowl of cold water, and set aside.

4 Squeeze the juice from the orange and pour over the peaches together with the wine.

5 Let the peaches marinate and chill in the refrigerator for at least 1 hour.

6 Remove the orange rind from the cold water and pat dry with paper towels.

7 Garnish the peaches with the strips of orange rind and serve immediately.

Peaches & Mascarpone

If you prepare these in advance, all you have to do is pop the peaches on the barbecue when you are ready to serve them.

NUTRITIONAL INFORMATION

Calories 301   Sugars 24g
Protein . . . . .6g   Fat 20g
Carbohydrate . . .24g   Saturates 9g

 10 MINS   10 MINS

SERVES 4

INGREDIENTS

4 peaches

¾ cup mascarpone cheese

½ cup pecan or walnuts, chopped

1 teaspoon sunflower oil

4 tablespoons maple syrup

1 Cut the peaches in half and remove the pits. If you are preparing this recipe in advance, press the peach halves together again and wrap them in plastic wrap until required.

2 Mix the mascarpone and pecans or walnuts together in a small bowl until well combined. Leave to chill in the refrigerator until required.

VARIATION

You can use nectarines instead of peaches for this recipe. Remember to choose ripe but firm fruit which won't go soft and mushy when it is barbecued. Prepare the nectarines in the same way as the peaches and barbecue for 5–10 minutes.

3 To serve, brush the peaches with a little oil and place on a rack set over medium hot coals. Barbecue for 5–10 minutes, turning once, until hot.

4 Transfer the peaches to a serving dish and top with the mascarpone mixture.

5 Drizzle the maple syrup over the peaches and mascarpone filling and serve at once.

Sweet Mascarpone Mousse

A sweet cream cheese dessert that complements the tartness of fresh summer fruits rather well.

NUTRITIONAL INFORMATION

Calories 542   Sugars 31g
Protein ....14g   Fat 41g
Carbohydrate ...31g   Saturates 24g

1¹/₂ HOURS   0 MINS

SERVES 4

INGREDIENTS

1 pound mascarpone cheese

½ cup sugar

4 egg yolks

14 ounces frozen summer fruits, such as
   raspberries and red currants

red currants or berries, to garnish

amaretti cookies, to serve

1 Place the mascarpone cheese in a large mixing bowl. Using a wooden spoon, beat the mascarpone cheese until quite smooth.

2 Stir the egg yolks and sugar into the mascarpone cheese, mixing well. Leave the mixture to chill in the refrigerator for about 1 hour.

3 Spoon a layer of the mascarpone mixture into the bottom of 4 individual serving dishes. Spoon a layer of the summer fruits on top. Repeat the layers in the same order, reserving some of the mascarpone mixture for the top.

4 Leave the mousses to chill in the refrigerator for about 20 minutes. The fruits should still be slightly frozen.

5 Serve the mascarpone mousses with amaretti cookies.

Panettone & Strawberries

Panettone is a sweet Italian bread. It is delicious toasted, and when it is topped with mascarpone and strawberries it makes a sumptuous dessert.

NUTRITIONAL INFORMATION

Calories 227	Sugars 11g	
Protein 5g	Fat 13g	
Carbohydrate ...19g	Saturates 8g	

35 MINS   2 MINS

SERVES 4

INGREDIENTS

8 oz strawberries

1 oz superfine sugar

6 tbsp Marsala wine

½ tsp ground cinnamon

4 slices panettone

4 tbsp mascarpone cheese

1 Hull and slice the strawberries and place them in a bowl. Add the sugar, Marsala, and cinnamon to the strawberries.

2 Toss the strawberries in the sugar and cinnamon mixture until they are well coated. Leave to chill in the refrigerator for at least 30 minutes.

3 When ready to serve, transfer the slices of panettone to a rack set over medium hot coals. Grill the panettone for about 1 minute on each side or until golden brown.

4 Carefully remove the panettone from the grill and transfer to serving plates.

5 Top the panettone with the mascarpone cheese and the marinated strawberries. Serve immediately.

Orange & Grapefruit Salad

Sliced citrus fruits with a delicious almond and honey dressing make an unusual and refreshing dessert.

NUTRITIONAL INFORMATION

Calories 217	Sugars 33g
Protein 4g	Fat 9g
Carbohydrate . . .33g	Saturates 1g

  2¼ HOURS   3 MINS

SERVES 4

I N G R E D I E N T S

2 grapefruit, ruby or plain

4 oranges

pared rind and juice of 1 lime

4 tablespoons liquid honey

2 tablespoons warm water

1 sprig of mint, roughly chopped

½ cup chopped walnuts

1 Using a sharp knife, slice the top and bottom from the grapefruits, then slice away the rest of the skin and pith.

2 Cut between each segment of the grapefruit and remove the fleshy part only.

3 Using a sharp knife, slice the top and bottom from the oranges, then slice away the rest of the skin and pith.

4 Cut between each segment of the oranges to remove the fleshy part. Add to the grapefruit.

5 Place the lime rind, 2 tablespoons of lime juice, the honey and the warm water in a small bowl. Whisk with a fork to mix the dressing.

6 Pour the dressing over the segmented fruit, add the chopped mint and mix well. Leave to chill in the refrigerator for 2 hours for the flavors to mingle.

7 Place the chopped walnuts on a cookie sheet. Lightly toast the walnuts under a preheated medium grill (broiler) for 2–3 minutes or until browned.

8 Sprinkle the toasted walnuts over the fruit and serve.

Vanilla Ice Cream

This homemade version of real vanilla ice cream is absolutely delicious and so easy to make. A tutti-frutti variation is also provided.

NUTRITIONAL INFORMATION

Calories 626   Sugars 33g
Protein . . . . .7g   Fat 53g
Carbohydrate . . .33g   Saturates 31g

5 MINS   15 MINS

SERVES 6

INGREDIENTS

2½ cups heavy cream

1 vanilla bean

pared rind of 1 lemon

4 eggs, beaten

2 egg yolks

1 cup sugar

1 Place the cream in a heavy-based saucepan and heat gently, whisking.

2 Add the vanilla bean, lemon rind, eggs, and egg yolks to the pan and heat until the mixture reaches just below boiling point.

3 Reduce the heat and cook for 8–10 minutes, whisking the mixture continuously, until thickened.

VARIATION

For tutti-frutti ice cream, soak 3½ ounces mixed dried fruit in 2 tablespoons Marsala for 20 minutes. Follow the method for vanilla ice cream, omitting the vanilla bean, and stir in the Marsala-soaked fruit in step 6, just before freezing.

4 Stir the sugar into the cream mixture, set aside and leave to cool.

5 Strain the cream mixture through a fine strainer.

6 Slit open the vanilla bean, scoop out the tiny black seeds, and stir them into the cream mixture.

7 Pour the mixture into a shallow freezing container with a lid and freeze overnight until set. Serve the ice cream when required.

Ricotta Ice Cream

The ricotta cheese adds a creamy flavor, while the nuts add a crunchy texture. This ice cream needs to be chilled in the freezer overnight.

NUTRITIONAL INFORMATION

Calories 438	Sugars 39g
Protein 13g	Fat 25g
Carbohydrate ...40g	Saturates 9g

 20 MINS 0 MINS

SERVES 6

INGREDIENTS

¼ cup pistachio nuts

¼ cup walnuts or pecan nuts

¼ cup toasted
   chopped hazelnuts

grated rind of 1 orange

grated rind of 1 lemon

2 tablespoons crystallized ginger

2 tablespoons candied cherries

¼ cup dried apricots

3 tablespoons raisins

1½ cups ricotta cheese

2 tablespoons Amaretto,
   or brandy

1 teaspoon vanilla extract

4 egg yolks

½ cup sugar

TO DECORATE

whipped cream

cherries, nuts, or mint leaves

1 Roughly chop the pistachio nuts and walnuts and mix with the toasted hazelnuts, orange and lemon rind.

2 Finely chop the ginger, cherries, apricots, and raisins, and add to the bowl.

3 Stir the ricotta evenly through the fruit mixture, then beat in the liqueur and vanilla extract.

4 Put the egg yolks and sugar in a bowl and whisk hard until very thick and creamy—they may be whisked over a saucepan of gently simmering water to speed up the process. Leave to cool if necessary.

5 Carefully fold the ricotta mixture evenly through the beaten eggs and sugar until smooth.

6 Line a 7 x 5 inch loaf pan with a double layer of plastic wrap or baking parchment. Pour in the ricotta mixture, level the top, cover with more plastic wrap or baking parchment and chill in the freezer until firm—at least overnight.

7 To serve, carefully remove the ice-cream from the pan and peel off the paper. Place on a serving dish and decorate with whipped cream, glacé cherries, pistachio nuts and/or mint leaves. Serve in slices.

Lemon Granita

A delightful end to a meal or a refreshing way to cleanse the palate, granitas are made from slushy ice, so they need to be served very quickly.

NUTRITIONAL INFORMATION

Calories	102	Sugars	27g
Protein	0.1g	Fat	0g
Carbohydrate	27g	Saturates	0g

5¼ HOURS   6 MINS

SERVES 4

INGREDIENTS

LEMON GRANITA

3 lemons

1 cup lemon juice

½ cup sugar

2¼ cups cold water

VARIATION

To make coffee granita, place 2 tablespoons instant coffee and 2 tablespoons sugar in a bowl and pour over 2 tablespoons hot water, stirring until dissolved. Stir in 2½ cups cold water and 2 tablespoons rum or brandy. Pour into a shallow freezer container with a lid. Freeze for at least 6 hours, stirring occasionally.

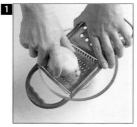

1 To make lemon granita, finely grate the lemon rind.

2 Place the lemon rind, juice and sugar in a pan. Bring the mixture to a boil and leave to simmer for 5-6 minutes or until thick and syrupy. Leave to cool.

3 Once cooled, stir in the cold water and pour into a shallow freezer container with a lid.

4 Freeze the granita for 4–5 hours, stirring occasionally to break up the ice. Serve as a dessert or palate cleanser between dinner courses.

Rosemary Cookies

Do not be put off by the idea of herbs being used in these crisp cookies—try them and you will be pleasantly surprised.

NUTRITIONAL INFORMATION

Calories 50   Sugars 2g
Protein . . . . .1g   Fat 2g
Carbohydrate . . . .8g   Saturates 1g

45 MINS   15 MINS

MAKES 25

I N G R E D I E N T S

4 tablespoons butter, softened

4 tablespoons sugar

grated rind of 1 lemon

4 tablespoons lemon juice

1 egg, separated

2 teaspoons finely chopped fresh rosemary

1¾ cups all-purpose
   flour, sifted

sugar, for sprinkling
   (optional)

 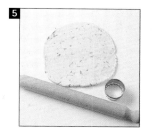 

1 Lightly grease 2 cookie sheets.

2 In a large mixing bowl, cream together the butter and sugar until pale and fluffy.

3 Add the lemon rind and juice, then the egg yolk, and beat until they are thoroughly combined. Stir in the chopped fresh rosemary.

4 Add the sifted flour, mixing well until a soft dough is formed. Wrap and leave to chill for 30 minutes.

5 On a lightly floured surface, roll out the dough thinly and then stamp out 25 rounds with a 2½-inch cookie cutter. Arrange the dough rounds on the prepared cookie sheets.

6 In a bowl, lightly whisk the egg white. Gently brush the egg white over the surface of each cookie, then sprinkle with a little superfine sugar, if liked.

7 Bake in a preheated oven, at 350°F, for about 15 minutes.

8 Transfer the cookies to a wire rack and leave to cool before serving.

COOK'S TIP

Store the cookies in an airtight container for up to 1 week.

Chocolate Biscotti

These dry cookies are delicious served with black coffee after your evening meal.

NUTRITIONAL INFORMATION

Calories	113	Sugars	.........9g
Protein	.........2g	Fat	...........5g
Carbohydrate	...15g	Saturates	.......1g

🍳 20 MINS   🕐 40 MINS

MAKES 16

I N G R E D I E N T S

1 egg

½ cup sugar

1 teaspoon vanilla extract

1 cup all-purpose flour

½ teaspoon baking powder

1 teaspoon ground
   cinnamon

1¾ ounces dark chocolate, chopped
   roughly

½ cup toasted slivered
   almonds

½ cup pine nuts

1 Lightly grease a large cookie sheet.

2 Whisk the egg, sugar and vanilla extract in a mixing bowl with an electric mixer until it is thick and pale—ribbons of mixture should trail from the whisk as you lift it.

3 Sift the flour, baking powder, and cinnamon into a separate bowl, then sift into the egg mixture and fold in gently. Stir in the chocolate, almonds, and pine nuts.

4 Turn onto a lightly floured surface and shape into a flat log, 9 inches long and ¾ inch wide. Transfer to the cookie sheet.

5 Bake in a preheated oven, at 350°F, for 20-25 minutes or until golden. Remove from the oven and leave to cool for 5 minutes or until firm.

6 Transfer the log to a cutting board. Using a serrated bread knife, cut the log on the diagonal into slices about ½ inch thick and arrange them on the cookie sheet. Cook for 10-15 minutes, turning halfway through the cooking time.

7 Leave to cool for about 5 minutes, then transfer to a wire rack to cool completely.

Florentines

These luxury cookies will be popular at any time of the year, but make a particularly wonderful treat at Christmas.

NUTRITIONAL INFORMATION

Calories 186   Sugars 19g
Protein ....2g   Fat 11g
Carbohydrate ...22g   Saturates 5g

20 MINS   15 MINS

MAKES 10

INGREDIENTS

4 tablespoons butter

½ cup sugar

¼ cup all-purpose flour, sifted

½ cup almonds, chopped

⅓ cup chopped mixed peel

¼ cup raisins, chopped

2 tablespoons candied cherries,
  chopped

finely grated rind of ½ lemon

4½ ounces dark chocolate,
  melted

1 Line 2 large cookie sheets with baking parchment.

2 Heat the butter and sugar in a small saucepan until the butter has just melted and the sugar dissolved. Remove the pan from the heat.

3 Stir in the flour and mix well. Stir in the chopped almonds, mixed peel, raisins, cherries and lemon rind. Place teaspoonfuls of the mixture well apart on the cookie sheets.

4 Bake in a preheated oven, at 350°F, for 10 minutes or until lightly golden.

5 As soon as the florentines are removed from the oven, press the edges into neat shapes while still on the cookie sheets, using a cookie cutter. Leave to cool on the cookie sheets until firm, then transfer to a wire rack to cool completely.

6 Spread the melted chocolate over the smooth side of each florentine. As the chocolate begins to set, mark wavy lines in it with a fork. Leave the florentines until set, chocolate side up.

VARIATION

Replace the dark chocolate with white chocolate or, for a dramatic effect, cover half of the florentines in dark chocolate and half in white.

Florentine Twists

These famous and delicious Florentine cookies are twisted into curls or cones and then just the ends are dipped in chocolate.

NUTRITIONAL INFORMATION

Calories 28   Sugars 15g
Protein ....1g   Fat 7g
Carbohydrate ...15g   Saturates 4g

20 MINS   20 MINS

MAKES 20

I N G R E D I E N T S

6 tablespoons butter

¾ cup sugar

½ cup blanched or slivered almonds,
  chopped roughly

3 tablespoons raisins,
  chopped

¼ cup chopped mixed peel

¼ cup candied
  cherries, chopped

3 tablespoons dried apricots,
  chopped finely

finely grated rind of ½ lemon or
½ small orange

4½ ounces dark or
  white chocolate

1 Line 2–3 cookie sheets with nonstick baking parchment; then grease 4–6 cream horn moulds or a fairly thin rolling pin, or wooden spoon handles.

2 Melt the butter and sugar together gently in a saucepan and then bring to a boil for 1 minute. Remove the pan from the heat and stir in all the remaining ingredients, except for the chocolate. Leave to cool.

3 Put heaped teaspoonfuls of the mixture onto the cookie sheets, keeping them well apart, only 3–4 per sheet, and flatten slightly.

4 Bake in a preheated oven, at 350°F, for 10–12 minutes, or until golden. Leave to cool until they begin to firm up. As they cool, press the edges back to form a neat shape. Remove each one with a spatula and wrap quickly around a cream horn mould, or lay over the rolling pin or spoon handles. If they become too firm to bend, return to the oven briefly to soften.

5 Leave until cold and crisp and then slip carefully off the horn moulds or remove from the rolling pin or spoons.

6 Melt the chocolate in a heatproof bowl over a saucepan of hot water, or in a microwave oven set on HIGH for about 45 seconds, and stir until smooth. Either dip the end of each Florentine twist into the chocolate or, using a pastry brush, paint chocolate to come about halfway up the twist. As the chocolate sets, it can be marked into wavy lines with a fork. Leave to set.

Mini Florentines

Serve these cookies at the end of a meal with coffee, or arrange in a shallow presentation box for an attractive gift.

NUTRITIONAL INFORMATION

Calories 75	Sugars 6g	
Protein 1g	Fat 5g	
Carbohydrate 6g	Saturates 2g	

20 MINS   20 MINS

MAKES 40

I N G R E D I E N T S

6 tablespoons butter

¼ cup sugar

2 tablespoons golden raisins
   or raisins

2 tablespoons candied
   cherries, chopped

2 tablespoons crystallized
   ginger, chopped

2 tablespoons sunflower seeds

1 cup slivered almonds

2 tablespoons heavy cream

6 ounces dark or milk
   chocolate

1 Grease and flour 2 cookie sheets or line with baking parchment.

2 Place the butter in a small pan and heat gently until melted. Add the sugar, stir until dissolved, then bring the mixture to a boil. Remove from the heat and stir in the golden raisins or raisins, cherries, ginger, sunflower seeds, and almonds. Mix well, then beat in the cream.

3 Place small teaspoons of the fruit and nut mixture onto the prepared cookie sheets, allowing plenty of space for the mixture to spread. Bake in a preheated oven, at 350°F, for 10-12 minutes or until light golden in color.

4 Remove from the oven and, while still hot, use a circular cookie cutter to pull in the edges to form a perfect circle. Leave to cool and crispen before removing from the cookie sheet.

5 Melt most of the chocolate and spread it on a sheet of baking parchment. When the chocolate is on the point of setting, place the cookies flat-side down on the chocolate and leave to harden completely.

6 Cut around the florentines and remove from the baking parchment. Spread a little more chocolate on the coated side of the florentines and use a fork to mark waves in the chocolate. Leave to set. Arrange the florentines on a plate (or in a presentation box for a gift) with alternate sides facing upward. Keep cool.

White Chocolate Florentines

These attractive jeweled cookies are coated with white chocolate to give them a delicious flavor.

NUTRITIONAL INFORMATION

Calories 235   Sugars 20g
Protein . . . . .3g   Fat 17g
Carbohydrate . . .20g   Saturates 7g

20 MINS   15 MINS

MAKES 24

I N G R E D I E N T S

14 tablespoons butter

1 cup sugar

1 cup walnuts, chopped

1 cup almonds, chopped

3 tablespoons golden raisins, chopped

1 tablespoon candied cherries, chopped

1 tablespoon mixed candied peel,
   chopped finely

2 tablespoons light cream

8 ounces white chocolate

1 Line 3–4 cookie sheets with nonstick baking parchment.

2 Melt the butter over low heat and then add the sugar, stirring until it has dissolved. Boil the mixture for exactly 1 minute. Remove from the heat.

COOK'S TIP

A combination of white and dark chocolate Florentines looks very attractive, especially if you are making them as gifts. Pack them in pretty boxes, lined with tissue paper and tied with some ribbon.

3 Add the walnuts, almonds, golden raisins, cherries, candied peel and cream to the saucepan, stirring well.

4 Drop heaped teaspoonfuls of the mixture onto the cookie sheets, allowing plenty of room for them to spread while cooking. Bake in a preheated oven, at 350°F, for 10 minutes or until golden brown.

5 Remove the cookies from the oven and neaten the edges with a knife

while they are still warm. Leave to cool slightly, and then transfer them to a wire rack to cool completely.

6 Melt the chocolate in a bowl placed over a pan of gently simmering water. Spread the underside of the cookies with chocolate and use a fork to make wavy lines across the surface. Leave to cool completely.

7 Store the Florentines in an airtight tin, kept in a cool place.

Italian Chocolate Truffles

These are flavored with almonds and chocolate, and are simplicity itself to make. Served with coffee, they are the perfect end to a meal.

NUTRITIONAL INFORMATION

Calories	82	Sugars	.........7g
Protein	.........1g	Fat	..........5g
Carbohydrate	....8g	Saturates	.......3g

 5 MINS   5 MINS

MAKES 24

INGREDIENTS

6 ounces dark chocolate

2 tablespoons almond-flavored liqueur (amaretto) or orange-flavored liqueur

3 tablespoons butter

¼ cup icing sugar

½ cup ground almonds

1¾ ounces grated milk chocolate

1 Melt the dark chocolate with the liqueur in a bowl set over a saucepan of hot water, stirring until well combined.

2 Add the butter and stir until it has melted. Stir in the icing sugar and the ground almonds.

3 Leave the mixture in a cool place until firm enough to roll into 24 balls.

4 Place the grated chocolate on a plate and roll the truffles in the chocolate to coat them.

5 Place the truffles in paper candy cases and chill.

Index

Index compiled by Sandra Shotter.